Open to God, Open for All

William Tyndale window in the south transept

Open to God, Open for All

The History of
Tyndale Baptist Church, Bristol
1868 – 2018

Edited by John Briggs

Tyndale Baptist Church and the Baptist Historical Society

ISBN 978-0-903166-47-8

Published in the United Kingdom by Tyndale Baptist Church, Whiteladies Road, Clifton, Bristol and the Baptist Historical Society.

Contents

Preface

John Briggs, Editor

Tyndale Baptist Church celebrates its 150th anniversary this year. Its foundation in 1868 occurred in a year which saw the end of transportation of British criminals, some for only petty crimes, to Australia; the last public hanging in Britain; the founding of the Trade Union Congress; and the first traffic lights in the world, installed outside the House of Parliament to control horse-drawn traffic in the area. Operating rather like railway signals, but using gas illumination at night, in less than a month a gas leak caused these to blow up, involving serious injury to the operating policeman, and the lights were withdrawn until the arrival of the motor car made the introduction of electric lights an urgent demand. Tyndale has fared better. Notwithstanding the efforts of the Luftwaffe to blow up the sanctuary, the church has witnessed resurrection and new life in further years of service to the people of Redland and Clifton.

Many things have changed in those 150 years. No longer does the congregation contain knights of the realm and the leaders of Bristol's most significant businesses. The inhabitants of the genteel suburbia of the late nineteenth century have given way to a much more diverse population, living in those same suburban villas but now divided into flats and apartments, with the least fortunate in society even making their residence in the church porch, with Tyndale playing a leading part in the Bristol Churches' winter night shelter programme providing accommodation for rough sleepers for twelve weeks in the winter months.

It is the story of that change with which this history is concerned, the story of how a church seeks to maintain a faithful obedience to its God-given mission and ministry, summed up in its motto which we have taken for the title of this book: *Open to God, Open for All*. This is a message which finds visual focus in the mural in the apse of the church where the focus is on the centrality of the cross and the sacrifice of the Son of God for sinful humanity. Here its message of forgiveness and new life stands above the waters of baptism symbolising the ever-present invitation to all who will to enter into Christ's forgiving love and to find there new purpose for living. That is the constant affirmation that the church stands for in a context which often seems so unstable and given to turmoil and confusion in a world of deceit and fake news.

Chapel histories can all too easily become an account of clerical comings and goings, and certainly the leadership offered by those called and ordained to the Christian ministry in building up the people of God in faith and commitment are vital parts of the story, as is the ministry of prayer and intercession, of word and sacrament, of worship and service occurring within the sanctuary. But what happens after the benediction, when the gathered congregation scatters back into the world of home and family, work and leisure, service of the community and the search for justice in a world divided by all too many unjust structures must also be told. This book must tell that story as it tracks the paths taken by the whole people of God who covenant with one another and with Almighty God in the fellowship of this church in the service of their neighbours, near and far, discovering God already at work in his world.

The church has a very rich archive which has been most diligently calendared with almost 900 items listed by Michael Youings for whose labour and skill we are most grateful. We are likewise indebted to the help of librarians, particularly Mike Brealey of Bristol Baptist College and Emily Burgoyne of the Angus Library, Regent's Park College, University of Oxford. The authors are also very grateful to those who have shared both memories and written and graphic sources with them which have been added to the archive. We are grateful to those who have provided written commendations of the book and to the Baptist Historical Society for its support. The member of the team who is not an author of a chapter who has made an immense contribution to its production is Ian Waddington who has cast his critical eye over everything and deployed his technological skills to produce our various researches in the form of an attractive readable text. The authors are very privileged to have been entrusted with the task of telling this story but are very conscious that much more could have been written. Their hope and their prayer is that what they have written will encourage this part of God's family to continue to write new chapters in this story of seeking to continue to be faithful to their calling, as the first 150 years of being church recede into the past, but as a green light shines ahead into the future, assuring them of the accompaniment of the Risen Christ as they seek to incarnate his body in the world in which he has placed them.

About the Authors

David Roberts was a Deputy Regional Director of the Open University. He attended Tyndale as a student in the 1950s and has been a member since 1975. He served as Church Secretary for seven years and subsequently as Secretary of the former Bristol and District Association. A member of the Baptist Union Council for 25 years, he also served on a number of ecumenical bodies at national and local level.

John Briggs, an Emeritus Professor of the University of Birmingham, has served on the Baptist Union Council and the Executive of the World Council of Churches. From 1985–2008 he edited the *Baptist Quarterly*, and in 2001 became the founding director of the Baptist History and Heritage Centre at Regent's Park College in the University of Oxford. Chairman of the Heritage Commission of Baptist World Alliance, 1990–95, and a Visiting Research Professor at the International Baptist Seminary in Prague, 2002–12, he is a Vice President of the Baptist Historical Society having previously served as President. He has been a member of Tyndale from 2015 and is also an Honorary Research Fellow of Bristol Baptist College.

David Bell was formerly Head of Religious Studies at Tewkesbury School. A trained youth leader, and Boys' Brigade training officer, he spent many years in voluntary youth work. A member of Gas Green Baptist Church, Cheltenham, for 38 years, he came to Tyndale in 1997 as student in ministry while studying at Bristol Baptist College. He has been a deacon at Tyndale for the last ten years.

Keith Clements is a Baptist minister who was a tutor at Bristol Baptist College 1977–1990, during which time he was Editor of the Baptist Historical Society for five years, and subsequently worked in the ecumenical movement at national and international level. He has been a member of Tyndale since 1977.

Michael Whitfield became a member of Tyndale in 1967 and was a general practitioner covering the area around the church for about 30 years. During the last half of this time he was a senior lecturer in general practice in the University of Bristol based in Canynge Hall, just opposite Tyndale. Since retiring, he has developed an interest in medical history and has written a number of books on the subject.

Michael Docker has been the minister of Tyndale since 2002. He had previous pastorates in Leicester and Southampton, prior to which he prepared for the ministry at Bristol Baptist College after a previous career in manufacturing. He has been chairman of the College's Council for the last 18 years and is the Baptist Chaplain to the University of Bristol.

Rachel Haig has been the Community Minister at Tyndale since May 2013. Prior to that she was at Horfield Baptist for 15 years as Student Minister (while at Bristol Baptist College), Associate Minister with responsibility for under-40's and then Senior Minister. She has chaired the Women's Justice Committee of the Baptist Union as well as serving on the Baptist Union Council and Faith and Unity Committee. Rachel is part of the team at the University of Bristol Multifaith Chaplaincy.

Further Reading

Those wishing to read further about this congregation and its service of the community are invited to consult the following texts:

Richard Glover – Teacher's commentaries on *Lectures on the Lord's Prayer* (1881), *The Gospel of St Mark* (1884), *The Beatitudes* (1888), and *The Gospel of St Matthew* (1889); and *The Comforts of God: Lectures on the Fourteenth Chapter of the Gospel of St John* (1908); "Our Mission in China" in *The Centenary Volume of the Baptist Missionary Society 1792–1892* (1892); *Herbert Stanley Jenkins, Medical Missionary, Shensi, China* (1914).

Dorothy Glover and Richard Glover, *Tyndale Echoes* (1954), containing brief excerpts from Glover's payers and sermons.

Dorothy Glover, *Set on a Hill: The Record of Fifty Years in the Lushai Country* (1944).

F. C. Bryan, *The New Knowledge and the Old Gospel* (1930); *Concerning Believers Baptism* (1943); *Concerning The Way* (1946).

Secondary Sources

Rosemary Chadwick, "Richard Glover" in *The Oxford Dictionary of National Biography* (2004).

L. G. Champion, *Bristol and District Association of Baptist Churches 1823–1973* (1973).

L. G. Champion, *Tyndale Baptist Church Bristol 1868–1968* (1968).

Bernard Darwin, *Robinsons of Bristol, 1844–1944* (1945).

Mike Richardson, *The Bristol Strike Wave of 1889–1890 Part 1* (Bristol Radical History Group, 2012).

Mike Richardson, "Rapprochement and Retribution: The Divergent Experiences of Workers in Two Large Paper and Print Companies in the 1926 General Strike" and "Work Relations: Compositors' Experiences in a Family-Owned Printing Company: J.W.Arrowsmith, 1918–39" in Mike Richardson and Peter Nicholls (eds), *A Business and Labour History of Britain* (2011).

D. T. Roberts, "Mission, Home and Overseas: Richard Glover of Bristol" in *The Baptist Quarterly,* Vol. XXXV, No. 3 (July 1993).

David Roberts: "Thomas Howe, Bristol Missioner" in *The Baptist Quarterly*, Vol. XXXVIII, No. 4 (October 1999).

David T. Roberts: "The Great War 1914–18: A Houseful of Belgians" in *The Baptist Quarterly*, Vol. 46, No. 1 (January 2015).

H. L. Taylor, *Edward Robinson, J. P. of Bristol* (The Carey Press, 1942).

Linda Wilson, "Citizens of No Mean City: A Study of Women in Two Baptist Churches in Late Victorian and Early Edwardian Bristol", in A. R. Cross, P. J. Morden and I. M. Randall (eds), *Pathways and Patterns in History* (2015), the Tyndale portion of which is expanded in her unpublished "Work, hospitality, fund-raising and opening bazaars: a look at the lives of Tyndale Baptist women between 1880–1911" (2015).

Chapter 1.

In the Beginning

David Roberts

> I was glad
> When they said unto me
> Let us go into the house of the Lord

These words from Psalm 122 were the first to be sung, as a chant, in the new Tyndale Baptist Chapel at midday on Wednesday 30th September 1868. The preacher at that opening service was the Hon. & Revd Baptist W. Noel, a former President of the Baptist Union (in 1855 and 1867), on the text Matthew 28 vv 18–20. At seven o'clock that same evening a second service took place at which the preacher was the Revd Nathaniel Haycroft of Leicester, who had for the previous eighteen years been minister of Broadmead Baptist Church in Bristol, and had been inducted to the pastorate of the new Victoria Road church in Leicester only two months earlier (where Baptist Noel had also been the preacher at its opening service). Only a few years earlier Noel and Haycroft had been on opposite sides of a controversy concerning C. H. Spurgeon's attack on certain practices of evangelical Anglicans. Haycroft's text was 1 Corinthians 1 vv 3–24. Between the two services a "cold collation" (a light informal meal) was held at the Royal Hotel, College Green. Less than two weeks after the opening, the church hosted a session of the Baptist Union Autumn Assembly, which was being held in Bristol. When the church was formally constituted on 6th April the following year there were 39 members. Apart from the new minister, Richard Glover, and his wife, Anna, all the foundation members of the new church were transferred from other local churches, 24 of them from Broadmead. Of the others, six came from Old King Street, another six from Counterslip and one from Pill.

Bristol had seen Baptist witness for more than 200 years. Two congregations contended for being considered the first Baptist church in Bristol – and still do! Broadmead had been founded in 1640 and Old King Street (then meeting in the Pithay chapel) ten years later, in 1650. However, in its early years the Broadmead church had practised both infant and believers' baptism and, indeed, some members of Broadmead moved to the Pithay in consequence. In fact the Old King Street church had moved twice from its original meeting place in Quakers Friars and then the Pithay, where it met for more than 100 years, until its new building was opened in 1815. Then in 1834 the Pithay chapel became the home of a new congregation which in turn eventually built a new chapel in City Road in 1861. After that the Pithay chapel was bought by another church which had been meeting in the Cooper's Hall (much later incorporated into the Theatre Royal). This church, however, did not prosper, with a number of disputes among the membership and with a succession of ministers. In 1867 they moved to a rented building in Park Street, but the church closed in 1869. Meanwhile a breakaway group from the original Pithay (future Old King Street) church met in Tailors Court until it opened a new building in Counterslip.

So in 1866 there were five Baptist churches in the central area, albeit one struggling and destined to close in 1869. In addition there were other churches further out of the city. The Downend church had been founded in the 1780s and the Fishponds church in 1841, moving into its permanent building in 1851. The Kensington church had been founded in 1831, originally in Thrissell Street. The St George church began in 1830, that in Stapleton in 1833 and Philip Street, Bedminster, in 1855. There had been a Baptist chapel in Westbury On Trym (Trym Road), founded about 1830 and flourishing in the mid-1840s, but this had closed and the building was sold to the Methodists probably in the 1850s. In 1847 some members from Old King Street founded the Buckingham church in Clifton, which would be the nearest Baptist neighbour to the new Tyndale church.

So why was there a need for another Baptist church? This was, of course, a period when all towns and cities were growing rapidly, although Bristol did not experience the almost explosive growth of some of the newer industrial towns. Nevertheless, between 1861 and 1871 (the census years) Bristol's population grew from 154,093 to 182,686, an increase of more than 18% – a greater rate of increase than in England and Wales as a whole (13%). A recent study has looked at the population changes within what is the modern Bristol Unitary Authority area, and this shows an increase of more than 17%, during the 1860s, which suggests that the local population growth was not confined to the city area. More significantly for the establishment of a new church in the area, Clifton over the same period was growing faster than either measure – by more than 23%. Speaking at the stone laying ceremony for the new church on 17th July 1867, the Mayor, E. S. Robinson, pointed out that since 1856 the rateable value of this portion of the parish of Westbury On Trym (the site of Tyndale was just over the boundary from Clifton) had increased from £21,000 to £40,000, and he was in no doubt that the population had increased correspondingly. Why was this so? This was largely because of the migration of many of the more affluent citizens away from the city centre, where they had frequently lived close to their business premises, out to the growing suburbs, especially Clifton and the adjacent Redland. In fact the population of the central area decreased by about 5% during the 1860s.

Elisha Smith Robinson, paper merchant, Mayor of Bristol and a founding trustee of Tyndale

Since around the 1760s Clifton had been the fashionable district – indeed, almost a separate town – for the most wealthy. Now the socially aspiring middle-class professional and business people sought to join them. But there was not much space left in Clifton and property there was correspondingly expensive. Therefore enterprising builders and landowners saw an opportunity on the fringes of Clifton, in Redland and Cotham especially. There was another factor that made a move in this direction out

15

of the city desirable. With the coming of the railway, there had been expansion to the east of the city, principally of industry, closely followed by the less affluent workers. Moreover, until 1867 travel into the city from the surrounding districts meant using toll roads, with the consequent cost. One of the turnpike gates, where the tolls were levied, was immediately south of the site of Tyndale, a spot still known as "Whiteladies Gate". However in 1867 turnpikes in the Bristol area were abolished and so it became more attractive to commute into the city from the suburbs. That event seems to have accelerated the rate of building. One contemporary observer commented:

> During the summer of 1867, building operations were carried on with unusual vigour in the suburban districts. In July a number of fields and nursery gardens near Redland and Hampton roads were laid out in new streets.

The area between Pembroke Road and Whiteladies Road was largely built up from the 1850s onwards, at an accelerating pace, and the spread of what a contemporary observer referred to as "what are called semi-detached villas" (in contrast to the terraces of central Clifton) continued further east into Redland and Cotham. This was an on-going process for some years after Tyndale was built – according to Dorothy Glover (writing on the occasion of the church's 80th anniversary in 1949) the land on the western side of Whiteladies Road between Apsley and Alma roads was still the site of a market garden. The east side of Whiteladies Road was likewise undeveloped. She also wrote of her mother with her visiting sisters being helped by "the Senior Deacon gracefully handing the young Mrs Glover… over stile after stile and along small field paths as they made their way to the new church" from their first home in Elm Grove Road (now known as Elmgrove Road) in Cotham.

It was to serve these new suburban developments that the various Christian denominations founded new churches. The Anglicans had already opened St John's in Whiteladies Road in 1841, followed by All Saints in Pembroke Road in 1868. The Congregationalists had built Highbury Chapel (now Cotham Parish Church), further east, at the top of St Michael's Hill in 1843 and then Redland Park in 1861 and Pembroke Chapel in Oakfield Road in

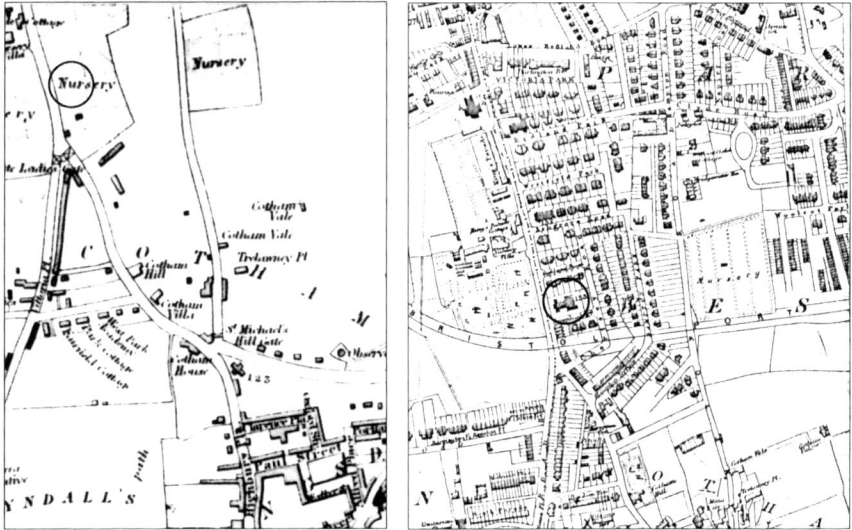

Two maps showing the development of the area around the church from the 1840s (left) to the early 1870s (right). The second map dates from between 1868 and 1874 and shows the new church (without the lecture hall) just north of the Bristol Port Railway. The location of Tyndale is marked with a circle. The maps are of approximately equal scale but are offset from one another.

1866. The Methodists built two churches in Whiteladies Road – Victoria in 1863 and Trinity, Tyndale's closest neighbour on the corner of Ashgrove Road, in 1866. It was against this background that the Revd R. P. Macmaster, minister of the Counterslip church, delivered an hour-long address at the stone laying ceremony:

> Seeing the goodly number of chapels with which the locality is already adorned, some friends might ask why build another here instead of in some destitute neighbourhood? The answer is this – the Baptists have their own church members to accommodate, and their distinctive principles to advance. Everybody knows that in the present day the tendency of wealth is to the suburbs, and yielding to this tendency many members of the Baptist churches in the city have come to reside in this charming neighbourhood. The consequence is that the distance is far too great to allow those of them who have young families to continue to attend city

churches, and therefore, like other denominations, the Baptists have to choose between losing the money of our wealthy members altogether, or uniting with them in providing accommodation near their residences. The fitter alternative is preferred, and this building is to be erected, certainly not with the view of robbing sister churches, but in order to retain the members of the Baptist denomination.

He concluded by pointing out that the Baptists had not neglected those districts where less wealthy citizens resided since, apart from the Buckingham chapel, all the Baptist places of worship "are located among the masses of the people".

The Revd Frederick William Gotch, Principal of Bristol Baptist College and founding trustee of Tyndale [© Illustrated London News Group. Source: British Newspaper Archive and British Library Board]

It all started at a Broadmead Church Meeting in the early months of 1866. After some discussion concerning the desirability of forming a new church to serve the rapidly growing area of Clifton, a sub-committee was set up to consider the idea. On 13th March the committee met, chaired by Dr F. W. Gotch (Principal of the Baptist College) and chose Joseph Eyre as its secretary and Edward G. Clarke (an accountant) together with E. S. Robinson as joint treasurers. An appeal to the Broadmead members was made for funds and when the committee met the minister, Nathaniel Haycroft, he expressed satisfaction at the response, but urged a wider appeal. By the end of March £1,890 had been contributed. Although the idea of a new church in the Whiteladies Road area was still considered "highly desirable", it was becoming clear that, while the minister was keen for the two churches to be in some way united under his leadership, and, indeed, had suggested that

Broadmead itself move out to the suburbs, there was growing unhappiness within the membership at this idea of their minister serving two churches. At this point a wider meeting "of interested friends and donors" was convened for 5 April. However, before this could happen, the committee reported to the Church Meeting that the idea of a new cause connected with the Broadmead church was "not sufficiently practicable".

At this point E. S. Robinson took up the cause. There is more about him in Chapter 4, but suffice it to say here that in 1866 he was Mayor of Bristol. While having a strong Baptist "pedigree" he was then a member of Highbury Congregational Church, but he and his wife joined the new Tyndale on 2nd November, 1869. A new committee was recruited and met on 9th May at Old King Street (hence that church's claim to be Tyndale's "mother" despite Robinson making clear that this was simply "a convenient place" of meeting). The new committee did not delay! Ten meetings were held between October and the following January. A small sub-committee was also put in place to deal with detailed matters between meetings of the main committee. Not that everything moved forward smoothly – at one meeting it was resolved that the "Gothic" style was unsuitable! This may reflect the unease among some non-conformists who saw this style as too closely associated with the High Church revival initiated by the Oxford Movement in the Anglican church. Clearly this decision was later reversed. Whiteladies Road was not the only site considered. The representatives of the Buckingham church feared this was too near their building, although in the end their objections were overcome. The principal alternative site being considered was on the edge of Woolcot Park. This was the name given to a development of a few roads to the south of the present Chandos Road, now the site of Brighton, Lansdown and Stanley roads. However, this was still rather difficult to access from the other developments. A contemporary observer, writing in 1867, commented: "The only outlet westward from the estate [i.e. Woolcot Park] was an old footpath, known as Nettle Lane" – this was the line of part of the future Chandos Road. In fact the developer was in dispute with the local authority about providing access, which it did not provide until 1877. There may have been another factor which influenced the committee against this site. The building plots here were smaller than most in Redland and this led to smaller, terraced houses being built. They may have anticipated that these would be occupied by less affluent families than those who were the "target" congregation. Indeed, a few years later the census shows that the occupants were in what would be regarded as working-class occupations. If Tyndale had been built there it would have been fairly isolated for its first decade and been in what might be regarded as a comparative "backwater" still today, instead of in a prominent position on a busy thoroughfare.

However, in the years immediately before the church was built there, Whiteladies Road was little more than a country lane. It had been created as an extension to the new Park Street around 1760, when it was known as the road to Wales – the route continuing across Durdham Down and on to Cribbs Causeway. At the northern end, on the hill was the Blackboy Inn, which was demolished in 1874, although its memory is perpetuated in the name of "Blackboy Hill". Just below it, on the western side, was King's Parade and a few cottages on either side of the road – the rest of the road was lined by nursery gardens on both sides for most of its length. In the 1850s it was still not a very pleasant thoroughfare having an open gutter down which house drainage flowed to the junction of several open sewers not far from the future site of the church, overflowing onto a field where Alma Road would be built. In 1852 the southern part of the road had been widened and it was at this time that the road was given its name – for many years "White Ladies Road", taking its name from White Ladies House which stood on the western side of the road opposite the later Aberdeen Road. By the time the church site was purchased other building was under way on the eastern side. Indeed, the trust deed described the site by reference to several new roads which bounded it – Oakland Road, Chertsey Road and Greenbank (later renamed Imperial) Road. By 1871 the whole of the eastern side of Whiteladies Road was lined with houses with side roads for most of its length. The site itself measured 240 feet by 110 feet (just over half an acre) and was part of a 9½ acre plot formerly known as "Mariners Path".

The earliest recorded owner of this land was John Hodgkiss, who died in 1740, leaving the land to be divided between his four daughters. Three of these quarters (including the future church site) were later re-united after being mortgaged in 1747 for the benefit of Hodgkiss' widow. When the loan was due to be repaid neither she nor her daughters had the funds, so it reverted to the lender, George Daubeny. After his death in 1764 his son of the same name inherited the land. He served as an MP for three years after an election which had erupted in a riot. In 1788 he allied himself with Caleb Evans, Principal of the Baptist College, in forming a local committee to campaign for the abolition of slavery. This was surprising given that his business was as a sugar refiner, and, less surprisingly, the following year he switched sides, having realised the potential commercial consequences of abolition! Subsequently the land was sold to the Queen Anne's Bounty (a fund to augment the incomes of poor Anglican clergy) and its income was assigned to the Vicar of Clifton (who was, in fact only a "perpetual curate" and therefore not entitled to the income from the tithes). Most of the area was leased as a market garden. Benjamin John Stickland, who lived in the nearby recently built Hampton Terrace, bought it in 1863 for £7,243 in order to build more houses, in collaboration with William Lyddon, a builder, and it was from them that the church plot was purchased, subject to a "fee farm rent" of £60 per year. Another builder who was a partner with Stickland in developing this area was William Coates. The committee had to agree to pay him £40 compensation for his loss of interest in the site. Once the site was secured a notice board was erected announcing that the new chapel was to be built there and giving the names and addresses of the treasurers – clearly in the hope of attracting more subscriptions.

The architect appointed was Samuel Hancorn of Steven Street, Bristol and Dock Street, Newport, who sadly died three months before the building was opened. It was originally hoped that the total cost would be around £3,000 and the building should be capable of holding up to 580 worshippers. The expected cost of the building was subsequently revised upwards to £4,170, and then the tender was finally let for £5,652 (some £900 less than the highest tender) to Messrs Marquis & Munro of Old Market, Bristol, whose Clerk of Works, Mr Hotham, oversaw the work. It was decided to omit the tower, thus saving about £500, but, even so and with a few additions to the original scheme, the final cost was £6,378. The tower was eventually built 25 years later to a modified design by the nonconformist architects, Crisp and Oatley. Henry Crisp (1826–1896) was the son of Thomas Steffe Crisp, the Principal of Bristol Baptist College from 1825 to 1868 (and tutor before that from 1818). Although he never became a member himself, two of Henry Crisp's older sisters were members of Tyndale for many years. George Oatley (1863–1950) was the partner of Crisp from 1888 until Crisp's death and went on with a new partner to design the new buildings for Bristol Baptist College in Woodland Road (now housing the University of Bristol's Anthropology and Archaeology Department) as well as many of the University's buildings. Another choice which had long lasting consequences was to omit a basement from the scheme. Mary Willoughby, owner of nearby properties, offered to purchase part of the site if it was not used, in order to build more houses. This option was considered alongside the decision about the basement and the plans do show the eastern portion of the plot as the possible site for a villa. It would appear that the "basement" would probably have been for a hall (as at Victoria Methodist church). However, since that was not included, and could clearly not be added later, the committee fortunately did not accept Mrs Willoughby's offer. Had they done so the Lecture Hall could not have been built a few years later, nor Tyndale Court a century later!

Just four months before the opening, there was still a shortfall of about £2,500 in the money raised. As a contribution towards this, a bazaar and a madrigal concert were arranged by a group of ladies (mostly the wives of committee members) at the Victoria Rooms. It was only two weeks before the stone laying that it was finally agreed that the name "Tyndale Chapel" should be adopted. William Tyndale had been closely associated with Bristol – preaching on College Green, for instance – as the Tyndale window in the church illustrates. However the name was adopted principally to celebrate the rare 1526 edition of Tyndale's New Testament, owned by the Baptist College since 1784, which was shown to the congregation at the stone laying ceremony – one of the few occasions it was allowed out of the college. It was later sold by the college to the British Library in London in 1994; the Library has described it as "the most important printed book in the English language".

The stone laying ceremony took place on 17th July, 1867. The Mayor, E. S. Robinson, presided and the congregation was accommodated in a large tent on the site, at the entrance of which a collection was made. Among those present were several local clergy and ministers and leading citizens. The

> # TYNDALE CHAPEL, WHITE LADIES' ROAD.
>
> The FOUNDATION STONE of the NEW BAPTIST CHAPEL in the WHITE LADIES' ROAD will be Laid on WEDNESDAY Next, the 17th July, by the Right Worshipful the MAYOR OF BRISTOL (E. S. ROBINSON, Esq.)
>
> The Ceremony will commence at Half-past Three in the Afternoon, and the following Ministers, with other Friends, have promised to take part in the proceedings:—Rev. W. MORLEY PUNSHON, M.A., Rev. URIJAH THOMAS, B.A., Rev. F. W. GOTCH, LL.D., Rev. R. P. MACMASTER, and Rev. CHARLES CLARK.
>
> A large Tent will be erected, with Reserved Seats for Ladies. There will be a Collection in aid of the Building Fund.

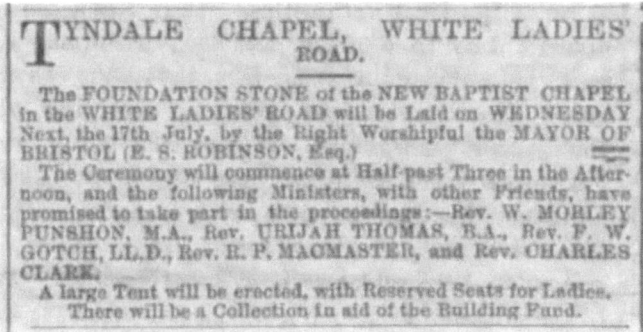

Notice in the Western Daily Press

Mayor was presented with a silver trowel with which he formally laid the foundation stone, before making a speech explaining the reason for building the church. Below the foundation stone a "time capsule" was buried. After Robinson had spoken came the address by the Revd R. P. Macmaster (minister of Counterslip church) and briefer addresses by three other ministers from other denominations. As well as the addresses, prayers were offered and three hymns were sung.

On 21st March 1868 the committee agreed to adopt a Trust Deed based on that of the Bloomsbury church in London and suggested the names of the trustees. It is remarkable that this decision was not made until building work was well under way and, in fact, the trust was not "declared", signed and sealed until 7th February 1869, some four months after the building was opened! The terms of the trust are largely unremarkable. As is usual in such documents it recites the details of the purchase of the site and its purpose. It also refers to the annual fee farm rent of £60 (most of the building plots in Redland were sold on this basis at that time) and to the Indenture (that is the document by which the ownership was conveyed to the trustees) which laid down that if the church should be destroyed it must be rebuilt within 18 months or the site could be used for more houses! (Fortunately by the time the church was destroyed in 1940 the freehold had been purchased and there was no threat of this being enforced.) The deed established a church with open membership and open communion and made it clear that it was a Baptist church and that the minister had to be a Baptist. One clause which has caused difficulty down the years was the requirement for a two-thirds majority of those present and voting at a

Tyndale before the clock tower was added

Church Meeting to elect deacons. There have been many different sets of rules drawn up from time to time to try to prevent this leading to a shortfall in the desired number of deacons. It also provided that the trustees should continue to control the affairs of the church until there was a membership of at least fifty. Because of this there were no deacons elected until 1871. Unusually the "ultimate trust" (that is what was to happen if the church closed) gave the authority to the trustees to dispose of the assets "for the benefit of the Baptist Denomination" rather than naming the particular organisation which would benefit. The trust deed named 21 trustees. Future trustees all had to be members of a Baptist church and some of the first trustees became members of Tyndale – eight of them serving as deacons. The trust deed lists their occupations – twelve of them were merchants or otherwise engaged in commerce, seven were professional men (four of those were accountants), one gentleman (in fact a retired businessman) and the Principal of the Baptist College, Dr F. W. Gotch. Appendix 1 contains some biographical notes on these first trustees.

In the months leading up to the opening of the church various members of the committee travelled to hear a number of ministers preach in their own churches. However it had been decided that the church would not be formed until a minister had been called. Richard Glover of Glasgow was invited to preach on two Sundays in January and February 1869, following which a meeting of the congregation resolved to invite him to become their pastor. The building committee was asked to continue in the role of deacons until the membership reached 50, at which point, in accordance with the Trust Deed, deacons could be elected. On 6th April the Revd J. A. Wheeler

Inside the church of 1868

of Old King Street presided at a meeting at which the church was formally constituted. The next evening Dr William Landels (who had baptised Richard Glover) delivered a charge to the church and Dr Gotch delivered a charge to the minister.

The building committee, now acting in its new role, first met a week later. There was still a shortfall in the funds for the building and at the following meeting it was agreed to take out a loan in the form of a mortgage of £2,500 from E. S. Robinson (mortgages from private individuals were a common way of funding building projects at the time). The other principal concern at this second meeting was the resignation of one of the committee members, Philip Henry Williams, who was also a trustee. He felt he had to resign because he had been declared bankrupt. Williams had been in an iron-trading business, but a few years earlier had started a business as a stockbroker. At first the other members of the committee accepted his resignation "with regret and sympathy for him and his wife in the circumstances which had rendered this course needful". However, after Charles Townsend and William Polglase had investigated the circumstances, they reported to a subsequent meeting that there appeared to have been transactions "which evince a want of Christian honour greatly to be regretted". It appears that Williams had been acting for a client who had been involved with illegal share dealing and his client lost a civil action brought by the company concerned. The extent to which Williams himself was culpable is not clear, although Townsend and Polglase were certain that he was – they were "not satisfied with the statement given by Mr Williams in explanation of his part in this transaction". There was an exchange of letters between Williams, his wife and several of the committee members and the minister, Richard Glover. From Williams' letters, between October 1869 and the following February it is clear that Williams was becoming increasingly unhappy with the actions of all the church people involved, not least the minister, to whom he wrote no fewer than fourteen letters over that period. The Church Meeting adopted a resolution expressing regret that "in some of Mr Williams's transactions there have been features which these brethren disapprove" and went on to urge him "to more earnestly avoid all 'appearance of evil' for the future". Williams suggested that the church members should "pull out the beam out of thine own eye" and "he that is without sin let him cast the first stone" (although without actually accusing anyone of any wrongdoing) and then he and his wife resigned their membership. The family moved to Bath and although Mrs Williams and other members of the family subsequently returned to Bristol, living quite nearby, they never returned to Tyndale.

By 1871 the membership had reached the required number of 50 to enable a diaconate to be elected. Thus on 30th May the first six deacons were elected. All the members of the Building Committee became deacons, with the exception, for obvious reasons, of Philip Williams. He was replaced by David Joseph and William Sherring was also elected. So the new diaconate consisted of Edward Clarke, Joseph Eyre, Elisha Smith Robinson, Charles Townsend, David Joseph and William Sherring. Charles Townsend replaced Edward Clarke as Secretary – a position he held for 21 years, only resigning when he was elected to Parliament.

Appendix 1: The First Trustees

The Trust Deed of 27th February 1869 named the 21 foundation trustees. The Trust Deed only gives their names and occupations, listed in the following order. Additional biographical details have been appended, where these are known. An asterisk* denotes those trustees who became members of Tyndale. There is more in Chapter 4 about those men marked with a plus⁺.

The Revd Frederick William Gotch, President of Bristol Baptist College (aged 61). The College was then sited in Stokes Croft, where Gotch lived in the President's residence adjacent to the College. He had become President in 1868, having served as a Tutor since 1845 while Thomas Crisp was President. Gotch had himself been a student at the College and also at Trinity College, Dublin. From 1836 to 1845 he was minister of Boxmoor Baptist Church in Hertfordshire and in 1868 he was President of the Baptist Union. He was born on 31st August 1807 in Kettering, Northamptonshire and his parents were John Cooper Gotch and Mary Ann (née Davis). He married Sarah Hannah Foster, who died in 1862. Their daughter, Katherine, married Edward Robinson. Gotch died on 17th May 1890.

Elisha Smith Robinson*⁺, Paper Merchant (aged 52), Clare House, Westbury On Trym.

William Polglase*, Wholesale Tea Dealer (aged 50), Ivor House, Durdham Park, Westbury On Trym (having moved there from Cotham Hill in 1868). His business was in Bath Street, Counterslip (until 1859 as a partner in the firm of Morris & Polglase) and later in St Stephen Street. For many years he was a leading member of the Bristol Chamber of Commerce. He was born on 28th April 1818 to a Quaker family in Bristol and in 1841 he married Sarah Till-Adam (who died in 1893). He served as a Tyndale deacon from 1871 until his death at the age of 61 in 1880.

Edward Gustavus Clarke*⁺, Public Accountant (aged 35), Woodside, Redland Grove.

Charles Townsend*⁺, Chemist (aged 36), Avenue House, Cotham Park.

Crosby Leonard, Surgeon (aged 40), Rockleigh House, Whiteladies Road. He was born on 16th May 1828 and died on 13th October 1879. He was the son of another surgeon, Isaac Leonard and his wife Mary Ann (née Crosby). Like his father before him, he was a well-known and highly regarded member of the medical profession in Bristol. He held a number of significant medical posts, including that of senior surgeon at the Bristol Royal Infirmary (BRI). Suffering from a form of paralysis, he sustained a fall in August 1875, in which he broke his leg. This may have contributed to his early death at the age of only 51. He left legacies to the BRI, the Bristol City Mission Society and the BMS.

David Stodhart Oliver, Wine and Spirit Merchant (aged 47), Arundell House, Cotham New Road (later Tyndall's Park Road). He was born in Shoreditch, London in April 1822 to Thomas and Barbara Oliver. His business address was 1 Temple Street. In 1850 he had married Henrietta Lemon and they had two children. He had been made bankrupt in 1860. He died on 13th May 1891. His wife outlived him and died in 1905.

Alfred Amor Taylor, Linen Draper (also a silk mercer) (aged 43), Frostan House, Redland. He carried on his business (Snow & Taylor) in Wine Street, where he and his wife also lived for some years. He was born in Trowbridge, Wiltshire in 1826 and in 1846 married Elizabeth Lovering Barron, who came from Ilfracombe in Devon. He died on 25th February 1871 aged only 45. His wife died ten years later at the age of 47.

William Hole Williams, Public Accountant (aged 43), Grove House, Durdham Park. He was the brother of Philip Henry Williams. He practised in Cardiff as well as in Bristol and had many other business interests in Gloucestershire and South Wales, becoming a director and chairman of various companies concerned with railways and collieries. He died in Gunnersbury, Surrey on 20th April 1892.

John Hare Leonard, Iron Merchant (aged 45), Fairfield Villa, Pembroke Road. He was born on 13th August 1823, the son of Robert Leonard and Martha Ann Hare. [His father, Robert Leonard was the senior deacon at the Counterslip church and worked closely with the minister of Counterslip, the Revd Thomas Winter. Winter had been one of the instigators of the Bristol Baptist Itinerant Society, along with Thomas Roberts of Old King Street and John Ryland of Broadmead, and Robert Leonard was the Society's treasurer for many years as well as being treasurer of the College for 25 years in succession to his own father. He was the owner of an iron business and also a coal mine, as well as being a City Alderman and Magistrate.] John inherited the iron business from his father, but moved to London to a new interest in the oil trade, importing and refining petroleum. In 1851 he married Ellen Perrin in Clutton (Somerset) and they had four sons and a daughter. John Leonard died in Islington, London, on 19th January 1895 and was buried at Arnos Vale Cemetery in Bristol. Ellen died in London on 1st November 1914.

George Hare Leonard, Colliery Proprietor (aged 42), 2 Wellesley Villas, Pembroke Road. He was the brother of John and was born 26th August 1826. For some years the brothers lived next door to each other. He married Sarah Grey on 6th March 1853 at St Matthias church. Whereas John inherited the iron business from their father, George inherited the Easton Colliery. He was a JP and one of the original trustees of the YMCA when it was established in 1853. He died in Bristol on 12th October 1913. John and George were two of a large family of 12 children of Robert and Martha Leonard; a younger brother, Frederick, had been a student at the Baptist College between 1849 and 1852.

Alfred Roberts Tratman, Ship Chandler (he also described himself as a "ship owner" and on another occasion as an "oil merchant") (aged 47), Easton Villa, Victoria Road. His wife, whom he married in 1851, was Marianne Sanders, who came from Barnstaple in Devon. They had six sons and one daughter. When he retired he went to live in Kensington in London, but later returned to live in St John's Road, Clifton. He died on 19th December 1903, aged 82, leaving his estate of more than £12,500 to members of his family.

William Sherring

William Sherring*, Nail Manufacturer (aged 40), Fairfield Road. Born in 1828 to parents who were members of Broadmead (his father was a publican in Lawrence Hill), he ran a very successful business manufacturing nails and similar iron goods in Wilder Street, employing over 100 workers. In 1856 he married Millicent Price and two of their three daughters married sons of Charles Townsend. Both their sons joined their father in the family business. He was one of Tyndale's first deacons, serving for eleven years. For some years he was secretary of the Society for Aged and Infirm Baptist Ministers and the Baptist Western Widows and Orphans Society. He donated a number of books to the library of Bristol Baptist College and also helped the college with fabric matters. He died on 10th November 1921, aged 93. At his funeral at Tyndale the address was given by the College Principal, Dr W. J. Henderson.

Samuel Miles Phillips, Gentleman (aged 52), no fixed abode! He was, in fact, a retired Iron Merchant who was living in a series of hotels. He was born on 31st August 1817 to William (a linen draper) and Elizabeth Phillips (née Pollard), who were members of Broadmead and lived on Welsh Back (his birth was recorded in the records of the Broadmead church and signed by the minister, John Ryland). He met a tragic death in July 1883 when he was staying at the Dragon Hotel in Hereford. He returned to the hotel about 8 o'clock and was found about two hours later by a maid, lying on the fender in the sitting room fire. It was thought that he had got up to ring the bell, slipped and hit his head against the mantelpiece. He was knocked unconscious and fell into the fire where he received fatal burns.

Owen Smith*, Commercial Traveller (aged 41), 9 Redland Park Villas. The description of his occupation seems misleading as in the 1871 census he is described as a wholesale stationer and later he described himself as a "retired wholesale stationer". He was born in Bicester (Oxfordshire) on 12th December 1827 to James and Elizabeth Smith and was christened at Water Lane Independent chapel. His father was also a stationer and a printer. He was married in 1857 at Westbury-on-Severn to Mary Ann Vorley who came from Wellingborough (Northamptonshire). He served as a deacon at Tyndale from 1886 until his death, and for many years was on the committee of the Bristol Female Refuge. He died on 19th February 1902 and was buried at St Nathaniel's church, Redland. His wife died in January 1913.

William Pethick, Tallow Merchant (aged 37), Lanoy House, Clifton. Born in Bideford (North Devon) to Thomas and Susan Pethick, on 8th November 1831, he was christened in the local Wesleyan chapel. In 1850 the family moved to Bristol where his father was a hide merchant. In 1857 he married Ellen Haycroft, also from Bideford, and they had three children. They married in London where two of their children were born, before returning to Bristol. He became a partner in the firm of Haycroft and Pethick, a South American import house. In 1866 he was elected a Councillor for the Bedminster ward and in 1894 became an Alderman and served as High Sheriff of Bristol in 1894–95. He was a founder of the Bristol Liberal Unionist Association and served as a JP both in Bristol and in Cornwall where he had a second home in Lanoy. In 1885 he stood for Parliament, but was narrowly defeated. He died on 12th November 1902 at his home, Woodside, Stoke Bishop and his funeral (attended by Richard Glover and other Tyndale members) was at Christ Church, where his wife's funeral also took place following her death on 18th August 1915.

Philip Henry Williams*, Stockbroker (aged 39), Corn Street (business address). Brother of William Hole Williams. He became a member of the committee which was appointed in April 1869 to run the church before deacons were elected. However, he resigned a month later having been declared bankrupt and also resigned his membership of the church. He was born on 8th June 1829 at

Williton in Somerset and had been a manufacturer of iron goods before moving on to being a stockbroker. In December 1861 he had married Martha Winter, daughter of the minister of Counterslip and eventually they would have nine children, all born between 1864 and 1877. Following his bankruptcy he and the family moved first to Bath and then to Swansea, where his three youngest children were born. However some time before 1881 he became an inmate in the private Northwoods Asylum at Frampton Cotterell, an institution describing itself as "An establishment for the reception and cure of a limited number of insane patients of the higher classes of society". Meanwhile his family had returned to Bristol, living in various places including Chandos Road and Clyde Park. It does not appear that any of the family became members of Tyndale.

Oliver Ransford, Accountant (aged 34), 4 Camden Terrace. He was born in 1836, the son of another Oliver Ransford and Henrietta (née de Castro, from a formerly Jewish family). His mother died at the early age of 28. On 23rd May 1863 he married Emma Mary Claypole at the church of St Mary Magdalene, Stoke Bishop. Like his mother, his wife, a member of Tyndale, also died young, aged just 35, in 1876. As well as practising as an accountant, he was Secretary of the Albion Building Society of which fellow Tyndale trustees E. G. Clarke was Chairman, E. S. Robinson a Trustee and Charles Townsend a Director. He died on 15th January 1889 aged 53.

Joseph Freer, Accountant (aged 35), 6 Cotham Terrace. He was born in Upton-on-Severn, Worcestershire in 1834 and lived most of his life in the Cirencester area of Gloucestershire. However, he lived and worked in Bristol for some years and also in Keynsham where he was a commercial clerk. In Bristol he was a cashier employed by the Bristol and Exeter Railway (which merged with the GWR in 1876) and was Superintendent of the Cotham Sunday School. He never married and lived in a series of lodgings. When he retired he went to live in Cirencester with his cousin, Edward Blundell (Professor of Agriculture at the Royal Agricultural College). One of his great interests was nature study, especially collecting wild flowers. On 30th November 1906 he went for a country walk near his cousin's home and suffered a fatal heart attack.

James Livett Daniell*, Solicitor (aged 23), Newton Villa, Wellington Park. He was born in 1845, son of John and Martha (née Tuckett). (Livett was his grandmother's maiden name – his grandparents were married at Broadmead in 1813). Starting as a Solicitor's Clerk he practised as a solicitor in partnership with his younger brother, Edward Tuckett Daniell, in Whitson Chambers, Nicholas Street. In 1898 he was President of the Bristol Law Society. On 13th January 1870 he married his cousin Sophie Day Baynes in London. They had two sons and a daughter. Their older son, John Arthur Helton Daniell, later joined the partnership and also served in a local territorial unit – the 1st Gloucester Volunteer Artillery – and was killed in France on 1st July 1917. James was a local preacher and a member of the Bristol Baptist Itinerant Society, serving mostly village churches and from 1900 to 1915 he was a deacon at Tyndale. As well as being a trustee of Tyndale he was also a trustee of the Mission premises and a member of its Management Committee. He died on 14th February 1919, aged 74. At his funeral at Canford Cemetery, Herbert Morgan referred to his wonderful versatility and the way in which he combined qualities which often seemed opposed – he was both serious and humorous. His widow died in London in 1931, aged 83.

Chapter 2.
Richard Glover

David Roberts

At the front of the sanctuary, facing the congregation, is Tyndale's only personal memorial tablet within the church. It reads, "To the glory of God in grateful memory of Richard Glover... the first minister of this church".

Richard Glover was born in South Shields on 6th January 1837, the eighth and youngest son of Terrot Glover, who came originally from Scotland, and his wife Anne (née Reaveley). Glover senior was a prosperous ship owner, who was actively involved in local politics as a Liberal, served as Mayor of his borough on three occasions, and as a Justice of the Peace. Several of Richard's brothers followed their father into shipping and related businesses. The eldest, Sir John Glover, served as Chairman of Lloyd's Register. Their devotion to the Liberal cause may be gauged by the fact that the first ship bought by Glover Brothers & Co. (three of Richard's brothers) in 1865 was named *The W. E. Gladstone*! The family were

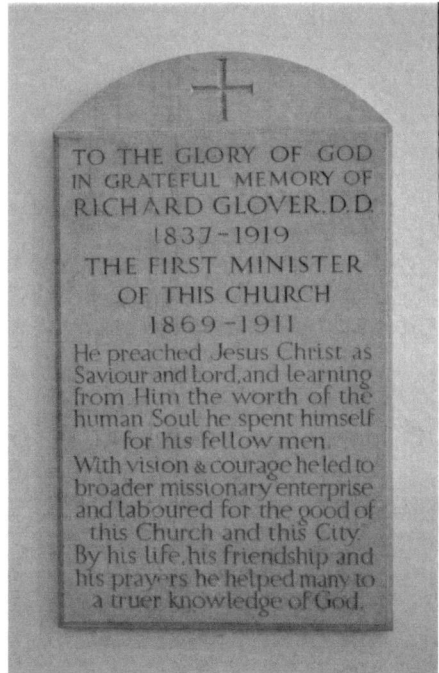

Richard Glover memorial tablet in the sanctuary

Presbyterians and Richard was baptised at East Street Presbyterian church, South Shields at twelve days old. Towards the end of his lengthy student career, however, Richard turned his back on the family's church and became a Baptist. At the age of seventeen he had begun his studies at the University of Edinburgh. After two years he moved to London, studying for a year at King's College and then at the Presbyterian College, where he was training for the Presbyterian ministry. Half-way through his four-year course, in 1859, he came to the conclusion that the Baptist rather than the Presbyterian denomination recognised most fully the dignity and responsibility of the individual Christian and the organisation and spirit of the New Testament, which emphasised personal response and personal responsibility. More than twenty years later he wrote: "I am comparatively indifferent to forms of church government, personally preferring those which give most scope to individual action and possess most elasticity". Much later (in 1898) he wrote: "The way in which the Saviour individualizes men... impresses me greatly... There is in Christ's teaching no suggestion of gregarious or corporate salvation".

Thus Glover's decision to become a Baptist was not simply a negative rejection of the Presbyterian doctrines, but the outcome of a positive identification with the ideas he found in Baptists doctrines. Glover's tutor at the Presbyterian College was Dr Thomas McCrie. In 1850 McCrie had published *Lectures on Christian Baptism* in which he forcefully defended the practice of infant baptism, questioned the necessity for total immersion and attacked the writings of the Revd Baptist Noel (himself a convert to the Baptist cause, having been an Anglican clergyman until 1849). So perhaps it is understandable that McCrie described Glover's changed views as "crotchety and erroneous", while at the same time giving him a lukewarm commendation as being "constitutionally candid, though given to speculation". It was in these terms that in 1859 McCrie referred him to Dr William Landels of Regent's Park Baptist Chapel, by whom he was then baptised. Landels would, no doubt, have had a special sympathy for Glover's position since, like Glover, he had started life in a different denomination, in his case the Primitive Methodists, and had also changed his views on baptism to embrace believers' baptism, being baptised himself at the age of 23 when already an ordained minister. Fourteen years senior to Glover, he became a close personal friend – the only person known to have referred to him as "Dick"!

Recommended to the church by William Landels, Glover began his first pastorate in 1861 at Blackfriars Street Baptist church in Glasgow, where he ministered for eight years. On 27 March 1866 he married Anna Finlay of Govan (a burgh rapidly growing and being swallowed by Glasgow), daughter of the proprietor of a textile manufacturing business. According to his daughter, Dorothy, it was through the influence of William Landels that the as yet unknown young Richard Glover was invited to preach one of the missionary sermons in London during the BMS Spring Assembly of 1867. He made such an impact that "people were moved to a new sense of the reality and importance of missionary work". Of more immediate significance for Glover himself was the call which followed to become the minister of the newly established Tyndale Church. Not that it was straightforward – he was also invited to become minister of another new church at Clapton in London. Happily (for Tyndale) he chose Bristol. Meanwhile the Downs Baptist Church in Clapton called the Revd Thomas Vincent Tymms as their minister – he later went on to be Principal of Rawdon College and to serve as Baptist Union President in 1896.

Richard and Anna Glover moved to Bristol in 1869, arriving from Glasgow at 1.00 am on the morning of 6 April – the day the church was constituted! Soon afterwards their first child was born – Terrot Reaveley, destined to become well-known as "T. R." – a classical scholar and prominent Baptist layman. For the first few years they lived at 6 Elm Grove Road in Cotham, but soon moved to 15 Westfield Park, which was to be Richard's home for the rest of his life. The family grew with the births first of Elizabeth in 1872 and then Dorothy in 1875. When she was in her 80s, Dorothy wrote an account of life in the family home when she was a child. She painted an idyllic picture – playing quietly in her father's study as he worked; being taken for walks by him on Durdham Down. Glover clearly had practical skills, making toys for his children, including two dolls' houses. Again Dorothy recalled:

> He could make paper things – trains, people, animals, ladders, wheelbarrows… in his own home with lathe, wood chisel and fretsaw; with paper, a press and paste; with chalk moulds and melted lead, he would cause children to create all manner of

things themselves that fascinated them and filled them with pride of accomplishment.

He retained these skills all his life, as evidenced by his entertaining the Belgian refugee children many years later (see Chapter 3). In a tribute after Glover died, his friend, the Revd J. G. Greenhough (formerly of Cotham Grove, Bristol), commented in the *Christian World*: "His knowledge of music was the envy of his brethren, and his artistic and mechanical genius their despair".

This is also an indication of his fondness for children. He was very conscious of the importance of working among children: it provided an opportunity for teaching the faith, which should not be missed, because "childhood is naturally the age of faith" and "a church, like a house, without young people is apt to be very dull". Glover seemed to have the ability to communicate well with children and to attract and hold their interest. Often he succeeded in sharing with them his own enthusiasm for practical skills and activities. He pointed out that many of those who had served as missionaries had been converted at an early age, but "I would do nothing to hasten church membership until the age is reached of, say, fourteen or sixteen". However, his own son had been baptised and become a church member at the age of thirteen, his daughters even younger, Elizabeth at the age of twelve, and Dorothy at eleven!

Once a month he devoted the morning service to the children and he recommended that there should be a children's address every Sunday. In the *Sunday School Chronicle* he contributed several series of "Notes for Teachers", and in 1888 he accepted an invitation to deliver the

Richard and Anna Glover with their children, Terrot (later known as "T. R."), Elizabeth and Dorothy.

Ridley Lectures at Regent's Park College on the subject "The Ministry of the Church to the Young". In teaching children, it was essential to stress the love of God for the idea "that the love of God should be fatherly, motherly, is to children the most credible of verities". He pointed out that the scholastic spirit that so dwarfed the mind of the church and imprisoned it, passed over from the Church of Rome into the reformed Churches, and into the minds of our Puritan fathers, and the idea that was dominant in their souls was the thought that God's motive power was not Love but the manifestation of His glory. In the nineteenth century the love of God had been rediscovered and "we have a theology better fitted to give to the children than in former days", not least because of the return from "misreading" the Epistles to reading the Gospels, which provided a simpler form of truth. So, through learning of the love of God, children were to be brought to Christ: "The only thoughts that are of use to child or man are those that set him thinking on his own lines, or that assist the struggling birth of thoughts within his soul".

While Glover stressed the importance of addressing the children in the Sunday congregation, it was as a gifted preacher that he became respected within and beyond his own church. Above all, he was considered to be effective in the pulpit. His daughter commented:

> What kind of preaching did the young minister address to his hearers? Having been brought up under it, I must rely on others who had a different background. They told me, "it was quite different". I can speak for it that his sermons never had twenty three heads, as was not unusual in those days. Chiefly he proclaimed the love of God, the grace of our Lord Jesus Christ, the responsibility of man to Him, love for our neighbour, and concern for his needs. The doctrines as he taught them were not something in a book or creed but living forces – becoming flesh. He had a gift for imaginative reconstruction. He did not use second-hand phrases. He made his own with vividness and freshness. Simplicity and depth and poetry were features. Those taught by him had nothing to unlearn in later life.

A more disinterested observer commented on a missionary address in 1883:

> The vast congregation... seemed spell-bound as Mr. Glover poured forth an address so full of sanctified eloquence and lofty inspiration that it is difficult to find terms in which adequately to characterise it.

Of his Presidential Address to the Baptist Union in April 1884 it was reported:

> Mr. Glover's "Inaugural" fully answered our expectations. An address of logical precision is not to be looked for from him. His thinking does not move in a logical groove; but he is a thinker of rare power, nevertheless, and his address abounded with thoughts of beautiful freshness and of priceless value.

While someone who did not always agree with him, speaking mainly of his preaching during his first pastorate in Glasgow, wrote:

> There were doubtless more learned, more brilliant, and more eloquent preachers than he, but none exactly like him. Without the slightest approach to eccentricity, or a spark of affectation, his personality was yet unique.

The same writer also commented:

> His speeches at Exeter Hall in 1880 and 1884, at Leicester in 1883, at the City Temple and at Broadmead in 1886, will not soon be forgotten by those who heard them... His two presidential addresses... reveal the essential spirit of the man, and are among the manliest, most reverent and Christ-like, as well as the most practical utterances to which we have listened.

Clearly the comment about his lack of logical thinking was made by one who had not heard his Inaugural Address as President of the Bristol Association in 1881. It consisted in the main of a closely argued thesis that there had been a decline in church life, and Baptist life in particular, in England during the nineteenth century and during the previous forty years especially. He quoted population and church membership statistics and he referred in detail to the level of giving in the context of the wealth of the nation as measured by tax revenue. He identified the reasons for this decline as "want of organic unity", the "distraction of our times", especially preoccupation with political issues and doctrinal controversy, a "general enfeeblement of the sense of the equal priesthood of all believers" leading to "in almost all our churches the almost exclusive discharge of many of our functions by the ministers" and, most importantly, a lack of depth in personal godliness. In response to this:

> Let us repent of these faults and imperfections, and lay warmer hearts in more unreserved sacrifice on the altar of our Saviour. Let us awake to the claims of our fellow-men, and deepen our concern for the glory of the Saviour. Let us be solicitous to receive a full reward, and we shall at length find in our Saviour's grace, in His Gospel, His smile, His help, we have power sufficient to achieve a success that will infinitely surpass all that is now conceivable by us.

Twenty years later he was more specific in identifying how the mission of the church at home might be addressed:

> Oh, if at home we would address ourselves to those absolute outsiders of whom we despair, I have the feeling that our churches would soon be filled by more virile souls, with larger convictions and consecration than are to be found in our midst today in the hearts of those more easily converted. It is not Sunday-school children only that we are to speak to, nor the aspiring, and the honourable, and those half converted by nature before grace touched them, but "every creature", to the drunkard, and blasphemer, to the lewd, the ignorant, the out-of-the-way, the heathen.

The work of the Tyndale Mission gave practical expression to his words, as will be seen in Chapter 5.

A side of Glover of which little is heard, and yet was much appreciated, was his sense of humour. Nowhere is this better illustrated than in an address he gave to the Bristol South Nonconformist Choirs Association. Speaking of the advantages of being accompanied by an organ, he observed: "It conceals silences and permits lazy people to go without singing" but "sometimes it is a steamroller crushing the congregation beneath its voice". Speaking of the choice of hymns:

> It is generally thought that the minister is responsible for all the bad tunes and the organist has the credit of all the nice ones. It is a case of "heads you win, tails I lose"! My idea is that the tunes should be chosen by a committee of two. The first should be a devout musician, who would select none but the good tunes, and the second should be some devout old woman, who enjoys hymns but who doesn't know much about music. She would see that the congregation is not robbed of the privilege of singing. Sometimes the minister might take the place of the old woman.

While his words were well received with laughter and applause, nevertheless some of his audience might have considered his humour a little "barbed" as he used it to convey a serious message.

Glover had come to the Baptist denomination through his own reading and convictions and this had involved a rejection of the Presbyterian view of the faith in which he had been brought up. Nevertheless he never rejected co-operation with people from other Christian denominations. Indeed in 1892 he was one of the two Baptist representatives at a remarkable conference at Grindewald in Switzerland to discuss closer co-operation between the various denominations in Britain. Very soon he had involved himself in Baptist life and also its controversies, while making it clear what he had rejected in moving on from his Presbyterian roots. This is clearly illustrated by his opposition to a scheme proposed by Baptist Union General Secretary, J. H. Shakespeare in 1909 for a ministerial settlement scheme which Glover saw as threatening the central independence tenet of Baptist churchmanship. In the *Baptist Times and Freeman* he wrote: "I frankly and with deepest conviction oppose this scheme on various grounds", which he went on to enumerate – it abandoned the Congregational principles of the Baptists, granting authority to a central committee and, in any case, it was likely that only the poorer churches would join the proposed "Federation" and to have two different schemes within the denomination would be divisive. For him this smacked too much of the Presbyterian ecclesiology from which he had departed; what was needed was spiritual renewal, not new organisation. Such a position is all the more remarkable when it is set within the context of Tyndale's contribution to the Twentieth Century Fund, part of which was to be used to fund these new central agencies. Tyndale's contribution which fell just short of £4,000 meant that Tyndale was the third most generous church in the denomination with only the church at Histon, near Cambridge where the Chivers family had large orchards for their jam-making business, and Heath Street, Hampstead giving more. At the Assembly where Shakespeare hoped to announce the success of the appeal he was still £326 short as the delegates awaited the news, and so he wired both Herbert Marnham, the treasurer of the Union, and Edward Robinson, pointing this out and both replied positively, so in the end they shared the honour of raising of the last monies needed. More than half of Tyndale's contribution came from the Robinson family.

Glover was also clear that he rejected Calvinism, and especially its teaching of predestination:

> Is it the doctrine of Scripture that all God's desires and purposes invariably obtain fulfilment? I think not. On the contrary *some* plan of God's is always and invariably realised, but that he has many alternative plans, less, more, and most good; and that whether *the* will of God – i.e. the very best – be done, or *a* will of God – the best possible in unyielding circumstances depends on us.

Further, "It is recognised through all Scriptures as the most solemn fact of human condition that the gracious will of God depends for its accomplishment on our concurrence and co-operation".

That was in 1880. Four years later, in his much praised Presidential Address to the Baptist Union he appears to have gone even further, when he stated:

> Man can inspire God, and charge the Divine Father with all his feelings, making Him participator in the thoughts, cares and

> desires of his heart, and in a limited but sufficient degree can
> mould the action and purpose of God.

Lecturing in 1883 on the Epistle to the Ephesians, chapter 1, he specifically rejected a Calvinist interpretation of verse 4 ("According as he hath chosen us in him before the foundation of the world…") and counselled his hearers to "avoid the darkness of Calvinism". By this sweeping aside of Calvinism, he set himself at odds with many of his contemporaries within, as well as beyond, the Baptist denomination, and notably with C. H. Spurgeon. They claimed to maintain their Calvinist roots, and held this to be the basis for their evangelical stance. Yet, of course, much of what Glover was denouncing in Calvinism had long since ceased to be part of what Spurgeon and other evangelicals within the Particular Baptist tradition thought of when they proudly labelled themselves "Calvinists". Similarly, Glover questioned the Puritan heritage which he saw as emphasising God's might and power at the expense of God's love. Surely it is Glover's much loved sense of humour coming through, however, when, around 1890 in his notes on chapter 17 of St John's Gospel, he wrote: "The hour is come – the hour that divides the history of the world. Until then it may be said to have been 'on the Down Grade', since then on the Up Grade". Clearly a reference to the "Down Grade" debate – a controversy which was dividing Baptists at the time. But there was more! For Glover also epitomised other attitudes which were perceived by some as inconsistent with an evangelical faith. Not only was he one of the growing number of nonconformist ministers who accepted biblical criticism, but he was generally open to the modern scientific teaching. In his thinly disguised tribute to his father in the *Daily News*, T. R. Glover stated: "he was frankly interested in Darwin, and it never seemed to occur to him that you could not be friends at once with Darwin and St. John". Yet in his later years he may have become less certain of this. In 1901, when he was aged 64, he expressed unease at the predominance of "laws" as the explanation of everything. He remarked: "For our progress to be sound, the supernatural should grow with the natural in our regard; but as it is, law is pushing out God more and more". However, in 1880 he had gone so far as to comment in an address to the Autumnal Assembly of the Baptist Missionary Society:

> I wish that the history of the religions of mankind could be written by a devout Darwinian; and I tell you why. Because it seems to me that in no field of observation will he find a firmer and nobler series of instances of the law of the survival of the fittest than in the study of the creeds of men. The heart of man has always opened to that which was best to live and die by.

This was in an address which sought to encourage missionaries in their task by arguing that mankind had a natural affinity for the divine. Throughout his ministry, Glover maintained this as one of the principal bases for his approach to mission. If mankind had a natural inclination to seek for a god figure, then it was the task of the missionary to point people to the true God: "We can tell men where they can find Him, infallibly and assuredly". He did not see this as simply a theoretical concept, for example: "A missionary has told of some few on the west coast of Africa who, in his judgment, sought after God even before the Gospel reached them". Therefore, he argued, Christians should not doubt that mankind was receptive to the Truth, and needed to show compassion towards all unbelievers, who lacked the consolations of the Christian faith. Furthermore:

> However man may be sunk in degradation, man is made in the image of God; and, however he forgets that Divine origin, there is in him, by virtue of it, an infinite capacity and an immortal force. Man everywhere is a generation that seeks God's face.

Perhaps more controversially, Glover did not simply write off all other faiths as without value. This needed to be understood if the church was to be successful in its mission to bring all people to Christ. Having understood it, then the approach to mission followed. He once wrote:

> I recognise that some heathen have virtues in which we are weak – such as submission to filial piety. There are truths we may learn from other creeds also. So I should urge on all heathen and all Christians the study of comparative religion.

In 1905 Glover was invited to give an address at the first Congress of the Baptist World Alliance under the challenging title, "The inadequacy of Non

Christian Religions to meet the needs of the World". Boldly he introduced his theme by averring, "the title of my subject must not be held to imply a belief on my part that the salvation of God is limited to those exclusively who know the Gospel story." Affirming that it was not for the church to limit the Holy One of Israel, he contended that Abraham knew no more than many heathen when he became the father of the faithful. He argued that God was not only the God of the Jews but of the heathen also, though compared with the noon-day light of the Gospel, the heathen only enjoyed a starlight experience. Accordingly the greatest need of the heathen world was the Gospel, and the greatest duty of the Christian world to utter it. Only the religion of the Bible provided a worthy conception of God and spoke of a Saviour to all people.

> It meets all the longings of our heart that God should save; and all the reverence of our reason that he should refuse to save cheaply; and all the instincts of our being that he should save us from the curse by sharing it – for sharing sorrow seems to be the one secret of securing it, both for God and man.

As a young man, Glover appears to have taken full advantage of the family shipping connections. While still a student he travelled widely. At the age of 21 he went to South Africa. There he visited the Moravian mission station at Genaden Dal. Subsequent voyages took him to Russia twice, the Mediterranean area, including the Holy Land, the South Sea Islands and even to the Arctic Ocean. Nor did his voyaging stop as he grew older. In 1890–91 he visited China on behalf of the Baptist Missionary Society. His daughter, Dorothy, later suggested that he was not altogether sure that he should go, feeling uncertain whether the visit had the full support of the BMS Committee, since that committee was uncertain of what strategies to pursue in China. Originally the visit was to take up to ten months, but in correspondence with the church Secretary, Charles Townsend, the BMS agreed to scale it back to six months. This fitted in with a resolution already passed by the Church Meeting to grant Glover six months leave of absence to mark the 21st anniversary of his pastorate. During this visit he sent frequent and lengthy accounts of his travels and experiences in China to the church secretary. These were then printed and, presumably, made available to the members of the congregation. Thus it was not simply through his

The Revd Dr Richard Glover

wide reading alone, but through his many travels, that he became aware of the tenets of other faiths and learned to respect them.

In a lecture at Bristol University College in 1883, Glover set out the biblical basis for this view. Commenting on Galatians chapter 4, verse 9 ("But now, after that ye have known God, or rather are known of God, how turn ye again to the weak and beggarly elements, whereunto ye desire again to be in bondage?"), he argued that St Paul saw some value in all religions: "Paul teaches that they [heathen religions] are all better than nothing and all preparing the way for Christ". He then proceeded to enumerate the services which those religions "we know most of" will render. These included inculcating many of those characteristics which are indeed looked for in one who follows the Christian faith, but he also suggested that many "heathen religions" also came near to Christian ideas of sin and atonement. He concluded by seeing this as an encouragement to Christian missionary work, since all these other "systems" prepared the way for the Christian Gospel. In other writings and addresses he enlarged on these ideas. With regard to Mohammedanism, he suggested that it was: "received not because of its error etc. but because it called man from idolatry to God". Gandama, the founder of the Buddhist religion, he saw as "the Martin Luther of India".

It is interesting also in this context to recall an incident which happened in Bristol. The Glover household was noted for its hospitality – an "ever-open door", as Dorothy later described it – and one visitor, in 1885, was Pandita Ramabai, an Indian convert from Hinduism to Christianity. While she was in Bristol, Glover took her to visit the tomb of the notable Hindu, Rajah Rammohun Roy (sometimes known as the father of modern India), who had died while on a visit to Bristol in 1833. He is buried in Arnos Vale cemetery (and many years later, in 1997, a statue of him was erected outside Bristol Cathedral).

It is, however, in the context of China that Glover showed the greatest respect for the "heathen religions". After visiting China, he was confirmed in his view and spoke of the Chinese as the "uppermost of all heathen people". He spelt out both how earlier missionary work in China had initially succeeded but later the faith had been corrupted, yet at the same time elements of it had been absorbed into some Buddhist sects. However, "we have a larger creed" and they "wait for the knowledge of God". So this was in no way to be seen as making the Christian Gospel redundant. On the contrary:

> The great people of China have come to a pass where the old and enfeebled religion of Buddhism and the somewhat secular moral teaching of Confucius no longer meet their need. There has always been a craving for higher truth in the hearts of Chinamen. The Temple of Heaven – i.e. of the one supreme God – in Peking has held there in Eastern Asia a position somewhat analogous to the position held by the Temple of Jehovah in Jerusalem – a witness to the one supreme God. It is our calling, and it is within our power, to give to that vast and strenuous and commanding people

> the light of life as it streams from the face of Christ and lives in His teaching.

This was said in the context of his address at the Memorial Service in 1901 for the Baptist missionaries killed in the Boxer Rebellion two months earlier. This rebellion (between 1899 and 1901) was an anti-foreign and anti-Christian movement that emerged in a period of drought and economic depression in China, representing an aggressive Chinese nationalism that targeted missionaries as the agents of a corrosive western culture. Writing earlier, in 1892, Glover had explained some of the background:

> They hate us; they misconceive the doctrines, rites and meaning of Christianity. The absence of all doctrine and practice expressive of reverence for the dead seems to denote on the part of Christians a disgraceful lack of filial sentiment.

It was in the light of these views that he saw the way for the Gospel to be proclaimed especially overseas. It was important for the missionary to seek to understand the people among whom he was going to work, and to respect their beliefs. So, "becoming Indian to the Indian is the duty of every missionary there", and, having thus come alongside the people, "believe in Man, in heathen man; believe that there is something in him which you have to find out." Indeed, "there are bits of the Gospel which only the heathen can see, and which, in our atmosphere, we cannot". Furthermore, "Remember that God has been there before you". Nor should conversion be seen in any sense as mechanistic: "Seek conversion, but cherish growth and build up character, that the whole nature fairly, evenly, and sacredly developed, may in harmony of a great service be a joyful song to God".

This advice was given in the context of evangelising the young, but was characteristic of his concern that conversion should be part of a process which included the nurture of any new Christian. On his return from visiting China, he urged that revival of religion should be "not of the nervous, hysterical sort".

Increasingly Glover was convinced that the churches at home must put more and more resources into overseas mission. The main emphasis of his

Report on the Deputation to China in 1890–91 was the need to send more missionaries, especially to build up work in the Shensi province. Frequently he gave his support to appeals for money, stressing the need to send more missionaries to China and elsewhere. He could envisage no substitute for sending people to witness to the heathen – "twice one are many more than two when it is two disciples sent forth". He maintained, however, that they must be properly trained and prepared for their mission. Of course they must be inspired – "only the inspired man can properly preach the Gospel of Christ". Inspiration notwithstanding, he firmly rejected a proposal to send untrained missionaries, and urged the colleges at home to "set themselves more diligently to train men for missionary work as well as for the ministry at home". Glover himself had become Secretary of the Bristol Baptist College in 1873 (and served in that capacity until his death), the same year that the young George Grenfell arrived as a student, from which date there was a marked increase in enthusiasm for overseas mission in that college. Glover also warned that what he perceived as a lack of calibre in the home ministry might be reflected in the quality of the missionaries. This view is, perhaps, a little surprising at a time when the general uplift in the educational standard of Baptist ministers was well under way. One reason for his concern was probably his observation that, especially in the case of China, of which he developed a special knowledge (he contributed the chapter on China in the centenary history of the Society in 1892), there was little contact with the better educated and more prosperous sections of the population. This he attributed to "the age-long and world-wide tendency of the poor to seek a gospel of comfort and partly because missionaries have almost exclusively addressed themselves to that class". In this he appears firmly to side with his friend, Timothy Richard, to whose biography Glover contributed a fulsome "Appreciation" ("Dr. Richard has been a man of immense influence in China. He had proved the greatness of his love for her people, and amongst rich and poor was trusted as few foreigners or natives have ever been"). Richard advocated concentrating the efforts of the missionaries on the education and reform of Chinese society as a necessary preparation for the evangelistic task, which was best undertaken by Chinese Christians themselves. Richard was also anxious to continue educational work in China, which the BMS had not fully supported, until Glover intervened on his behalf and secured BMS support for Richard's editorial and publication work.

Glover was aware of the dangers of the missionary "following the flag", where this might lead to the Gospel being associated with the less worthy aspects of colonial conquest, such as the events surrounding the Opium Wars in China – two sets of wars in the mid nineteenth century concerned with trade in broader terms than opium whereby Britain, later assisted by France, forced the Chinese to open their markets to western trade leading later to the western powers dividing China in a quasi-colonial fashion into defined areas of western influence. Glover commented:

> We have injured them, as probably no nation ever injured another, by the opium traffic, which has demoralised a large proportion of this vast Empire with a vice as bad as that of drunkenness.

Nevertheless, he saw the opportunities which were being opened up by colonial expansion:

> We reach them with our army, our commerce, our oftimes imperious wars. Near enough to do these things, are we to rule them, slay them, injure them. Near enough to do these things, are we near enough to save them?

At the conclusion of his Presidential Address to the Baptist Union Autumn Assembly in 1884, on the theme of "The Work of the Church Today" he commented: "It seems as if God meant it to be wrought chiefly by the English people, and had set us a nation of kings and priests unto God to rule and raise our fellow men".

This may grate on twenty-first century ears but was in the spirit of its time. Indeed it was a sentiment echoed by his successor as minister of Tyndale, Herbert Morgan, more than 30 years later in 1918 when he addressed the North Glamorgan English Baptists: "Our Empire is a trust committed to us for the extension of God's Kingdom and the furtherance of God's purposes".

Yet, in seeming contrast, in 1898 Glover strongly advocated the creation of native churches. Missionaries must "let forms of church life be native to the place" and "you must teach your converts to be independent of you". In 1892 he wrote approvingly in reference to China: "Directly three or four in any place became interested in the truth, the one with most of the spiritual and intellectual qualities of leader about him was made 'Leader'". In this way those missionaries in China in touch with Glover were promoting principles of a church which was self-governing, self-propagating and self-supporting which became the hallmarks of the Three-Self Movement, one branch of the Chinese church which learnt how to survive when foreign missions withdrew and a national promotion of communism prevailed.

It should not be thought, however, that Glover was merely a spectator of mission overseas. He may never have served as an overseas missionary, but was nevertheless actively engaged in the work of the Baptist Missionary Society at home. There was one point when he might have gone overseas to serve. In 1879 he was invited to go to India to become the BMS India Secretary and minister of the Circular Road church in Calcutta – the invitation assured him that the Committee "fully contemplate such arrangements as shall secure their esteemed and honoured brother ample scope for the exercise of his rare gifts as English preacher". His decision to decline the invitation was greeted with considerable thanksgiving by Tyndale – so much so that they took the admirable decision to make a presentation to him on the occasion of his not leaving! (Many years later, in 1901, he also declined an invitation to become minister of the Mansfield Road church in Nottingham.) However, his decision in 1879 certainly did not mark any decline in his involvement in the work of the Society. He attributed his interest in overseas mission to his wife during his first pastorate at Blackfriars Street in Glasgow. Yet it is not unreasonable to speculate that the seeds of this interest had been sown during his youthful travels to many parts of the world. Later he was to recall that early involvement in Glasgow. Addressing the Baptist Union of Scotland Assembly in 1884, he claimed that when he went to Blackfriars Street the church's annual donations to the BMS amounted to no more than £10, but that by introducing a monthly giving scheme, he soon increased this to £80. Whether he could claim similar credit for the generosity of Bristol Baptists very soon after he moved to the city must be open to question, but within a year of his arrival it was noted that almost £1,000 had been given – the largest amount ever and the best outside London.

Be that as it may, the following year Glover became a member of the Society's Committee and he soon became a frequent speaker at BMS assemblies and similar events. The pages of the *Missionary Herald* record his name as speaker or preacher at a variety of such occasions, especially during the 1880s and more particularly in later years on the subject of China. He was, as were others, perpetually concerned about the finances of overseas mission. This concern showed itself both locally and nationally. In 1886 he proudly reported gifts which had been secured towards the current deficit from people in and around Bristol. When he spoke in a debate about the current debt which the Society had run up in 1884, his suggestion of an immediate collection was acted upon and raised some £1,200, and, when the Society was again in financial difficulties in 1898, it was he who wrote on behalf of the Committee setting out the situation and explaining the proposals for its solution. In all this he worked closely with A. H. Baynes, Secretary of the BMS, and later recalled, "we had begun to dream that we must equalise expenditure and income by spending less", but Baynes "taught us the more excellent way of giving more". So highly was their partnership regarded, that in 1904 their names were linked as "the chief of our missionary enthusiasts".

Later that same year it was a member of Tyndale, Edward Robinson, who became treasurer of the Society. Indeed, in addition to the service which he rendered to the Society himself, Glover also influenced others to serve it in various ways. Thus members of his congregation, such as Charles Townsend and Herbert Ashman, were to be found presiding at national missionary events, while Mrs Robinson (Edward's wife) served as President of the Zenana Mission for several years. He also encouraged especially the more wealthy to give generously, notably Sir Charles Wathen, whose munificence in financing expeditions to the Congo was recognised by the naming of one of the mission stations after him, but who also, for example, guaranteed half the cost of sending eight new missionaries to India in 1880 and a further fourteen to China from 1883 onwards. While Wathen is principally remembered for his generosity to the work in Congo (indeed the senior missionary from the Congo, Holman Bentley, attended Wathen's

Queen Victoria Jubilee Convalescent Home

funeral) it is possible that his contributions to the work in China were greater. In his chapter on China in the 1892 centenary history of the BMS Glover makes no mention of the generosity of Wathen. This may because other people in Bristol also made substantial contributions or possibly because Wathen was still alive when he was writing (he died the following year). During Glover's pastorate at Tyndale, at least fourteen members of the church went to serve overseas with the BMS, to be followed by several others in the years immediately following, so that at the time of his death, eight years after his retirement, there were no fewer than eighteen members of the church thus serving.

It is difficult to assess how far it was Glover's leadership which accounted for the outstanding record of service to the community by members of Tyndale, a topic to be dealt with in Chapter 4. There can be no doubt, however, that this man, whose father had given distinguished service to another community, was in tune with such people and would certainly have encouraged them in this aspect of the mission of the local church. Glover himself was involved personally to an extent. For example, when there was a scandal over election bribery in 1880, Glover spoke at a public meeting in the Colston Hall in Bristol, calling attention to the responsibility of the minority who had the vote, towards the vast majority who did not, both in Britain and throughout the Empire.

His most notable contribution to the local community, however, arose from his membership of the Bristol Infirmary Committee. Seeing an unmet need, he took an initiative to raise funds and then served as secretary of the committee of distinguished citizens, some of them members of Tyndale, which arranged for the building of the Queen Victoria Jubilee Convalescent Home, on the corner of Blackboy Hill and Redland Hill, on the edge of Durdham Down. It was opened by Queen Victoria herself in 1899, when Richard Glover read the address to the Queen.

This concern for the less fortunate majority is illustrated by an incident which occurred on a Sunday morning in November 1889. That and the following year were a time of considerable industrial unrest throughout the country, and Bristol saw a number of strikes by workers in various industries. One such was a dispute between the mainly female workforce of the Great Western Cotton Works in the Barton Hill district. They were seeking increased pay and also some improvement to their working conditions. One of the leaders of the strikers was Miriam Daniell – a solicitor's wife who had chosen to go and live amongst the poorer people and became well-known (some would say notorious) as a socialist agitator. On 10th November more than 1,000 workers marched through the city centre and up the hill to Clifton. There they divided into two groups to visit churches where more affluent citizens could be found, probably in the hope of enlisting their sympathy and possibly some financial support. The choice of Tyndale might well have been influenced by Mrs Daniell's family connection with the church – her brother-in-law, James Livett Daniell, was a trustee of the church and would later serve as a deacon. Another reason for the choice of Tyndale was probably Glover's earlier involvement in the dispute.

A few days earlier three delegates from the Strike Committee had met a group of forty non-conformist ministers, including Glover. The ministers showed some sympathy for their cause, but then met the management and examined the company's accounts. Glover then led a smaller group who met the Strike Committee again and advised then that, in their view, the company could not meet their demands.

Led by a drum and fife band they paraded to the church and some 300 women came in just as Glover was about to address the children. Clearly he had not been forewarned of this "invasion". Nevertheless he addressed the strikers, firstly referring to Ephesians 6, verse 5 ("Servants, be obedient to your masters...") he pointed out that this text referred to slaves, for whom such an injunction might have been more difficult. He had refrained from becoming involved in industrial disputes as he feared that such intervention might cause difficulty – the resolution was best left to the parties concerned. He pointed out that working conditions had improved considerably during the last 50 years with a more equitable distribution of wealth than had formerly been the case. Nevertheless there were circumstances when a strike was justified, although it was a clumsy weapon and could be dangerous. He acknowledged that he had never known "how hard it was to make ends meet" and warned the more affluent members of the congregation to "be on their guard about preaching to those who were worse off". He concluded by assuring his listeners that he prayed that each side in the dispute would treat the other with "brotherly fairness and mutual forbearance, which would result in more comfort and happiness to all". Finally, he commended the strikers for their demeanour throughout the procession and at the service.

The other group who went to All Saints church were ignored! On subsequent Sundays similar marches were held to other churches. The strike lasted about a month and the strikers' demands for certain improvements in their working conditions and for payment at time-and-a-quarter for overtime were granted. However they had to accept that there would be no increase in their ordinary wage rates.

Despite all his wider involvement in local civic affairs and in Christian mission both at home and further afield, Glover's ministry at Tyndale remained his primary concern. An early initiative was the establishment of the Mission in St Augustine's parish in 1872 (the subject of Chapter 5). He also wrote a series of tracts. They are mostly undated, but appear to have been begun within a few months of the start of his pastorate. They were

The lecture hall built in 1880

each headed *Tyndale Tracts*, and this fact, together with their probable date, indicates that they were not designed for use amongst the people with whom the Mission was in touch, but rather within the context of Tyndale Church itself. Indeed, while their message is mostly simple and straightforward, the language suggests that they were aimed at a rather better educated audience than they would have found in the vicinity of the Mission. This was a clear indication of Glover's evangelising zeal. During the 42 years of his pastorate 420 new members were admitted following baptism or confession of faith, as well as many more by transfer from other churches. From the original 39 founder members, the membership had grown to over 250 by the time he retired. Worship at Tyndale, moreover, provided a key part of a Bristol college student's training, one student noting that a side pew was especially reserved for their use.

In 1894 the church celebrated the 25th anniversary of both its foundation and of Glover's ministry. When the church was built the proposed clock tower had been omitted in order to keep the cost down. So it was now decided to build the tower (to a slightly altered design) as "a grateful commemoration of his services to this Church and the Denomination". A legacy formed the basis of the fund-raising and the nearby Redland Park Congregational church also contributed. That church had also planned a clock tower, but when it learned of Tyndale's scheme it resolved to abandon its scheme and pass over to Tyndale the funds so far raised. As a further commemoration the wooden pulpit was replaced by a grand stone one. This was the second major building project during Glover's pastorate (in addition to the Mission premises). When he arrived the premises offered limited facilities, so in 1880 the Lecture Hall was built behind the church at a cost of about £4,000. This enabled a Sunday School to be formed the following year, developing from the previous "Minister's Class" which had met in the vestry. It also provided scope for a number of weekday activities. By the time Glover came to the end of his pastorate there was a regular pattern of meetings. On Mondays the fortnightly Women's Prayer Meeting and the Young People's Guild (originally a Christian Endeavour society); a mid-week service was held on Wednesdays, with the Church Meeting once a month, and also a choir practice; on Thursday afternoons the Dorcas Society and Zenana Working Party alternated; and on Fridays there were occasional meetings of the Sunday School Zenana Working Party.

Early in 1906 Glover became ill – he claimed he had not been ill for over 40 years! In January that year he was in Bournemouth on holiday and gradually his condition deteriorated. Eventually it became clear that this was more than simply a bad cold or bronchial catarrh as had been thought at first, but was a more severe problem caused by a thickening of his vocal chords. In May he went to London to stay with his brother, James, who was a doctor and who referred him to a Harley Street consultant, Greville MacDonald. He was ordered to refrain from speaking for an extended period and there was concern that he might not recover sufficiently to be able to preach. This might have led to him having to retire. Already the suggestion of appointing an assistant had been discussed, a suggestion with which Glover was not altogether happy. However, in the changed circumstances he agreed and the search for a suitable man began. Fortunately his health did recover and he was able to resume preaching at the end of October.

Herbert Burdett

Several possible candidates were considered, but in the end the person chosen as assistant was Herbert Burdett. Born in Leicestershire in 1878, he had trained for the ministry at Rawdon College. When he came to Tyndale he had already served a pastorate at Wednesbury in the Midlands for five years. He remained at Tyndale until 1912, and shortly before he left he married a nurse, Ethel Jenkins, daughter of the Tyndale church secretary. When Herbert Morgan arrived, Burdett moved on to Shipley in Yorkshire. After the war, in 1918, he went to China as a BMS missionary, returning in 1939. His last pastorate was in the small village of Niton (at the very southern tip of the Isle of Wight), after which he retired to Bristol, and resumed his membership of Tyndale, in 1945. He died in 1976.

Glover's long ministry and service to the local community did not go unrecognised. In 1884 he was chosen as President of the Baptist Union and in 1891 Edinburgh University, where he had studied as an undergraduate, conferred on him the honorary degree of Doctor of Divinity (DD). He was presented at the ceremony by Professor Archibald Charteris, a leading member of the Church of Scotland, and Glover's near contemporary. In his speech, Charteris mentioned especially Glover's Teachers' Commentaries on the Gospels of St Matthew and St Mark. Then in 1912 Glover was one of a distinguished group of men awarded the honorary degree of Doctor of Laws (LLD) by the University of Bristol. The degree was conferred at a ceremony when the new Chancellor of the University, Lord Haldane, was installed. Similarly honoured on the same occasion, amongst others, were the Principal of the Bristol Baptist College, William Henderson and the

Prime Minister, Herbert Asquith. It is strange that on his memorial tablet in the church only the DD is shown after his name, but not the Bristol LLD!

In 1911, shortly after his 74th birthday, Richard Glover retired. The church would not let him go quietly! A subscription list was opened to which 442 people subscribed – local dignitaries (including the Bishop of Bristol), 48 ministers (mostly, but not all, Baptists) and current and former church members from across the world. Altogether £1,119.12s.6d was contributed. After various expenses were paid for, and gifts for Mrs Glover and Dorothy, a monetary gift of £1,052.12s.0d was presented to Dr Glover. A "Farewell Meeting" took place on 12th April at which the presentation was made along with an Illuminated Address. It was chaired by the prominent local Quaker and philanthropist, Joseph Storrs Fry. After the presentations and messages read from those unable to be present, there were 13 "short addresses" – each scheduled to last four minutes (although all but three were recorded as over-running!). The proceedings concluded with a brief speech of thanks by Richard Glover. A tribute in the Canadian Baptist magazine referred to him as "a Baptist Archbishop" who was retiring from his "Baptist cathedral"! It went on to remark: "He was old when he was young and he is young when he is old" and especially commended his preaching. The tribute was written by the Revd Thomas Phillips of Bloomsbury who, in a rather different mood wrote that "the only grudge we can bear against him is that, like Edmund Burke: 'He has narrowed his mind / And given to committees what was meant for mankind'"! This was probably rather unfair as Glover had always seen committees and meetings as simply a tool to be used for the Gospel. He once commented that God did not expect every man to form a society, "Some believe that in the millennium all life will crystallise in societies, and every saint be a secretary"!

Glover continued to be involved in the life of Tyndale after he retired – even putting in an appearance at the Mission children's Christmas party as Father Christmas (no need for a false beard and his hair had been white since the age of 35!). In 1916 the whole church joined in the celebration of the Glovers' Golden Wedding. The following year he had a fall and broke his arm and he was less active after this. He died on 26th March 1919, shortly before the church celebrated its Golden Jubilee.

Chapter 3.

Herbert Morgan: Tyndale at War

David Roberts

The first intimation of Richard Glover's forthcoming retirement is a resolution passed at a Church Meeting on 1st February 1911. This was a response, with appropriate words of appreciation, to a letter Glover had written tendering his resignation. At the same meeting thanks were expressed in a further resolution to his assistant, Herbert Burdett, who was also tendering his resignation. This second resolution also expressed gratitude for Burdett's willingness to continue his ministry until a new minister was called or until he himself was called to another church. From this it is quite clear that there was no suggestion by either the church or Burdett of his succeeding Glover – indeed Burdett chaired several of the Church and Deacons' Meetings which dealt with the question of calling a new minister. At a subsequent Church Meeting it was agreed that a Selection Committee should be established to bring a nomination for a new minister. The membership of this committee had been agreed by the deacons to consist of themselves plus five others – one to represent the Sunday School, one from the Men's Society, one from the Zenana Working Society and two from the Mission.

When the committee met, a list of six names of possible candidates was drawn up and from this the Revd Allan Marshall Ritchie of Blenheim Baptist Church, Leeds was invited to "preach with a view". Ritchie accordingly preached at Tyndale and at a subsequent Church Meeting it was resolved to call him to the pastorate – 90 of the 95 who voted were in favour. However, within two weeks Ritchie declined the invitation. That was reported to the church on 1st November 1911 and at the same meeting it was reported that the Revd Herbert Morgan of London had been invited to preach – Morgan had not been on the original list of six suggested names. In accepting this invitation, Morgan made it clear that he was not committing either himself or the church to "any further steps". Nevertheless following his visit, on 5th February 1912 the Church Meeting resolved to extend a call to him to become the minister – 71 voted in favour, one against and three abstained (a note was made in the minute book that attendance at the meeting had been reduced because of very bad weather). In his letter of acceptance on 24th February, Morgan wrote: "No choice that I have ever had to make has been so difficult or so painful and I can only hope that the course of events in the future may prove that I am obeying God's call". He confessed that he knew "so little of the life in your city and in your suburb"

The Revd Herbert Morgan

and that his acceptance "need not mean the surrender of my many interests in Wales", but that he would put his ministry at Tyndale first.

Morgan was a Welshman, born in a village near Neath in 1875. From there his family moved to Porth in the Rhondda, where he spent his schooldays. He came from a family who were members of a local Baptist church. They could not afford to pay for his education to continue, so he left school to work in the local Water Board office. Quite soon he was recognised as having a call to the ministry and as having exceptional intellectual gifts. So, with the assistance of friends, he was enabled to attend the Pontypridd Academy and qualify for university. He went to the South Wales Baptist College, affiliated to the University of Wales. There he gained his BA, with honours in philosophy and Greek before going on to Mansfield College,

Oxford, subsequently being awarded a scholarship which enabled him to go to Marburg University in Germany for post-graduate theological study.

Bilingual, he was able to preach in both English and Welsh and in 1906 he was called to his first pastorate at the Welsh Baptist Church in Castle Street, London. There the future Prime Minister, David Lloyd George, was among his congregation. He served there for six years before he responded to the call to Tyndale. Morgan was unmarried and in Bristol he lodged in Upper Belgrave Road.

To be the minister of a church during those war years must have been a challenge to anyone. For Morgan the challenge was all the greater because he held pacifist views. In the September 1914 edition of the church's monthly magazine, the *Tyndale Messenger*, he wrote:

> How has it come to pass that the blast of the trumpet was sounding throughout Christian Europe the call to the deadliest war that ever made the earth groan? Is it not the stultification of modern diplomacy, with its subterranean shifts and its hollow catch-words and professions, that the whole of Europe should be dragged into Armageddon through a petty quarrel between a barbarous and war-intoxicated state like Servia and an ancient tyrant like Austria?

He went on to refer to the "refuge of lies" behind which European nations had been "lurking" and the "perfidy" and "falsity" of diplomacy. Not that such views were necessarily confined to pacifists. In fact Morgan was careful, while not abandoning his views, to avoid parading them, while offering pastoral support to those whose families were torn apart by the war. Indeed, one month into the war he wrote:

> We are proud of the valour of our forces and of the leadership of our generals, but our hope for victory rests ultimately not on the excellence of our military equipment or strategy, but on the justice of our case. If war is ever justifiable for an age like ours, that boasts of its civilization and progress, then this war in defence of the neutrality of Belgium is, perhaps, the most honourable that we have ever conducted.

He did go on to qualify this by pointing out that the independence of Belgium happened to coincide with Britain's national interest! It is also interesting to see here, well before the war had settled down into the attritional trench warfare that characterised most of it, that Morgan was already referring to it as "the deadliest war ever", seeing it as a potential "Armageddon" – a word very much used in hindsight later!

Morgan was largely in tune with some other Baptists who, while deploring the prospect of war, had begun to see some justification for it when they learned of the suffering especially of the Belgians. Early in the war a group of German Protestants sought to justify Germany's actions and sent an appeal to Evangelical British Christians. On 23rd September 1914 several Baptists were among a group of 42 British church leaders who responded to this: "It has not been a light thing for us to give our assent to the action of the Government of our country in this matter" they wrote and "We have taken our stand for international good faith, for the safeguarding of smaller nations". One of those who signed this statement was T. R. Glover, the distinguished son of Richard Glover.

On St David's Day in 1916 the Bristol United Welsh Sunday School held a special service (in Welsh) at Tyndale. Herbert Morgan was the preacher. He addressed the subject of patriotism, contrasting "false patriotism", which was negative, with "true patriotism", with its need to recognise the aspirations of other nations and to work for international co-operation. He made a similar emphasis the following year when he addressed the newly-formed Redland Association for the Study of Social Problems: "The nations ought to labour together for the common good of the world". Later in 1917 he addressed the Bristol Operatives' Radical Association, speaking of favour of "Peace by Negotiation". By August 1918, after four years of war, Morgan, like so many, appeared to despair of the war ever ending:

> The ghastly tragedy drags on from year to year and from land to land, an awful commentary on our civilization and on Christianity. People are no longer looking to the Church to bring about peace, but to International Labour. Churches must say that war, all war, is immoral and unchristian.

62

In March 1916 the Military Service Act had come into force introducing conscription for the first time in Britain. The Baptist Union Assembly in April 1914 had unanimously passed a resolution opposing a proposal to introduce conscription, partly on the grounds that it would be seen as provocative by other countries. However, by 1916 the situation was completely different. The Act provided for exemption to be granted on various grounds, including conscientious objection to engaging in "combatant service". Baptists were divided in their attitude to conscientious objectors. Some, such as John Greenhough of Leicester (who had been minister of Cotham Grove Baptist Church in Bristol in the 1870s) considered that those who fought were better Christians than those who did not. Herbert Morgan, not surprisingly, given his pacifist views, was more sympathetic. Writing in the *Tyndale Messenger* in June 1916 he regretted that Free Church leaders had been slow to react. However, he did not address directly the question of whether men were right to object, but rather pointed out that their objecting was within the historic Nonconformist tradition – "a refusal on the grounds of conscience to obey what was felt to be a tyrannical interference on the part of the State authorities". He did complain, as did many others, of the contempt with which conscientious objectors were often treated by the tribunals which had been established to consider applications. He went on to cite Basil Robert, the son of the Revd G. W. Robert, Minister at the Tyndale Mission, who was "manfully and cheerfully bearing his testimony at Gosport". His service record (under his full name, George Basil Robert) clearly records that he had been "exempted on conscientious grounds from serving as a combatant". His harsh treatment led to him being cited twice in Parliamentary questions to the Under Secretary for War. In May 1916, Joseph King (the MP for North Somerset and himself a pacifist who had opposed the introduction of conscription) asked whether Robert and two others had been subjected to military punishment at Horfield Barracks. The Minister declined to respond! The following month Charles Hobhouse (MP for Bristol East and clearly not a pacifist as he later became Honorary Colonel of the Tank Regiment!) asked whether Robert had been required to "drill with a rifle, and, if so, whether orders will be given to prevent such rifle drill being given in the case of members of the Non-Combatant Corps". The Minister responded that he was making enquiries, but there appears to be no record of any result. This may be because the question was overtaken by a much more high profile argument in Parliament, involving the Prime Minister, concerning the fate of some non-combatants who had been sentenced to death by courts marshal (their sentences were commuted to lengthy imprisonment). Basil Robert had enlisted in the Dorset Regiment in April 1916 and by the time Morgan wrote about him he was in the detention barracks in Gosport. After the war he became a Rural Industries Organiser in Stroud and served as an ARP Warden during the Second World War. He died in 1960.

As soon as the war started, German troops invaded Belgium. Within days of the start of the war Belgian refugees began to arrive in Britain and were soon being dispersed to various parts of the country. A substantial number of Belgian refugees came to Bristol. Given the involvement of many of its members in public affairs in the city (see Chapter 4), it is not surprising that Tyndale was one of the churches which decided to provide assistance to them. Throughout the war years the *Tyndale Messenger* gave news of these refugees and published an account by one of them of their experiences. By early September 1914 thousands of Belgian refugees had reached Britain – mostly coming into the port of Felixstowe. On 10th September the President of the Local Government Board told Parliament that the government had offered hospitality to Belgian refugees and that they were being brought to London. However he also expressed the hope that "the country generally would co-operate in this work". In Bristol the response was initially by the Voluntary Services Bureau which invited people to telephone with offers of accommodation and other help. Within a very few days the Bureau reported "an abundance of offers" such that "many homeless, destitute, bereaved Belgians will be looked after in Bristol and the neighbourhood". Not surprisingly, the Roman Catholic community was at the forefront of these offers, most Belgians being of that persuasion. Indeed, the Roman Catholic Bishop of Clifton offered the use of a large mansion in Bath to accommodate refugees. Unfortunately he was unable to fulfil his offer as the place was commandeered for military use. Meanwhile, a reception centre was opened in Clifton by the Belgian Consul in Bristol.

Local councils were encouraged by the government to set up committees to deal with the refugee problem. Bristol responded immediately. In order that this committee might be widely representative of the city, it had 40 members. There was no representative of Tyndale on the committee, but the minister of Broadmead Baptist Church (the Revd F. G. Benskin) was among its members. A set of rules was agreed, and approved by Lord Lytton, the government minister responsible. Within days the trickle of refugees coming to Bristol had become a flood – a trainload was welcomed by a crowd of local people when they arrived at Bristol's Temple Meads railway station. Most of these arrangements were concerned with "destitute persons" while it was hoped that "persons of good families" would be offered homes and treated as guests. It was to these "good families" that Tyndale offered hospitality.

The church was offered the free use of a house in nearby Pembroke Road – number 73. The local utility companies also offered free water and gas and the Council exempted the house from domestic rates. The Homeopathic Hospital provided free medical care for the refugees. Work started immediately to prepare the house for the "guests" – "zealous people have been setting besoms and scrubbing brushes in motion". Meanwhile income was being raised both to purchase furniture and for the running costs, and an appeal was made both for money and for useful items of equipment. Members of the Tyndale Mission also contributed, through their own collecting box. Once the first Belgians arrived, "Miss Turner and her maid went into residence... and it is impossible to estimate how much they did

Belgian refugee house at 73 Pembroke Road

not only for the physical comfort of the household, but more especially for their happiness". She stayed with the refugees in the house for the first week, helping them to settle in and frequently visited the house after that. Miss Turner was Dorothy Turner, a 23-year-old nurse and church member, who went on to serve as a nurse in India with the BMS. Fifty years later, when she was back in Bristol, living in retirement, she received an unexpected visit from some of the surviving former refugees, including a "baby" who had been born there. They came to reiterate their thanks for the welcome and hospitality which she and others had given. They enjoyed what she described as a "hilarious lunch" at a local restaurant, speaking a mixture of English, French and Flemish. She was told: "We came to say thank you to Tyndale. We shall never forget".

At the end of their first week in residence, the Belgians were welcomed with a house-warming party during which hosts and guests entertained each other with songs. It is not clear how many of the Belgians could speak English (although one of them, Henri Bertholet, certainly could) nor whether any of the church people spoke French. The guests were made welcome in similar ways throughout their stay – as, for example, with the provision of an annual Christmas tree and Christmas meal, when new clothes were also donated. Amongst those who helped to entertain the visitors was the retired Richard Glover. Many years later his daughter, Dorothy Glover, recalled his visits to the refugees:

> My father was constantly there, arriving with a bag of apples for the little boys, and "asking for scissors". This meant he was prepared to sit down and cut out toys for the children till they were tired.

Henri Bertholet expressed appreciation in the *Tyndale Messenger* – "Thanks especially to *le très honorable le docteur Glover*".

On 30th October sixteen Belgians had arrived at 73 Pembroke Road – which rapidly increased to seventeen, when a baby was born on 10th November. There were two family groups. One consisted of Georges Dereere and his wife, together with her two sisters and their maid. The Dereere family came from Courtrai (later to be the scene of a major battle in 1918). Gustav August Georges Dereere was the baby who was born soon after their arrival and his birth and baptism, presumably in a Roman Catholic church, were reported in the *Tyndale Messenger*. Dorothy Glover recalled that their guests never ceased to wonder that Protestant ministers, her father and Herbert Morgan, should do all this for them, Roman Catholics. The other family group consisted of Madame van de Weghe who had three daughters with her, one of whom was married to Henri Bertholet, who was also among the group with their four children. Mme Van de Wegh and her two unmarried daughters came from Ostkamp (near Bruges). Her other daughter, Mme Bertholet, and her family had been living in Hay (between Namur and Liege) but were originally from Dinant-sur-Meuse. They had moved from their home town because of Henri Bertholet's work – he was an official of the Belgian Agriculture Ministry. Many of the Bertholet family had still been living in Dinant at the outbreak of war, and were consequently caught up in the terrible events which took place there.

Ruins of Dinant-sur-Meuse

It had started on 13th August 1914. A troop of French soldiers was trying to defend a bridge over the river Meuse. The officer in charge, Lieutenant Charles de Gaulle (many years later to be President of France), was wounded in the engagement, as were most of his troop. More than a week later, on 21st August, the Germans were repairing the bridge when they came under fire. These Germans claimed that they had been fired on by armed civilians and were therefore entitled to retaliate. The Belgian account asserts that the shooting came from some French soldiers and that the German troops, as they entered the town, immediately began shooting randomly at the houses as they passed. What is in no doubt is that many were shot in the doorways of their houses and, while most of the women with some children were herded into the local prison, a large number of men were summarily executed in the town square in full view of their wives and children. Over the next few days there were further, apparently random, killings. One claim was that some 800 inhabitants were killed. Some, who were not executed, were taken prisoner and a few people managed to escape into the surrounding countryside. Subsequently the town came under prolonged artillery bombardment and many of the

prominent buildings as well as houses were destroyed – only about 300 of
the 1500 houses in the town were left standing.

Henri Bertholet emerged as the leading personality among the refugees in
Pembroke Road – his offer to give church members French lessons was
accepted by about twenty people, although how proficient they became is
not recorded. He also gave a talk about Belgium to the Tyndale Social and
Literary Society. Clearly his own command of English was good, as he also
gave a detailed account in the *Tyndale Messenger* of the experiences of his
family members who had been caught up in the terrible events in Dinant.
The family there was in three households in the same street. One consisted
of his father, Alexis, and Henri's two siblings; a second was that of his sister
and her husband and their two-year-old son; the third an uncle and aunt
and their six children. After the battle on the bridge, they all lived in their
cellars for the next ten days. On 23rd August a German soldier knocked on
the door and, when she answered, threw Henri's sister into the street before
he and his companions looted the house. The families fled to another
building from where a number of men were taken out and shot. From there
the survivors were taken to the local prison, where they could hear what
proved to be the execution of at least 148 men (they later counted the
bodies). That evening more men, including Henri's brother and brother-in-
law, were taken out and lined up to be shot. Henri's father tried to
intervene, but was prevented by the family. Somehow the younger men
avoided being shot and the family were again reunited. There appears to
have been some random shooting, as a result of which Henri's aunt was
fatally wounded. The family were then among a group who were taken to
the scene of fighting between the Germans and the French and used as a
human shield – at least one person was killed before the French stopped
firing. After this the remaining men were led away and, apparently, taken as
prisoners to Germany. The women managed to escape to a nearby wood
where, two days later, Henri's sister gave birth to a baby girl. They
remained in hiding for a month until Henri himself was able to find
somewhere safe for them to go. He described his own experiences as
comparatively "insignificant". When Belgium was invaded he and his wife
and children were on holiday near Bruges. He worked for the Red Cross for
two months and, after providing for his female relations, as he had

described, he took a week to escape across Holland and join his family who had by then reached London. They had escaped from Ostend to Boulogne in a fishing smack and thence made their way via Folkestone to London. There was at least one happy and unexpected reunion as described in the *Tyndale Messenger*:

> On Monday, Feb 8th [1915], towards seven o'clock in the evening, there was a ring at the bell [at 73 Pembroke Road], and in walked, unheralded... Monsieur Alexis Bertholet... The family was astonished... the joy of the reunion may be imagined.

It was an astonished Dorothy Turner who happened to open the door to him. He had been imprisoned in Cassel in Germany for three months, but what led to his release is unexplained. At supper that evening a prayer of thanksgiving was offered. However, the family reunion was short lived as Henri was ordered by the Belgian Minister of Agriculture (his employer) to move to Pont l'Eveque in France to work with farmers restocking the farms in what little of Belgium was unoccupied. Now that he was earning again, he sent regular donations to the church towards the expenses of the Pembroke Road house. Later his wife, children and father joined him in France. However, Henri's uncle and his six children took the place of the departing Bertholet family – he had lost his wife in Dinant as Henri had recounted. Previously they had been living in a house provided by another Bristol church. At about the same time the Dereere-Vandenbroucke family moved to another house to join others of their family, including a son who was a priest. In October 1915 a cousin of the Van de Wegh family, Pierre Lootens, who had been wounded and discharged from the Belgian army joined the group until late in 1916, when he left to work in the Belgian Munitions Works in Newcastle. Another arrival in 1915 was a young theology student, M. Van de Maele, who had been training for the Roman Catholic priesthood. Later he went to France to work in a Belgian ambulance team as a stretcher bearer. Meanwhile another of the residents had trained to do munitions work and by the end of 1917 four of them were engaged in some form of war work.

Money was constantly being raised during the war to support these refugees, although towards the end people needed to be reminded on

French class run by Henri Bertholet; Herbert Morgan is seen in the back row

several occasions of the continuing need. Altogether some 26 refugees lived in the house during those four years, and when the war ended there were probably still nine residents in the house. However, the owners decided at this point to sell it, so the remaining Belgians moved to another house (15 York Gardens) while they awaited repatriation to Belgium. On 28th February 1919 a social gathering was held at the church to bid their visitors farewell. As a token of their gratitude the Belgians presented to the church a picture of their king. In January 1919 the Belgian Consul had warned the group that they might have to wait several months before being granted passports. In fact the repatriation of the Belgian refugees took about six months – the official estimate of the number of Belgian refugees in Britain was about 200,000. The government appointed Basil Peto (a member of a well-known Baptist family – his father had served as treasurer of the BMS although there is no evidence that Basil was a Baptist) as Commissioner for Repatriation and ships were commissioned to undertake the task. By mid-May 1919 it was reported that the process had been completed.

The hospitality given to these Belgian refugees was the principal way the church contributed to the wartime needs "on the home front". Meanwhile church life continued much as normal. The Church and Deacons' Meetings were held at the usual times and the various societies continued to meet – the *Tyndale Messenger* regularly included a detailed account of the proceedings of the Social and Literary Society. However there were other war-related activities, as well as the voluntary work done by many individuals through organisations such as the Red Cross and the YMCA. Very early on in the war the Imperial Hotel, opposite the church in Whiteladies Road, was commandeered by the military. The church offered to provide recreational facilities for the troops billeted there, but were advised that this was not needed. However, much later, in 1917, a large group (reported as hundreds) of members of the Women's Army Auxiliary Corps was billeted there and in nearby houses. Tyndale co-operated with four nearby churches to make facilities available. One afternoon and evening each week the Lecture Hall was turned over to these young women who were supplied with books, magazines, games and other recreational material. The other churches made similar provision on the other days. Comforts were offered sometimes in response to an unexpected situation, as when, on a snowy day in February 1916, a fleet of transport wagons temporarily stopped outside the church. Tea, coffee and cakes which had been prepared for members at the church's Annual Meeting were given to the hungry soldiers!

By 1917 food shortages were becoming serious and people were being encouraged to grow as much of their own as possible. So, jointly with nearby Redland Park Congregational Church, Tyndale acquired a field which was turned into allotments, each of which was cultivated by one family or group of friends – including the minister. On at least one occasion (and probably on others which were not reported) groups of wounded soldiers, as many as 120, were guests of the church for a day. Morgan reflected that: "Something of the reality of war came home to us as we saw a young lad being carried out by a comrade because he had lost both his legs".

Meanwhile, many of the young men needed no such reminder as they were on active service with the armed forces. Tyndale men served in a wide variety of Army units, including the new Flying Corps, as well as in the Royal Navy, and they held a wide range of ranks from Private and Seaman to Colonel. All those who were commissioned as officers were connected with Tyndale rather than with the Mission, which probably reflects the social differences between the two congregations. At the end of the war, the church's Jubilee Handbook, published in 1919, listed no fewer than 71 men associated with the church and the Mission who had served. Of these 19 were killed or died on active service, but only six of them were named on the memorial stone which was erected in the church. After this was destroyed, when the church was bombed during the Second World War, it was replaced by a commemorative window in the rebuilt church listing these same names. Those named were just the men who were actually church members – thus members of the Mission, Sunday School scholars and members of church families were not included. The full list shows that some families lost more than one member.

The present window is also a replacement for one given by the Robinson family, which commemorated the three members of that family who had been killed. Two Robinson brothers were killed on successive days in 1915. Geoffrey, a 2nd Lieutenant in the Gloucester Regiment was killed on 25th September at Hulluch; Edward, a 2nd Lieutenant in the Somerset Light Infantry, was killed the next day at Loos. Ten weeks later, on 8th December, another brother, Clifford, a Lance Corporal in the New Zealand Rifles, was killed in Gallipoli. Meanwhile, their oldest brother, Arnold, served briefly with the Artists Rifles before being released to manage a shell factory, while the fifth brother, Gilbert, who had been working in Madras, served as a provost marshal in Bangalore. So out of these five brothers only two survived the war. Their three cousins, who also served, all survived.

The first Tyndale member to enlist following the outbreak of war, was Arnold Kerry – the Secretary of the Young People's Guild. He had first joined the Grenadier Guards, but was then commissioned in the Devonshire Regiment. Later he transferred to the Manchester Regiment and was Mentioned in Despatches – just "one down" from a gallantry medal. The incident which led to this award, in 1916, also saw him severely wounded and sent back to England. Here he spent time in hospital before being sent to Cambridge as an Instructor. However, it appears that he had not fully recovered and he was admitted to hospital again, where he died in February 1918. Alfred Whitewright was a member of a prominent missionary family. He had been in China immediately before the War, but returned early in 1915 in order to enlist. He was commissioned in the Notts and Derby Regiment. What led to his death is not clear, but he died very suddenly, back in England, in June 1916. Private Cyril Prewett of the Wiltshire Regiment had been an apprentice upholsterer before he joined the army in 1917. He was serving as the Commanding Officer's batman and orderly when he was killed outright by a bullet to the head after only being at the front for a few weeks. In 1914 he had married and so left a widow and also a daughter who was born a few months before he was killed. His sister married William Hockey, and through her he is linked to a family that has been prominent in the church right down to the present day.

Those were the six commemorated in the memorial window – four of them officers and two "other ranks", which is a reflection of the social make up of the church – except that it is surprising that one of the Robinson brothers was not commissioned! Amongst the others were C. E. Stewart, killed in 1914 and interred in Holland. He had been a member of the Naval Brigade – sailors sent to serve with the army at the front. In September 1916 the death of Rex Kerry was reported in the *Tyndale Messenger*. In 1917 Kenneth Leonard, a former bank clerk, was killed and then a few weeks later Francis Tratman, a 20-year-old former Sunday School scholar. A few months before the end of the war, in May 1918, Kenneth Jenkins died from the injuries he received in a battle on the Somme. He was the youngest son of Frederick Jenkins, Secretary of Tyndale. In 1914 he enlisted with the North Somerset Yeomanry with the rank of corporal. He was one of some twenty members of Tyndale families who had enlisted by the end of 1914. By May 1915 he had been promoted to the rank of sergeant. In May 1915 he wrote an account of his experiences in the trenches, which was published in the *Tyndale Messenger* the following July. The North Somerset Yeomanry was part of the 6th Cavalry Brigade and the events he described took place in the area around Ypres on 13th May 1915. The Yeomanry occupied trenches in front of Bellewaarde Farm. There were 16 officers and about 300 other ranks. Here are some extracts from what Jenkins wrote:

> At 3.30, dawn on Thursday, they started shelling us and from then, continuously till dark... We could do nothing but stand and keep a sharp look out for over fifteen hours, expecting to be blown to Hades every minute... Our trenches were being blown in, kit and ourselves being buried time after time. As soon as a breach

was repaired with sand bags etc., another would come and breach it in another place. Men were falling practically all up and down the line... Our line originally was about 800 yards long, but gradually we had to concentrate owing to losses and blown-in trenches, and of the 290 men and officers who went in, only 170 came out, just 24 hours later... As a regiment we are practically without officers. But in spite of it all, the spirit of the men is fine...

It seems that the 13th was an exceptional day, and I heard a regular officer say that it was a longer and fiercer bombardment than he had ever seen men undergo... The weather was rotten – cold and raining, and our coats are still sodden, indeed, the trenches were about as bad for wet and mud as in November, and we had the same trouble with rifles jamming as we had then... I had 10 casualties out of 27 in my troop. I will endeavour to tell you what it was like. It will not be easy though, even then, as such a hammering as we had is apt to leave one's mind rather vacant on some points; but the horror of the constant stream of wounded that struggled past me in the narrow trenches, on their way to the dressing station is still vivid. But there are things one will never be able to forget. I lost one man in my troop, and eight were wounded, two badly. It was truly awful, and yet, you know why, I had little feelings of actual fear...

We are now camping in a brick field, and having built little houses with bricks and tiled them, are fairly comfy. I don't know what they are going to do with us, as we are minus our Colonel (wounded), our Adjutant (killed) and both the others wounded. I have never spent such a long day as I did on Thursday. We stuck to our trenches, however, and this morning, on a Church Parade we had, our Brigadier thanked and complimented us on the fine work we did.

Two months later, in July, Jenkins was commissioned as a Lieutenant in the same regiment. In September 1916, he resigned his membership of Tyndale and joined the Church of England (which is why his name was not included on the memorial) and, shortly afterwards, he married Julia Louisa

Coulbourne, a dance teacher. At the beginning of 1918 he was attached to the new Tank Corps, which had seen action on the Somme. Soon afterwards he was mortally wounded and died on 31st March 1918, aged 31. He had no children and his widow did not remarry. She lived to the age of 87 and died in 1978.

Frederick A. Jenkins

The Jenkins family made a distinguished contribution to Tyndale. In 1888 Frederick Jenkins, his wife Emma and three of their children, Percy and Marion and Vaughan joined the church at the same time. Both Percy and Vaughan, who were training in accountancy, were on the Mission management committee and their father was a teacher in the Sunday school. Percy Jenkins was the secretary of the Lads' Institute. By 1913 Frederick was a deacon and treasurer of the Sunday school at Tyndale. This was not surprising as he was by then the senior partner in one of the largest of the Bristol accountancy firms, Curtis Jenkins and Co. who looked after the finances of many important Bristol firms such as the Wills tobacco family and were involved in many railway and water companies in the city. In 1905 Frederick Jenkins was elected to the Council of the Institute of Chartered Accountants. In a book about the history of the Curtis Jenkins firm it states that "he was the father of numerous children (15) and it was alleged that he was unable to count them at breakfast which resulted in frequent absenteeism!" And there was an apocryphal story that he was wont to smoke in bed till the very end of his days. Certainly he and his children made Jenkins a name to conjure with in the City of Bristol for fully forty years. In 1903 Frederick was elected Tyndale secretary, serving until his death in 1919 when he was succeeded by his son, Donald, for a further five years. The family lived at 58 St John's Road in Clifton and two other children influenced Tyndale in important ways. Ethel Grace became a nurse and married Herbert Burdett, Richard

Glover's assistant minister, in 1912 before becoming missionaries to China for many years. Her brother, Stanley Jenkins trained as a doctor in Bristol and also worked in China, dying there at the tragically young age of 38 (see Chapter 10); his biography, *Herbert Stanley Jenkins, Medical Missionary, Shensi, China*, was written by Richard Glover.

The end of the war passed with scarcely any mention in the *Tyndale Messenger*, which was more concerned with the forthcoming celebrations for the Jubilee of the church. One important development in 1918 which failed to receive any mention was the decision that women could be elected as deacons. The following year the first two were duly chosen – Miss Christina Culross and Miss Dorothy Glover. However equality was still a long way off, as for many years only single or widowed women were elected and it was only in the last quarter of the 20th century that women deacons began to serve communion!

Immediately after the war ended in 1918 with the Armistice signed on 11th November, the government called a general election, which took place on 14th December. Herbert Morgan decided to stand for election. He had always shown a keen interest in social issues. In 1911 and 1912 he had written three publications: *The Church and Social Problems, Housing and Public Welfare* and *The Social Task in Wales*. At a time when the state had been increasingly making provision for the social problems that had emerged during the previous century and more of the Industrial Revolution, Morgan was keen to point out that the church still had a pivotal role. In his "Letter" to church members in the 1913 *Tyndale Handbook* he had written:

> Much zeal for social reform is shewn in Parliament, in Social Settlements and elsewhere outside the Church – in the narrow sense – but she has her own great place, and it is not to be ousted by any of these. For she has a supreme function to fulfil in the realm of motive and character from which the social problem originates and from which also all real reform is to emanate.

This was an age when the Church of England was often referred to as "the Tory party at prayer". While this is clearly an exaggeration, certainly there was a degree of correlation between the two. The other side of the coin was the identification of Non-conformity with the Liberal party. Morgan, however, could see "the writing on the wall" as far as the Liberal party was concerned. In his view the Labour party, rather than the Liberal party represented the future. He was not alone in this. Especially in Wales, confidence in the Liberal party was waning and being overtaken by support for the Labour party. Morgan had been an active member of the Independent Labour Party for some years and, along with some other young Welsh non-conformist ministers, had shared electoral platforms with Keir Hardie. It may well be that Hardie's strong pacifist views influenced Morgan. Perhaps it was surprising that a man with his clear political outlook should be called to the pastorate first of Castle Street, with Liberal leader Lloyd George in its membership as well as another Welsh Liberal MP (John Hinds), and then of Tyndale, among whose members were leaders of the Liberal cause in Bristol. It was a natural move for him to stand as the Labour candidate for his home constituency of Neath. Sadly for him he failed to win the crucial support of the miners, who, apparently, found his pacifist views unacceptable in the aftermath of the war in which so many of them had lost family members. He did not help his own cause when, at an electoral meeting, he made reference to the "Poor Old Kaiser" who had gone into exile. The meeting broke up in disorder after, according to a press report, the audience broke into singing "Rule Britannia"! So he lost to the Liberal candidate, securing only 35% of the vote. Thus, in the view of one biographer: "Welsh Labour representation lost a figure of outstanding calibre".

How far this setback contributed to his eventual decision to leave Tyndale, it is difficult to assess. More likely he saw his move as positive. After the war Aberystwyth University College had decided to establish an Extra-Mural Department. According to his old friend, Waldo Lewis "he was persuaded by the late Professor J. H. Davies to return to his native country and become the first Director of Extra-Mural Education". So, in 1920, after eight stressful years, Morgan left Tyndale.

In 1923 something occurred which precipitated an end to Morgan's bachelor existence. A Tyndale member, William James, a draper and furrier with a business on College Green died. Two years later Morgan married his widow, Clara Churchill James (née Durham). The wedding took place at

Tyndale, conducted by Morgan's successor, Revd G. W. Harte. Sadly, their marriage was destined to be short lived. Not much more than a year after they married, Clara died, aged only 51.

Morgan remained at Aberystwyth until he retired in 1940. He was very much involved in Welsh life both within and beyond the Baptist denomination. One commentator wrote that under his leadership the Extra-Mural Department had "an especially powerful impact on the cultural and intellectual life of mid-Wales". A biographer wrote: "He was in great demand as a preacher in Welsh and English, though not in the style regarded as 'popular' and as a lecturer". His wider interests are reflected in his writings on social matters and he was keenly involved in the development of social services. In 1945 he served as President of the Baptist Union of Wales. Morgan died in the Aberystwyth General Hospital on 22nd September 1946. At a Memorial Service in Bethel Baptist Chapel, Aberystwyth on 3rd October his life-long friend, Waldo Lewis, gave thanks for "this great and good man – for this loyal and warm-hearted friend and companion on life's road. For this true and faithful servant of our Lord Jesus Christ".

Morgan is not forgotten in Aberystwyth. Even today, many years after his death, students compete for the annual "Rev Herbert Morgan Scholarship" worth £1,000 a year.

Chapter 4.

Tyndale in the Life of the City

David Roberts

In her book *Leisure and the Changing City, 1870-1914* (1976), Professor Helen Mellor wrote (p. 81):

> Tyndale Baptist Chapel only had a congregation of about 200 members, but a high proportion of them were involved in social and philanthropic work in the city. Many of these had formerly been associated with Broadmead Baptist Chapel, but the close-knit, socially cohesive group at the Redland Chapel were able to pursue socio-religious work with a single mindedness which brought greater influence.

She then goes on to mention several prominent members of the church, who are the subject of this chapter, and then concludes: "With men like this in its congregation, Tyndale Baptist Chapel had an influence far exceeding its numbers".

She had, however, preceded these comments by saying:

> Perhaps the most outstanding fact was that there was no sectarian discrimination in Bristol. The governing élite was drawn from the Church of England, the Quakers, Congregationalists, Baptists, Wesleyans, even Roman Catholics.

Her view is supported to some extent by something written towards the end of the period she is concerned with. Writing in 1909 G. F. Stone wrote in *Bristol as it was and as it is: A record of fifty years progress* (p. 139):

> There has been a lowering of denominational barriers. The distinction may remain but the differences are far less accentuated than formerly and points of agreement are so

important that the fullest and friendliest cooperation has grown up among members of what are often known as "the Evangelical Free Churches".

Mellor's book is clearly concerned with the period down to the outbreak of the First World War and, indeed, it was in the first fifty years of its life that Tyndale included in its membership such an accumulation of "the great and the good" of Bristol. She could also have included the business life of the city in her summary, but that was outside the scope of her book. Most prominent here was the Robinson family. There were members of this family in membership of the church and also serving as deacons from the start until the death of Katherine Robinson in 1985. Elisha Smith Robinson, as shown in Chapter 1, took a prominent part in founding the church and he served as a deacon until his death in 1885. He had been named after his maternal grandfather, Elisha Smith, who had been a friend of William Carey and was himself minister of Baptist churches at Chipping Campden and Shipston-on-Stour between 1780 and 1819 (while at the same time running a grocery shop). Smith's daughter, Maria, married Edward Robinson who owned a paper mill at Overbury (near Tewkesbury). Their son, "E. S.", was born on 20th March 1817, his birth being recorded by his grandfather in the records of the Chipping Campden church. For a short time he worked for his grandfather in the grocery shop, until his father sent him to gain business experience in various places, but then decided he was not good enough to take on a management role in the business and appointed someone from outside the family. At this point Elisha decided to branch out on his own and, in 1844, moved to Bristol. With £90 of his own savings and a loan of £100 he founded the firm which became E. S. & A. Robinson after his younger brother, Alfred, joined him in 1848. This was a paper, printing and packaging company which prospered and grew to become one of the major employers in Bristol as well as an international company until it merged with John Dickinson Stationery in 1966 to form the Dickinson Robinson Group, one of the largest businesses of its kind in the world.

Alfred Robinson took no part in public affairs but E. S. Robinson rose to prominence in Bristol in 1857 as the first Chairman of the Corporation of the Poor on the occasion of its becoming a Poor Law Union. This change

This cartoon refers to E. S. Robinson's action as Chairman of the Corporation of the Poor when he agreed to it being incorporated in the Poor Law structures in 1857

had been forced on the Corporation (founded in 1696) after more than 20 years resistance when the Corporation lost its fight with the central government for its continued existence as an anomaly under the Poor Law structure, which had been put in place in the 1830s. So to be its Chairman was controversial at the time. Nevertheless after three years Robinson was able to boast that the Union had successfully coped with an influx of poorer people into the city centre without increasing the rates! However, how far he could claim the credit for this is debatable since, with the rapid expansion of Bristol at that time, the rateable value of the city was increasing and thus the yield became greater each year – so much so that the poor law rate was actually reduced each year for several years. His civic activities gradually widened – he became Chairman of the Port & Pier Railway (which became the Severn Beach Line) and took an active part in the establishment of the Avonmouth docks. Meanwhile he had been elected as a Councillor and Magistrate and served as Mayor in 1866.

After completing his mayoral term, he tried to persuade the Bristol Liberal party to adopt him as their parliamentary candidate. There were some extremely unpleasant incidents surrounding the elections in 1868. There were two parliamentary elections in Bristol that year – firstly a by-election in April followed by a general election in November. The first was occasioned by the resignation of one of the two Bristol members, the prominent Baptist, Sir Moreton Peto (who had been one of Bristol's MPs since 1865), following the failure of his company (Peto, Betts & Co.). Robinson was anxious to be adopted as the Liberal candidate, but the Liberal establishment in Bristol chose another candidate from outside the city. Robinson did not seek to be selected for the subsequent general election – which was probably just as well since it was marked by a great deal of intimidation of both candidates and voters. However, only two years later one of the members died thus precipitating another by-election in March 1870. This time the Liberal party decided to hold a "Test Ballot" (rather like an American Primary) and the outcome was that Robinson was selected. In the ensuing election he won the seat by a narrow margin, despite the abstention of about a thousand Liberal supporters who were unhappy with the choice of candidate. However, the Conservatives petitioned against the result and a court of enquiry was convened. It transpired that two of Robinson's agents had bribed some of the electors (the sums expended only amounted to £18) during the "Test Ballot". The case was referred to the Court of Common Pleas where the judge ruled that Robinson's election was invalid. He was unfortunate in two respects. Firstly, although the bribery had not been during the election itself, the judge ruled that the "Test Ballot" was an integral part of the election, and secondly it was only a few years earlier that the law had been changed. Previously only bribery in which the candidate himself was involved could lead to a challenge, but now the result could be overturned even if the candidate had not been personally involved in the bribery. In giving his verdict the judge expressed some sympathy for Robinson as he doubted whether these small bribes had influenced the outcome! He did try again on further two occasions. In 1878 and 1880 he failed to secure the Liberal nomination but in 1880 he stood as an independent candidate, coming bottom of the poll. So Robinson never did become an MP.

Robinson was married twice and twice widowed. In 1845 he married Elizabeth Frank Ring. She was the daughter of Richard Ring, a member of a Quaker family and proprietor of a pottery business in Brislington. He did not consider Robinson to have sufficient prospects to be worthy of his daughter, so they eloped and were married in Cornwall. During the 26 years of their marriage they had seven children. Elizabeth died in 1871 and the following year he married the much younger Louisa Thomas, the daughter of the Revd David Thomas, minister of Highbury Congregational chapel, where Robinson had formerly been a member. Louisa's health was poor and their marriage lasted less than four years as Louisa died at the age of only 34 in April 1875.

E. S. Robinson died on 29th August 1885. More than fifty private carriages processed to his funeral at Arnos Vale Cemetery a few days later, conducted by Richard Glover. Despite the heavy rain, the processional route was lined with spectators, and flags on business premises were flown at half-mast. So many people, including the leading citizens and many of the firm's employees, attended that the service was held in the open air. Shortly afterwards a bust of him was placed in the Colston Hall, the favoured venue for Liberal assemblies – the Conservatives favoured the Victoria Rooms.

Kossuth, named after the great Hungarian nationalist who sought his country's independence in the 1848 revolution, and Edward were the members of the next generation of the Robinson family to be most actively involved in the life of Tyndale. As a young man Kossuth ran a farm at Almondsbury, but most of his life lived as a gentleman "of private means" in Clifton and Stoke Bishop. In 1887 he married Maria Selina Wathen, niece and adopted daughter of Sir Charles Wathen, another member of Tyndale (see below). He served Tyndale as a deacon for many years and as treasurer of the Mission, whilst Maria Robinson was a leader in the church's women's work and in the Tyndale mission.

However, it was Edward who in his service to Tyndale, to E. S. & A. Robinson and to the city was most clearly the successor to his father. He was born in 1853, the fourth of the seven children. At the age of 16, in 1869, he entered the business in a lowly capacity (starting work at 7.30 am!), gaining experience in each of the departments of the business, but rapidly was given more responsibility. Two years after joining the firm he went on its behalf to South Africa as part of a drive to explore the potentials for overseas business. Subsequently he visited Australia and New Zealand. Over the years other representatives of the firm built on these early contacts and subsequently separate overseas companies were formed and trading

Edward Robinson

contracts established in a range of countries worldwide. Another parallel with his father was that he was joined in the business a few years after his own arrival by his brother Arthur, but it was clearly Edward who was "the boss" even before Arthur's death in 1913. It was after his father's death in 1885 that Edward assumed the leading role. He also built on his father's paternalistic style of management. As early as 1858 E. S. had instituted the Saturday half-holiday and to that, in 1889, Edward added a week's paid holiday. Then in 1901 he donated the substantial sum of £5,000 as the nucleus of a pension scheme for the employees and subsequently added further amounts to it as also did his brother, Arthur. A further step was taken in 1912 when a profit sharing scheme was introduced and in 1920 an issue of Workers' Shares bearing an interest rate of 8%. This last development was possible because in 1893 the firm had become a limited company when Alfred Robinson retired, its directors being recruited from among the more senior employees. Edward continued as Chairman until the age of 76, retiring in 1929 when his son Foster Robinson succeeded him as Chairman and, as in the previous two generations, he was joined by his brother, Harold and later, after he left the army, by Percy, a member of Tyndale.

Edward also followed his father's example in giving service to the city, not only through the Council – he was Lord Mayor in 1908 – but through many other organisations in and around Bristol. Along with Richard Glover, he was one of the prime movers in establishing the Convalescent Home on Durdham Down. Other bodies in which he was actively involved included the Council of Bristol University, the Colston Research Society (supporting research at the University), the Chamber of Commerce and the Anchor Society (an organisation founded in 1769 to care for the elderly). To celebrate their Golden Wedding in 1926 Edward and his wife, Katherine, donated a piece of land in Bedminster for the provision of a public park.

It might seem surprising that, with all his responsibility for an expanding international business and his involvement in so many aspects of the life of Bristol, he had any time (let alone energy) to make a contribution to church life. Yet Edward served, not only as a deacon at Tyndale for 54 years but as its treasurer for almost as long. He also succeeded his father as treasurer of Bristol Baptist College for fifty years and of the BMS for ten years from 1904. It is said that one of the office clerks at Robinson's spent almost all his time doing the book-keeping for Edward's various treasurerships! Beyond the denomination he was an active supporter of the Bristol City Mission Society (and its President in 1927) to which he donated £2,500 during his lifetime together with a mission building in Bedminster and then from the trust fund following his death two gifts totalling £8,500 (part of which the Mission used to pay off its overdraft). In 1876 Edward had married Katherine Frances Gotch, daughter of the Principal of Bristol Baptist College. Both Edward and Katherine were active supporters of the BMS. When the BMS celebrated its ter-jubilee in 1942, Edward was the subject of one of a series of twelve biographical booklets published to mark the occasion (written by H. L.Taylor – a fellow Tyndale member and former senior member of the staff at Robinson's). With her husband's support, Katherine served as President of the Zenana Mission (which became the Women's Missionary Association) in 1901 having served on its committee since 1894. The Robinsons were also generous with their hospitality and frequently entertained missionaries who were home on leave at both their Bristol home and their country home on Dartmoor.

E. S. Robinson may have been frustrated in his attempts to become an MP, but one Tyndale member who succeeded – indeed the only one – was Charles Townsend. He was born in Edgbaston, Birmingham on 6th June 1832 and christened at Carrs Lane Independent (Congregational) church. His parents, John and Hannah, had been married in Doncaster (his mother's home town) where Charles' older sister was born – his younger brother was born in Leeds. His father was a commercial traveller at the time his children were born, which may explain their different birthplaces. All of them were christened in Independent churches. However, by 1841 the family was settled in Bristol, which was his father's home town, and Charles was a pupil at Christmas Street City School (better known as Queen Elizabeth's Hospital). However, in Bristol it was to Broadmead Baptist Church that they went rather than any Congregational church and, indeed, Charles' father, John, served as a deacon and Sunday school superintendent and Charles was baptised there. His father worked for Ferris & Co. – a wholesale pharmaceutical business and Charles joined the same company. At first he also worked as a commercial traveller, mainly in Wales and the west country, but eventually became a director. In 1859 he married Anna Maria Holden, whose father was a sugar refiner in Bristol, and they had four children. Two of their sons married daughters of fellow deacon, William Sherring. The Townsend family lived for some years in Avenue House, Cotham. Many years later this became a Residential Home where a number of Tyndale members have been resident and it was also where Dr David Russell, former General Secretary of the Baptist Union, spent his last years.

We have already seen that Townsend was one of the leading men in the establishment of Tyndale (see Chapter 1). He was among the first deacons in 1871 and continued until 1903, when he was made a Life Deacon. He was also Church Secretary from 1871 until his election to Parliament in 1892. As well as being an active member of Tyndale, he served as President of the Bristol Baptist Association in 1888 and was involved with the Bristol City Mission Society, serving as one of the secretaries for some twenty years. He used his position in Ferris & Co. to help the BMS, making supplies available for missionary dispensaries in the Congo.

Like so many of the Tyndale members at this time he was an active member of the Liberal party; indeed, although it was not a formal position, he came to be regarded as the Leader of the Liberals in Bristol. He was elected as a Councillor for the Bristol North ward in 1872 and was re-elected unopposed for twenty years. One of his main interests was the docks, with a number of major schemes being undertaken at that time. He became Chairman of the Docks Committee in 1880, the same year that he was appointed as a magistrate. Education was another of his concerns, both technical education and schools, serving as a Governor of Bristol Grammar School for six years. Other responsibilities included chairing the Chamber of Commerce in 1874. On the occasion of the 1892 election, when he was a candidate, a pamphlet was published giving details of each of the six candidates for the three Bristol constituencies. It includes a list of the political causes which Townsend espoused, including Home Rule for Ireland, disestablishment of the Church in Wales and Scotland, Free Trade, electoral reform ("one man, one vote"), Sunday closing, shorter working hours for underground miners, international arbitration and the abolition of the hereditary principle in the House of Lords. Much of this echoed Gladstone's party manifesto known as the "Newcastle Programme" following its launch in that city in 1891. He was also a supporter of the Peace Movement and at a meeting shortly after his death a memorial resolution was adopted, which included: "Alderman Townsend was always a consistent, devoted and wise advocate of peace principles". The Chairman recalled that during the South African (Boer) War he was one of their truest and best friends.

Charles Townsend

It is well known that after 1886 the Liberal Party was divided over the issue of Irish Home Rule. Townsend was a fervent admirer of William Gladstone, who was now advocating Home Rule, and Townsend was persuaded to stand in the 1892 election in opposition to the sitting member, the well-known Quaker (and chocolate manufacturer), Lewis Fry. Following the split over the issue Fry had sided with the Liberal Unionists who opposed Home

Rule. In the poll Townsend won a narrow (4,409 to 4,064) victory over Fry and so entered Parliament. However, his sojourn at Westminster was short lived. At the next election in 1895, although he polled slightly more votes, his 4,464 was not enough to beat Fry's 4,702. During that time he also served on the Executive Committee of the National Liberal Federation. It may have been some consolation that two years later he was elected as an Alderman. Townsend died on 4th November 1908 having lived long enough to be present when the King opened the Royal Edward Dock in July that year.

A member of Tyndale who was born the year after Townsend, in 1833 was Charles Wathen, but his membership of the church was not for such a long period – he became a member on 27th December 1881 and resigned on 21st May 1890. More than most, he was associated with several churches, all of them in Bristol. He was a principal supporter of the building, in 1859, of a United Presbyterian church in the Horsefair area. When he died the then minister recalled that "during the first pastorate of this church he was a regular and devout worshipper here". (When the building was damaged in the 1940 Blitz the congregation worshipped in Broadmead Baptist Church before returning when it was rebuilt; it was demolished in 1988 and only the tower remains today next to the bus station). After resigning from Tyndale, Wathen joined the congregation at the Mayor's chapel for the rest of his life and was a generous contributor to the cost of its restoration. In fact Wathen was noted for his generosity, not least to Baptist overseas mission work. On his

Sir Charles Wathen

death the (Baptist) *Missionary Herald* reminded its readers that he had given some £1,200 for work in the Congo and an additional £500 for building a school there. In gratitude a missionary station on the Congo was named after him. Then, following Richard Glover's visit to China, when he advised that more missionaries were needed there (see Chapter 2), Wathen donated half the amount needed – some £2,100. Nearer home, when the Baptist Union held its Autumnal Assembly in Bristol in October, 1886, Wathen, then Mayor, (and while he was a member of Tyndale) gave a reception for the delegates at the Colston Hall.

Charles Wathen's family came from the Stroud area of Gloucestershire, although, for a reason which is not clear, he was actually born in Waterford in Ireland on 19th March 1833. Whether this influenced his decision to oppose Gladstone's proposals for Irish Home Rule and support the Liberal Unionists can only be a matter of speculation. His parents were another Charles and Mary. The Wathen family was settled in that part of Gloucestershire for many generations and the family connections are quite complicated! When Charles died, his obituary in the *Western Daily Press* said that he:

> had for an ancestor Sir Samuel Wathen, of Stroud, whose son was Sir Paul Bagot, he having assumed that name. A large mill near Stroud was called "Paul Wathen's Mill" and the deceased's father, one of the firm who owned it, subsequently came to Bristol, as the firm was dissolved.

Certainly Charles (aged 9) was with his parents and an older brother (James) and a younger sister (Elizabeth) in Bristol by the time of the 1841 census and in the following census, ten years later, his 71-year-old father's occupation is given as "retired victualler" while Charles' own occupation is "Clerk to linen warehouse". Then, in 1862, he joined John Gardiner in a business which his family had founded in 1805, as a retail clothier which had a substantial export business, especially exporting ready-made clothes to Jamaica using "puncheons" – rum barrels, which were then filled with rum for the return voyage. The firm then became known as Wathen, Gardiner & Co. and gradually expanded into the manufacture of uniforms.

In 1898, after Wathen's death, the firm moved to new premises in Staple Hill, where it still trades today.

Wathen became a Councillor in 1877 and an Alderman in 1889. Between 1884 and 1890 he was Mayor no fewer than six times! Like the two Robinsons and Townsend he took an active interest in many aspects of local politics and charitable enterprises (in 1888 he was President of the "Grateful Society"). He also "put his money where his mouth was"! There was concern that the museum and library were struggling financially and the intention was that the city might take them over. The problem was that such a move would land the city with a large debt, so Wathen paid off their debts from his own pocket thus enabling the transfer to go ahead. This was only one example of his generosity to the city – in 1887, for example, he presented the Corporation with two elegant pieces of plate (weighing nearly 300 ounces) for use in the Mansion House. Wathen's attitude to working men was less generous. In 1886 (when he was Mayor) a deputation from the Bristol Socialist Society delivered a petition to him which had been passed at a public meeting. This called upon the Council to open a "registry office" (i.e. labour exchange) and to provide employment through a programme of public works. Wathen's response was to deride the resolution and suggest that "the working men come down to the same level as the working men on the Continent, work more hours and for less pay".

In the New Year's Honours in 1889 Wathen was knighted. This followed a royal visit by Prince Albert Victor, Duke of Connaught, who, as eldest son of the future Edward VII was heir presumptive to the throne (he died a few years later and his brother eventually succeeded as George V). This visit was during one of Wathen's mayoral years and seems to have been part of a pattern – in 1897 the Lord Mayor, Herbert Ashman (see below) was knighted by Queen Victoria during her visit to the city, and in 1908 the then Lord Mayor was also knighted following the visit of Edward VII!

Wathen married twice, but had no children. In 1853 he married Mary Selina Chase and two years after her death in 1881 he married the much younger Mary Ann Sexton of Ashburton in Devon. Again there were no children. However, Wathen adopted three of his first wife's nieces (their widowed father had been left to look after ten children) who all took the

Wathen name – Mary Selina married Kossuth Robinson in 1887 (see above); Edith married Henry Vipond Bate (a civil servant) in 1894 and had three children; and the same year Mary Ann married the Revd Montague Blamire Williamson (an Anglican clergyman) and they had four children. (It appears that the Chase/Wathen girls were attracted to unusual names!) Although Edith and Mary Ann became members of Tyndale in 1887 they both resigned in 1890 and became Anglicans. The Wathen family lived at Ashley House on Ashley Down. However, shortly before his death he had bought the Cook's Folly estate and planned to renovate the house as a new home. In the event it was subsequently bought by his fellow Tyndale member, Sir Herbert Ashman (see below).

Wathen died on 14th February 1893. That day he was on his way to a Council meeting and had been seen by a fellow councillor leaning against the wall of Lloyd's Bank in Corn Street, clearly in some pain. However he insisted on going to the meeting (the Council House was then on the corner of Corn Street and Broad Street) and at 4.00 p.m. made a speech. Half an

Tyndale with the Wathen pulpit

hour later he collapsed. Another Councillor, Dr Cunningham, immediately attended to him, but he could not be revived and died there in the Council Chamber – perhaps a fitting end for one who had served the city so well. His funeral was at the Mayor's Chapel conducted by the Mayor's Chaplain and the Dean of Bristol gave the address. At Arnos Vale Cemetery Richard Glover led the final prayer. Also present was the Revd Holman Bentley, the senior missionary at the BMS Wathen station in the Congo. In his memory a new stone pulpit was given to Tyndale. Sadly, as with much else, it was destroyed when the church was bombed in 1940. Despite all his generosity to Baptist and other causes, at his death his estate was valued at more than £147,000.

Herbert Ashman could not rival Wathen's six terms as Mayor, but he had the unique distinction of becoming Bristol's first Lord Mayor, an office he held for two years. It was on 2nd June 1899 that Bristol was given the privilege of so designating its leading citizen. This was followed by a visit by Queen Victoria, as part of her Diamond Jubilee celebrations, on 15th November. On that occasion Ashman was able to claim another distinction, being the last person to have a knighthood conferred by the Queen in person and in public. This took place outside the Council House, the Queen leaning out of her carriage to "dub" the new knight. There was one further distinction for him when in 1907 he was created a Baronet.

Herbert Ashman was born in Yeovil on 11th June 1854, the son of Thomas Nathaniel Ashman and Henrietta née Vaters. He was educated at Taunton School, one of the few nonconformist boarding schools of that period so presumably came from a nonconformist family. The family moved to Bristol where he joined his father's leather business and then, in 1876, with his brother (who retired in 1899) set up the firm of R. H. & H. Ashman, Leather Factors. It became a private company in 1909. In 1904 he was President of the Leather and Hide Trades Provident and Benevolent Institution. On 2nd April 1874 at St Barnabas church in City Road he married Eliza Lorenzen, whose father (born in Denmark) was foreman in a tan yard. They had six children but three of them died in infancy. However, one daughter married fellow Tyndale member Sir Percy Sargent. The newly-wed couple became regular worshippers at Tyndale and ten years

Sir Herbert Ashman dubbed by Queen Victoria

later were both baptised (on the same occasion as the minister's son, T. R. Glover).

It was Richard Glover who is said to have encouraged him to become involved in civic affairs. In December 1890 he was elected to the city council and became Mayor in 1898. In 1900 he became an Alderman. He was President of the North Bristol Liberal Association for twenty years and of the city-wide Liberal Association for three years. There were some among the Liberal party who encouraged him to stand for Parliament, but he steadfastly refused. As with Tyndale's other city councillors he served on a variety of committees and other bodies within the city such as the Anchor Society (see above) of which he was President in 1898. He was also involved in a number of sports clubs, serving at various times as President of a golf club and a rowing club. And he was an early motorist too. He took an especial interest in the recruiting of soldiers for both the Boer War and the First World War. However, in the case of the Boer War, his concern went beyond recruitment and extended to the welfare of the families of the soldiers, especially those who had been killed. In 1914 he chaired the Citizens' Recruiting Committee, but his sudden death meant that he was unable to be concerned with welfare issues after 1914.

In September 1914 he was taken ill with appendicitis and, despite urgent surgery, died in the early hours of 26th September at the family home, Cook's Folly. His funeral took place at Tyndale a few days later. The account of it in the *Western Daily Press* included a list of those who processed in the 40 carriages as well as all the others who attended and the organisations that many of them represented – the list reads like a catalogue of Bristol's voluntary societies and of the "great and the good" of the city. Soldiers of the newly formed Bristol Battalion lined the route and the robed choir from the Lord Mayor's Chapel led the singing. Then on 4th October a Memorial Service was held at the Colston Hall and subsequently a memorial resolution was passed by the council which referred to his "beneficent influence in commercial, social, educational and philanthropic circles". On his death the baronetcy passed to his son, Frederick (a member of Tyndale from 1898). However he was too ill to attend his father's funeral and he died at his home at Clarence Croft, Weston-super-Mare on 22nd December 1916, aged 41, at which point the baronetcy became extinct as he had no heirs.

Many of those who attended Ashman's funeral may have recalled being in Tyndale for a similar occasion less than two years earlier. On 23rd January 1913 a congregation including nearly all the same distinguished citizens assembled for the funeral of J. W. Arrowsmith. Like Ashman, he had been baptised in later life together with his wife. When they were baptised in 1903 he was aged 63 and his wife was 48 and they had been attending Tyndale for many years.

James Williams Arrowsmith had been born in Worcester on 6th November 1839, the fifth of the seven children of Isaac Arrowsmith and his wife, Louisa. Isaac was a newspaper proprietor and printer. He moved to Bristol in 1854 where he entered into a partnership with Hugh Evans, a stationer and bookseller in Clare Street. However, the partnership only lasted three years and he then moved to new premises in Quay Street and James joined him in a business of which the principal work was printing railway timetables and the Bristol Channel Tide timetables. When Isaac died in 1871 James took control of the business and began to develop the publishing side. This rapidly grew and a number of books were published which would become popular – *Three Men in a Boat* (Jerome K. Jerome),

Prisoner of Zenda (Anthony Hope) and *The Diary of a Nobody* (George Grossmith) were, perhaps, the best known examples. In addition many books of local interest were published including, for many years, a Christmas Annual. In the later years of the 19th century it was said that the majority of books sold on railway bookstalls were published by Arrowsmith's.

A recent historian assigns the business to the category of "benevolent paternalism" alongside similar enterprises run by Quaker entrepreneurs:

> Like his father, he was keen to help workers to develop an ideology of self-help. However, he recognized that trade unionism had a role to play in his firm. He supported the benefit purposes of trade unionism where workers made their own insurance arrangements to provide for unemployment, sickness and old age.

Arrowsmith was prepared to go the extra mile in terms of compassion for his workers so that when the union superannuation fund ran into difficulties in 1906, he made a donation of ten guineas indicating that if necessary he would turn this into an annual non-contractual payment in order to keep the scheme running. But on issues of control and managerial authority he resisted change as is demonstrated by a robust letter to the Bristol Typographical Association which had in 1874 demanded an increase in overtime rates: "I cannot too strongly express my disapprobation that the profession of printing in Bristol is descended to the low ebb of requiring an agitator to come amongst them for the purpose of spreading discord". The Union was quick to deny any personal attack on Arrowsmith, acknowledging that it regarded his firm as a model

James Williams Arrowsmith

employer. In practice his style of paternalism managed to accommodate the development of trade union representation at the workplace by granting better and more wide-ranging benefits than those secured by union agreements elsewhere. Thus around the turn of the twentieth century a sports club was opened for the sole use of his workers in a corner of Gloucestershire County Cricket ground, and more substantially, from 1876 all his workers received a week's paid holiday, and by 1894 they were working a 48 hour week. Benevolent paternalism practised by the firm before the First World War minimized conflict and seemed to have been happily embraced by the workforce. Nothing less than this could be expected of a member of Tyndale.

J. W. Arrowsmith was one of the founders of the Liberal Club in Bristol but, despite frequent invitations to do so, never stood for elected office. He did, however, become a magistrate in 1896. Despite his increasing business responsibilities, he continued his service in the City of Bristol Rifle Corps, which he had joined in 1859, until 1881. In this he not only served as Quartermaster, but also became an award-winning marksman. Shooting was only one of his many sporting interests. Cricket was probably the foremost of these and he, with others, played a large part in securing the County Ground in 1888 at Ashley Down for the Gloucestershire County Cricket Club, of which his friend, W. G. Grace, was, of course, a prominent member. Not surprisingly he served as a member of the County Cricket Club Committee for many years. In his later years he also played golf.

Although never a councillor, he nevertheless was prominent in his public service. He was one of the group who promoted an Industrial and Fine Arts Exhibition in 1893, which involved the erection of a large temporary building (520 by 110 feet) in Colston Avenue, using the recently covered section of the river Frome at the northern end of what is now known as the Centre. A few years later he was similarly involved in the erection of the Cabot Tower on Brandon Hill. His most important involvement, however, was with the establishment of Bristol University. In the chapter on the history of the University in *Bristol and its Adjoining Counties*, published in 1955 for the visit of the British Association for the Advancement of Science (the Association had previously come to Bristol in 1836, 1875, 1898 and 1930), Professor A. M. Tyndall wrote:

> In the spring following the 1898 meeting of the British Association
> in Bristol… a Bristol printer, James W. Arrowsmith took a leading
> part in founding the University College Colston Society… It is
> believed that this Society, now the Colston Research Society, has
> no parallel in university history. It has supported special
> investigations in various departments and faculties… In its first
> ten years the Society not only brought money and new friends to
> the College, but through a succession of guest speakers, it helped
> to convert the pipe-dream of a future university in Bristol into a
> live issue.

When major buildings were erected in University Road in 1911 one of their prominent features was named "The Arrowsmith Tower". Arrowsmith served on the University Council and, predictably, on its Athletic Ground Management Committee.

On 31st August 1882 the 41-year-old James married Kate Adams, who was 27. They married at St Andrew's church in Plymouth, where her father ran a drapery and tailoring business. They lived at various addresses in Bristol – 99 Whiteladies Road and then 24 Westfield Park (next to Edward Robinson) and finally in Upper Belgrave Road. Kate died in 1907 and James' health began to deteriorate around the same time. On 19th July 1913 he died following a stroke. They had no children and one of his nephews took over the business, which continues today having moved to Winterstoke Road in 1954. In announcing his death, the *Western Daily Press* said that he was "interested in literature, local history, art, education, politics, philanthropy, volunteering and all kinds of amateur athletic sport". At his funeral, Richard Glover gave the address, gently giving an insight into another side of his character: "He had no diplomacy, no tact, but great charm and high integrity". He was interred at Redland Green with his wife, the Bishop of Bristol sharing the committal with Herbert Morgan.

Like his friend Charles Townsend, E. G. Clarke was the son of a commercial traveller, which resulted in his siblings being born in a variety of places as the family moved around the country. Townsend and Clarke had become friends when they attended the same school and remained friends for the rest of their lives – living as near neighbours for some years. Edward

Gustavus Clarke was born in Newton Abbot in Devon on 31st May 1833 and christened at Salem Independent Chapel a few months later. His parents were Gustavus Clarke and Elizabeth née Bliss and he was their oldest child. By the time he was 9 the family had moved to Bristol.

Edward Clarke joined a firm of accountants, Messrs Barnard & Thomas and, having qualified as a chartered accountant, became a partner in the firm in 1873. When the new Bankruptcy Act came into force in 1883 a new post of Official Receiver was created and Clarke was appointed to that office for an extensive area which included Bristol and Bath. He served for 17 years, only retiring a few months before his death. Clarke's father was more closely associated with Liberal politics than his son, serving as Chairman of a ward Liberal Association (in which he was succeeded by Charles Townsend). Nevertheless, like Arrowsmith, Edward Clarke was much involved in other public and charitable organisations. In fact he was joint secretary with Arrowsmith of the committee which built the Cabot Tower and also worked with him on the Industrial and Art Exhibition. He was active in the Chamber of Commerce, the Anchor Society, the YMCA and many sporting organisations, including the County Cricket Ground. In reporting his death, the *Western Daily Press* commented: "So many sided was Mr. Clarke that there were few undertakings started in Bristol which had for their object the benefit of the people that did not obtain his support and interest". He also gained a reputation as a popular after-dinner speaker. Clarke was the Joint Treasurer (with E. S. Robinson) of the first committee set up by the Broadmead deacons to consider the establishment of what became Tyndale (see Chapter 1). He continued to serve on that committee until the church was established and was then one of the first deacons in 1871. However, he only remained on the diaconate for three years, resigning soon after becoming a partner in the accountancy firm.

Clarke married twice. On 20th February 1862 at Broadmead he married Mary Phillips. However, soon after their daughter, Edith Mary, was born in 1863 Mary died. Then on 2nd March 1865 at Frogmore Street Baptist chapel in Abergavenny he married Emma Harris Conway. Abergavenny was her home town, although she had been at school in Bristol. In 1868 their son, Arthur Conway Clarke was born. Edward Clarke died on 19th January 1901 aged 67 and his funeral at Arnos Vale cemetery four days later was conducted by Richard Glover with civic representatives present, together with members of the various voluntary organisations that he had served. He had died just three days before Queen Victoria and in his address Glover reminded the congregation that their sorrow at Clarke's death was in the context of the national mourning for the Queen. After Edward's death his widow returned to Wales and died in Pontrhydyrun in Monmouthshire on 6th July 1907.

In later years there have continued to be members who have made notable contributions to many aspects of the life of the city right down to the present day. But after the death of Herbert Ashman in 1914, there were never so many prominent citizens to be found together in the membership of this one church.

Chapter 5.
The Tyndale Mission

David Roberts

Only two years after the church was constituted it began work in one of the poorest districts of the city. This was the area to the south and west of the Cathedral within the parish of St Augustine's – the medieval east end of the cathedral had originally been an Augustinian priory. Alongside the Cathedral stood the church of St Augustine the Less (demolished in 1962), which served as the parish church for the district. By the 1870s most of the more affluent citizens of the area had moved north towards Clifton, many of them to houses on the southern slopes of Brandon Hill. And it was to serve their spiritual needs that a new parish church – St George's – was built in 1823. This splendid building is now used as a concert venue. Thus by 1870 most of the remaining former grand houses had become multi-occupied tenements with other poor quality dwellings around them.

In 1868 work had started to enlarge the Cathedral – a nave was added to the medieval choir and transepts thus extending the Cathedral westwards. Around the same time the north wing of the Deanery, itself a replacement for the old Deanery which still remains as part of the Choir School, which stood to the west of the Cathedral, was demolished and the new Deanery Road was created leading west towards Hotwells. Despite all these improvements, most of the area around the Cathedral, and between it and the river, was best described as a slum. However, most of the housing stood back from the river and was thus protected from the worst effects of sewage in the floating harbour. Describing the district many years later, Dorothy Glover wrote:

> The hollow between Brandon Hill and College Green had become
> a sink into which had drained some of the city's dregs. The

> dignified streets, where notable people like Samuel Taylor
> Coleridge and Friese-Green lived, now had their houses let to
> many tenants and almost all concealed tragedies of poverty and
> sin.

The area served by the Tyndale Mission was rather larger than she described, and consisted of some 35 or 40 streets and courts in which most of the inhabitants were poor. Many of the houses were occupied by more than one family. Typical was 15 Stephens Court, where in 1891 three families totalling twelve people aged from 6 to 50 lived in four rooms. There were, however, a few streets where conditions were slightly better, notably St George's Road. There were always a substantial number of unemployed men to be found on the streets of the district, while those who had jobs were in a wide variety of employment, with some having to travel well outside the immediate area to find work. The other feature of this, like many similar districts, was the proliferation of public houses. The growing emphasis on temperance meant that these were a feature of great concern to those running the Mission, as it was to many others, not in order to seek to deprive these people of one of their few pleasures in what was often a miserable life, but out of a very real concern for the well-being of their families. A father, when employed, spending his wages on drink or a mother neglecting her children when drunk were both situations which were harmful to the whole family, especially to the children. Even where there were no children, the excessive spending on drink could leave households destitute.

Missions in the more deprived parts of the city were by no means a new concept. The Bristol City Mission Society (confusingly there was also a Methodist "City Mission") which worked in several areas, had been founded in 1826 by a group of Baptist and Congregational ministers and laymen. One of those who took the initiative was the Revd Robert Hall, Minister of Broadmead. During the next century and beyond many lay people, mostly Baptists and Congregationalists were supporters of the Mission – prominent among them Edward Robinson and Charles Townsend of Tyndale. Other Tyndale people served the Mission in various ways at different times. In his history of the City Mission (*Mission of Mercy*) in 1979, Ronald Cleves wrote: "The City Mission, by its nature and calling, is two handed. With one hand it has always carried and presented the Gospel – with the other, it has also brought relief to those who were in need".

This might serve as a description of many such missions, not least that which Tyndale established in St Augustine's parish, one of the few deprived areas where the City Mission did not establish a work. Indeed it was a leading member of the City Mission, Peter Fabyan Sparke Evans (a businessman – a tannery owner – and a councillor as well as President of the Bristol Sunday School Union), who drew the attention of Tyndale to the potential for a Mission in that area.

On 2nd July 1871 a Sunday School began meeting in Stephen's Court, Lower Lamb Street. The work expanded quickly and within two months there were about 100 children led by some ten teachers, so larger premises had to be found. These were in a former Jewish Synagogue in Lower College Green. Here a Mothers' Meeting and a mid-week service were also held. In February 1876 Dean's Cottage adjacent to the Deanery in Lower College Green was leased from the Dean of Bristol for 12 guineas a year. One condition of the lease was "not to allow ingress or egress through the entrance in Lower College Green for any school children". So they had to use the back door! This was, presumably, to ensure that none of the mission children intruded on the area frequented by the cathedral clergy. Further expansion of the work led to the renting of a former public house (The House of Rest). By the late 1880s there were more than 300 children enrolled in the Sunday School as well as many other activities, and Sunday congregations of about 140.

By this time the Mission was also struggling to operate in four different buildings. So it was decided that the time had come for the Mission to have its own premises. A site was chosen in Deanery Road, taking advantage of the topography whereby that road was carried over Lamb Street on a bridge, so that the main entrance, leading to the principal 300-seater hall opened onto Deanery Road. Below the hall were two further floors; the middle one had six classrooms and another large room with the capacity to seat about 120. On the lowest floor, with an entrance also at street level onto Lamb Street were two rooms which between them could accommodate 150 children. There were also toilets (on each floor), a kitchen and a central

Tyndale Mission in Deanery Road

heating system. The site was purchased for £625 and Mr Sparke Evans laid the foundation stone. The building, which cost £2,600, was opened on 22nd June 1888 (by coincidence the day after the now extended nearby Cathedral was opened), and registered for public worship on 10th November that year, but it was not registered for marriages until 1896. Even before the Mission had its own premises a library had been created with more than 400 books, which scholars could borrow. The rules of the library stated that each scholar had to subscribe one penny a quarter, which entitled them to borrow one book a fortnight and which must be returned in good condition after 14 days. The Catalogue of the library shows a bias towards "improving" literature, including several by Old Humphrey (the pen name of the popular author of children's books and religious tracts, George Mogridge). Not all the books were of a religious nature – for example there were books on natural history and biographies of historical figures.

In November 1880 it was recorded that the "Church Commenced". It never became a fully independent church, but from that date there were Church Meetings and members were admitted – the first recorded on 23rd November 1880 when Miss Dora Clarke, who lived at 5 Lower College Green Avenue, was admitted following baptism. She died in 1885 and a note in the church roll describes her as "useful consistent, earnest" and that "her end was peace". Of the 18 members admitted in the first year, 16 were "by baptism". It would appear that there was no baptistery at the Mission since baptisms took place at Tyndale, usually on a Wednesday evening – the normal time for Tyndale baptisms. The first recorded Church Meeting at the Mission took place on 29th September 1881. As at most future meetings, the first item discussed was applications for membership. However, a memo attached to the front of the membership roll stated:

> Copy of resolution passed at Deacons Meeting May 9 1881:
>
> Mission Church
>
> That before any candidates for membership are submitted to the Mission church; a report upon each case be presented to the Deacons of Tyndale with the opinion of the Teacher or Visitor to whom the candidate is known & such report may be presented to the Deacons after any service & without waiting for the monthly Deacons meeting.
>
> Charles Townsend, Secretary

It is significant that this memo clearly indicates that it was the Tyndale deacons who had to receive the report since there were also deacons at the Mission. Over the years their membership varied, but there were always some who were Tyndale members, usually also on the Tyndale diaconate. Many Tyndale members were involved in the work of the Mission, not all of them in leadership roles. Many of these were women. In 1892, for example, four of the 12 members of the Management Committee and 22 of the 41 Sunday School teachers were women. However, not all the teachers were from Tyndale – Mrs Elizabeth Norman, for instance, was, with her husband (a mason) a member of the Mission who lived locally. Writing many years later Dorothy Glover recalled:

> There were in such a work inevitable tensions between the helpers and the helped and between fellow workers of varied opinions, but it was a healthy outreach of the church's life and those who took part learned to express their faith and to find treasures of Christ among the poor. Some vignettes come to us out of the misty past:

Edward Robinson in white shirt sleeves fighting a gang of youths who were molesting the children coming to Sunday School.

Edward Robinson, a member of one of the wealthiest families in Bristol, went on to become Lord Mayor (see Chapter 4). His brother, Kossuth Robinson, served as treasurer of the Mission for some 25 years. One of the most prominent workers was Frank Shoard (a bank clerk), who served as one of the Mission deacons and as Superintendent of the Sunday School for many years. When he died tribute was paid to him in the *Tyndale Messenger:* "The Tyndale Mission may be said to have begun with him. In it he lived and moved and had his being. He helped and comforted the aged and played with the boys". But it was not only the more affluent Tyndale people who helped – in 1893 it was reported that the Servants' Bible Class sent a hamper containing some 100 items of clothing for the people connected with the Mission.

Frank Shoard

By 1891 the Mission was a very active place. The Annual Report for that year reported attendances at morning and evening Sunday services averaging 35 and 200 respectively. There were also children's services on a Sunday with some 40 attending in addition to a Sunday School with 432 children enrolled and an average attendance of 255 – however only four of the 41 teachers were members of the Mission, the rest were from Tyndale. There was a wide variety of activities on every night of the week as well. There was a mid-week service with an average attendance of about 40. Then there was a Prayer Meeting, Choir Practice, Mothers' Meeting, Band of Hope for children and Gospel Total Abstinence Society for adults, Factory Girls' Club, Lads' Institute (which became a Swimming Club in the summer), Men's Night School, Junior Girls' Club and Penny Bank (with 75 "depositors"). The Mission had its own cricket team which won 12 of its 17 matches that year. There were then 43 local members of the Mission.

In view of all this activity, it was decided to appoint a full-time Missioner. The man chosen was Thomas Edward Howe. A 30-year-old Londoner (born in Hackney on 30th June 1860), Howe had no formal ministerial training. He had been baptised at the age of 12 at Old Providence Chapel, Shoreditch by the Revd William Cuff. Very soon he became a lay preacher and frequently led worship at Hope Mission, Haggerstone until he received the call to Bristol. Howe was married to Emily (née Dowse) and they had four children (William, Lilian, Florence and Jeannie) – a fifth (Thomas) was born while they were in Bristol. Howe kept a detailed diary or log of his work, with daily entries. This is a unique record, not only of Howe's work, but also of life and conditions in that small area of Bristol during the five years he was there. The first entry is dated Monday 1st June 1891:

Thomas Howe

> Today I've commenced in the Lord's name and on behalf of the 24 districts connected with the above Mission, a work sorely needed, in the five hours spent in visitation, with tracts obtained from the R. T. S. Depot. I found the people in a positively dead condition before God & where they lived at all in a low state of spiritual life. I was enabled to visit about 100 houses, in many of which are 2, 3 & sometimes 4 families living in a most degrading condition without God & without hope in the world & careless as to eternity.

He then goes on the list the 13 streets and courts he visited that day and concludes: "Roman Catholicism & Church of England seem to hold great sway, but no 'churchism' is in greater power. May God own & bless the visitation to the Glory of His own great name".

On the Saturday at the end of that first week he recorded that he had visited 413 houses! That week he also held the first of a series of weekly services for the workers during their "dinner hour" in a local factory – about 20 attended. This was Fuller's Coach Works, a newly built factory in St George's Road in which this long established company (founded in 1770 and by 1891 the largest manufacturer of quality carriages in Bristol) had created an innovative production line. Clearly the management was sympathetic as they not only allowed these services on their premises, but also provided a harmonium for the services as well as a library for the workers. Some of these men became involved in the life of the Mission – in February 1892 two of them gave their testimony and sang at a meeting of the Total Abstinence Society. This was one of a proliferation of temperance organisations in Bristol. Eventually, shortly after Howe left Bristol, these came together under the umbrella of the Bristol United Temperance Council in 1897.

Howe was constantly coming up against problems caused by excessive drinking. Very soon after coming to the Mission he reported:

> It was our painful duty to separate a man and his wife, who were fighting desperately, but we succeeded in offering a little pacification, which stopped for the time what might have been a most deadly conflict, both being determined to end the days of the other – and such is the life of many about here.

The aim of temperance societies was to encourage people to "sign the pledge" – that is to make a promise to give up drinking altogether. Howe did his best to encourage this, though not always with lasting success:

> A case of drunkenness and indifference came under my notice today. A Mrs Deveral, so addicted to drink that she sold her pail, teapot, lamp and her husband's trousers to satisfy her craving. We have twice got them to sign the pledge, but each time they broke it afterwards.

Howe continued his regular visitation around the area and while he registered some positive outcomes, he never lost his sense that more needed to be done for both the spiritual and material welfare of the people –

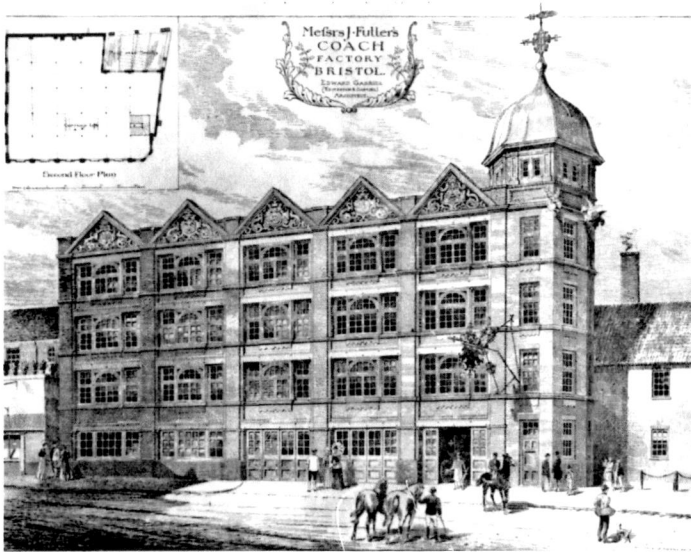

Fuller's Coach Works on St George's Road

on one occasion after helping a man find work by providing some suitable clothes, he commented "it is a poor Christianity which does not consider the temporal needs of the people seriously". On another occasion he commented: "Empty cupboards are unfit companions for empty hearts". Unemployment – or more often sporadic casual employment – was a constant challenge. One of his earliest entries in his diary tells of such situations:

> A man out of work we visited and prayed that work might be sent. The next day he had some to do and, although temporary, yet gave relief. Another man, ill for some eight weeks, had been praying all day for help as they had no money and would want for food on the morrow.

There was little improvement during his five years at the Mission. Towards the end of that time he reported:

> In one house I found a man out of work with six children depending on them. No food in the house and the woman pacing the room with a young baby, who was crying for milk, and the

> woman had not a penny to buy any. I have asked nearly a dozen
> employers of labour to give the man work, but all reply: "We do
> not require labourers". It is most painful to go from house to
> house and find so many in a similar condition.

Despite the difficulties, there was clearly some improvement in the
situation for some of the people, often because of persuading them to be
more careful with what little money they had. In his Annual Report towards
the end of 1892 he was able to report that a gradual improvement was
discernable and, for example, many were now paying their rent more
regularly.

Sometimes Howe was able to offer some practical help, frequently coupled
with spiritual advice:

> One case of Mr Rowe, a tailor, was very sad. Out of work, five
> children and five weeks behind with his rent, and the door of his
> room off its hinges, to the common danger of his children. We
> helped him a little and, purchasing a new pair of hinges, managed
> to hang the door safely and spoke of Christ and his righteousness,
> as Noah did while he made the ark.

Inevitably those who were too old or infirm to work were also of concern
and he gave what help he could:

> Found one of our church members, an old Welsh woman, having
> an income of 3/6 a week, of which she pays 1/6 rent, gathers her
> fuel on the banks and begs, if she has no other means of supply.
> She was prevented from attending our services on account of her
> boots requiring mending. This we have agreed to have done.

Not that all the elderly were unable to earn some sort of living, especially if
given some help. One case illustrates this very well, although it did not go
smoothly:

> We have for nearly a year been collecting a subscription to help a
> poor man and woman, 70 years of age, to buy a donkey and cart to
> enable them to carry on their trade – coke and wood. We have
> succeeded in finding the thing required and have sealed the

> bargain by paying 10/- deposit. The whole is to cost £3, of which the old man pays £1.

Then, a week later:

> We have completed the purchase of a donkey, cart and scales for the aged couple mentioned last week, and, having found a suitable stable wherein to lodge it, handed it to its future owners and wished them God's speed.

All went well for about six months, then:

> A poor man, whom, some time ago, we set up with a donkey and cart, has told me that, through giving him too much rope in the stable, the donkey hanged himself. So that too much rope is bad for donkeys as well as people! Two gentlemen have agreed to give 5/- towards the part purchase of another.

Probably an entry in the diary some two years after he arrived (9th May 1893) sums up his general experience of the conditions in the area:

> During the seven hours I spent among the people I was greatly distressed. The first house was to give advice to a woman summoned for assault. Second to hear an account of one of our elder girl scholars who stole 13/- from her mother on Saturday. Third, a woman who locked her family in the house the day through while she went out washing – nearly £25 have been got rid of in two months. Fourth a list of twenty houses, each more or less filled with complaints. Fifth a drunken husband and an indolent slovenly wife and five or six children, almost destitute. Sixth a starving woman and a drunken husband (just out of prison). I tried to comfort the poor woman and gave her some counsel. Next follow a series of out of work people in great distress. Seventh a man, whom I have just brought home drunk on licensed premises and desired me to see a lady who will befriend him – to whom I went in Stokes Croft, but only to fail. Eighth a man here lying in a dying condition and his wife has been brought home, helplessly drunk, with her head cut open. Ninth, a man

whom I have asked many times to come to our meetings and give himself to Christ, usually answers: "I have so little time".

Relations with other denominations were mixed during this period. Howe appeared to welcome the arrival of the "Slum Sisters" of the Salvation Army. With regard to the Roman Catholics he commented in 1894:

In one or two Roman Catholic families I was well received and helpful conversation was engaged in, although the reading of the Word of God is not relished, except by their own priests. We often get these people to our meetings and hope to do them good.

As to the Anglicans, relationships fluctuated. In 1891, for example, an elderly woman fell and broke her leg on the Mission premises. The Vicar of St George's refused her any help, telling her she must get help where she broke her leg. Soon after that someone told Howe that the Vicar only visited his parishioners once a year. However, the next year St George's provided a bath chair for a crippled woman and the Mission provided an attendant to take her out. Many years later relations had clearly improved when, in 1918, the vicar of St Peter's Hotwells invited regular communicants of the Mission (together with those from another Free Church in his parish) to share in a joint communion service.

Howe's years at the Mission saw much growth. After his first year membership had increased from 43 to 51 and by 1895 it had reached 100. The Sunday School had seen similar growth and a few months before his departure, Howe was able to report that there were now 479 scholars. Howe concluded his ministry at the Mission in March 1896, after almost five years. His hard work was recognized by the Tyndale deacons who encouraged him to take some time out before taking up his new pastorate in London. They resolved that between his official leaving and the commencement of his new ministry "the interval between the above dates be used for a much needed rest" – in effect giving him a month's paid leave. Special services were held to mark his farewell and he was presented with a purse containing £38.2s.6d together with an illuminated address. The Mission congregation had initiated a collection for this "testimonial", to which Tyndale members were also invited to contribute and to which the deacons added £5 from church funds.

With his family he returned to London where he ministered at the new Ilderton Road Baptist Church in Bermondsey for some 22 years, seeing its membership grow from 62 to 350. Then in 1918 he moved to Hornchurch in Essex where he served for 12 years before retiring to Wickford (also in Essex) in 1930 and continuing to preach in local churches until shortly before his death. It was here that he died on 27th November 1936, aged 76, following a ten-week illness and having gone blind some months previously. His obituary notice in the *Baptist Handbook* spoke of him as "a sympathetic and indefatigable visitor among the sick and poor, and was therefore trusted by the well-to-do to be their almoner" – a tribute which certainly summed up his work at the Tyndale Mission.

Soon after Howe departed another Missioner was appointed. The Revd George William Robert came from a very different background. A Channel Islander, born in Guernsey in 1856, and son of a pastor, as a young man he had begun preaching in French and then trained for the ministry at the Metropolitan (later Spurgeon's) College and had already had two pastorates in Northamptonshire – Weston-by-Weedon (1887–1891) and Kingsthorpe (1891–1896). Unlike his predecessor both he and his wife (Maria – also from Guernsey) together with their eldest son, Percy, became members of the Mission. They arrived with four children – Percy, Ethel, Maude and George Basil. At first they lived in Sandford Road, Hotwells but later moved to Somerset Street and then to Queen's Parade, Brandon Hill. Over the 19 years that Robert remained at the Mission his family circumstances changed. We have already seen that George (usually

The Revd George Robert

known by his second name, Basil) became a conscientious objector (see Chapter 3); in 1908 Percy married, as did Maude in 1910. Ethel did not marry and in 1934 returned to Bristol and to membership of Tyndale; she died in 1940. Her sister, Maude, then widowed, also became a member of Tyndale at the same time but transferred to Knowle West, a new cause in the south of the city in which Tyndale had a great interest, the following year. George's wife, Maria, died in 1912 at the early age of 58, but two years later George married Alice Carver – a member of Tyndale, an active worker at the Mission, and a younger sister of Mrs Emily Porteous. In April 1915 their son, Cecil William, was born.

Under Robert's leadership the Mission work continued in the pattern that had been established over the recent decades. The *Tyndale Handbook* for 1901 details five separate meetings on a Sunday starting with a prayer meeting prior to morning worship which was paralleled by a separate children's service. The afternoon was occupied with Sunday School and Bible Classes. At 5.30 p.m. there were Cottage Meetings and at 6.30 p.m. Divine Service and a Children's Service running in parallel. The day finished with a "People's Pleasant Hour" (as over against the Wednesday afternoon "Women's Pleasant Hour") with the note that it was replaced by "Open-Air Meetings" in the summer months, but on the first Sunday in the month both gave way to Communion. During the week, women were well catered for with a Mothers' Meeting, a Girls' Club meeting in junior and senior divisions, a Dorcas Society with the exceptionally lengthy meeting time given as 3.00–7.45 p.m. so one imagines that knitters and sewers came and went during this period, a Pleasant Wednesday Afternoon, and a Young Womens' Club. Discipleship was nurtured in both a junior and an ordinary Christian Endeavour Society, whilst temperance was nurtured by a branch of the Band of Hope and the Gospel Total Abstinence Society. Parallel to the Girls' Club, the Lads' Institute also met in junior and senior sections, the former meeting twice a week and the latter three times, in addition to which there was a Boy's Brigade Company. Mid-week worship was on Wednesdays at 8.00 p.m. followed by Choir Practice, whilst Saturdays saw the St Paul's Penny Bank in operation.

Gradually living conditions in that part of Bristol were improving and the population was reducing at the same time. Already before the Mission was established the population of the area had begun to decrease and in the 20 years from 1871 to 1891 the population of the St Augustine parish declined from about 10,000 to 8,500 and in the following decade to 7,000. Nevertheless the membership of the Mission had increased to 141 by 1909, but the number of children in the Sunday School had decreased to 285, by 1916 to 216 and by 1918 to 190. Indeed the Annual Report in 1914 commented on there being fewer scholars because the neighbourhood was "less crowded". On the eve on the First World War the Mission continued to be a very busy place. In addition to the regular services for adults and children and a Sunday School, there was a Girls' Club, a Mothers' Meeting, a Pleasant Afternoon Meeting, a Band of Hope and a Tract Society. However, in retrospect it is possible to detect the beginning of a change.

The 1913 *Handbook* also listed a number of "Auxiliary Institutions" which the Mission hosted, mostly of a generally educational nature. However these were not simply organisations that used the Mission premises. George Robert was Secretary of the College Green Men's Adult School and Financial Secretary of the St George's Road Men's Institute and Club, of which Edward Robinson was President. Herbert Morgan was Chairman of the Lads' Institute and two of Robert's children were joint secretaries. A list of the activities in 1916 showed various organisations meeting every weeknight and many also in the day. Within less than a decade the nature of the Mission would have changed considerably with the new stress very much on education. Probably the events of the First World War played a significant part in that transition and the obvious interest of Tyndale's minister, Herbert Morgan, in adult education may have encouraged this shift (see Chapter 3). One important consequence of the war was the loss, between May 1918 and the following April, of the use of part of the Mission premises which were commandeered by the government. Another was the loss, either temporary or, sadly, permanently of many of the young men including some from Tyndale who were helpers and by 1918 there was a shortage of teachers for the Sunday School, although this was partly occasioned by the curtailment of the Sunday tram service making it more difficult for people to travel to the Mission from the Redland area. In 1916 it was feared that the Men's Club might have to close as the shortage of members was causing financial problems – other similar clubs in Bristol had closed. Then in the summer of 1915 George Robert left on leave of absence to do chaplaincy work for the YMCA on Salisbury Plain (Hamilton Camp). However, soon afterwards he resigned and in October a farewell gathering took place at which he was presented with a cheque for £50 – the speakers on this occasion included the Vicar of St George's, Brandon Hill. Towards the end of 1916 he was inducted as minister of Kilmington in Devon. In 1919 his health began to deteriorate and he died in Kilmington on 18th September 1921, aged 65.

Soon after Robert's departure a Deaconess was appointed to serve the Mission. This was Miss Emma Beatrice Clapson (known in accordance with the conventional style as "Sister Emmie"), a young lady aged about 32. The original intention was for her to work at the Mission during one winter, but in the event, as George Robert was not going to return from his chaplaincy work, she stayed for six years. During that time, from 1915 to 1921, things changed considerably. In the summer of 1916 a fundamental change to the constitution of the Mission was made to try to create a closer relationship with Tyndale. To this end the office of deacon was abolished and instead there was to be a Membership Committee. By 1919 the list of activities shows a narrower focus with the emphasis clearly shifting towards adult education. The Sunday services and Sunday School continued while the Men's and Women's Adult School, together with the Men's Club and Lads' Institute are listed in Tyndale's *Jubilee Handbook* as "Auxiliary Institutions". From these activities evolved the Folk House, an independent adult educational institution. It had become clear by 1926 that the trustee body for the Mission was ineffective, probably because it had not been required to act for some years and some of its members no longer lived in Bristol. So the Tyndale church secretary, Spencer Murch, set about tidying it up – giving some of the older trustees the opportunity to retire (which several of them did) and recruiting some new ones (20 was the number constitutionally required). Following this an appeal for £2,000 was made to pay for redecoration and various alterations which were made within the building, which was then leased to the Folk House for a nominal one shilling a year.

By that time Sister Emmie had moved on. She worked for Moseley Baptist Church in Birmingham at the Hope Street Mission (now Highgate Baptist

Church) for the next 25 years, and died in Birmingham on 3rd December 1966, aged 83. Her obituary in the 1968 *Baptist Handbook* was written by a fellow deaconess. Inevitably she wrote principally about her much longer period of work in Birmingham. However her conclusion that "she was a humble-hearted follower and servant of the Lord" is a worthy tribute to this lady who served the Mission during a period of adjustment to the very different world after the First World War.

Chapter 6.

G. W. Harte: Setting the People of God to Work

John Briggs

On returning to Wales in 1920, Herbert Morgan left behind in Bristol a strong church of some 290 members. His successor, George William Harte, was a Londoner by birth, born in 1884 in East Ham where his family were members of the Baptist Church. He trained at Spurgeon's College and had his first pastorate at Tewkesbury, where Tyndale's Robinson family had their origins. He came to Tyndale after a successful ministry at Albany Road, Cardiff, a church in the northern suburb of Roath of very similar strategic importance to Baptist witness in Cardiff to that of Tyndale in Bristol. It was there that he married Gwladys Pritchard in 1912. However, much of his eight-year pastorate in Cardiff saw him serving as a chaplain in war-torn France from 1915–1920, so that de facto he came from chaplaincy service almost direct to Tyndale, with a markedly contrasting attitude to issues of war and peace to that of his predecessor, for he was noted as having been present both at the battle of Loos and that of the Somme, where his work for British soldiers was spoken of in the highest possible terms. His recalling of his first experience under fire in the front line was memorable, for he confessed he was shaking with fear until he heard the voice of the senior Padre in his ear, "Steady Harte, underneath are the everlasting arms". Chaplaincy experience gave him a ready rapport with men so it is not surprising that his activities beyond his Tyndale pastorate included acting as a major promoter of the Laymen's Movement nationally, being at the time of his death the only minister appointed to its presidency. So it was that as Tyndale bade farewell to one minister to a life's work of serving adult education in Wales, it received from Wales a talented minister in the prime of his career.

In due course Tyndale would come to celebrate the contribution made by young men associated with the church in defence of the nation. During the war years the *Tyndale Messenger* had faithfully recorded the serving and the fallen, both members of the church and those associated with the Tyndale Mission though Morgan did not hesitate to express his pacifist and anti-war conscience. After the war Kossuth Robinson convoked a special meeting of the diaconate at his house at which he announced that he and his wife wished to donate a stained glass window at Tyndale in memory of the three sons they had tragically lost in the war, a design for which had been prepared by Arnold Robinson, another of Kossuth Robinson's sons. Such was the limited vision for the original window in the old church. Accompanying it was a stone memorial to the church's other fatalities. When a new window was provided for the rebuilt chapel this commemorated all church members who had died in the war, but not those associated with it or its agencies, and in particular the Tyndale Mission. Significantly the losses to the church came mainly from commissioned officers reflecting the nature of the church's membership.

In those days things happened fairly rapidly, albeit thoroughly. Morgan announced to a Church Meeting on 26th September 1920 that he had been unexpectedly invited by the University of Wales to be the first Director of its Extramural Department, an invitation of such exceptional potential that he did not think he could refuse. He preached his last sermons at Tyndale on 19th December. The deacons were nothing if not ambitious in their idea as to who might succeed him: M. E. Aubrey of Cambridge and Tom Phillips of Bloomsbury were suggested, but especially appealing was Bristol-trained Dr Charles Brown of the large Ferme Park church in North London, notwithstanding the fact that he had already reached the age of 65. Not surprisingly, Brown, although giving careful consideration to the invitation, replied negatively to the delegation that went to meet with him in London.

The Selection Committee, meeting on December 17th 1920 was told that, fortuitously, the Revd G. W. Harte, whose name had already been mentioned in earlier conversations, and had been warmly supported by S. R. Timmins, was shortly to preach at Horfield. Accordingly a large delegation was asked to attend that service and advise their colleagues on what they heard. Subsequently Harte preached at Tyndale and met with the

Sunday School. In addition, Harry Taylor was asked to see Harte operating in his present church in Cardiff on which he subsequently reported most favourably, noting the large number of people recently received into membership and the number of young men in the congregation with whom Harte seemed to have a special rapport. This favourable response led to the Church Meeting issuing a call to the pastorate adding that the salary would be £500 per annum. This was five times the salary the church paid Sister Emmie for her work at the Tyndale Mission which was increased in 1920 to £100 in line with a Baptist Union recommendation. The figure of £500 a year indicates a desire to provide some comfort for the minister of Tyndale but not great wealth: by contrast Hugh Stowell Brown of Liverpool was paid £900 in the late nineteenth century and at Bloomsbury Baptist Church, London the minister received up to £700 at that time, the same sum as was paid to Dr Glover at the end of his ministry. Mr Linton at neighbouring Buckingham Chapel, Clifton, voluntarily reduced his £390 to £350 in 1935 but Buckingham provided its minister with a manse.

By April 1st 1921 it was announced that an invitation had been sent to Harte which he soon accepted. Under recommendations from the Baptist Union the pastorate was to be for a period of seven years in the first instance, and in this respect the church deferred to the Union, though there is no record of the superintending minister for the area playing any part in filling the vacancy. Harte's induction on 31st May was followed by four prayer meetings on successive days seeking blessing on the church as it received "this new gift from God". At the induction service significantly Charles Brown (who had previously declined the pastorate) issued the charge to the church and D. J. Hiley, like Harte a veteran of chaplaincy service, a former minister of Broadmead and President of the Baptist Union in 1920, issued the charge to the minister. Harte saw the task of the church essentially as winning "the world for Christ", for which task he identified three elements: first, "Faith in God, in His Person, His promises, and His power to save through Calvary". The second ingredient was comradeship based on a common experience in Christ, whilst thirdly there was the need for an emphasis on personal evangelism. This, he believed, should be written through the different biographical narratives of Christ's disciples in the contemporary world each one incarnating the story of the mission of the

THANKSGIVING.

TYNDALE BAPTIST CHURCH,
(Whiteladies Road), **BRISTOL.**

——TUESDAY, May 31st, 1921——

TO WELCOME THE

Rev. GEORGE Wm. HARTE.

TEA AND RECEPTION. (5.45)
IN THE LECTURE HALL

Chairman . . Mr. Ed. ROBINSON, J.P.,

who will introduce the following as representing the offices and organisations of the Church.

The Secretary	Mr. D. F. JENKINS.
The Deacons	Those present.
The Stewards	Mr. S. MURCH.
The Sunday School.. ..	Mr. A. J. HASLER with OWEN PARSONS and MARGARET MURCH.
Women's Missionary Work ..	Mrs. Ed. ROBINSON.
Baptist Women's League ..	Mrs. KOSSUTH ROBINSON.
Dorcas Society	Mrs. NEWMAN and Mrs. W. H. SMITH.
Literary Society	Miss D. PORTEOUS.
Choir	Mr. W. MAKER.
Girls' Auxiliary	Miss K. HASLER.
Tennis Club	Miss NEWMAN.
Folk House	Mr. FOYLE and SISTER EMMIE.
Caretakers	Mr. and Mrs. JOINT.

The following will speak:—

Mr. Ed ROBINSON ..	.. for the Church.
Mr. C. J. WATERFALL ..	.. for the Folk House.
Mr. F. J. BRISTOW ..	} for the Albany Road Baptist
Prof. T. W. CHANCE, M.A., B.D.	} Church, Cardiff.
Rev. GEO. JARMAN ..	.. for the Baptist Ministers of Bristol.
Rev. Dr. ARNOLD THOMAS ..	.. for Congregationalists of Bristol.
Rev. DAVID WALTERS ..	.. for Redland Park Church.
Rev. JOHN CONWAY ..	.. for Presbyterians of Bristol.

Letters of regret for absence have been received from—

Rev. T. G. ATKINSON, Trinity Wesleyan Church,
Rev. H. R. WILKINS, Vicar, St. John's Church.

Mr. HARTE will reply.

THE DOXOLOGY.

Induction service for G. W. Harte

church in its endeavour to bring people to Christ. The invitation to every church member was to write: "The Gospel according to you".

A concern for the prayer life of the church was to be a keynote of the new pastorate. Indeed this had been part of the preparation for his induction, whilst Herbert Morgan had already instituted a prayer meeting before morning worship in 1918. Harte indicated how important it was for him to know that the deacons were praying for him daily as he assured them he would be praying for them, and as he wished they would offer specific prayer for each other, a sure way he believed to create harmony in the leadership of the church in the interest of wining souls for Christ. He also asked the deacons that they not allow anyone in their presence to wrongly criticise or cry down the church. The deacons stood silently, hand clasped in hand to signify their agreement to Harte's wishes.

Harte had already, to the satisfaction of the deacons, shown himself "alive to all the difficulties of our position at Tyndale". Since these were not spelt out one can only guess as to their nature. The first two decades of the new century, much taken up with foreign war, witnessed a move away from old securities in politics, thought and social behaviour. The old uncritical belief in unstoppable progress was itself a casualty on the blood-strewn fields of Flanders. In particular the great days of the alliance between Non-conformity and the Liberal Party, in which many of the leaders of Tyndale had played a critical part, were on the wane. Non-conformists now began to split their votes between the Liberals, the Labour Party and the Conservatives and with such split affections, were accordingly less influential. The attractions of the old agenda of the "Non-conformist Conscience" with its concerns for temperance, sexual morality, the problems of mass gambling, Sunday observance and its opposition to state support for church schools, had now to compete with the larger more complex issues of unemployment, the problem of slum housing, and the increasingly explicit conflict between capital and labour. United and in alliance with the Liberal Party, Non-conformity was a force to be reckoned with, but with the allegiance of its members split between all three parties its influence was greatly diluted just when the Free Churches were beginning to face numerical decline.

Thus the new minister of Tyndale was coming into a world of change. On a more mundane level he was apparently expected initially to find his own accommodation, but this was difficult as a salary of £500 a year did not make for easy house purchase, and the large houses around Tyndale were very expensive. For Glover with a forty-two year pastorate owning a house was hardly a problem whilst Herbert Morgan as a bachelor only needed modest rented rooms, but Harte with two children had different needs. Tyndale deacons with some difficulty bought a house in Clarendon Road, Redland. Indeed they were only able to do this by diverting the £1,000 then standing in the Jubilee Fund, deemed insufficient to undertake the desired work on the organ and the re-ordering of the church interior, so the acquiring of a manse became the Jubilee project. But when the house then deemed appropriate came on the market, a further £350 needed to be found, £300 was to be borrowed from a Building Society to be serviced by an annual rent to be paid by Harte, who also made a personal gift of £50 to the Jubilee Fund to achieve the required purchase price of £1350. Although described as "greatly liked by Mr Harte", "a desirable property" and "an excellent property" at the time of purchase, the house was never ideal, and there are later frequent comments in the deacons' minutes about its unsuitability, being too big and damp, leading to repeated requests from Harte for a smaller more serviceable house. The Hartes' two children, Brian Grenfell (born 1919) and Ruth (born 1925) were brought up in the Clarendon Road premises.

The diaconate was split on the issue which made decision-making difficult. Some deacons argued that now pastorates had an expectation of a limited period coupled with the size of salary, it was impractical for the pastor to either take out a mortgage or to rent an appropriate property. In Harte's case an initial period of seven years was extended by a further five, the extension being accompanied by the gift of a purse of money collected from the church and congregation. Over against the church providing a house for its minister, Edward Robinson is recorded as saying "he was not at all pleased with the idea of purchasing a manse as what will suit one minister will not suit another and that in buying and selling houses [the church] was bound to lose", proposing instead that the church rent a house for the minister's use. However the house in Clarendon Road had already been deemed by the Inland Revenue to be a manse, as of 1927, prior to which Harte had been paying a rent of £55 per annum, for now it was reported that the revenue claimed there was an arrears of income tax due from Harte of just over £30 in February 1930. Indeed the failure of the deacons to resolve this problem of housing, which took more time on their agenda than any other item, may have strengthened Harte's positive response to the invitation to the pastorate of the church in Beckenham, London. On his departure the house was sold but only achieved half the purchase price.

Tyndale was a church with many wealthy, indeed very wealthy, members but was not a wealthy church, agonising over frequent and recurrent deficits of fairly small overspends, leading the deacons to impose severe restrictions on Tyndale expenditure partly in curbing the number of external causes seeking support from its membership and partly through austerity measures, failing to deal with the issue of the minister's house, delaying even essential maintenance and decorating to the next financial year when hopefully funds would be available. On other occasions the size of the deficit was such as to require more immediate focused attention in terms of the holding of Gift Days or a programme of diaconal visitation of all members to explain the situation, pointing out the responsibility of church membership in these circumstances. The church's long-serving treasurer was Edward Robinson whose views on such matters were treated with the utmost respect. He and his brothers could have easily dealt with these crises out of their personal wealth but to have done so might have created a dangerous reliance on such benevolence and accordingly there is no evidence that they ever created such a degree of dependency, although Edward Robinson did pay £12.19s in 1927 to eliminate the debt on the *Tyndale Messenger* rather than it be made a charge on church funds, and they were very generous supporters of other Baptist causes. Perhaps this is how Robinson dealt with his conscience on the responsibilities of wealth, for Bernard Darwin recorded of him that he was a quiet, retiring man "who was troubled by the thought that he was making too much money".

One strategy used by Harte was to convoke a meeting of the men of the church and congregation but this produced no startling proposals to remedy the church's financial problems – the treasurer was soon telling weekly offering contributors that to avoid a deficit an increase of one third over the present level of giving would be necessary. Harte, described as a tall, upright man with straight eyes and an engaging smile, had a particular ministry to men. This was not perhaps surprising as his faith had been tempered, when as a young man, he served as a Padre in the trenches in the 1914–18 War, giving him a particular gift in securing their support. His ministerial style was not flashy but none the less determined. An extract of Harte's response at his induction service to his Beckenham pastorate, recorded in *The Beckenham Journal*, is perhaps illustrative of his approach to ministry which was worked out whilst at Tyndale:

> My method is just a persuasive method, it is not to argue, intimidate or assume but to go alongside men and persuade them if I can. To me the Church is not an institution; it is a communion. I look on the Church as a family.

This language is significant; not only was the church to be conceived of as a family but it was essentially made up of a network of families. Dorothy Porteous, writing for the centenary, pictured Tyndale families sitting in their pews: "fathers and mothers, sons and daughters of all ages, elderly folk, devout and yet so friendly to all".

Harte's concern for ministry to men found ready expression in the establishment of a Men's Contact Club first at Tyndale in 1928, then more famously at Elm Road, Beckenham, where the club attracted a hundred members in two months and the movement subsequently swept the country. Contact Clubs, which sought "to win men outside the churches for the service of Christ and his kingdom", began to be formed in quite a number of churches, and in 1936 a conference of men's organizations which was held in London under Harte's chairmanship resulted in the founding of the Baptist Men's Movement almost 30 years after the founding of the Baptist Women's League (BWL), amidst an increasing consciousness that the denomination was increasingly losing contact with men. Under Harte's leadership, Contact Clubs had been formed in 72 Baptist churches by the end of the Second World War.

At the same time women were becoming increasingly vocal in the life of the church. The first lady deacons were listed in April 1919 when Miss Christina A. Culross and Miss Dorothy Glover commenced long years of valuable

The Revd G. W. Harte

service. By the time of Harte's departure there were four female deacons, and women generally were ever more active within the Tyndale branch of the BWL re-launched with new vigour. In its minutes a number of energetic women appear making major contributions to Tyndale's life – prominent among them were Miss Marion Jenkins, Mrs Maria Robinson, Mrs T. H. Barnett and Mrs F. J. Burgess.

The deacons were increasingly wary of allowing retiring collections for good causes – individual chapel appeals or certain denominational funds. They were more generous in allowing other churches and charities the use of the premises, including the hosting of Association meetings. An exception was the allowing of a retiring collection on Christmas Sunday 1921 in favour of the victims of a Russian Famine Appeal, whilst exception was also made in

August 1922 in favour of the Lord Mayor's Fund, where the visibility of Tyndale support was important. Such retiring collections as were allowed were first clustered to certain limited dates and then by placing in the pews special envelopes for the cause approved by the deacons. This method was used for gifts towards the funding of a memorial to William Knibb, famed for his part in securing the emancipation of Jamaican slaves – although Knibb was born in Kettering, the family moved to Bristol when he was 12. On this occasion the Revd R. A. L. Knight of Jamaica preached at Tyndale. As was common in many Baptist churches of the time, Salvation Army Officers in uniform were welcomed once a year to collect for their work after morning worship, probably in recognition that the Army was able to work effectively amongst people unlikely to participate in the life of a suburban chapel. The holding of a Whist Drive by the Girls Auxiliary at Mrs Porteous' house raised different issues and it was suggested that the auxiliary might want to consider alternative means of raising funds to further the cause for which they were founded.

On the other hand the deacons were concerned that there was an accumulation of funds in the Lord's Supper Account since such monies were contributed to alleviate hardship within the church fellowship, a position fiercely defended in the early years when payments out of this fund to other good causes were suggested. Later this seems to have been relaxed when small subscriptions were paid from this fund to the Bristol Sunday School Union and the Bristol Civic League. It was further agreed that a small part of these funds be placed in the hands of the minister so that he could more immediately respond to any need that he might encounter. An indication of the uses of this fund is to be found in a deacons' minute in November 1925 when it is recorded "that we assist Mr Edney, our organ blower, out of the poor fund owing to his being out of work". His successor, Mr Chapman, was similarly helped at a later date. An earlier example of the use of this fund was when it was agreed to reimburse Miss Ellen Shoard who had paid medical expenses incurred by Miss Nicholson, a founder member, by reason of a recent accident. The limited call on these funds is a clear indicator of the financial security of most church members. The Folk House had its own Poor Fund. Miss Shoard in her will left £100 to the church to be used as the pastor and deacons should decide and a second

£100 to be invested by the Church and the income used to subscribe to the Bristol Dispensary or such other institution as the pastor and deacons may determine "for assisting the poor residing or formerly residing in the district covered by the work of the Tyndale Mission". On another occasion Tyndale's help was sought by the Bristol Crippled Children Society for help with the treatment of Ernest Snook, a member of the Folk House Sunday School, thus showing how Bristol charities worked together to fulfil their aims.

The changing needs of different groups within the church called forth different responses – for example in the autumn of 1922 the deacons gave unambiguous support to Miss Lane starting an initiative on Thursdays to help young women, and so the Thursday Club, principally supported by the many women "in service" in the big houses in the area before the invention of washing machines and vacuum cleaners, was born. An early reference to work amongst students appears in September 1921 when Harry Taylor funded the printing and distribution of a brochure providing notices "of our Church's engagements in the student Hostels in the City". In 1930 it was proposed by the Church Meeting that a document be produced setting out the objects for which the church stood, together with a list of its activities. The deacons thought the first proposal might be too off-putting to visitors and new members but the second proposal worth pursuing.

G. W. Harte had an outstanding gift of preaching which young people in particular appreciated. He enjoyed meeting them in informal surroundings, whilst he, like other ministers who had served as chaplains in the war, was happy to be called "Padre". However, Harte was worried about integrating young people into life-long church membership emphasising that "The Young People of Today will be the Church of Tomorrow". This tomorrow he foresaw as containing many social and cultural challenges, prompting him to ask the question: "Is our present method of training and reception of young people into Church Membership sufficient to guarantee that the Church of tomorrow will possess conviction rooted in knowledge?"

Concern to secure a profession of faith from young people without an equal concern to nurture them in robust discipleship meant that all too many young lives were lost to the Church. All this was particularly important for a church that was sustained by an intricate pattern of family networks, suggesting that the church was having increasing difficulty in holding on to the younger members of its leading families. There was stern criticism of the Sunday School: special prayer was sought "to rescue the Sunday School from the general inadequacy which has prevailed in it for all too long" though it has to be admitted that the church was on occasions rather grudging in funding this crucial activity. There was work to be done here and so the injunction: "Let us be serious about this work and not play at it" (October 1921). Many youngsters were admitted to church membership at too young an age when, although "intentions were sincere", "our knowledge of what it demanded was sadly deficient".

It would be difficult to dissent from such a diagnosis of the problem of securing young people's allegiance to the Church which was far from being a new problem, for it has been a kind of repeated chorus written into so much Sunday School history. However, the remedy proposed by Harte, a system of Graded Membership devised by the Congregationalists, seemed rather unimaginative and mechanical. It was basically to introduce three levels of membership. Junior Membership was for those aged 13 to 15 years old who, with the consent of the church and their parents, committed themselves both to regular worship and a course of instruction, but without either vote at Church Meetings or participation in communion. Young communicant members who might be aged from 15 to 18 who would similarly promise regular attendance at worship and to undertake more advanced instruction would now be able to take part in communion though still not to vote at Church Meetings. Through this process it was hoped many would in time graduate to full, intelligent, committed church membership. On paper all looked well – there would be a steady transition from Sunday School through to full church membership. In its various grades the young were to be under expert instruction and in the body of the Church able to enjoy the riches of fellowship so that "a type of church member with conviction rooted in knowledge is developed", leading to the Church itself focusing more attention on their development which in its turn would provoke the interest of parents. In Harte's book some such scheme was necessary to protect the Church's future. The scheme was thoroughly rehearsed but it was not clear that it was ever fully implemented.

Associated with this need to reach out to young people Harte proposed the institution of a "definitely religious service", to meet on those Mondays when the Social and Literary Society did not meet. There was hesitation about proceeding in this way because it seemed like establishing an occasion which would compete with the Wednesday evening service and it was suggested that focusing that service more definitely on the needs of young people might be a better way to proceed with appropriate Bible Studies and discussion. For his part Harte proposed services specially focused for the seasons of Advent and Lent.

At the same time Harte thought that whilst the church had institutions to touch the lives of its young members spiritually, intellectually and socially, it lacked a point of engagement with their physical energies, save for the Tennis Club which anyhow was not a wholly Tyndale enterprise. Related to this was a request in a letter from Harry Taylor from some members of the Church and Tennis Club for the use of the Lecture Hall for two nights a week in the winter months to play badminton. The proposal was sympathetically received but the deacons wondered whether the playing of badminton might be part of the wider functions of a Recreation Club and set up a small committee to formulate proposals for such an initiative. The deacons were quite clear that such an enterprise needed to be seen as a specifically church-based activity rejecting the notion of anything like leasing out the hall to a secular badminton club, but the need to provide church-based recreation especially for young people was recognised, catering for a wide range of interests. The club was not altogether successful – by October 1923 the Tuesday night sessions were abandoned for lack of support which was perhaps part-compensated for by opening on a Saturday at 3.00 p.m. rather than 5.30 p.m. with facilities granted for the serving of light meals. However a request to open the membership to a limited number of "outside members" was rejected since such experiments elsewhere had led to a loss of control, it being noted that "we had ourselves experienced the difficulties created of retaining sufficient control under such circumstances in connection with one other of our church organisations", presumably a reference to the Folk House.

But changes were already happening. Shortly before Harte's arrival, in response to recent history and the nature of the international situation after the conclusion of hostilities in Europe, the church, partly at the request of members of the Young Men's Bible Class, had decided to inaugurate a Tyndale Branch of the League of Nations Union to campaign for future conflicts to be resolved by negotiation rather than by military action. Other prominent Baptist churches acted similarly in taking a small positive step in establishing a culture seeking the rule of peace. The officers of the new society, which mustered some forty members at its first meeting, bore names familiar to the Tyndale congregation with Edward Robinson as President. Its first meeting was convened on 11th July 1921. At a meeting at the end of October two members, Dorothy Porteous and Susie Adams, reported on a peace conference they had attended in Salzburg speaking under the title of "Education in Internationalism". In due course the Bristol branch of the League expressed pleasure in admitting the Tyndale branch to its membership. The church also agreed to make an appeal in the *Tyndale Messenger* for volunteers to take part in a street collection on behalf of the League. However by the end of 1930 the minister noted that the church's subscription to the League had not been paid for three years.

The Redland Collegiate School or simply The Collegiate School represented a significant network of people within the Tyndale fellowship. Leading the enterprise was the family association of the Adams, the Horlicks and the Hopes. The School was founded in 1903 by Miss Susie, Miss Dora and Miss Florence Adams. The principal energy came from Susie who in due course married Rex Hopes, artist, poet and actor, who for a time was the principal window dresser for Austin Reed and who was a member of the Fabian Society. He joined Susie in running the enterprise. Dora married Arthur Horlick, a Bristol-born and Bristol-trained Baptist minister who had been pastor of Coleford, in the Forest of Dean, where the Adams family had their origins, from 1897–1916, and thereafter at Shirehampton, later serving as secretary of the Bristol Baptist Union, which he seems to have combined with duties at the school and being a member of the congregation but not the church at Tyndale. The school had an international dimension, for Susie Adams had a very close friend, Fraulein Schlenker, who had to return to Germany during the First World War. This friendship provides one reason

Susanna Hopes

for Susie's passionate commitment to the League of Nations, and the cause of World Peace, seen in the school's presentation of a Peace Pageant which she had choreographed in the Victoria Rooms, now home to the University's music department. In 1926 a first group of German pupils arrived in Bristol and were housed in Iddesleigh House with the Horlick family: on return to Germany they created an informal Iddesleigh Circle which for many years kept them in touch with the school. Staff members such as Dulcie Emery who retired in 1938 after 15 years service were also church members, whilst the boarders had a walk on the Downs before attending morning worship. At least one pupil was baptised at Tyndale.

New activities had to be set alongside the traditional work of organisations like the Literary Society which seemed to maintain a fairly high standard of intellectual debate and reflection, the ever-active Dorcas Society which effectively supported one part of the outreach work of the Tyndale Mission, the Medical Missionary Auxiliary Association, and the newly established Baptist Women's League. There were also a variety of regional, national and international societies supported by Tyndale. Regionally, the Belgian Hospitality Fund, the local Baptist Association and the Bristol Baptist Itinerant Society, the Bristol Sunday School Union and the Bristol City Mission Society all made their claims, whilst collections were regularly made for the Red Cross, for medical charities, the Sunday School and Tyndale's own mission. The church has always been a major supporter of the Baptist Missionary Society both in terms of personnel serving overseas, participation in the society's committee work at home, and in finance. Support was also given to the Baptist Union in its major fund-raising enterprises, for the Home Work Fund (later renamed "Home Mission" in 1970), and for its specialised funds such as that to provide ministers with pensions. Visiting speakers commended causes such as the Lebanon Hospital in Syria, the work of the YMCA, the United Board supporting Free Church chaplains to the forces, and the Religious Tract Society.

In June 1918 a Forward Movement Committee had been formed as part of Tyndale's preparations for the celebrations of its Jubilee. A meeting of the church and congregation agreed to the suggestion that open-air work might be undertaken on the Downs in conjunction with neighbouring churches on Sundays after evening services in July. It seems that this was too late for events to be arranged in 1918 but in June 1919 it was reported that the open-air "conferences" on the Downs had made a good beginning and it was hoped that:

> This bit of aggressive work will have good results even though we may not be able to register them in detail. It will be a good thing if we can give the impression that Christianity is ready to come out into the open, and that it is meant for the rough and tumble of practical life.

The first service was led by Dr Platt of Trinity Methodist supported by friends from Trinity, Redland Park and Tyndale, making a goodly crowd attracting a number of strangers. Well-loved singable hymns led by a harmonium created atmosphere for Platt to speak comprehensively about "The Fatherhood of God", focussing on God as the Father of our Lord Jesus Christ who was near and loving to each one – "the approachable Christ". His address was followed by questions from "A Man in the Crowd". Whether this was engineered or not it provoked lively discussion. Eight further meetings followed, stretching from the last Sunday in July until 21st September. Four of these occasions were led by a Mr Harrison, two by Platt and one each by Mr Walters of Redland Park and Herbert Morgan whose theme was "Liberty".

Ecumenical experiments date back to Herbert Morgan's pastorate. In October 1918 Trinity Methodist Church devoted its Wednesday evening meetings to a series of lectures and conferences on Reunion and Tyndale decided where possible to cancel its own activities and join with Trinity in this exploration. At the same time the Revd Gladstone Sargent, vicar of Christ Church, Virginia Water, was welcomed to the pulpit of Tyndale. It was agreeably noted that on the same Sunday T. R. Glover was occupying an Anglican pulpit in Cambridge. Gladstone Sargent was one of the eight children of E. G. Sargent, bank manager and long-serving deacon of Tyndale; his elder brother was the distinguished surgeon Sir Percy Sargent who married a daughter of Sir Herbert Ashman; another brother, Douglas Sargent, was also an Anglican clergyman and when Assistant Secretary of the Church Pastoral Aid Society chaired the meeting of the Religious Tract Society at Tyndale in May 1919. Sir Percy, it was noted, was born into a non-conformist family but became an Anglican later in life. The leakage here to the established church of at least four children of prominent Tyndale members is to be noted.

In 1925, the Council of Christian Churches in Bristol of which Tyndale was a member (as also of the Bristol Free Church Council), had proposed a non-profit making Housing Scheme. The deacons recommended the church should purchase five £1 shares but the Church Meeting changed this to a collection in favour of the scheme with the encouragement of individuals so minded to purchase shares. In the event the collection was used to purchase shares but Edward Robinson suggested he not be one of those to hold shares on the church's behalf as he already held shares in the enterprise, now known as the Bristol Council of Churches Tenement Association, and it was agreed that the church as a charity should not benefit from this investment and that therefore any return be gifted back to the association. The work was successful, for there is record of additional properties being purchased, but with changing times these church-owned properties were, with the consent of the original donors such as Tyndale, transferred to Bristol Corporation in the autumn of 1950. Funding the general work of the council was not easy and when a deficit put the post of secretary to the Council at risk Tyndale invited him to speak at a Sunday morning service so that a retiring collection might be taken for the Council's funds.

Harte himself discerned the special need of the many in domestic service who lived and worked in the area, for whom the Thursday Club was established. A more general club was instituted on Tuesday and Saturday evenings in an endeavour to meet the needs of all associated with the church (December 1921). An increase in numbers worshipping at Tyndale especially at the evening service, where there was steady and sustained improvement, was noted. The Social Hour following the service had not proved numerically successful, but for those who did attend it provided an opportunity to deepen fellowship. Resort to advertising to extend the church's outreach did not command significant support. Rather, it was noted, "One by one is the New Testament method and each bringing another will double the congregation".

Tyndale participated in a Bristol Crusade in the early summer of 1925 and contributed very modestly to its costs. This was to be followed up by ecumenical services on the Downs once more until the end of July and Harte anticipated a baptismal service at Tyndale at this time. A note in the deacons' minutes records Harte's judgment that a lack of "corporate fellowship" among Bristol Baptist churches was hindering extension work in terms of the building new churches to cater for "the extending circumference of outer Bristol".

Statistics submitted in 1925 showed a fairly static membership of 226 members at Tyndale plus about a further 25 at the Folk House; 108 Sunday School Scholars were recorded at Tyndale plus a further 160 at the Folk House. Both the published membership lists for 1925 (Church Members and Seat Holders) and 1931 (Church and Congregation) show a considerable number of asterisked names indicating that these were the names of people either serving as missionaries or for other reasons not in regular attendance. Some had moved to other parts of Bristol or surrounding rural areas. Some may well have been students elsewhere; members of the medical profession – both doctors and nurses – seem to have been particularly mobile. The statistics for 1927 show a net loss of 19 though this was masked by the integration of the Tyndale and Folk House figures, then numbered at 43, giving an overall membership of 249.

Whilst Tyndale had abandoned the charging of pew rents fairly early in its history (in favour of disciplined giving to church funds through the use of dated envelopes) it did have seat holders and a Seat Warden to administer the scheme, which accounts for notes that at five minutes before a service commenced and for the evening service all seats should become free. Although the church was now emphatic in rejecting pew rents, the seat holders clearly indicated a constituency to which appeals for funding were regularly addressed. It had also up to 1931 used communion cards as a means of checking on those in regular attendance but then decided to give them up though uncertain as to what should take their place. Unlike other similar Baptist churches Tyndale never seems to have developed a large fringe congregation, particularly for evening congregations, of sermon tasters such as happened at Queens Road, Coventry or indeed Broadmead. The lack of baptisms in some years suggests that the church was very dependent for its good health on "biological growth" within the network of church families rather than evangelistic impact on the neighbourhood, and hence the importance of the church's work with children and young people. A rather strange note appears in the deacons' minutes where it is remarked that "the parking of cars in front of the church was not desirable" making the suggestion that motorists park in Imperial Road instead. Later a more positive note is sounded and it was suggested that a rota be established of car- owners willing to drive older and disabled members to church.

The need for a committee to maintain pastoral contact with missionary members and those living out of Bristol was identified. At that time the election of deacons took place every three years. In 1933 there were difficulties because Dr W. J. Henderson, on retiring as Principal of Bristol Baptist College, indicated he did not wish to continue as a deacon,

Dr W. J. Henderson

and E. J. Taylor wished to resign "owing to his going to the country to reside" making his attendance at Tyndale less regular – his address was soon shown as Abbot's Leigh. His fellow deacons readily framed a resolution thanking him for past services and were gratified that, though moving from the immediate area, he was anxious to maintain contact with the Church.

When all its many activities were listed, Harte discerned a missing dimension in the Church's life:

> There is however one great need which must be supplied if our manifold activities are to be ultimately effective in bringing individuals to a definite commitment of their lives to Jesus Christ. What we lack is a live Prayer Meeting. Prayer meetings are not in favour with those who do not attend them, and often disappointing in their lack of purpose to those who do. May be many are not convinced of the purpose, power and method of prayer. It is our urgent business to remedy this.

Early in 1924 at Harte's suggestion, it was proposed to open the chapel daily for "prayer and meditation". Eighteen months later he proposed a series of four meetings for silent prayer.

On arrival at Tyndale, Harte had expressed his concern about the church's weakness in effectively nurturing its young people into effective and dedicated discipleship. That same concern occupied his last months at Bristol. In September 1930 a joint meeting of deacons and Sunday School teachers and officers was convened to plan a forthcoming Youth Week in October. The starting point for discussion was general agreement that "the church had failed to hold its young people". Harte reported on what young people had confessed to him at a prior meeting in his home that they judged that Sunday services did not do enough to cultivate the devotional life, arguing that services ought to offer a greater possibility for congregational participation, for example by use of responses, the provision of pew Bibles as well as hymn books, and the use of directed Silent Prayer. Young people did not want "stunts" to attract their peers – better to make the services that already existed more attractive and worthwhile. Whilst young people asked for the challenge of being assigned some difficult task, they had not shown themselves willing in any great numbers, for example, to support the evening service or help with the activities of the Folk House especially the Sunday School. Beyond that there was no more relevant or difficult task than to engage in the care of other young people.

When discussion was sought topics should be announced in advance together with some suggested reading so that people could prepare themselves to participate. There was a request for doctrinal sermons which were deemed most important and that issues which troubled the mind such as the nature of sin should be dealt with; the cultivation of spirituality was not easy and young people needed help here. Harte and others thought church members were in danger of taking too much for granted – in fact there was much ignorance even of the "ABC" of the faith. With regard to the devotional life help was needed with such things as the use of devotional aids and the discipline of daily Bible reading which might be related in some way to Sunday worship. Suggestions included a series of devotional meetings early in the morning and an early communion on Sunday mornings. The taking up of the collection was seen as an unnecessary intrusion into the worship with the suggestion that this be undertaken during the singing of a hymn – but this was contested, and in fact it was agreed that more be made of the collection by the minister receiving this from the stewards as a deliberate liturgical action. "Unmeasured criticism of the praise portion of the service" was particularised in criticism of the choice of hymns, a general dislike of chants, and of the role of the choir which was not seen as aiding worship, whilst the format of the communion service needed further thought. The discontent revealed by these investigations came as a challenge to both minister and deacons who confessed their failure in not unmasking these profound difficulties earlier, but were thankful that this concern was now on the agenda. The solution lay not in more meetings but rather fewer, though with a concentration on making the various agencies of the church truly effective with greater endeavours at establishing deeper personal relationships with more sharing of hospitality.

Young people found Literary Society meetings intimidating in the presence of so many older people. The format of the Sunday School was unattractive – even the name was off-putting and the question asked – why not call it a

Crusader Class, presumably with little thought that this would mean signing up with a non-denominational para-church movement? Criticism of the Sunday School was once more considerable and it was underlined that in facing them the deacons should rid themselves of all preconceived ideas. The Sunday School officers said they were thinking of launching a campaign "To catch my pal" which might include taking a census of those living in the surrounding area. This was not well-received – for it was judged that any idea of canvassing the area should be done on the basis of a joint endeavour of all the churches and should be undertaken by adults and not by youngsters themselves. Harte believed that if the church were able to resolve the problem of the spiritual life of the young people attending Tyndale that would provide the remedy for such a deepening of commitment would place on them an obligation to reach out to their peers. Youngsters thought Sunday School yet another occasion on which they were talked at with little opportunity to make their own contribution – a series of study circles or properly focused discussions might be better. It was suggested that the school be moved to Sunday mornings so that young people had some time at their own disposal. Tyndale youngsters did not have a sense of being valued and would welcome being given specific tasks to do, and it was suggested that they be invited to run the Tuesday evening service and that they take a greater part in the evening service though Harte would still deliver the sermon.

The problem was grave enough to cause the deacons to have six special meetings, though the proposed youth week seems to have been confined to a Sunday evening conference for young people, which was not as helpful as had been hoped. Some sixty attended but the age range was too wide to make for effective discussion since the needs of those in their teens were different from those in their middle to late twenties. Opinions forthcoming were much the same as had been earlier rehearsed. It was not something like an institute that they were seeking, rather what was being expressed was a desire for "a distinctly spiritual movement" enabling them to remain in the church, developing their own spirituality and discovering how best they might loyally serve the church. The training of leaders amongst the church's young people was an urgent task which was already being partly treated within the activities of Christian Endeavour.

It was at Tyndale that Harte became involved in the Baptist Missionary Society becoming a member of the General Committee in 1922 and was later chairman of the China and Home Organisations sub-committees of the Society. Thus he was never slow to seek the involvement of Tyndale members in the work of the society, or their generosity in sustaining its activities. Particular interest was sought in the work of those Christian schools which provided for the education of the children of BMS missionaries abroad, as also for Carey Hall, Selly Oak, Birmingham, a United Missionary College for the training of women in which Dorothy Glover had a special interest. In June of 1921 the changed mood of mission activity in Asia was noted in a quite remarkably optimistic assessment of the missionary scene which was now, arguably, to be characterised by a new emphasis on reconciliation or mutual sympathy, in line with sentiments Glover had expressed at the beginning of the century:

> Buddhist and Christian pastor work together. Hindu, Mohammedan and Jain find in Christ's messengers a peace-making power; Confucianist takes a leaf out of the Christian's book and institutes a species of worship, where leisure and self-examination or self-recollection take the place of the sermon and prayer. These things represent a very different atmosphere from the hatred and suspicion in which much of the earlier work of missions had to be done. It seems as if the Spirit of God were breathing 'like morning air', making miracles possible.

Harte was rather embarrassed when in the autumn of 1926 *The Missionary Herald* revealed how much time he, alongside other ministers, was giving to the work of the BMS which was calculated as the equivalent of one day a week. Very surprised that this had been made public, he assured Tyndale that it did not involve his being absent from Tyndale on a Sunday. Because of this and other commitments, when an invitation came to him through Edward Robinson for him to serve as chaplain to the Gloucester and Worcester Brigade of the Territorial Army, although attracted by the task, he deemed it best to decline the offer.

When in 1928 the renewal of Harte's ministry was discussed by the deacons, whilst it was renewed for a further five years, two deacons failed to give him support. In 1930 he received an invitation to move to Elm Road Baptist Church, Beckenham, at a salary of £600 per annum. In a letter dated December 19th, he wrote,

> I cheerfully accept the invitation which I regard as a conclusive indication of God's will. You will appreciate that I do so under a clear sense of duty when I say that my coming will probably mean a financial disadvantage to me. But I am confident of the future and quite happy that it is the Master's will that we should work together for His glory.

This is an interesting comment given the problem he had when arriving at Tyndale to be able to afford appropriate housing.

In 1948 G. W. Harte retired from the ministry of the local church but continued to serve Spurgeon's College as its energetic Secretary, an office he had taken up in 1937 and which he held until 1953, a year before his death, three years after the tragic early death of his son. Grey Griffiths, Home Secretary of the BMS, in his obituary notice concludes his tribute:

> These are bare outlines of a life utterly devoted to the cause of Christ, whether at home or abroad; an effective preacher of the Word, a clear expositor of Scripture, and organiser of no mean ability, a seeker of souls, a delightful friend, and a promoter of all things that would make for a more efficient ministry.

Chapter 7.

The Robinson Stationery Enterprise, Senior Employees and Tyndale

John Briggs

Great changes took place in society as the remarkable achievements of the nineteenth century gave way to the emerging challenges of a new century and as the focus of the war effort was supplanted by the need to build a new world following the coming of peace in 1918. The great Robinsons paper bag empire, founded by Edward Robinson's father in 1844 was necessarily caught up in these changes. In an old-fashioned paternalistic way the Robinson brothers cared for the welfare of their workers, though it seems they were not so committed to the temperance cause as to outlaw the demands made on newly qualified apprentices, who, it is said, had to give each journeyman in the department "a loaf, a saveloy and a pint of beer". Expansion of the business, embracing the manufacture and printing of bags, boxes and sacks, was rapid and extensive; by 1885 they were employing 600 at their Redcliffe factory and two years later a new factory was added in Bedminster, which, amongst other functions, specialised in offset colour lithographic printing in which Robinsons led the field. The opening of the Bedminster factory in particular increased the scope for women's employment in the area.

The Robinsons were early to grant their labour force a half-day holiday on Saturdays which they instituted in 1858 and which was followed in 1889 by a week's paid holiday granted to all those who had twelve months' service. The Robinsons lived happily with the ministry of Richard Glover, who, though anxious for the church to work out its mission in the world, is on record as saying "that the Free churches should keep out of all disputes between employer and employed and should concentrate all efforts on the

Robinson's first factory at No. 2 Redcliffe Street

proclamation of the Gospel". But nationally Edward Robinson was noted as one of those non-conformist leaders in industry who made an outstanding contribution to the welfare of their workforce and in 1901 contributed £5,000 (later greatly increased) to launch a pension fund for elderly and disabled former employees, support for the employees' sick club and the building of a convalescent home. In 1912 he introduced a profit-sharing scheme (which by the time of his death had distributed half a million pounds to Robinson workers) and five years later a family allowance scheme. In the early twentieth century the working week at Robinsons was rather less than that in comparable firms. This was further reduced in the 1920s with preferential hours for men over 60, women over 55 and those with 40 years' service, together with rewards for good time-keeping.

In 1912, a rest room was established for the girls employed at Bedminster with a matron to care for their welfare. A year before that, girls who were convalescent after illness had been able to go to the Arthur Robinson Cottage Home, near Henbury. At the same time works canteens were

"New" Robinson's factory in Redcliffe Street

introduced to the various Robinson factories which soon became the location for a range of social events. The company paid the fees of those who wanted further education by way of evening classes. Sporting activities were formalised in 1912 under the aegis of the Athletic Club but company sports had existed before that, not surprisingly given the Robinson family's delight in cricket.

But change was on the way with the recognition of Trade Unions. Although the family business had become a limited company in 1893, family members were still prominent amongst the shareholders. In 1920 Robinsons arranged for an issue of workers shares in the company yielding 8%. At the same time Robinsons was becoming a global enterprise with subsidiary companies founded all round the world. When they opened their new factory in Fishponds in 1902 – which focused on the making of boxes and cartons – they were mindful of the welfare of their female employees many of whom lived in the Bedminster district or St Philips, the site of another early Robinson factory. Thus they had to catch the train to work

Robinson's factory in Bedminster

every day and home again in the evening. They were allowed to leave the factory at 5.00 p.m. "on the dot" to race down Filwood Road to catch the 5.05 train to Bristol, singing,

> We are the Robinsons girls, we are the Robinsons girls, we pay our tanners, and we know our manners, we are respected where ever we go...

At that time to get taken on at Robinsons it is said that a girl had to show a certificate of good attendance and good conduct from her Sunday School plus a sample of her sewing. For more mature workers there were company houses built in Maple Avenue, Fishponds, where many of the workers lived, of which it has been said "factory and suburb together make as good an example as need be of modern working conditions such as would have astonished both masters and men of an earlier age".

All in all the management style of the Robinson company has been described in terms of benevolent paternalism. A recent analysis by Michael Richardson suggests that the main elements of this were

146

> providing welfare benefits and stimulating a sense of economic well-being that fostered self-help rather than discouraging it. It was a relationship that promoted a sense of righteousness and superiority in the company owners.

Robinsons, father and son,

> believed strongly in the free market economy and employers' rights to complete managerial authority. They promoted a kind of community capitalism in which they saw themselves as the leading lights.

But in a changed economic situation the company's pre 1914–18 paternalism with its considerable welfare and social provisions had later to compete with membership of trade unions for employees' loyalty. For its part Robinsons, although endorsing the establishment of The South West Alliance of Master Printers' Association in 1905, delayed joining the organisation until 1917. The company had already granted recognition to the Typographical Association in 1910 and by 1917 the National Society of Operative Printers and Assistants had recruited semi-skilled workers including a sizeable number of female employees into membership. The National Union of Bookbinders and Machine Rulers opened its membership to women in 1917 and again attracted a considerable number of Robinsons' female employees into membership, so that by the end of the First World War trade unions were well established within the company. Not all their demands were well received in the Robinson board room but by 1926 the company had joined the Bristol Master Printers' Association which sought to provide a vehicle for amicably settling industrial disputes.

Although wanting the best for their employees the Robinson management, committed as they were to the principles of laissez-faire, did not take kindly to anything which they deemed to be interfering with their rights to exercise complete managerial authority whether it be demands made by trade unions or the intervention of government. The virtues of thrift and hard work were readily rewarded, with the firm providing secure employment, good working conditions and a sense of belonging to a worthwhile industrial community. Such a pattern of management worked well within an expanding economy but was more open to question in times of trade depression as occurred in 1921 when Robinsons reluctantly made 114 of its 3,000 workers redundant. Conflict between management and unions in such a situation was all but inevitable. As technologies changed so demarcation disputes between different trade groups became more frequent. One works manager at Robinsons was on record as saying "to obtain the best result from mechanization in the future there must be some breaking down of the walls which divide these various craft unions". On the overall relationship between management and labour it has been suggested that "the religious values of Robinsons' directors... may have had some bearing on acknowledging workers' rights to have an independent representative voice", with the same forces moderating the paternalist authoritarianism of the company which had a more benevolent tradition than that of rival companies, with union recognition conceded to certain categories of workers before 1914 and then extended to the company's many women workers during the war. Robinsons, rather than entering into out and out conflict with the unions, accommodated them but only to a limited degree, recognising that they had legitimate rights and interests but by the 1930s there was a closed shop of union membership in operation at the company.

At its peak the Robinson group employed some 6,000 people. The company suffered extensive war damage which brought out once more the company's Baptist connections for some of its offices were temporarily transferred to the Baptist College of which Edward Robinson was the long-serving treasurer. At the same time the company with its advanced printing processes undertook some vital war work.

Edward Robinson was greatly involved in civic affairs. A magistrate from 1889, he also served as Vice Chairman of the Bristol Chamber of Commerce (1880–83), Vice Chairman of Bristol South Liberal Association, a Liberal Councillor from 1906 until 1924 when he became an Alderman until 1929. His work on the city council necessarily brought him into contact with the local trade union leadership so that he was well aware of their goals and ambitions. His year as Lord Mayor in 1908 saw him very engaged with relieving distress at a time of much unemployment for which he raised substantial sums. Out of this emerged a more lasting work with the founding of The Bristol Civic League on whose council he served until 1929, offering help and relief to a large number of citizens who had encountered various misfortunes. To celebrate their golden wedding Edward and Katherine Robinson gave the city a capital sum to be used for slum clearance and the creating of a park and the re-housing of those whose homes had been demolished. His other offices included Presidency of the Anchor Society (1887), and Chairman of the Colston Research Society which fostered research in the new University College and, after 1909, the University of Bristol.

Edward and Katherine Robinson were vitally involved in the work of Tyndale. Of Edward, member, deacon and treasurer for many years, it was said,

> No one served Tyndale with greater devotion or loyalty. He loved his church and was proud of it and its place in the community... Even in later years to see his erect figure walking up one of the aisles bearing a collecting bag to the Communion Table was to realise that here was a man to whom all worthwhile things were sacred and to be handled with reverence.

To mark his golden wedding his business colleagues commissioned his relative, the Newlyn artist, Thomas Cooper Gotch, to paint this doyen of nonconformist business propriety. Edward's response to his relative was, "But you have made me look so serious", to which the painter replied, "But then you are a serious man!" And that was true but in the company of children he enjoyed delightful merriment. He served for 50 years as treasurer of Bristol Baptist College and in this was supported by his wife who, given her parentage was also greatly concerned for ministerial education and together had the vision of moving the college from its limited site in Stokes Croft to an impressive suite of building in Woodlands Road adjacent to the University and an institution well funded for future needs.

Likewise they were both greatly concerned for the welfare of the BMS, both locally and nationally. At Tyndale Katherine Robinson served as missionary secretary and was one of the most persuasive of collectors for the BMS. She was for many years secretary-treasurer of the local branch supporting Zenana work amongst secluded women in India and China. In 1901 she was elected the national president of the Baptist Zenana Mission and was conspicuous in her work to integrate its activities more completely in the work of the parent society which was successfully accomplished under the new name of Women's Missionary Association in 1913. Her missionary concerns were not limited to the BMS – her ecumenical concern being seen in the fact that on at least one occasion she chaired and spoke at a meeting of the Anglican Bristol Missionary Society, "remarking that they were all working for one aim... She spoke of the importance of the women's work as a department of missionary effort". Tributes to her character were widespread: "A woman of wide interest and catholicity of taste, many good causes owed very much to her thought,

Katherine Robinson

labour and gifts". Indeed Harry Taylor argues that with Miss Angus as secretary of the Zenana Mission and Lady Pearce Gould its treasurer, that "the place accorded to women in the counsels of the denomination today [1942] owe an inexpressible debt to their progressive outlook and ability".

In 1904 Edward Robinson was elected treasurer of the BMS, a post he held with distinction for ten difficult years, successfully despatching annual deficits. It was his privilege to serve as treasurer when the society benefited from the munificence of the Robert Arthington legacy to the value of around half a million pounds "for the purpose of spreading God's word amongst the heathen (excluding Mohammedan populations)". But the Robinsons' work for the society was not only though formal office but is seen in their personal care of missionaries, many of whom they entertained at their home in Bristol or at their country home on Dartmoor, where a warm welcome always awaited missionary friends. This joint effort and beneficence was recognised in the naming of the college and museum in Tsingchowfu, "The Gotch Robinson Training School", after the names of their parents, its first graduate being ordained by Richard Glover on his visit to China in 1891. When in 1904 this institution became an integral part of Shantung Christian University Robinson was once more prominent amongst those who made this financially possible. Amongst acts of personal kindness which only came to light long after the event was their funding of a Chinese student to complete his PhD in London which enabled him to become a senior member of the Chinese Diplomatic corps. But as with his wife his interests were not confined to Baptist causes, serving for many years as president of the Bristol City Mission.

Edward Robinson died on September 7th 1935. His funeral took place in a packed church with many civic and business dignitaries in attendance with an overflow gathering in the Lecture Hall when the eulogy was given by the veteran minister, Dr Charles Brown, whom the deacons had tried to secure for the Tyndale pastorate. His words, arising out of 55 years of friendship, offered unqualified tribute:

> Neither I nor any other man has known anything mean or unworthy or doubtful in character or conduct. He was one of the most interesting of men because he was always interested in other people and was always willing to learn. He was one of God's gentlemen, and a man of transparent sincerity, without pretence or guile, of stainless honour, unblemished integrity and unaffected piety. Edward Robinson proves in his own person that a man can be a Christian and a successful business man – that a man can be in a great way of business with all its thronging cares, and can keep his soul alive and his faith sweet and strong.

The number of families beyond the several generations of Robinsons who were employed by the firm is of real significance. Life deacon, Harry Langford Taylor (1877–1951) worked for the company for 53 years from the age of 13, rising from office boy to becoming a director of the company (his father had also worked for Robinsons for some 38 years and later his son also joined the firm). Taylor was commissioned as a 2nd Lieutenant in the City of Bristol Volunteer Regiment in May 1917. In Bristol church life he was for many years president of the Bristol City Mission, and the first lay president of the Bristol Free Church Federal Council. Nationally he served as treasurer of the BMS (1930–1946) playing a decisive role in their property purchasing decisions, opposing Robert Wilson Black's attempts to bring the BU and BMS under one roof in Russell Square, because both the building was too large and it was only available on a leasehold contract. In 1937 he became one of a line of distinguished lay presidents of the Baptist Union. He joined with Gilbert Laws of Norwich in raising questions as to whether younger Baptists wanted, as Baptist ecumenists suggested, a United Free Church in Britain, questioning whether in United Churches candidates were readily coming forward for believers' baptism, worried that in such a church distinctive Baptist teaching and practice would be lost. But his minister, F. C. Bryan, in his previous pastorate, had come out in favour of greater unity.

The Bodey family provided two secretaries/directors of the Robinson company. The first was William Thomas Bodey (1865–1928), whose father, also William, was minister of St George's Baptist Church in Bristol for 31 years, where the younger William served as a deacon for 27 years. Forty-five years with Robinsons, he also served as president and/or chairman of the Bristol Master Printers & Allied Trades Association and the National Cardboard Box Makers Association, and was a member of the National Council of Master Printers. An anonymous tribute printed in a local newspaper after the report on his funeral said of him:

> Such men as he are the very salt of business life. Of exceptional ability, he was the most modest and unassuming of men; the most tireless and conscientious of workers, he yet conveyed an impression of being always calm and unhurried. No matter how great the press of his own duties, he was always ready to give not only a courteous hearing but wise and practical counsel... He was a man of the gentlest and kindest nature, of broad and generous sympathy.

Harold Bodey (1901–54) was educated at Clifton College, leaving at the age of 18 to join the staff of Robinsons but after only seven years with the parent company, he was sent to Devon as manager of its subsidiary, the Ottery Bag and Paper Company. Whilst there he became a member of the Sidmouth Congregational church and, even though he had been brought up a Baptist, he refused to get involved in the founding of a Baptist church in

Harold Bodey

Sidmouth as he felt it would interfere with the work of the other Sidmouth churches. In 1930 Harold was brought back to Bristol to become the manager of the paper bag factory in Bedminster until 1944, when he succeeded another Tyndale deacon, H. L. Taylor, as Chief Buyer for the Robinson Group. Having served in the Home Guard as a major during the Second World War, he was appointed Company Secretary in 1946 and joined the Board in 1948 as Director in charge of bag sales and production. The Revd F. C. Bryan, the minister of Tyndale, wrote of him in 1944:

> All too often, the pleasure of a minister in the business promotion of his laymen is tempered by anxiety as he observes how 'the cares of this world and the deceitfulness of riches' begin to impair the quality of their Christian service and witness. But Harold Bodey gives rise to no such qualms. As his powers developed under the challenge of his business opportunities and responsibilities, so the more consecrated to the service of Christ he became.

Bodey married Christine Morris and together they had three children, John and David, who both went to Clifton College and then joined the Robinson firm, and their daughter Ruth (known as Pixie) who taught at Clifton College. He was a deacon at Tyndale, an able lay preacher, and took a great interest in and played a major part in the project to establish a new church at Westbury On Trym. He had a particular interest in the Baptist Missionary Society and was treasurer of the local district and also treasurer of Bristol Baptist College. By then the Robinson company had provided the College with treasurers of the college for the previous 84 years. He died in 1954 aged only 53. His funeral, after all too short a life, was attended by 900 and had to be held at Broadmead Chapel where F. C. Bryan testified that he was "religious but did not parade his religion. He was a man of unflagging zeal". His wife, Christine, continued at Tyndale as a deacon and ran the women's meeting and two of his children have had major roles within the life of Tyndale: David serving as both deacon and secretary. And so the link continues into recent times. When the church was rebuilt in 1955 following the bombing, the new upper room, which had been created where there had formerly been a gallery, was named after him and to this day retains the name: the Harold Bodey Room.

Thomas and Emily Porteous had been married by Richard Glover but spent their early married life in Wales before Emily retuned to Bristol to live in Chertsey Road as a widow with her mother and six children sometime prior to 1911. Dorothy Porteous (1889–1977) was the chief welfare officer of E. S. and A. Robinson in Bristol and lived at 13 Chertsey Road. Her younger sister, Ella, another devoted member of Tyndale, also worked in the Welfare Department of Robinsons. Awarded the MBE for her work in personnel management, Dorothy served as church secretary from 1949 until 1970, continuing on the diaconate as life deacon from 1970 until her death in 1977. Thus she was a key person in the church during World War Two, the re-building of the church and the centenary celebrations. She pioneered "Children's Church" at Tyndale and also served as a Local Preacher. County Commissioner for the Girl Guides, she was a member of the Collegiate School Council and Chairman of the Old Girls' Association, a member of the Baptist Missionary Society and even a candidate in an election to the Bristol City Council. Ronald Cowley said of Dorothy:

> Her support for the Missionary movement was phenomenal and she was at the heart of the Missionary Supper and Everybody's Effort for many years, but her pastoral work in caring for, praying for, and visiting so many people was impressive.

But by the time Dorothy Porteous retired, the old Robinson firm had become part of a large international group, for in 1966 Robinsons merged with John Dickinson Stationery to form the Dickinson Robinson Group (DRG), creating one of the world's largest stationery and packaging companies. Products with a high public profile included *Sellotape* and *Basildon Bond*. The Porteous family home in Chertsey Road, sometimes seen as a kind of annex to Tyndale for all the activities that took place there, was bequeathed on Dorothy's death to the Tyndale Housing Association. Two of Dorothy's sisters, Marjorie (Mrs Harmon) and Hilda both undertook missionary service, the one in China and the other in India but

Edward and Katherine Robinson

returned to the UK to live with Dorothy.

Kossuth Robinson, with his wife, the adopted daughter of Sir Charles Wathen, played a major part in the life of Tyndale and the Mission. He served as a Justice of the Peace for the County of Gloucestershire and at one time had kept a 100-acre farm. On his death on 9th February 1928 he left an estate worth some £27,000. But with wealth came tragedy for he lost three sons in the First World War, memorialised in Tyndale's stained glass. One of Kossuth Robinson's surviving sons was the stained-glass window artist Arnold Robinson whose artistry adorns a large number of west-country churches, including Bristol Cathedral and the old Baptist College in Woodland Road but nowhere more prominently that at Tyndale where his membership lasted for nearly fifty years until his death in 1955, following his retirement as a deacon a little earlier to make way for younger candidates. His son, Geoffrey Robinson, also a stained-glass window artist, although brought up and married at Tyndale, became a worshipper and church warden of St Mary, Redcliffe.

Edward Robinson's offspring also made their contribution to Tyndale: Colonel Percy Gotch Robinson, DSO, CB, CMG, who had a very distinguished war record with the acting rank of Brigadier General, Master of the Merchant Venturers in 1934, was approached in September 1922 to act as a steward to replace Spencer Murch on the latter's election to the diaconate, but he declined to act, although in March 1923 he did unveil

Tyndale's war memorial, but in the 1925/1931 *Handbooks* he is shown as residing at Queen Charlton, near Keynsham, and therefore not attending Tyndale regularly, but his sisters did. Frances Gotch Robinson, who died in February 1954, was quite a formidable woman: "Her big frame matched a large and generous heart and mind". County Commissioner for the Girl Guides, a city magistrate when few women sat on the bench, she was deeply interested in the welfare of young people. A member of Tyndale since 1892, she was generous to the BMS, the College, the Bristol City Mission and to her church.

Frances' younger sister, Katherine Gotch Robinson, a life deacon of Tyndale, a musically-gifted, philanthropic, but often considered eccentric, woman did not want to see Cote House and its beautiful grounds fall into the hands of commercial developers, so she bought the house and land on the death of her brother, Harold, in 1954 for £12,500. Having witnessed the devastating effect of his wife's death on Harold, Katherine wanted to provide a place for older people to live to help ease their loneliness. She approached the Society of Merchant Venturers for assistance. As some of her brothers and uncles were Merchants she knew that they were helping many other charities in Bristol and were known for their pioneering philanthropy. Thus in 1968 the Cote Charity was born. Katherine turned the house into flats for older people who needed small, manageable and convenient accommodation. She was offering potentially lonely older people a chance to be a part of another kind of family in the beautiful setting of Cote's grounds. A purpose-built home for older people constructed next door was opened in 2009 under the name of Katherine House.

Chapter 8.

The Ministry of F. C. Bryan

John Briggs

The remarkable thing about the call to the next minister, Frank Colin Bryan, a candidate of special interest to Edward Robinson, was that a call to the Tyndale pastorate was issued twice. The first invitation was sent in December 1931 at a salary of £600 p.a. with the new minister making his own arrangements as to housing, with the understanding that if he chose to live at Clarendon Road an appropriate rent should be charged. This was graciously declined but the invitation sent a year later was accepted with Bryan's induction taking place at the beginning of May 1933, some twenty-six months after Harte's departure. So impressed were the deacons by Bryan that they were prepared to suspend their search for a minister pending their later attempt to secure him. On neither occasion was there any evidence of advice being given by the Superintending Minister for the Western Area, though the church contributed to the presentation made to the Revd Gummer Butt on his retirement from this office. Without resort to area officers there was within the diaconate a number of people who knew their way around the denomination with sufficient skill as to bring before the church a rich list of potential pastors.

The deacons' specification of the qualities needed in the new minister were that he should be

> one who is young but who has a certain amount of reputation and who will take a real interest in us and concentrate on Tyndale at least for a time, a good preacher, a scholar who thinks for himself, and has a real spiritual experience, and has a keen missionary interest.

Bryan was not exactly young – he was 42 – when he arrived at Tyndale, his fourth pastorate. His mother was a member of the famous Norwich Jewson

Baptist family and his father a Baptist minister trained at Spurgeon's College. He was educated at Christ's Hospital and Jesus College Oxford where he read mathematics, represented the university at chess and rowed for his college. He stayed in Oxford to complete his theological and ministerial preparation at Mansfield College under the Congregational theologian, the Revd Dr W. B. Selbie.

One of those who played a crucial part in the securing of F. C. Bryan's services for Tyndale was the world-renowned mathematician, Professor (later Sir) John Lennard Jones, whose membership at Tyndale

The Revd F. C. Bryan

dated back to 1926 when he was Professor of Theoretical Physics at the University of Bristol. A member of the Selection Committee, he was one of those delegated to travel to Clapton Downs to hear Bryan preach in his own church and it was he who proposed a second visit to Tyndale. Whilst seconding the motion to invite him to the pastorate he argued that the church should give Bryan ample time to decide – almost six months in fact. However before Bryan took up the pastorate Lennard Jones had moved to Cambridge to become Professor of Theoretical Chemistry, before succeeding Lord Lindsay as the second Principal of the University College of North Staffordshire (now Keele University) in 1953, where unfortunately he died prematurely the following year. The University Chapel at Keele is named in his honour.

The pastoral vacancy called forth a diaconal letter to the membership accompanied by a personal visit wherever possible. Tyndale was fortunate in being able to enlist the help of the Revd W. W. B. Emery, a former minister of Queen's Road Coventry and recently retired from the pastorate of Cotham Grove Baptist Church, to undertake midweek services and undertake pastoral care of the congregation, virtually acting as moderator of the church during this extended pastoral vacancy. At the same time the church sought the help of Dr Arthur Dakin, principal of Bristol Baptist College, with Sunday services as often as he was able. Bryan's "preaching with a view" at Tyndale took place on a weekday in the lecture hall. He began by addressing the gathered congregation with these words: "You know why I am here, I know why I am here – now we will forget it. We will worship God". Dorothy Porteous records:

> The atmosphere changed completely. I think we knew at that moment that God had sent him to us and so it was throughout his ministry. He lived near to God; his preaching and praying reflected it.

Those who remembered him when this history was being written recalled a man of conspicuous holiness.

Effective pastoral ministry was an ongoing concern. Bryan left behind him the reputation of a pastor committed to the systematic visitation of his people. A mixed gender Visitation Committee had responsibilities in this area, but early in Bryan's ministry it was suggested that elders be appointed to undertake this task. However the two men and two women nominated to serve, declined and the idea was abandoned at that time. In the pulpit Bryan presented firm convictions, the product of thoughtful and imaginative study. Witness to this is to be found in the small book he was to publish in 1946, *Concerning the Way,* which, reflecting his ministry at Tyndale, gave practical guidance and counsel with clear insight into the nurturing of the Christian life. Whilst his thoughtful sermons attracted students to Tyndale, he was equally at home with children's ministry and it was he who initiated the Children's Church. From 1936 a senior student at the College was appointed as assistant minister on an annual basis.

Towards the end of 1931 both a monthly youth service and a monthly prayer meeting after the evening service were suggested, though the former does not seem to have been implemented. In June/July a series of specially advertised late night Sunday evening epilogues at nine o'clock was proposed, hoping to persuade those leaving the Downs to come in for a half-hour service with special soloists. A second proposal to leave the church open for prayer was considered but issues of insurance and the caretaker's remuneration had to be considered. In the autumn months it was proposed to have a social hour following the evening service concluding with Family Prayers once a month.

Bryan reported enthusiastically on a conference concerning work amongst young people held at City Road Church in the autumn of 1934. In 1936 a similar conference was held at Tyndale and requests were made for offers of hospitality for visiting youngsters. Although there were encouragements, the future of work amongst young people remained a concern to the minister and deacons alike, leading to Bryan convoking a conference for young people early in 1937 which led him to set up a Young People's Council, whilst in 1939 two young people were appointed to represent Tyndale on the Bristol Young Baptists' Union. At the same time Bryan played a major role in the development of the young people's work of the Baptist Union nationally and was much sought after as a speaker for Summer Schools and retreats.

Tyndale paid its dues to the Bristol Council of Churches through a Free Church apportionment. In 1932 the church wardens of St John's invited Tyndale to be present at the induction of their new vicar, an invitation reciprocated the following year when the vicar of St John's together with the ministers of Redland Park and Trinity Methodists were invited to bring greetings on the occasion of the induction of F. C. Bryan. Tyndale members were vitally involved in the West Bristol Free Church Council which the church had joined in 1935, the year that Mrs F. J. Burgess, whose husband was a councillor and a deacon, served as president. In the winter of 1937–8 the church's winter programme included a series of studies of what the different denominations stood for, "so that we might hear what the other denominations had to say". As an introduction, the Baptist position was to be explored with presentations by Bryan, Christina Culross and J. W.

Brighton. At the conclusion of the series a meeting on Church Union was called to explore what possibilities there were in North West Bristol.

As early as March 1935 a first approach was made by the treasurer of Cotham Grove Baptist Church enquiring whether the congregation in Cotham might join Tyndale, suggesting that a group of equal numbers from each church be set up to explore the possibility. This met and whilst no decision was taken, Bryan was anxious to write to the Cotham diaconate indicating that if they did wish to explore the issue further they could be sure of a cordial response. In the event the voting at Cotham's Church Meeting was 48 in favour of continuing as a separate cause and 28 opposed to this. In due course a new minister was called and Tyndale sent greetings on his settlement, but the issue was to return to the agenda later. An interesting note in the minutes of the Deacons' Meeting records allowing the Mount of Olives Church on Blackboy Hill to use Tyndale for a baptism service and this was granted conditional on the service not being advertised. In March 1935 the YWCA on Whiteladies Road was closing with some members transferring to Tyndale's Thursday Girl's Club. They also sought the use of the church parlour on Sundays from 4–6 p.m. for their weekly Bible Class, and this was granted at a charge of 2/6d a week.

Hospital Sunday in 1932 was to be led by Mr Emery with the address given by Sir Percy Sargent, a distinguished London surgeon, who was still a member of Tyndale. He was married to Mary Louise, daughter of Sir Herbert Ashman, the first Lord Mayor of Bristol, and another of Tyndale's aristocracy. The deacons wrote a letter of condolence to Sir Percy on Lady Sargent's death in 1932.

Starting with support for the League of Nations at the conclusion of the First World War, the cause of international peace was an issue of great importance to a number of Tyndale members. In 1931 a Deacons' Meeting minute notes a request from the Bristol Disarmament Council requesting that the church make available a table for signatures during the week commencing July 20th – presumably for those to sign who opposed the increasing stockpiling of armaments in Europe. Messrs Hopes and Murch were appointed to a sub-committee to investigate with power to act, but unfortunately there is no record of consequent action, but given the Hopes' concern for peace this may well have been a subtle way of agreeing to the proposal, for the Hopes were known for their commitment to World Peace which Mrs Hopes, as principal of the Bristol Collegiate School, often made the theme of her school assemblies. Further to this Tyndale, by a modest subscription, joined the World Alliance for International Friendship Through the Churches, founded in 1914 in the context of Anglo-German tensions. References to further subscriptions to this organisation are to be found in the inter-war years. In May 1935 Mrs Hopes and her sister, Agnes Horlick were appointed church delegates to the United Peace Conference. In 1937 the church affiliated to the Bristol Peace Council, and adopted its peace resolution as its own, and in June 1939 made its premises available to the Quakers for a peace meeting. Tyndale was still paying an annual subscription to the League of Nations even after the outbreak of war in 1939 and after the war supported the United Nations Association. In October 1947 Mrs Hopes hired the church hall for the showing of a peace film and a lecture by J. Keith Killby, secretary of the "Federal Movement for the United States of Europe".

Nearer at home Tyndale joined the Bristol Civic League for Social Services, an organisation of which Edward Robinson was a founder, in 1932, and faithfully paid annual subscriptions thereafter though rather strangely the deacons agreed to pay this out of "the Lord's Supper Fund" hitherto robustly defended for the pastoral needs of the members of church and congregation. The use of this fund is evidenced by Mr Elson returning the £10 he had received at the time of his severe accident, "hoping that somebody else might benefit", in February 1950. In the context of the economic slump, Bristol's unemployed came on to the church's agenda in October 1932 at the request of the Council of Christian Churches. Whilst one deacon suggested that the chapel should be put at the disposal of the unemployed, a counter argument was that the Folk House was better located to undertake this work so Tyndale representatives on the Folk House Council were asked "to take such steps as they may see fit to speedily do whatever is within their powers to help the unemployed", for which Tyndale raised immediate finance with the expectation that greater resource would be needed in the coming winter. Concern for areas of social distress in South Wales led the BWL to combine this concern with helping the work at Knowle West in a kind of triangular trade. Tyndale collected goods for a jumble sale; this was held at Knowle West in the summer of 1937. The £7 raised was given to the South Wales Distress Funds whilst a parcel of clothing was sent to the Baptist Church in Treforest for use there. Early in 1938 a further initiative was taken when, through the services of the Superintendent Minister for South Wales, a partnership with Hawthorne Baptist Church, Pontypridd was initiated. Tyndale members visited Pontypridd and a delegation from there was received at Tyndale together with the two ministers exchanging pulpits. There were visits by members of Tyndale BWL, and the Girls' Club knitted garments for those in need at the Hawthorns with wool provided by the BWL (which by 1940 was rationed), the BWL also adding their own gifts, so that several large packages were sent to the Hawthorns in addition to the money the church had raised for the Hawthorne Chapel Christmas Fund.

Within Tyndale's own fellowship, a collection was made to recognise the 22 years service given by Mr Joint with his wife as church caretakers. In February 1932 Joint, now aged 70, had been admitted to Ham Green Hospital and accordingly offered his resignation. The church collected about £90 for a presentation fund from which the deacons agreed to pay Mrs Joint five shillings a week to supplement her pension income as long as the fund allowed, and in the event of her death to expend the remainder in the interest of the family.

Traditional non-conformist conscience issues remained alive – thus a letter from the Bristol United Temperance Societies sought a Tyndale correspondent to help them formulate policy in respect of "renewed activity" on behalf of the brewers. A large Temperance demonstration was held at Broadmead in 1936 when it was reported that the brewers were spending six million pounds on advertising with the result that many more young people were frequenting public houses than eight years previously. The March Church Meeting had temperance on its agenda and the Temperance Society was congratulated on its successful objection to the extension of opening hours in Bristol, which led the Church Meeting to agree a retiring collection in their favour. In fact temperance remained a regular item on Church Meeting agendas and the passing of appropriate resolutions in the years prior to the outbreak of war. Drink and Gambling also appeared as topics for concern in the BWL programme. In 1940 it was decided that the gifts for the temperance cause should be split between the Baptist Temperance Society and the Bristol Temperance Society. A new matter of conscience emerging was the opening of cinemas on Sundays to which the Tyndale diaconate was opposed. The conscience issue which does not feature in the Tyndale agenda was the public funding of denominational education, which elsewhere in the denomination early in the century was strongly opposed through the Passive Resistance movement under the leadership of John Clifford.

Tyndale supported the Bristol Baptist Union in encouraging fellowship amongst local churches with the possibility of groups of young people going out to visit village causes. Funds were collected to clear the debt on the new church at Knowle West, and later to support the stationing of a deaconess to lead the work there. It also supported the Association's appeals on behalf of Hillfields Park, Bath, and Southmead, Bristol, as early in the century it had collected substantial funds for Horfield's Building Fund. At the end of the war Tyndale, at the Association's request, entered into a partnership with the country church at Woolard, exchanging visits and helping with pulpit supplies.

A brief note in July 1931 showed Tyndale deacons disinclined "to fall in with the suggestions" made by the Baptist Union's Commission on the Spiritual Welfare of the Churches. Such an attitude may have been influenced by a theological controversy threatening the Baptist Union at that time. In preparation for the Discipleship Campaign to be launched in 1932, T. R. Glover, who had been president of the Union in 1924 some 40 years after his father, had produced a pamphlet entitled *Fundamentals* in which he wrote brief notes on Sin, Punishment, Repentance, Conversion, Salvation, Atonement, Justification and Sanctification. The failure of the note on Atonement to affirm traditional understandings led to protests from the pastor of the Metropolitan Tabernacle and others, demanding the withdrawal of the pamphlet. Eventually Glover agreed to do this and a replacement pamphlet – *The Saving Work of Christ* – was composed by Dr Percy Evans, the irenic principal of Spurgeon's College, whilst Glover affirmed in Council his faith in Christ as Saviour and Lord. T. R. Glover remained very much a son of Tyndale, frequently preaching or lecturing at the church so that his being made the bête noir of conservative Baptists may have affected Tyndale's association with the Union for a time.

Tyndale did, however, take a part in the Discipleship Campaign, combining with Buckingham and Cotham Grove chapels for prayer for the enterprise. Leading up to this Campaign every Deacons' Meeting was preceded with specific prayer for its success, Eustace Davies arguing that discipleship was the primary duty of every church member arguing, "we had to bring it home to each individual including ourselves". The Tuesday evening service preceding the commencement of this initiative was thus to focus on "Tyndale and the Discipleship Campaign", with meetings on successive evenings in the three churches, but thereafter the work was to be progressed by Bryan in a Tyndale context. This new emphasis on outreach saw Bryan constructing a carefully thought-out winter's programme which he agreed to introduce to the congregation at a conversazione in the autumn, at the same time agreeing to preach a monthly topical sermon at the evening service. Quarterly Church Meetings were to include a substantial and well-prepared discussion of an aspect of church life which would occupy the whole of the evening, these innovations to be the subject of a pastoral letter sent by the minister to all members of the church and congregation. The first such Church Meeting had as its topic following on the Discipleship Campaign the not-too-helpfully phrased topic of "The Church's attack on the non Church-goer". Bryan also proposed a united week of witness at Tyndale to which Buckingham and Cotham would be invited when a team from the three churches would testify to "What Christ means to me". At a church social occasion Paul Sturge, Warden of the Folk House, was invited to update Tyndale members on the range of its current activities. Thus in its mission programme Tyndale managed to stress both issues of social responsibility and evangelistic outreach.

In 1934, references to baptismal services become more frequent in the church's minutes but the baptistery had a bad leak, losing about 1,000 gallons per baptismal service, leading to a proposal to construct a new open baptistery surrounded by a low balustrade. This together with the removal of the organ to the north transept and the movement of the pulpit and the construction of a sounding board was to be funded by the Jubilee Fund, now that the funds from the sale of the minister's house had been returned

The diaconate in 1946. Front: Miss K. G. Robinson, Miss D. A. Porteous, S. Murch, Revd F. C. Bryan, C. R. Dickens, Miss D. F. Glover, Miss C. A. Culross; middle: E. G. Seath, A. W. Robinson, W. H. Parsons, J. W. Brighton, F. D. Yeo; back: H. L. Taylor, F. J. Burgess, A. J. Finch, H. Bodey.

to it. Not all agreed with this expenditure arguing that the monies should instead be made the basis of a capital fund for the upkeep of the church. Nor were issues of design easily resolved, for an initial design based on the baptistery at Abbey Road Church, St John's Wood, failed to please. Revised designs were agreed by the deacons, with the apse beautified by the gift of a new communion table in memory of Mr and Mrs Edward Sargent (Edward had been a deacon for 34 years and Sunday School Superintendent for 26 years) and deacons' chairs by an anonymous donor, whilst another provided an alms basin and new collecting bags.

The new lay-out was to be presented to the church at a conversazione in October 1935 at which occasion members of the congregation were to be asked which sittings they would like. Clearly this change in the church's interior made a significant change to the worship space at Tyndale, and prompted the church to ask the Folk House for the return of its original Communion Flagon and Plate so that the breaking of the bread and the pouring out of the wine could be a more clearly visible liturgical action. Associated with this was a series of experiments to improve the acoustics of the chapel with various suggestions made: a sounding board, the deployment of curtaining and some alteration to the position of the pulpit, the last of which seemed initially to be fairly effective though it did not seem to resolve the hearing problems of an ageing Edward Robinson, so an experiment with a sounding board was agreed. At the same time the possibility of providing hearing aids to the deaf was discussed, but in the end it as judged that the numbers interested were too small to justify action.

Prior to Bryan's arrival the following items of perennial concern were already on the deacons agenda: Sunday music, Young People's work, activities for the men of the church. The moderator, William W. B. Emery (a retired minister from Cotham Grove), had comments to make on the music at Tyndale leading to a meeting with Walter Maker, the organist, the outcome of which seems to have been that professional singers were employed to lead the singing and sing solos to the apparent advantage of noticeably improving the standards of worship. Such employment seems to have also been the practice at other Whiteladies Road churches, since there are records of transfer of these singers, for example, to Victoria Methodist. Bryan early made it his practice to have prayer with the choir before Sunday services. When the Bristol Baptist Union and the Bristol Choral Society arranged a hymn festival promoting the revised Baptist Church Hymnal, Tyndale ordered 200 copies which were presented to the church by H. L. Taylor to commemorate his presidency of the Baptist Union. The introduction of the new hymnal was the occasion for considerable debate about the role of music in the church's worship.

Walter Maker, the church's organist and son of the more famous F. C. Maker who was organist at Redland Park, was concerned for high musical standards and to make music "a real ministry of the church". The minister, with somewhat different perspectives, said he had to consider the happiness of the congregation, taking into account how they could best express themselves in music thereby securing "the co-operation of the rank and file". To secure this he proposed holding a "Carolari" in the evening service, in which he would explain both hymns and tunes. Eustace Davies identified less than 25% of the evening congregation possessing the ability to read music and less than 50% accurately describing themselves as musical, leading him to suggest the dropping of chants and anthems. No less than seven other deacons joined in the subsequent conversation indicating how much feeling the topic provoked, but this did not resolve the issue for in June 1938 the deacons were informed of the "great dissatisfaction" with the singing at Tyndale, a complaint that was to re-emerge towards the end of the war, and again in the post-war period, even though paid choristers were reinstituted on the return of men from serving in the forces. An innovation in 1937 was the presentation of a Narrative Drama of the Nativity after evening worship on December 19th.

A pleasing minute from September 1935 presents an agreeable problem of "how to deal with the great number of strangers now coming [to services]... as it was realised Mr Bryan could not speak to them all". Existing members of the congregation were encouraged to make "tactful contact" with any newcomers sitting nearby. Growing congregations at morning communions also presented problems for seating people in alternate pews.

At the end of 1935 a minute reads: "At this anxious time in our church's life it was decided to suggest to Mr Emery to ask for the private prayers of the members at next Sunday's morning service". This seems to have related to Bryan's health since he had been absent sick from Deacons' Meetings since September. The situation was so serious that the receiving of new candidates into membership was delayed and in the event they were received into membership in January 1936 when the Revd Grey Griffiths, Home Secretary of the BMS, was preaching. It was not until the end of March that Bryan returned to his duties at Tyndale to the great relief of church and diaconate. That autumn Bryan reported that he had six candidates awaiting baptism and thereafter a regular stream of baptismal services are noted in the minutes, some coming from members of "the club, others from the Sunday School and others with no prior organisational connection".

Students begin to appear as part of the youth agenda with the Students' Missionary Association holding its annual meetings at Tyndale in 1934. At the same time Bryan made a special attempt to establish links with students in the university as part of Tyndale's outreach. Offers of hospitality here were deemed very helpful. He also noted that in Cambridge students were offered associate church membership, on the nomination of the minister of their home church, with the right to attend but not vote at Church Meetings. The deacons agreed to recommend that Tyndale do likewise. By the end of the 1930s the church was holding a social event before evening worship at the beginning of the academic year particularly to welcome students just beginning their courses in the university. A trickle of students took up associate membership and by the late 1940s church members were being encouraged to entertain students in their homes.

The reference to Cambridge is interesting because Bryan had a Cambridge attachment throughout his life. He was born in Bluntisham on the Cambridge/Huntingdonshire border where his father was the pastor in the early 1890s and it was Cambridge that became the base for his work as Eastern Area Superintendent, and there that he died. When in September 1931, the World Alliance for International Friendship through the Churches held its eighth International Conference in Cambridge, F. C. Bryan gave the welcome address on behalf of the Cambridge Free Churches. Bryan, very much the scholar-pastor, published three books, one before he came to Tyndale and two during his Bristol pastorate. Perhaps the most demanding was that first volume, *The New Knowledge and the Old Gospel*, published by the Kingsgate Press in 1930 which demonstrates a well-read intelligence well-able to set out balanced argument. Further publications were to come reflecting on Bryan's Tyndale years.

From time to time long-serving church officers offered their resignation largely on account of age or other commitments – thus presentations were made to retiring Church Secretaries, Treasurers, Sunday School Superintendents, Weekly Offering Secretaries. Most notable in this respect was the death of Edward Robinson on September 7th 1935 at the age of 82, having served as a deacon for 54 years. The last Deacons' Meeting at which he was present was that held in October 1934; in March and April 1935 his absence was explained by continued illness and the minister was charged with writing to him hoping for his speedy recovery, but this was not to be. Grieving a beloved friend, his fellow deacons paid tribute to "a supporter of all good causes" who "used his life and gave of his means for the uplift of mankind". "He loved to make others happy and he will long be remembered for his kindly sympathy by all who came into contact with him". In 1938 the church set about making a suitable memorial to this service and targeted the raising of £100 for the purpose. A very relevant memorial would be the improvement of arrangements for the deaf but the deacons also thought this ought to be accompanied by some more tangible recognition of Robinson's service. The money was raised, the hearing aids provided and a lectern commissioned on which a new Bible would be placed and a tablet would commemorate Robinson's work for the church.

A tantalizing minute from the April 1937 Deacons' Meeting reads: "Mr Bryan said that he was a delegate to a fortnight's conference at Oxford in July to which the deacons wished him God speed". The very important Universal Council for Life and Work (a forerunner of the World Council of Churches) met in Oxford in July but the only recorded British Baptist representation was that of Baptist Union General Secretary, Dr Melbourn Aubrey, and the Revd P. T. Thomson of Leicester, but it is likely that Bryan was present representing the World Alliance for International Friendship through the Churches. Critical for the work of this major conference on Church-state relations was the fact that whilst the German State churches were not allowed to send delegates, the Baptists and Methodists were, the Free Churches attracting much odium for disassociating themselves from the message of encouragement sent from the conference to the Confessing Church in Germany in its resistance to the attempted state take-over of the long established state churches in Germany.

Invitations began to come in for services from Tyndale to be broadcast on the radio. The first such was on October 29th 1933 from eight o'clock to a quarter to nine. In September 1936 a morning service was broadcast from Tyndale and since this was to be an earlier time than Tyndale's normal worship it was debated whether this should be followed by a Communion service or the dedication of the Children's Church which saw a transformation of the old Primary School room made possible through a generous gift from Miss Eleanor and Miss Marjorie James in memory of their parents. The new Children's Church was to accommodate worship for children in parallel to the main service in the sanctuary and was dedicated on a Saturday night in February 1937. A further broadcast service took place in May 1939 and the minister reported messages of appreciation had been received from China, South Africa, Australia, Ceylon, Crete, Portugal, Aden, Mauritius and Bechuanaland! Further broadcast services continued to take place including an evening service in March 1947 when Bryan's sermon was one in a series on the Life of Christ.

The church felt itself honoured when in 1938 Miss D. F. Glover was appointed chairman of the BMS at a time when the society was facing severe financial difficulties which led to Tyndale seeking to raise special funds to reduce the society's deficit. Two years later Tyndale held a special supper and thereby raised over £150 for the BMS. Additional to its support of the BMS, Tyndale showed an interest in Baptist work in Europe taking up collections for the continental mission in support of the work of Dr J. H. Rushbrooke, founding General Secretary of the Baptist World Alliance, who came to live in Bristol and joined the membership of Tyndale. The address at his funeral in 1947 was given by Dr Dakin who affirmed him as "a truly great man of our denominational history". Following the invasion of the Sudetenland by Hitler in September 1938 the church raised quite substantial funds for Baptists in Czechoslovakia. The Lord Mayor raised a special fund in aid of refugees and the offering taken up at the Civic Service

Children's church

held in Tyndale in May 1939, attended by the Lord Mayor and Councillors, was devoted to this. Tyndale also contributed to a food ship helping those in distress because of the Spanish Civil War, and for the Christian community in China following a special meeting for prayer in response to information about violence meted out to some Christian missionaries serving in that country. Later Bryan was given a free hand by the deacons to accept an invitation to visit the churches in Latvia in the summer of 1939 if he chose to do so.

Historical Consciousness began to make its mark on the church leadership as they began to be aware that 1936 would represent the 400th anniversary of William Tyndale's martyrdom. The church also secured Dr T. R. Glover, public orator in the University of Cambridge, to speak on the 100th anniversary of his father's birth. Two years later he was back at Tyndale for the church's 70th anniversary. At the end of Bryan's ministry the church contributed towards the placing of a plaque on Hanham Mount, some four miles east of Bristol, commemorating the persecuted Baptists who met there after the restoration of the monarchy in 1660, whose

T. R. Glover

witness is still commemorated by the beacon which stands there. The open-air pulpit on the site commemorates the preaching of George Whitefield and John Wesley to the nearby Kingswood colliers, celebrating at once both Bristol's puritan and evangelical heritage.

The deacons were often over frugal with church finances, sometimes unwisely putting off essential items of maintenance. A memorable occasion was the redecoration of the Lecture Hall in 1936 when a proposal from the church secretary, Spencer Murch, to have this done failed to find a seconder leading to the secretary's threatened resignation. At the same time his colleagues voted no action on the painting of the exterior of the church which had last been done seven years previously. Notwithstanding this second failure to command the support of his colleagues Murch remained as church secretary serving for 23 years. An architect not in private practice, Murch taught at the Bristol School of Architecture, the only undergraduate school in the provinces in the 1920s. He came from distinguished Baptist stock – his father was Baptist minister in Frome for many years and his grandfather, Dr W. H. Murch served as principal of Stepney (later Regent's Park) College from 1827–1843 during which time the college became affiliated to London University. Spencer Murch and his wife became members at Tyndale in 1913 on moving to Bristol, and thereafter filled a number of offices such as Sunday School secretary, property steward, looking after the church premises, a deacon and finally the church secretary. Having a qualified architect as church secretary was of immense value when the chapel was being rebuilt. He was elected a Life Deacon shortly before his death.

Breaking with frugality, early in 1938 the deacons agreed to install a telephone for Bryan. Whereas the parking of cars had once been seen as a problem they were now seen as an aid to Tyndale's ministry as ageing members of the congregation lived further away from the church – volunteers from the Contact Club were now to be invited to bring older members of the congregation to church.

Wider concerns were for the Bristol Baptist Discipleship/Forward Campaign, for the support of Mr Hurditch, a blind evangelist, and for the new church to be built as part of the Forward Campaign at Knowle West, for which cause Bristol women had pledged to raise the funds for the site, namely £450 of which Tyndale women were to raise £50. Rather than a series of teas and musical entertainments in people's homes, most preferred one major supper on church premises which raised almost £7 whereas £27 was raised by direct giving, and a bring and buy sale was held in Mrs Maria Robinson's garden. Further activities were proposed in conjunction with the men's Contact Club, and there were summer outings to organise. At the same time they made a very modest contribution towards paid help for work with babies and toddlers at the new church at Knowle West. In 1937 the Bristol Baptist Union sought to promote a Forward Movement among the churches with an anonymous donor offering £50 for each new church opened. At Tyndale Dr Dakin was invited to commend the cause alongside Mr Horsington from Southmead.

Back in 1932 the BWL had put itself on a more ordered basis with an elected committee and carefully compiled minutes and elected officers including the election of Mrs Bryan as President, with the ambition that every female member of the congregation should become a member of the BWL. Mrs Bryan's apologies for absence from the committee became more frequent in the late 1930s and a minute early in 1940 reports on her recent illness "and how thankful we all were that her life had been spared and that she was making a good recovery". She was, however, to the distress of the women of the church in particular, to die prematurely in 1942 leaving Bryan as a widower for the last thirty years of his life. She left behind a tribute to her warm and compassionate humanity, her sensitive response to every need and her wonderful courage in battling with ill health.

Tyndale Baptist women supported both local and national interests. A proposed amalgamation with Tyndale's Women's Prayer Meeting was negotiated with Miss Dorothy Glover, and Bible Study groups established. The committee of the BWL now assumed responsibility for preparing for communion services and organising hospitality and catering for events at Tyndale. All was not plain sailing, however, and in September 1935 serious consideration was given to closing the Tyndale branch of the BWL which had the effect of provoking a more deliberate programme of activities, albeit after a short period changing to quarterly rather than monthly meetings – though monthly meetings combined with a prayer meeting were soon reinstated. Replacing the Church's tea-ware became a BWL concern for which they sought the support of the Literary and Social Society and the Wives Comradeship group. In co-operation with the Women's Missionary Association (WMA) the BWL constantly sought to raise funds for the BMS. One step towards bringing all the women's activities into one organisation occurred when Dorothy Glover was appointed president of both the BWL and the WMA, with both groups studying her book, *Set on a Hill: The Record of Fifty Years in the Lushai Country* (Carey Press, 1944). Finance was raised to support the new Home for Unmarried Mothers at the Haven in Surrey (though the initial minute refers to the London Home for Girls in Stoke Newington, a BWL project established as early as 1912 on another site to provide accommodation for single women coming to London for employment). On a more personal level the BWL promised their help in canvassing the many newcomers who had come to live in the district.

A pencil note in the Deacons Minutes for 1939 reads: "War declared September 3rd", tragic news which was announced to the congregation during morning worship. Already the church was thinking about Air Raid Precaution Shelters. Those able to retreat to their homes were advised so to do. Those remaining were best accommodated in the basement or in the lobby adjoining the children's church, with further accommodation to be provided, it was suggested, by the digging of trenches in the church garden as the Council had done at College Green. A further option to be explored was whether the church could use the shelter at the University of Bristol's Canynge Hall on the opposite side of Whiteladies Road and a request to the Vice Chancellor was duly submitted, but the church then learned that the City Council was erecting a concrete shelter on the cul-de-sac part of Chertsey Road with space for 50 people. Lighting restrictions were best met by changing the timing of evening services. Initially it was not proposed to darken the windows of the Lecture Hall but the Girls' Club requested that this be done so that they could continue their Keep Fit and Drama classes. This was achieved through the generous provision of black-out materials by H. L. Taylor. A request from the BBC for the exclusive use of the Lecture Hall (at a rental of £175 p.a.) for the duration of the War did not prove practical. The Lecture Hall was however let out to the Red Cross from 10 until 5 o'clock five days a week at a charge of ten shillings a week in the summer and £2 per week when heating and lighting was required.

The Secretary told his fellow deacons that they should provide a stirrup pump, a first aid box and appropriate buckets to be kept on site to deal with incendiaries, whilst he proposed to keep the plans of the church at his home should they be required if the church were to be rebuilt. A duty deacon was to be present on church premises as much as possible for a month at a time. Dorothy Porteous was one of the first to undertake this, reporting that although the Girls' Club was doing excellent work it needed tighter controls, causing the deacons to ask them to work with a committee of management. Under wartime constraints it was agreed that the Girls' Club become a mixed club meeting on Thursdays and supervised by Bryan, assisted by Miss Glover and Miss Timmins. At the same time the Badminton Club was

TYNDALE BAPTIST CHURCH, RAID NOV. 24, 1940

The first heavy raid on bristol occurred on Sunday Nov.24, 1940. The service started at 6. O'clock & the Alert went at 6. 20 p.m. The signal was given & the servide was stopped, a few went home the remainder went down to the shelter in the Basement.

A prearranged

There was no question that we were in for a heavy raid flares were dropped overhead,& the guns opened up; then the incendiaries showered down all round the building, one fell on the lead flat over the Church Parlour, which burnt itself out, one came through the roof *of the church* & fell into the gallery, it was descovered by Mr Green the Caretaker and I with the stirrup pump & young Mr House with a pail of water rushed to the scene of action, the pitch pine pews were well alight but we got *the fire* out fairly quickly. By this time fires were burning all round us. One fire in Imperial Rd was put out by the Wardens, a house in Chertsey Road was blazing & a Fireman came & looked at it & went away, the mains had been hit & there was a shortage of water. The all clear went at 12. 10 a.m. on the way home on the Downs which were not in the raid, it was possible to read a paper by the light of burning Bristol.

Spencer H. J. Murch
Church Secretary

Report by Spencer Murch of the air raid of 24 November 1940

allowed the use of the hall on Wednesday evenings and Saturday afternoons and evenings. Added to the deacon on duty there was to be rota of fire watchers to take appropriate action if a siren were to go off during a service or a meeting. Later this was changed to the desire to secure paid Fire Watchers from black-out time until ten o'clock. Mr and Mrs Green, the caretaker and his wife, were asked to undertake the task with the provision of a self-contained flat either in the church or in Chertsey Road but they declined to serve. Instead a rota was drawn up with students from the college serving one night, the minister one night and Green, amongst others, serving two nights.

In September 1940 a letter of thanks was received from Redland Park Congregational Church for the gift from Tyndale towards the air raid damage done to their church. But Tyndale was not to escape. On December 1st there was an emergency Deacon's Meeting following the air raid on the previous Sunday which saw an incendiary bomb fall on the gallery of the church, which was successfully extinguished by the fire watchers on duty. Deepest sympathy was expressed to Mr and Mrs W. F. Shean (who both survived a direct hit on the shelter they were in) and to A. J. Finch and C. R. Dickens both of whom had lost their businesses. But worse was to follow: the next day, 2nd December, both Tyndale and the Folk House were destroyed by enemy action.

The living church at Tyndale did not simply bemoan the wickedness of bomb attacks and their impact on civilian life. On 12th December 1940 the deacons were already considering the issue of war damage, when a letter of condolence was received from the Baptist Union. A lot of action took place. Children's Church was suspended. At this time Dr T. R. Glover disposed of a considerable part of his library and sent a handsome cheque for a yet-to-be-established Rebuilding Fund. This was soon in place and regular appeals made to ensure that it reached a realistic sum. Windfalls by way of legacies, such as that from Miss Clara Gibson and the sisters of Miss Marion Jenkins in 1943 were quite logically assigned to this fund.

At the same time Tyndale also contributed to the Baptist Union's War Emergency Fund to help churches in difficulty maintain their pastors' salaries, as well as trebling their giving to the Sustentation Fund for the long-term provision for ministerial stipends. At home, following the destruction of the church building, Bryan's offer to forego £100 p.a. of his salary was reluctantly but thankfully accepted, but in 1943 the church voted Bryan a special gift, and in 1944 the level of his salary was restored, and from January 1945 increased to £700. With the destruction of the church, the services of the paid singers was discussed, and it was decided to terminate the contracts of the two male singers, one of whom was about to be called up, but to retain Miss Elsie Balmond because without Tyndale's services she would be in real need. Walter Maker, the organist, was to continue on his existing honorarium. Mr Green, the caretaker, agreed to a reduction of ten shillings a week in his wages. A war damage claim of £20,929 for Tyndale and £1,900 for the Folk House was lodged with the District Valuer. Given the complexities of all this, the trusteeship of the church was passed to the Bristol and District Association of Baptist Churches.

But this is to anticipate. The most remarkable baptismal service was that held in August 1941 when four candidates were baptised in the shell of the bombed out church, one of a series of baptismal services conducted in that environment. One case in 1943 of an elderly cripple seeking baptism and membership was resolved by a service in her home in the presence of some Tyndale witnesses. Baptism was by affusion, that is by pouring water over the head. In 1943, a year when Bryan's health once more gave cause for concern and he was again absent from the pulpit for several months, he edited a collection of essays, *Concerning Believers Baptism*, his own contribution being on "Preparation, Administration and Visitation", in which he set out a syllabus of the topics that ought to be covered in baptismal classes and the sensitivity required by the church in appointing visitors.

Bryan's writings may well explain why he was invited to speak at the Oxford Socratic Club and Socratic weekend conferences. He first appears in their records as a guest speaker in January 1943 on the topic "What Is Prayer?" Later that year a weekend Socratics' Conference on "Christian Faith" held at the Quaker Centre, Jordans, near Beaconsfield, Buckinghamshire, found Bryan again one of the speakers. Influential in this group were the Presbyterian Eric Fenn, then Assistant Head of Religious Broadcasting at

Baptismal service in the ruins of the sanctuary

the BBC, and the president of the Club, the literary scholar and Christian apologist, C. S. Lewis, with whom Bryan soon established a friendship. Two years later, in March 1945, the Socratic Club held another weekend conference on "Christian Faith", this time at Ridley Hall, Cambridge where Lewis, Fenn and Bryan each spoke twice. As in 1943, Lewis talked about "Presuppositions of Faith" and "The Church", whilst Eric Fenn spoke on "Faith in Christ" and "Prayer – before or after faith?" and Bryan on "The Nature of Faith" and "The Consequences of Faith", very possibly the same topics as he addressed in the previous conference. An examination of Lewis' and Bryan's writings shows that the two men shared what has been called "a compatibility of Christian thought that made their friendship all the more likely and all the more rewarding".

Back in his own pastorate the church was more immediately concerned about the D-Day landings in Normandy in June 1944, planning to make the day that the landings took place a day of prayer, with the Children's Church open all day and special services at 12 noon and 7 p.m. and with retiring collections the following Sunday for service personnel families. Confident of the success of this venture the church also began to plan how to receive home demobilised women and men from the forces. Further minutes in

October 1944 anticipated the signing of an armistice with the provision that if that were to be announced on the six o'clock news, a thanksgiving service would be held at 7.30 p.m. but if it were announced later the service would be held on the following day.

Another sign of the times was permission being given to the BWL to have a retiring collection to enable them to purchase materials to make garments for the troops which it was thought would best be done on Armistice Sunday. Getting sufficient wool in war-time conditions proved increasingly problematic, even though Tyndale women pledged clothing coupons as well as cash for this purpose. A meeting of local BWL branches at Broadmead, noted in the *Evening Post*, witnessed an officer express the men's thanks for these comforts, later accompanied by a brief newsletter together with a small gift such as a book token or a book of stamps. A further project by Bristol BWLs was to support the equipping of some YWCA huts to minister to women serving in the forces, whilst Bryan was diligent in sending periodic letters to forces personnel. With the end of the war, notes of demobilised men and women returning home appear in the re-established church magazine.

From time to time adjustments were made to the timing of services and meetings to fit war-time conditions, and various schemes to protect the remaining property from further damage were devised. Membership issues were handled sensitively, with an attempt to keep a realistic membership list. In July 1944, Dr and Mrs Johnson offered their resignation on Dr Johnson's adopting British Israelite views, which he subsequently withdrew, though indicating he no longer wished to receive weekly offering envelopes. A lady who wanted to transfer from Redland Park failed to secure commendation from her minister, causing Bryan and his colleagues to proceed with great caution to the extent that being visited by two lady members of the church caused this applicant to reconsider her desire to transfer. There are other references to members resigning to join another denomination.

In the midst of all these changes the minister expressed concern at "the practical cessation of the family life of the church particularly the Tuesday evening service." The problem was that war conditions imposed extra duties on many who could not therefore attend on Tuesday evenings, leading to the sending of a pastoral letter containing the suggestion that those older members who could not attend would nevertheless join in a fellowship of prayer. In an attempt to appeal to a different constituency Bryan instituted a short midday service on Wednesdays from 12 to 12.15 and was sufficiently pleased with a trial period to make them a permanent feature of Tyndale's diet of activities.

In the spring of 1944 several special Deacons' Meetings were convened to consider "the spiritual rebuilding of the church". A careful audit of the various meetings and organisations associated with the church needed undertaking with the priority being set on the Prayer Meeting and the week-night service, "these two being the powerhouse of the church". A second priority was a focus on family life with the possibility of making an appeal to the membership and suggesting a new covenant by them to secure the spiritual renewal required. Various factors impacted on the deacons' minds as they reflected on the situation in November 1946 – the break-up of family life, young men taken away from church to do their national service, a disruption of habits of worship, the unsettlement occasioned by cruel war experience.

At the beginning of 1944 the deacons of Tyndale received a letter from The Young Bristol Baptist Union urging the church to set up a Youth Council to which they readily agreed, suggesting that there should be a concentration on group work to head off the danger of over-large numbers and work that was over institutional. The deacons' minutes note that young people at Tyndale "showed vigour and vitality" but needed leadership which was not helped by the introduction of national service. Bryan indicated that alongside this review of youth work he also believed that there should be a review of the various women's organisations. All this led the deacons to conclude their meeting with a time of prayer and an injunction to prayerfully consider the future before reconsideration of the topic when it was suggested that this was an area of church life where students at the college could give help.

Negotiations over the rebuilding of the church were to take fifteen years before the rebuilt church was opened in March 1955. Whilst church

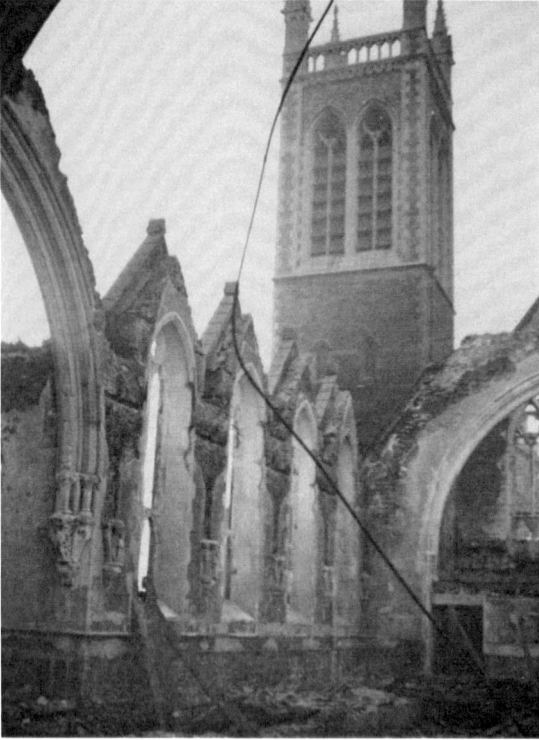

The tower stands above the ruins of the sanctuary

members had ideas about how a church for the second half of the twentieth century might be designed, the War Damage Commission at its first meeting with church representatives in the summer of 1946 insisted that there be a reconstruction within the then existing footprint of the ruined church using the extant foundations and such external walls as were still serviceable. The only alteration allowed was the replacement of the rear gallery with a class room as long as the cost was not more than plain replacement. However it was clearly indicated that it would be some years before any licence could be issued because houses and factories had a greater priority than churches. This meant that the use of the Lecture Hall for worship, originally seen as a temporary expedient, had now to be seen as lasting for a lengthy period and so its appearance was improved for that purpose, though the idea of installing Robert Halls' Broadmead pulpit was found to be impractical. Eventually an organ, the gift of H. L. Taylor, which he had originally intended should be anonymous, was secured from a large house in Sneyd Park, renovated and installed at Tyndale. At the end of 1948 it was intimated after earlier denials that there could be some compensation for the loss of stained-glass windows which the deacons passed on to Arnold Robinson and Spencer Murch for consideration.

In the summer of 1949 a note of hope from the War Damage Commission came in the form of a judgment that they could give earlier consideration to premises where there was likely to be deterioration to the remaining fabric if action was not taken and Murch affirmed that Tyndale would certainly fall into such a category. This was followed by a message from Taylor that if Tyndale wished for action in the first six months of 1950 they should act swiftly and this they did, appointing Eustace Button, an experienced Bristol architect who had already advised the church on the refurbishment of the church in 1935, to superintend the work whilst Spencer Murch, himself an architect, acted as liaison officer between the church and Button. The instructions from the church were three-fold – to provide a children's church capable of accommodating 80 children, to incorporate a large vestibule in which to welcome the congregation and a sanctuary to seat around 400 people about which there was some difference of opinion. Given the small size of the evening congregation most were wary of too large a sanctuary but Taylor thought the church of tomorrow would need more space. Button drew up plans which the diaconate approved but he explained that there could still be problems because timber and especially steel were in short supply and the national economic crisis could still delay the starting of any church programmes, causing the expensive drawing up of costings to be wasted. Accordingly the church submitted approximate estimates of costs to the Church's Main Committee and in January 1950 it was reported that Tyndale had been categorised as "No One Priority". But in the years since the destruction of the church it was so often hope and delay, and another five years would elapse before the rebuilt church was ready for worship, fifteen years after the bombing.

Work with young families would for the future be better based at Westbury On Trym where hopefully, with the blessing of the Free Church Council, a new church would be planted, following on the successful launching of a Sunday School in the area for which purpose Dr Henton Davies had initially offered his lounge, though it the event it was launched at Mr Appleby's. Clearly, however, what would be needed was the establishing of a new church and accordingly much of the deacons' time was taken up with identifying and purchasing a new site on Reedley Road, not in the centre of the "village" but strategically placed amidst the new housing being built to the west of Falcondale Road. A small sum of money paid by the War Damage Commission to Tyndale as the landlord of the old Mission premises was used to pay for the architect's initial fees for the Westbury venture. Some temporary buildings were purchased and erected on site so that the work could commence.

With new developments in hand at the end of the war, particularly the new work being established at Westbury, the strains on Bryan were considerable, leading to consideration of the possibility of appointing an assistant minister. If it were only a question of running the Sunday School and providing pulpit supplies that could easily be accomplished, but the church had pledged itself to establish a church in the fullest sense of that word and a Christian community centre meeting a variety of local needs. What Bryan envisaged was a young minister, or possibly a returning chaplain to the forces, working Tyndale and Westbury together with him until Westbury could secure status as an independent church. Bryan believed that some grant aid would be available. At Tyndale the assistant minister would have special responsibility for working with young people. Whilst there was much goodwill at Westbury, as yet lay leadership was not forthcoming. Conveniently, the Revd J. I. Carlyle Litt, a returning chaplain, already had a house in Bristol, though it was not long before a manse was purchased. Grant aid was only available for an "initial pastorate" and so H. L. Taylor thought it best to do without the aid, arguing that he thought

Westbury On Trym Baptist Church
[©churchcrawler.co.uk]

Tyndale could find £400 p.a. for 3–4 years providing Bryan with the help he needed. In the event Litt served the new church at Westbury On Trym from 1947 to 1960. The work got off to a good start with a strong Sunday School, Girl Guides, Scouts and Women's Meeting, with the prospect of opening a Contact Club for men in the autumn, and with a monthly church magazine to give publicity to the work. In March 1947 twenty-six Tyndale members were dismissed to become Foundation Members of the new church which was to be initiated in April.

Thus whilst many things were heartening such as the size of Sunday morning congregations and the new work started at Westbury, other developments were very worrying such as the unwillingness of members to take on office, and the collapse of the church's youth work. The church could not compete with much that was attractive in contemporary culture, but it needed to face up to the priority laid upon it to present the claims of Christ, and it was proposed that this challenge be put to the church, with the need to rebuild the family of the church, perhaps by committing themselves through some form of covenant. Was it possible in discussion to get people to say why they were not prepared to become church members? How could nominal members be challenged to more active participation? General education gave less attention to the Bible and so there was a need to nurture scriptural knowledge amongst the congregation and to offer special opportunities for leadership training, remembering that older members who found it difficult to attend meetings did support the church with their prayers. Whilst Litt thought that given time demobilised men and women would soon find their place in the church Bryan was not so sure. The identification of specific tasks to be undertaken by them and by the church's youth was urgent. The demands of everyday life during the week seemed in the post-war world to put more pressure on church members. Bryan was encouraged to preach on these issues, and to follow this up with a letter to church members to include an appropriate questionnaire, inviting folk to three follow-up sessions on Tuesday evenings. However these planned group discussions, with two groups to discuss Church Life, two the Church's Witness, whilst a fifth was to be confined to those under 30, kept being deferred. In a more mobile society it is not surprising that more transfers of membership are recorded but less happily more deletions for non-attendance.

When St John's Church celebrated their centenary in April 1941 the preacher in the morning was the bishop and in the evening the vicar was anxious to continue the celebrations through a united service involving all the Whiteladies Road Churches, which Tyndale readily agreed to join if the

After the bombing

other churches also did so. Trinity Methodist Church, which was relatively unscathed by the bombing, was anxious to join with Redland Park Congregational Church and Tyndale, both of whose chapels had been destroyed, in circulating the district with an invitation to the local families to come to church for purposes of worship and fellowship. At Tyndale, it was left to the minister to implement the church's happiness to join in such a scheme. Relations with the Anglican diocese were good: when Bishop Clifford Woodward was translated to Gloucester, Tyndale sent him a message indicating how much they would miss his leadership in the diocese, and contributed to his leaving present. Soon after his appointment they managed to secure Bishop Frederick Cockin to preach at a midweek service.

A suggestion that Whiteladies Road was over-churched and that the Free Churches should come together and form a Union church found little favour with the Tyndale diaconate, though a delegation was appointed to confer with Redland Park officers on this. There could, it was thought, be more scope for the churches combining to offer institutional work if a suitable location could be found. Redland Park's hall suggested itself for this purpose but since the building of a new church was some years into the future the release of the hall for such purposes could not presently be contemplated. However at the end of the war a united Contact Club for men was established with Redland Park. The deacons thought that a membership of 3–400 indicated an upper ceiling beyond which the family nature of the church would be lost. Clearly the social profile of the area was changing with family residences giving way to flats in multiple occupation. Whilst there would be fewer children in the area, it remained attractive to students and young professionals. Various proposals were made as to how the rebuilt church should be configured. All these considerations led to the deacons deciding that with the War Damage Commission providing two thirds of the cost of a substantial but plain rebuilding of the sanctuary, that this should be done, but all was to be undertaken coupled with the insistence that what was happening on Whiteladies Road should not jeopardise the sound establishment of the new work in Westbury On Trym.

After the war, the Church magazine was reinstituted initially as a monthly leaflet with Dorothy Glover once more editing it, now with the assistance of Miss Brayley. It was at this time that the deacons arranged for a rota of car owners to provide transport for Bryan when he needed it. It was also agreed to pay Margaret Bryan £100 p.a. for secretarial services to her father. Bryan suggested this sum should be deducted from his salary but the deacons were insistent that it be treated as an additional benefit.

Social events at post-war Tyndale included Christmas parties, missionary suppers, garden parties for deacons and their wives, New Year's socials, Sunday School parties, teas for new members to meet the deacons and their wives. In the winter months Guest Services took place on the first Sunday evening of each month and Young People's services on the second Sunday, hoping to address the continued concern to find ways to keep the church's own young people and to integrate new young people into the life of the church, which was also to be served by the founding of the Tyndale Youth Fellowship under the leadership of Rowland Brake. In the autumn of 1948 the starting of a cub pack was in prospect, but in the New Year Bryan was speaking of starting a Life Boys (as the junior section of the Boy's Brigade was then known) with the help of Michael Hamlin, indicating that in due course this would lead to the establishment of a Boy's Brigade Company. Such rapid changes of prospective strategy indicate a measure of desperation about finding the right recipe for youth work at Tyndale.

The most popular of all activities were the "Everybody's Effort" events which replaced the Bazaars and Bring-and-Buy Sales of an earlier generation. Everybody's Effort events not only raised large sums of money for Tyndale's charities, including particularly the BMS and the Rebuilding Fund, but expressed a deep sense of effort and achievement across the membership, leaving fragrant memories of good times of fun put to the service of the wider church. Special services included an annual service to which the Guild of the Handicapped was invited and there were periodic visits from the Bristol Collegiate School who had been regular attenders when the school was located in Redland.

Tyndale, though mainly a congregation of the comfortably off, also had concern for those less fortunate. Thus a concern for the poor is to be seen in the disbursement of the communion fund and in the creation of the post of "almoner" held for many years by Miss Christina Culross until the end of 1950, when she was ably succeeded in post by Miss Katherine Gotch Robinson, one of Edward Robinson's daughters. Four years later Katherine was to extend her charitable concern with the purchase of her brother's home, Cote House, to form the basis for a charity providing extensive care for the elderly. Katherine Robinson faithfully and discreetly served as almoner and her reports give an indication of the kind of help offered – such as were reported in June 1951 when there were three persons receiving weekly or monthly assistance, eleven who received Christmas gifts, with more occasional help given to emergency cases. Consultation with the treasurer and secretary was a regular part of her discerning where there was need and she encouraged deacons to pass on to her the names of anybody associated with the church who could do with help. In 1952 she reported what a pleasure this work gave her. She always emphasised that the gifts came from Tyndale and there was universal gratitude for the help afforded. There had been no cases of extensive financial distress during the year but the church did give regular help to three people and more occasional assistance to a further two.

In 1948 the BMS made two attempts to secure F. C. Bryan's services as Foreign Secretary of the society on the retirement of Dr H. R. Williamson. The initial response by Bryan was to resist nomination. But when the critical state of the society's work in all its separate fields was made known and when H. L. Taylor, one of his own deacons but also a member of the BMS Staffing committee, intervened on the society's behalf, Bryan was persuaded to give more serious consideration to the invitation, and indeed to allow his name to go forward. Led by Taylor, the Tyndale deacons who would have resisted Bryan going to another church, agreed that in the circumstances this was a "sacrifice" the church had to be prepared to make for the sake of the society. However when the General Committee postponed making a decision to July, Bryan came to the conclusion that he could not perceive the call of God in this move and withdrew his name, as did Ernest Payne in the same process. Eventually Victor Hayward, a China missionary, succeeded to the post in 1951 and provided the society with "a searching and remarkably perceptive" vision which some, however, found too radical.

1949 would see the 80th anniversary of the founding of the church and three days of celebration were planned – special Sunday worship with the minister presiding and preaching, on Monday a reunion for of Tyndaleans with light refreshments, and on Tuesday evening a public celebration with addresses by the Rt Hon. Ernest Brown, MP, as President of the Baptist Union, and by Dorothy Glover, with one of Edward Robinson's sons in the chair. Miss Glover's memorable address was subsequently printed.

A major concern in the later months of Bryan's ministry was the work of the organist who had served the church faithfully for so long, but now neither he nor the choir were giving the satisfaction to the congregation which they had once done. Various proposals of sub-committees to find a solution to the problem and various delegations to see Walter Maker were made but none provided a solution to a matter of such great delicacy and in the end Maker's resignation was only secured by suggesting that he had worked so closely in partnership with Bryan and that a new minister would be making a new start in a very different situation. Indeed behind the issue of church music there lay a tension between an old way of doing things and the culture of an emerging world which was very different; this issue took more diaconal time than any other. Eventually Maker was persuaded to intimate in September 1950 that he would resign before year's end, but in the event a minute records his death in December.

In March 1950 Bryan told the deacons that he had received the unanimous nomination of the churches of the Eastern Area of the Baptist Union to become their Area Superintendent and that, believing this to be the call of God, he would, if offered the appointment, feel bound to accept. The deacons, whilst reluctant to lose his services thought they had no option but to support him in this move. On Bryan's acceptance of that position, H. L. Taylor was appointed as moderator at Tyndale during the pastoral vacancy. Arrangements were made for a Farewell Meeting for Bryan on September 4th, but before that he had already arranged for a preaching visit to the USA so his last Deacons' Meeting was in June 1950. The arrangements for the September meeting were ambitious with the hope that the bishop would be present. Addresses were to be given by representatives of the Westbury Church, the Folk House, Bristol Youth Committee, the Bristol and District Baptist Association, the Baptist College and the four Whiteladies Road Churches, whilst letters of gratitude were secured from the University, Bristol Baptist ministers, Clifton High School, the Missionary Auxiliary and Wills Hall. A presentation had been made to Bryan's daughter, Margaret, at the previous Church Meeting and Bryan was presented with a parting gift of £300.

Chapter 9.
The Folk House, 1920–1966

John Briggs

How to shape the church's mission in changing times was already an urgent consideration when the First World War came to an end. Even before the war it had been agreed to move the activities in Deanery Road from a downtown mission type of programme to something more akin to what was being undertaken by various Christian settlements. Already the missioner, the Revd G. W. Robert, helped to found the St George's Road Men's Club and was also much involved in Adult School work at College Green both of which activities maintained close connections with the Mission. During the war years work at the mission continued under the guidance of Sister Emmie though this was made more difficult by the commandeering of the premises for military purposes. In the event this only served to strengthen the intention to reorient the work which was increasingly to focus on adult education. There were problems with running the Sunday School, which had around 200 children enrolled, as the call-up of men for the forces and the suspension of Sunday trams made it difficult to secure an adequate number of teachers. In the later months of the war the Mission congregation still mourned the loss of three of its men in combat. In April 1918 it was reported that the Scout Troop had to be suspended but happily had amalgamated with that run by the YMCA at Jacob's Wells with the note, "Never was the care of boys more necessary than now, as the reports of juvenile crime and the warnings of observant social workers testify". Even though its constituency was hard-pressed financially they were still mindful of other people's needs and put on a concert the proceeds of which went to "Wounded Soldiers' Comforts", a cause that also received gifts from the Mission's harvest celebrations. The senior Girls' Club entertained 30 orphans from Bristol South and West who had lost their fathers in the trenches, funded by money they themselves had raised. At the same time the Boys' Club reached its maximum membership of 80 with many would-be members turned away.

The *Tyndale Messenger* faithfully records the names of those who conducted evening services at the mission, so described from February 1918, the morning service apparently abandoned, for other activities were soon advertised for Sunday mornings. Many of the laymen who gave their time were very faithful in their regular ministry at Deanery Road. Some preachers were drawn from local clergy such as the Revd H. Leon Thomas of Wycliffe Congregational Chapel and the Revd J. W. Probert of Counterslip. H. H. Pewtress, a future Superintendent of the Western Area, presided at communion whilst still a student at the College. Others bear recognizable Broadmead names, and some were members at Deanery Road itself. Apart from the regular visits of the minister at Tyndale to conduct communion, relatively few Tyndale names appear, but in January 1920 Miss D. F. Glover appears as the first female preacher at the Mission apart from Sister Emmie; followed by Miss Funnel in February and Mrs Moore in May, with both of them reappearing in September.

Not all seemed to be well with the Sunday evening service, for whilst sometimes it was claimed that attendance was being sustained, that a good number of strangers were present in the congregation and that new folk were being welcomed into membership, church members were criticized for their laxity in supporting this service.

> If only the members of the Mission, themselves would set an example by regular attendance we should make a big step forward, but as it is at present, the increase is coming and coming rapidly from members of the outside public. Surely in these trying days one should not have to look in vain for sacrifice and support from those who are members of a Christian body. As loyalty is one of the essentials of church membership one can only feel disappointed at the indifferent attendance of many who have their names on the roll at the Mission.

In April 1920 it was reported that five of the older girls at the Mission had been baptised and added to the membership. In June sixteen girls left

The Folk House, Deanery Road

Hotwells on a steamer for Ilfracombe for the Club's annual holiday at Combe Martin.

In July 1920, Tyndale's Church Meeting decided that the old mission building was to be devoted to this new but allied use. To be known as "The Folk House", it was to operate as "an unsectarian, all-purpose educational settlement" which, it was hoped, would become a centre of valuable work. Tyndale, recognising the possibility of this new adult educational movement, entrusted the management to a council and executive of which the church and the Bristol Adult Schools Union nominated an equal number of members. The Mission was still located in an area of deprivation with Tyndale raising money for its Poor Fund and the Dorcas Society providing "warm and useful garments". Practical help in the neighbourhood continued to be needed especially in the winter months: "to many whose only income is an Old Age Pension, a parcel of grocery or a bucket of coal is a great boon". On several occasions those "passing through deep waters" testified: "If it hadn't been for the Mission I would have gone under".

A summer activity in 1921 was a garden party at the home of Mr and Mrs Edward Robinson. It was confidently stated: "Altogether the Folk House has become a community, working out the Social and Intellectual aspirations of its corporate life in strict and solemn obedience to a spiritual ideal".

In November 1920 the name of "The Folk House, College Green" first appears in the *Tyndale Messenger*, with Sister Emmie as minister and A. J. Foyle as secretary, both previously associated with Tyndale Mission. In the same month, the colourful Independent Labour Party member, campaigner for women's suffrage and defender of Conscientious Objectors, Councillor Mabel Tothill, who had Quaker connections, spoke at the evening service (and again in May and September), and in December one of the preachers was the very protestant Anglican, Thomas Inskip, newly elected MP for Bristol Central. In January 1921 Alderman Frank Sheppard, first Labour Lord Mayor, spoke; in May, Councillor T. Pearce of the Co-operative movement; in July and September 1921 Miss Shaw; October 1921 Miss Helen Sturge, women's suffrage campaigner and advocate of women's education; and in November Councillor A. W. S. Burgess, later chairman of Bristol Port Authority.

Mabel Tothill

Helen Sturge

A request from the Folk House in December 1920 to relocate the monthly communion service which took place after evening worship from the large hall to a room on a lower floor was strenuously resisted by the Tyndale deacons. Later Miss Glover confessed that there was probably a misunderstanding here as she had suggested the change of location to secure a quieter ambience for the communion service. She was frightened that the Tyndale deacons' response might have given unnecessary offence which it would be well to remove since Tyndale deacons "had now no jurisdiction over the conduct of affairs at the Folk House". Her colleagues encouraged Miss Glover to do what she could to rectify the misunderstanding.

In December 1920, the Folk House, which it was hoped would become "in some sense a University, in some senses a Church, and in some sense a Club", was reopened with a refurbished basement café, by Arthur Smith, Master of Balliol, a friend of the Workers Education Association and a champion of the cause of Adult Education. The chairman was the Quaker historian, W. C. Braithwaite. In sending apologies the Bishop of Bristol, the Rt Revd George Nickson summarised the new institution's function:

> The enlargement of the mental horizon; the illumination of life
> and its meaning; the interest and value which the study of the
> labours of the past, as well as the problem of the present and the
> possibilities of the future, means for us today; above all the sense
> of fellowship and the grasp of the spiritual basis of life, commend
> this movement to us all.

Sir Isambard Owen, Vice Chancellor of the University of Bristol, expressed the hope for the most cordial relations between the university and the Folk House. Mrs Katherine Robinson, representing Tyndale, spoke of the previous history of the work "and expressed the hope that the religious side of the work would be well maintained". Was this a *cri de coeur* and a foretaste of questions to come? In other respects the Folk House was flourishing – in February 1921 more than 1000 adults attended class.

Shortly after G. W. Harte's arrival, Sister Emmie accepted a call to Oxford Road, Moseley in Birmingham. At the same time the long-held desire for the work to be led by a resident warden was accomplished with the appointment of Paul Sturge, "a man of strong Christian character, with a passion for the Kingdom of God". Sturge, who was by training a surveyor and land agent, came from a well-known Quaker family and had recently been engaged in relief work among the starving people of Europe. After leaving Bristol Sturge would become a notable General Secretary of the

Quaker Friends' Service Council. His appointment to the Folk House was only announced to Tyndale deacons after he had begun work in Deanery Road. Other adjustments were made consequent on Sister Emmie's move to Birmingham. Miss Marion Jenkins took over the Wednesday activities which she had developed, A. J. Foyle the Sunday School once more and Harry Taylor the Sunday evening services. In 1931 Tyndale was still supplying a significant number of Sunday School teachers for the Sunday School.

It was not long, however, before Tyndale members began to feel disconnected from the work of the Folk House. Tyndale still elected twelve members to the Folk House Council. There was clearly concern that the educational purpose of the Folk House was becoming its dominant aim, rather than the more rounded mission of earlier years, which included concern for the soul as well as body and mind. In a re-organization of 1922, it was clearly stated that "the Folk House is a Settlement, the aim of which is to develop the Religious and Educational life of the individual and the community in the Spirit of Fellowship". The spiritual dimension was still there but with less specific theological content, and whereas until that date Tyndale held half the representation on the Council, Executive Committee and Programme Committee, in all these bodies, by revisions of the constitution, it was in the future to have only a substantial minority representation. One suspects that this was only a facing up to the reality of a decreased commitment to the Folk House project and that it was increasingly difficult to find 12 persons willing to serve on the Executive, that is to say a loss of active involvement by Tyndale members in the work on Deanery Road was the antecedent of less representation on the governing bodies.

The expense involved in running the Folk House was another issue. In October 1922 a request for Tyndale to take up a retiring collection to eliminate a small debt in the Folk House Sunday School accounts was denied, it being argued that "the responsibility of financing the Folk House Sunday School should rest on the Folk House Executive". More seriously Tyndale was legally liable for one third of the deficits incurred in the running of the Folk House. When this was raised in the diaconate in December 1929, Miss Jenkins and Miss Glover both defended the work and

Whilst in Bristol Adult School work, as well as a deep interest in the St. George's Road Men's Club which he had helped to form, engaged his attention. In this useful service he gained the respect and affection of many men. Much sympathy will go out to his widow and sons and daughters. Another old Tyndale link has been snapped, reminding us yet again of that "rest that remaineth" which is now his portion.

R. C. N.

THE FOLK HOUSE, COLLEGE GREEN.

Warden,
Mr. PAUL D. STURGE,
The Folk House.

Secretary,
Mr. A. J. FOYLE,
The Folk House.

Speakers on Sunday evenings :—October 2, Mr. H. L. Taylor ; October 9, Miss Helen Sturge ; Oct. 16, Mr. E. H. H. Jones ; Oct. 23, Mr. T. D. Heald.

SUNDAY, 9 a.m. Men's Physical Development Class
10 a.m. College Green Men's Adult School
11.15 a.m. Study Class, on " Economics "
3 p.m. Children's School
6.30 p.m. Meeting for Worship
7.45 p.m. Music, Recitals, etc.

MONDAY, 7.30 p.m. College Green Women's Adult School
7.30 p.m. Young People's Adult School
8 p.m. Course of Lectures, " West Country Poets " (commencing October 10th)

TUESDAY, 7.30 p.m. Adult School Training Class
7.30 p.m. Bible Study Class
7.30 p.m. Debating Society
8 p.m. Course of Lectures on " Old and New in Art and Life." (Fortnightly, commencing October 25th)
8 p.m. Tutorial Class, " Psychology "

WEDNESDAY, 3 p.m. Sisterhood
7 p.m. Dramatic Class
7 p.m. Folk Dancing Class (Beginners)
8 p.m. „ „ „ (Intermediates) Commencing September 28th,
7.30 p.m. Course of Lectures on " Foreign Affairs " commencing October 19th)

THURSDAY, 7 p.m. Women's Physical Development Class
7.30 p.m. Girls' Club
7.30 p.m. Crafts Class
7.30 p.m. Course of Lectures, " Psychology " (Fortnightly, commencing October 6th)

FRIDAY, 7.30 p.m. Speaker's Class
7.30 p.m. Singing Class
8 p.m. Eurhythmic Class (Commencing September 30th)

SATURDAY AFTERNOONS Dramatic Performances for Children
SATURDAY EVENINGS Popular Lectures, Concerts, Socials, Dramatic Performances, etc.

All interested are invited to join the Folk House. Membership Subscription 5s. per annum, dating from October 1st, 1921.

Contributions for the OCTOBER number of the *Messenger* should be sent to the EDITORS by WEDNESDAY, OCTOBER 19th.

Miss DOROTHY F. GLOVER, 15 Westfield Park, Redland.
Miss CULROSS, 16 Hartington Park, Redland.

Subscriptions for the *Messenger* for 1921 are now due and should be paid to Miss Evelyn Thorn, 73 Queens Road, *or to* Mr. C. Burris, 72 Pembroke Road. Minimum Subscription, 2/6 per year. Postage 6d. extra.

The Carlyle Press, 59 Park Row.

Folk House programme from October 1921 printed in the Tyndale Messenger spoke of the improved spirit there and believed that "quite a distinctive religious work was being done". In their assessment of the first three years of the new partnership in early 1923, the deacons were concerned, whilst not wishing to be over-critical, about the extent to which the original agreement that "the work would not lose its [sic] evangelical character" had been honoured. They also detailed statistics on the area being served, noting that only 20 of the 250 registrations for classes came from the "constituency originally intended", that is the run-down district around Deanery Road, with a majority of the users coming from the suburbs and as far distant as Weston Super Mare and Portishead, rather than the local area. They went on to record their worry that "it was regrettable that the religious object if the work was so little advertised publicly whilst the educational programme was given such prominence".

The leadership of the work at the Folk House seems to have passed into the hands of members of the Society of Friends who may have had different ideas as to how the religious objects of the work were to be defined. The deacons had diagnosed the main problems associated with the Folk House but seemed reluctant to take decisive action. Those most involved in the work of the Folk House claimed that none of the agencies in being at the time of the transition had ceased to function and some new work, especially amongst boys, had been added. Arguments were made that arrangements for the Sunday evening services and the Sunday School needed strengthening, whilst the Tyndale deacons were pleased to note that a new programme of systematic visitation of the district was about to be launched, but it was clear that the diaconate was divided on the issue, with both strong criticism and clear support being articulated, and so the deacons resolved to recommend to the church that it continue to support the Folk House, but in 1925 proposed an annual tenancy of the Deanery Road premises with the Folk House Council "in order to safeguard Tyndale's interests".

Another indication of changing relationships was that from the summer of 1925 it was proposed that the Tyndale membership and the mission membership be merged into one list as "Deanery Road and Tyndale were now one church". However those worshipping at Deanery Road were now a declining number and at the end of 1927 the deacons agreed to Sturge's suggestion that because the number of adults attending the evening service was small, it be made a children's service, whilst retaining the monthly women's service organised by Miss Jenkins, and also the Communion Service – although these seem to have become infrequent since, when Sturge asked that Harte should take the first Sunday evening service each quarter, the deacons replied that now there was not a Communion Service regularly on this Sunday, and because adult attendance was so small, Harte could not be released.

By 1932 the activities of the Folk House were becoming too extensive for the Deanery Road premises, and a number of schemes for expansion began to be aired such as acquiring land on the opposite side of Deanery Road on which a new building would be erected and connected with the existing premises by way of a bridge. There were complex legal issues about ownership and maintenance of the old building and the new. A revision of the Trust Deed was interpreted as meaning "in effect we give up the control of the Folk House", an admission of a further alienation of the work from that of the church, a process which some dated back to when Herbert Morgan was minister which some had opposed then as also at this later date. In the event the new proposal was rather different – the church was to grant a lease for 21 years to a company made up of 15 members of whom three were to be nominated by Tyndale, the other partners being Bristol University, the WEA, the National Adult School Union and the University Settlement Association. At this point the mathematics becomes rather problematical. According to the minutes of the Deacons' Meeting (June 1932), this body was to appoint five governors, of whom two should be Life Governors, one representing Tyndale and one the other 15 [sic]. But excluding the three members from Tyndale, there were only 12 other members.

In the early 1930s various proposals about the development of the buildings were entertained which were partly dependant on what the city council did with the land on the opposite side of Deanery Road, so although there was considerable talk, in the event no changes took place. A further proposal to change the Folk House constitution in 1936 caused further anxiety for Tyndale's deacons – in the new scheme Tyndale would only nominate 6 out of 34 members of the governing body, some 10 of which places were allocated to co-opted members. This caused considerable disquiet at Tyndale and led to an examination of the terms of the original agreement setting up the Folk House, but in the end they agreed and nominated J. W. Brighton, Miss Irene Cross, Eustace Davies, Miss D. F. Glover, Harold Hockey and Miss Ella Porteous to represent Tyndale. But *de facto* in the interwar years Tyndale was moving from being a co-sponsor of the work to being little more than a landlord.

At the end of 1934 Paul Sturge resigned as Warden. The deacons were anxious that Bryan secure the opportunity for Tyndale to approve any change of governance consequent on this. The Folk House replied that no change of scheme or extension of the premises was contemplated in the immediate future because of lack of funds. To help meet this need Tyndale gave the Folk House organisers the use of Tyndale's Lecture Hall for a sale to eliminate this debt. For the future the Folk House declared their intention to secure the patronage of a number of "Influential Citizens" to aid their cause. The first candidate reported to Tyndale for the wardenship was a Mr Read who had been a master at a Friends' School and was particularly interested in the problems of the unemployed and the deacons commended his candidature to the Church Meeting, but in the event the Folk House Council appointed Harold Bing of Hull, subject to their being no objection from the Education Settlement Association. It is difficult to read these minutes without a sense of the marginalising of the Tyndale interest, partly because of revised structures in the governance of the Folk House, but one suspects also because of a lack of personal involvement in the enterprise by Tyndale members except for that of a dedicated few. The movement of Paul Sturge to London was also critical since he had taken part in some Tyndale functions and carried the church's confidence.

By 1927 the limitations of the old Mission premises were becoming more and more apparent and the Folk House leadership brought forward plans for their radical alteration. The deacons, however, before any action was taken were concerned that the present suite of buildings should be valued, offering to contribute towards the cost of this. Arising from this they received a site valuation of £1,200 and £3,500 for the buildings as they stood with a possible valuation of £4,000 subsequent to alterations being successfully accomplished. An even more ambitious scheme involving the building of an additional floor was presented but withdrawn on the outbreak of war.

An address given at the Folk House by Neville Denis Pritt, MP, which it was claimed was little more than a glorification of developments in Russia, caused considerable controversy. The deacons in February 1920 indicated that they were very disturbed at this use of the Folk House premises, and mandated Bryan as chairman of the Folk House Council to enquire into the matter. Pritt, who came from a wealthy city family, was educated at Winchester and London University. A colourful character, he was a successful barrister who joined the Labour Party in 1918 and was elected MP for Hammersmith North in 1935. In 1932, he had visited the Soviet Union, and, according to Margaret Cole who travelled with him, "the eminent KC swallowed it all". Four years later he attended the first Moscow Show Trial penning an account of this in *The Zinoviev Trial* largely supporting Stalin in his purge of the Communist Party. Later, in 1940, he was expelled from the Labour Party following his support of the Soviet invasion of Finland. It is hard to believe that the Folk House leadership had exercised due diligence in making the necessary enquiries before inviting Pritt to speak. George Orwell thought him "perhaps the most effective pro-Soviet publicist" in the UK.

What Tyndale deacons had failed to achieve, namely a clear decision about Tyndale's on-going relation with the Folk House was in effect achieved by Hitler and his bombing of Bristol, including the Folk House, whose activities were consequently transferred to Read's Dispensary in St George's Road, Harold Bing taking a temporary post at Bristol Grammar School, thus removing the property tie between Tyndale and the Folk House. However, the deacons did spend around £250 providing a temporary roof, repairing the glazing and clearing rubbish largely to protect future war-damage claims. At the same time they received an enquiry from Messrs Sturge and Co. – Paul Sturge, the first warden, had been a surveyor by profession – enquiring if the deacons were considering selling the site on Deanery Road, to which they replied that they had no intention of doing so at that moment in time but they would be willing to consider any offer Sturge and Co. cared to make. In fact, the Folk House continued to use the Deanery Road premises until, in 1966, the premises were compulsorily purchased to allow for the construction of an extension to the Central Library located next-door. The Folk House moved to new premises in Park Street, where it is still based. The purchase money, £13,000, became the capital of the Richard Glover Fund within Tyndale's accounts which continues to make grants for various activities, primarily of an educational nature. Although the cause of adult education, providing invaluable opportunities for those denied a proper education in their youth to develop a full and rounded understanding of the world in which they lived, became more distant from the church as larger funding and sponsorship was sought from non-church sources, Tyndale can justifiably take pride in pioneering work in this crucial area. Much the same was to happen to the church's endeavours to provide comfortable and accessible accommodation for the elderly as the management of regulation became more and more complex and beyond the capacity of Tyndale's minister and deacons. Although secularized in later years, pioneering of both these initiatives remains to Tyndale's credit.

Chapter 10.

Tyndale and Missionary Outreach

John Briggs

Chapter 2 of this study has already demonstrated how central mission was to Richard Glover's ministry, both at home in the work of the Tyndale Mission in Deanery Road, and abroad in his commitment to the China mission of the BMS in particular. The concern of the minister rapidly became the concern of the whole congregation, surrounding which was much fund-raising, missionary suppers and addresses from missionaries on deputation not to mention full participation in the Bristol Auxiliary of the missionary society.

The chronology is interesting. Of the more than 30 missionaries listed in the several lists of Tyndale missionaries – the list on the honours board in the vestibule differs from that in the minutes – some 17 made their decision to serve overseas under Glover's ministry – nine going to serve in China, seven in India and one in Congo. Glover's arithmetic was slightly different. At his farewell gathering in 1911 he spoke with "profound thankfulness in my heart" of the 20 to 30 members of Tyndale who had gone out to serve on the mission field, speaking of the "fully 20 at work there today, besides those sleeping on the banks of the Congo or elsewhere". Maybe some went indirectly to the mission field or served with other agencies than the BMS. One of those asleep by the Congo River was James Henry Shindler, who came to Bristol Baptist College and to Tyndale in 1882, but who died of fever in 1887 only a few months after arrival in the Congo, one of a frightening number of missionary deaths at that time. It was a particularly bitter blow for the Shindler family, for his brother George had died in Shanghai in 1879. His less than seven months of service are of special interest as he was the son of Robert Shindler, Baptist minister in Addlestone in Surrey, the author of the original articles which appeared in *The Sword and Trowel*, the magazine of the Metropolitan Tabernacle,

Mr and Mrs Holman Bentley and their Congolese assistants

under the title of "The Down Grade", at just the time when his son was offering up his life in missionary service. That James Shindler, who made clear the influence of his father's friend, C. H. Spurgeon, in his Christian formation, should choose to train at Bristol, to worship in a church pastored by Richard Glover and to serve with the BMS, indicates something of the way the Baptist denomination held together even in times of considerable tension. When Shindler arrived in Bristol, F. W. Gotch – who had played a major part in the production of the Revised Version of the Bible, an enterprise which secured Spurgeon's approval – was still President of the Baptist College, but in 1883 he was succeeded by James Culross, a Baptist leader in whom Spurgeon continued to have confidence at a time when he separated himself from both the Union and the Missionary Society. It also illustrates the point that a number of Tyndale's missionaries came to Bristol for training at the Baptist College, then situated in Stokes Croft, before joining the church.

Another dimension of the missionary presence at Tyndale was the number of missionaries who worshipped with the Tyndale congregation. Dorothy Porteous captures this in her centenary reflection in which she imagines the

Revd J. S. Whitewright, veteran of the China field, taking down notes during a service to aid his work at Tsinanfu, and the tall dark Congolese, Nlemvo, "with stately head" walking up the aisle with the Bentley family. William Holman Bentley, grammarian and translator, who lived on Whiteladies Road for the last few months of his life after 27 years in Congo, did not become a member of Tyndale though he worshipped here together with his Dutch-born wife, herself the daughter of a China missionary, who with their daughter did become members. Brian Stanley, in his history of the BMS, notes Nlemvo's presence in England from 1884–6 but he came to the UK on further visits and was the only African present at the founding Congress of the Baptist World Alliance in 1905. By that time Bentley's work, impeded by his poor sight, sometimes occasioning total blindness, and the impact of the tuberculosis which was gradually consuming all his strength, was drawing to a close; the New Testament translation was complete and work on the Psalms was well-advanced with the aid of the ever faithful Nlemvo who was with Bentley in his final illness and was present at his funeral at the end of that year. Bentley's most celebrated work was the reduction of the Congo language to written form, and the compilation of a dictionary of the language followed by the translation of the New Testament. At his death he was still translating the Old Testament into Congolese. Glover wrote:

> It would be difficult to find anywhere a finer bit of missionary work than that which he has left behind him at Wathen station, on the Congo. A church of about 500 members, extraordinary for the activities of the members in carrying the Gospel themselves into all the district round about; and a noble school – the building for which was one of the last gifts of the late Sir Charles Wathen – remain his memento.

That he worked at the Wathen station of the BMS may explain why he spent his last few months in Bristol. His memorial service at Tyndale, conducted by Glover, was a major event after which a great procession of carriages proceeded to his internment at Arnos Vale.

The first missionaries listed on Tyndale's missionary board are the Revd and Mrs Isaac Allen, though their names are not found on any membership list. Allen was brought up in the Broadmead Sunday School where he was a classmate of William Sherring, later a deacon at Tyndale, whose father was an exceptionally generous patron of BMS work. Isaac became an apprentice at Messrs Llewellin and James, brass founders. Uncertain of what kind of education he could secure in this country he migrated to America where he enrolled at Oberlin College which had gained fame for its openness to black students, its participation in the abolitionist movement and, following its president, C. G. Finney, its concern for forthright evangelism. Whilst at college he wrote an essay on the "Abolition of Slavery" which won the prize offered by the Anti-slavery Society and followed this up by a trip "down south" to see how slavery worked. Unfortunately he was identified as the author of this essay whilst there and had to escape hurriedly. He joined the northern army when the civil war broke out but received a bullet wound on the parade ground that prevented him from taking part in the fighting. Back in England in 1863 at the age of 32 he applied to the Baptist Missionary Society and was sent to India, where he served at Dacca – now the capital of Bangladesh – where he encountered Pandita Ramabai, a brilliant Indian Brahmin woman, and introduced her to Christianity. She was baptised but continued to see herself as both Hindu and Christian. During Easter 1885, as resistance to her Anglican "handlers" reached a crisis, Ramabai managed to escape to Clifton, where Isaac Allen, her old Baptist mentor, was convalescing, recovering from malaria, in the home of Richard Glover. Allen retired to Bristol in 1892 and died in 1911. Because Glover was indisposed his funeral, which took place in the Lecture Hall at Tyndale, was conducted by H. W. Burdett, but Glover wrote his obituary.

The importance of Tyndale for the work of the BMS in the late nineteenth century is partly hidden in a couple of sentences in Brian Stanley's *The History of the Baptist Missionary Society* where he writes,

> By the end of 1883 the £2,100 required for the outfit and passage money of fourteen missionaries [for China] had been supplied, all of it from the city of Bristol. Half was promised by Charles Wathen, benefactor of the Congo mission, and the other half was raised by Richard Glover, pastor of the Tyndale Church and chairman of the Society's China sub-committee.

But not only so, for Stanley pays tribute to Glover's work in raising the whole profile of the China mission to a new level within the life of the Society, and since Wathen was a member of Tyndale in fact the whole of the China fund was Tyndale inspired. Moreover in the Congo, two mission stations had names associated with Tyndale – Wathen or Ngombe Lutete and the neighbouring Kibentele.

Veteran missionaries, Mr and Mrs Whitewright, were long associated with Tyndale. John Sutherland Whitewright was born in Edinburgh in 1858 and after six years working for the ordinance survey came to Bristol to train at the College, before proceeding to China. He arrived in the city of Chingzhou, Shandong province, in 1881 where he was in charge of the Theological and Normal Class leading on to the establishment of the Native Training Institution in Chingzhou to train pastors, evangelists and teachers, following Timothy Richard's conviction that the essential task of evangelism should be the task of an emerging self-supporting

John Sutherland Whitewright

indigenous church, though there remained a need for ex-patriot help in reaching that goal. When in 1893 new buildings were provided and the institution was renamed the Gotch-Robinson Theological College, of which Whitewright became the first Principal, its Tyndale connection was made abundantly clear. As the Principal explains, the new buildings were funded at the expense of "a gentleman in England" in memory of his father and his wife's father – E. S. Robinson and F. W. Gotch – with the object of helping to further work "to which they in their lifetime were devoted".

Back in 1887 Whitewright had established a small museum in Chingzhou where he assembled materials to illustrate, initially to his own students, the "customs, interests and inventions of the Western World", a venture which has been called "one of the most powerful evangelistic agencies in China". It was conceived of as "praeparatio evangelica" – visitors to the museum were soon numbering a thousand a day and all were invited to the neighbouring lecture theatre for evangelistic preaching and spiritual counselling. In 1905, he moved the museum to Jinan, where it became the extension department of Shantung Christian University, rather grandly described by the American mission leader, Robert Speer, as "the most effective piece of university extension work which can be found in Asia, if not in the world". That such work in China and through the Folk House in Bristol should be proceeding on parallel lines is most interesting, with people like the Robinson family promoting both. H. R. Williamson who succeeded Whitewright gave it as his judgment that the Institute did much to break down anti-Christian prejudice and thus prepare the way for the hearing of the Christian message.

Two further Tyndale missionaries played a key role in establishing a Christian presence in higher education in China. E. W. Burt, born in Yeovil in 1866, early took advantage of non-conformists being allowed to matriculate and take degrees at Oxford studying at Balliol, Oxford before proceeding to Bristol Baptist College, before serving in China from 1892 to 1932. His early years were spent in pastoral and evangelistic work but from 1904, when Shantung Christian University was brought into being, he served on its staff as Professor, Dean of Theology, and sometime Acting President, the only member of staff with continuous service over those 20 years. Tribute was paid to "his steady devotion to his work and his generous and catholic spirit" and to Mrs Burt's work amongst women in the extension department. Burt only resigned from the University staff, work which he thoroughly enjoyed, when he was appointed Field Secretary for China. Writing in 1917 in the *Missionary Herald* describing the relocation of the University to Jinan, the headline given to his article was "China must be won by Chinese". Although much engaged in higher education his main aim remained "to win Chinese to Christ and to see the Church firmly established among them". In a manuscript autobiography he drew satisfaction from the knowledge that many of his former students were exercising influential roles in Christian leadership throughout China. His *After Sixty Years* was an able study of the establishing of BMS work in Northern China from 1867 to 1927.

Evan Morgan was a Welsh student who came to Bristol to train for missionary service and was appointed to the China field in 1884, aged 24. He is noted as one of those who supported Timothy Richard's strategic missiological thinking and indeed joined him in the work of the Christian Literature Society in 1906, succeeding him in 1915 and continuing in post for another 20 years. This provided an excellent base for him to exercise his gifts as translator, writer and editor, making available to the vast Chinese market the best of the cultural treasures of the western world including works of Christian scholarship with such a degree of excellence that the University of Wales conferred on him the degree of Doctor of Divinity (DD). This justified him calling himself "an evangelist of heart and mind". He spent his retirement in Bristol.

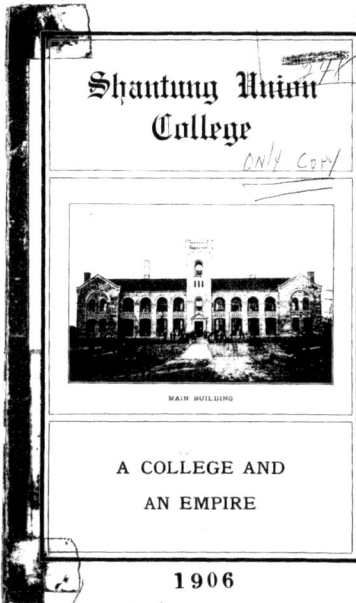

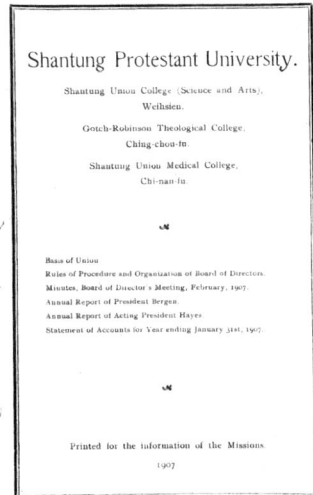

Shantung Christian University

Another Tyndale member who sailed to China with the BMS in 1884 was Samuel Couling, raised in the church in Totnes. As a Ward Trust Scholar his ministerial training was in part at Bristol College (1879–80) and in part at the University of Edinburgh from where he graduated with an MA degree. He served with the BMS for some 24 years in Shantung before resigning to take up a post as tutor with a Chinese family in 1908.

China was also the scene of the ministry of the extraordinarily-gifted Stanley Jenkins, son of Tyndale's church secretary, and a product of the student volunteer movement, who trained as a doctor in Bristol and at an exceptionally young age secured both his MD and FRCS. The great-nephew of Dr Robert Fletcher, of the Surgeon General's Library, Washington, Jenkins served as Assistant House Surgeon, House Physician, and Casualty Officer at the Bristol General Hospital and also House Surgeon at the Children's Hospital. In 1900–1901 he was House Surgeon at St Mark's Hospital, London, then Registrar, Pathologist and Resident Medical Officer at Mount Vernon Hospital for Tuberculosis, Northwood.

A leader in the Students' Christian Movement, he felt convinced of a call to serve as a medical missionary and went out to China under the Baptist Missionary Society, and in 1904 took charge of the medical work at Sian Fu, in Shensi, North China. The Chinese language presented no difficulty to him. China was just then settling down after the Boxer Rising when the Chinese had become now more ready to recognize that foreign missionaries only desired to help them. Jenkins' knowledge of their language made friends of his patients, and

Stanley Jenkins

they consulted him on other than medical matters, for there is nothing that pleases a Chinese as much as finding someone who is willing to listen to his story, and Jenkins was a patient listener. There was no railway and Sian Fu was a month's journey inland; there were the same diseases as at home and a few others, but all in a more advanced state – wounds full of maggots; malignant disease long past the operable stage; a dislocated shoulder of six months' standing covered by a plaster; needles previously inserted to let out evil spirits; common drugs in very crude form. The native doctors usually prescribed the infusion of a herb in a pint of water, so that concentrated drugs in the form of tablets were viewed with suspicion. Until he could train assistants, the missionary doctor had to be surgeon, house surgeon, nurse, and manservant, and dispense his own medicines. Until trained in antiseptic methods, Chinese assistants could not assist at operations; the Chinese were averse to major operations, particularly to amputations, whilst permission to open the abdomen was a novelty till the Chinese learnt that lives could be saved thereby. All this bore fruit on the spiritual side with conversions and baptismal services.

During his first furlough Jenkins was engaged in collecting appliances for his hospital, especially an X-ray installation, which was well on its way out to China when Jenkins fell ill. He had other improvements in mind, particularly the building of a new hospital. On his return at the end of 1912 he took up work in conjunction with Cecil Frederick Robertson, FRCS. However, Sian Fu had been exhausted by famine, fire, and snow, and typhus had become prevalent. Robertson caught the disease in the out-patient department. Jenkins took his share in faithfully nursing his colleague in his final illness. After twenty-one days Jenkins himself sickened. He did not give up but, with a temperature of 103°F, saw sixty out-patients, and went to bed with his Chinese attendant sleeping in his room. Mrs Jenkins had been with her children to the coast, but was able to reach her husband and nurse him for the last few days. Although after a fortnight the fever left him his weak heart was not to allow recovery and he died at the end of a three-week illness on 6th April 1913, aged only 38. He was buried in the Baptist Missionary Churchyard by his fellow-missionaries, many of his Chinese patients following his body to his grave. He had married the daughter of Mr and Mrs Thomas Liveridge, of Llandaff;

she was left with two young children, a boy and a girl, who both trained as doctors and spent many years with the Baptist Missionary Society. Testimonies to the quality of his service came in from many quarters – fellow Tyndalean, Evan Morgan, paid tribute not only to extraordinary medical skills but to high administrative and linguistic gifts. Richard Glover felt this loss deeply and wrote a sensitive biography of this young martyr to missionary service which also reflects his deep knowledge of the work of the China mission. A different kind of tribute is to be found in the work of the Jenkins-Robertson Memorial Hospital built on lsand donated by the Chinese government. Jenkins' sister, Grace, was also a China missionary, married to the Revd H. W. Burdett, sometime assistant minister to Glover. Unlike her brother she served for twenty years using both her nursing skills and her evangelistic skills amongst the leading women in that part of China.

Burdett came from that part of the Midlands that had given birth to the BMS but he trained for the ministry in Bristol. His first pastorate in Shipley was interrupted by work for the Soldiers' Christian Association in France but an underlying call to missionary service could not be denied and a fortnight after the armistice was signed in 1918 the Burdetts set sail for China where he was mainly concerned with building up local congregations and evangelistic outreach which caused the Chinese, with deep respect, to call him the "tramps the road pastor". The fruit of his Bible-based ministry was the building up of a strong indigenous self-supporting church, well established before he returned to England on furlough in 1939 when the uncertainties of the times led him to take a pastorate in the Isle of Wight from which he retired to Bristol in 1944. Although he transferred his membership to Buckingham, his obituary, celebrating 98 years of service was written by Ron Cowley. Mrs Burdett, who died in 1961, was an able coadjutor in all her husband's labours where her ministry to educated and wealthy women in the cities of the area as well as in lengthy itinerancies in the rural hinterland was well received as well as the assistance she gave to the overworked staff of the Jenkins-Robertson Memorial Hospital.

In all Tyndale provided eight China missionaries with their wives, or at least these men brought their wives into membership at Tyndale: Mrs Martha Whitewright (née Allen), Mrs Marion Morgan (née Weedon), Mrs Katherine Henderson Smith (née Lane), Mrs Helen Stonelake (née Carver),

*The Mission House in Chingzhou, with Martha Whitewright seated in
the wheel barrow, equipped for travelling*

Mrs Grace Burdett (née Jenkins), Mrs Gladys Rowley (née Shaw – her sister married the India missionary, Percy Bushill), Mrs Marjorie Harmon (née Porteous) and Mrs Gladys Lamming (née Warne). Some of these created missionary dynasties – for example, of the four sons and two daughters of the Henderson Smiths, two sons became missionaries in China and one in Congo, whilst one daughter served as a deaconess at home. The Stonelake story is one of overcoming tragedy. Helen Carver, baptised at the age of thirteen at Tyndale, met Henry Stonelake there after she had tragically lost her first husband after only weeks of marriage, and he his first wife after service in the Congo. They were married in Shanghai in 1909 after Stonelake's transfer to the China field and gave almost 30 years service in Shansi Province, living a most frugal life sharing the hardships of their Chinese neighbours in a district where reconstruction after the Boxer Rising was slow to accomplish, until retirement in 1937 just before the Japanese invasion. Hearing of the distress in the area they returned in 1938 and stayed for a further year until the advance of the Japanese forced their withdrawal to Shanghai, and later to the USA. But even that was not the end of their missionary service for the BMS sent the Stonelakes to Jamaica to report on the situation in the colony. After due study, they submitted a very sombre report. Fifty ministers were serving 200 churches; of these half were thoroughly reliable, a quarter in need of help, whilst the remaining quarter ought not then to be in the ministry, some because of extreme old age, leading to the suggestion that the society appoint a commissioner to spend three years assessing the situation and seeking remedies for the parlous state of the Jamaica Baptist Union. The Stonelakes finally retired to Bristol where Helen outlived her husband dying just short of her 96th birthday.

Educational work was also high on the agenda of the work in India. Stephen Thomas was born in neighbouring Wiltshire before coming to Bristol where he became a member of Tyndale with considerable involvement in the work of the Tyndale Mission. He entered the College in 1880 before setting sale for Delhi where he worked for 37 years serving as Director of the Boy's School and the Training Institute for Indian Preachers. The confidence that he won amongst both the Hindu and Moslem communities meant that the Government entrusted to him large sums of money to expend on relief work which led to the award of the Kaisar-i-Hind Medal for notable public service by Edward VIII. His lasting memorial was the institution he led for so many years which became the Union Christian School jointly sponsored by the BMS and the (Anglican) Society for the Propagation of the Gospel. Ill-health led to retirement in Bristol in 1922.

The work of some female missionaries leaves fewer records than could be desired. Marion Shaw met Percy Bushill when he was a student at Bristol and she spent 12 years with him in Delhi (1913–25), before ill-health compelled her husband to return to England where he had notable pastorates in Orpington and Eastbourne. Ethel Davies was born in Liverpool but came to Tyndale from Toxteth Tabernacle when her work as an art teacher brought her to Bristol. She sailed for India in July 1919 and "gave 32 years self-effacing steady service to the people of India" working in Delhi and then at Baraut and the hospital at Dholpur where for sixteen years she witnessed to Christ cycling out to do work in people's homes in the surrounding villages and amongst the hospital patients. Davies retired to Worthing. Emmeline Morgan's legacy is similar:

> there was nothing spectacular in her life and ministry, but she was rewarded by seeing that her labour in the Lord was not in vain

> and numbers of Indian women call her blessed as they remember
> her gracious influence and witness.

Bristol born, she served for 35 years with the Baptist Zenana Mission in Bhiwani and Delhi. Another single woman to serve in India was Hilda Porteous who was baptised at Tyndale and, after teacher training, went to India in 1912 giving outstanding service at Gange High School in Delhi, reputed to be the only European teacher who could teach mathematics in Urdu thereby securing excellent exam results. She graciously gave up her work in the school she loved, and transferred to district work in Baraut where she worked in complete harmony with the local Indian superintendent of missionary work, the Revd Haider Ali, whose mother had been one of her colleagues in the Gange School. Hilda Porteous retired to Bristol in 1947.

Tyndale's presence in India is also to be seen in the service of three further single women. Doris Timmins was a member of a significant Tyndale family. At school in Bristol, she was baptised at Tyndale and became a member and trained to be a nurse. Under the BMS she sailed for India in November 1924, serving for 17 years on the staff of the hospital at Chandraghona where she founded the Nurses' Training School in 1937. Her prominence in nurse education led to her appointment as Nursing Superintendent of the Campbell Hospital in Calcutta, serving there throughout the Bengal famine of 1943 when it is said she was instrumental in saving the lives of many babies whose mothers had died on the streets. In 1949 she rejoined the BMS serving at hospitals in Bhiwani and Patna before retiring in 1956. A daughter of the manse, Daisy Webb was born in Melksham, baptised at Downend, and studied at Bristol University when as a 21 year old she was challenged at a Student Christian Movement Conference to offer for missionary service. After a year at Carey Hall she sailed for India in October 1915 spending her first twelve years on the staff of Buckley House Girls' School, transferring in 1928 to Udayagiri in the Kond Hills where she initiated a programme of women's education in association with the Moorshead Hospital, also supervising a hostel for girls working at the hospital until she retired in 1947.

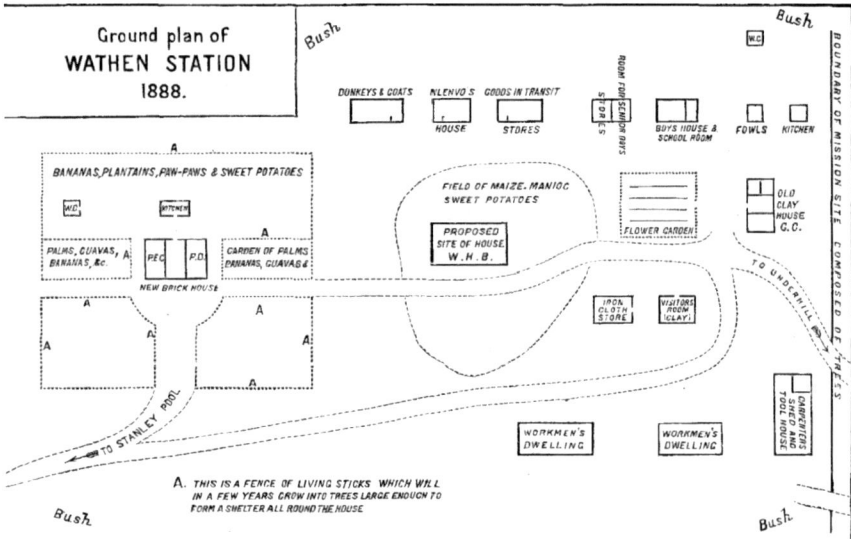

Ground plan of
WATHEN STATION
1888.

Bush
Bush
Bush

DONKEYS & GOATS NLENVO'S GOODS IN TRANSIT
HOUSE STORES

ROOM FOR SEMOUR RAYS

BOYS HOUSE & SCHOOL ROOM FOWLS KITCHEN

W.C.

BOUNDARY OF MISSION SITE COMPOSED OF TREES

BANANAS,PLANTAINS,PAW-PAWS & SWEET POTATOES
W.C. KITCHEN

FIELD OF MAIZE, MANIOC SWEET POTATOES

OLD CLAY HOUSE G.C.

PALMS, GUAVAS, BANANAS, &c. PEG P.O. GARDEN OF PALMS BANANAS, GUAVAS &

PROPOSED SITE OF HOUSE W.H.B.

FLOWER GARDEN

TO UNOERHILL

NEW BRICK HOUSE

IRON CLOTH STORE VISITORS ROOM (CLAY)

TO STANLEY POOL

WORKMEN'S DWELLING WORKMEN'S DWELLING

CARPENTERS SHED AND TOOL HOUSE

A. THIS IS A FENCE OF LIVING STICKS WHICH WILL
IN A FEW YEARS GROW INTO TREES LARGE ENOUGH TO
FORM A SHELTER ALL ROUND THE HOUSE

Bush
Bush

Wathen mission station, Congo

Dorothy Turner was born in Clifton, baptised at Tyndale and became a church member. She was educated at Clifton High School and Westfield College within the University of London. Having secured nursing qualifications she sailed to India for service with the BMS in 1920 serving in Delhi (1920–22), Dholpur (1922–5) and at the Women's Hospital in Palwal from 1925 until her retirement in 1953. Her missionary focus is to be seen in her establishing with a colleague a Prayer Room at the hospital. Her major contribution to Indian welfare was as a pioneer of modern nursing education in India serving for many years on the executive and examining board of an organisation which, founded to serve mission hospitals, later became the Punjab Nurses Registration Council. It was Dorothy Turner who designed the badge worn by those acknowledged as Trained Nurses of India. Her service to the women and children of the Palwal district was recognised by the Indian government who awarded her a silver Kaisar-i-Hind medal.

With the additional names of Miss Agnes Horlick (who served as an educational missionary in Ceylon for eight years), the Revd Jack E. Young (Congo) and Miss Barbara Gadd (also a missionary to Ceylon), the list of Tyndale missionaries ends. What becomes apparent is that a number of names appearing on the list are of those who worshipped at Tyndale for some of their student years but who had other sending churches. Jack Young was one of these. He had a background in banking and came from Bloomsbury and Plymouth. In his final year at College he served as student pastor with F. C. Bryan before becoming Tyndale's second missionary to work in the Congo, serving from 1938 to 1955 initially at Yakusu but latterly caring for the Missionary House in Kinshasa. On retiring from the Congo for health reasons he combined a part-time pastorate at Hanham, Bristol, with school teaching and when he finally retired he joined Broadmead where he became a deacon. A name that does not appear on the list is that of Mrs Lysbeth Brand (née Eadie) who served with the BMS in India where her parents had been missionaries. A very modest gift was given to her in September 1950 on account of her serving as "Brown Owl" at Tyndale for some years; she served in India from 1950–68 when the family returned to pastorates in this country.

An interesting incident which throws up wider issues is found in the minutes of the Deacons' Meeting for July 1950, concerning a recommendation that Lady Vera Horwill (née Walker) be received into membership. Brought up in the Portobello Church where her father was minister, she graduated from Edinburgh and was accepted by the BMS as a missionary doctor in 1932 and was assigned to the hospital at Berhampore, India. But she soon became engaged to (later Sir) Lionel Horwill (1890–1972), the last ex-patriot judge operating in the sub-continent whose family seemed to have lived in Pembroke Road. The marriage took place in May 1934 and occasioned Dr Walker's resignation from the BMS. Her offer of medical assistance after that date was not acceptable to the BMS even though it threatened leaving the hospital without medically qualified staff, though in the event a Syrian Christian colleague gave temporary cover. 1948 witnessed both the Horwills speaking at a missionary meeting at Buckingham Chapel. Bryan told the deacons that residence in India meant a transfer from a Baptist Church was not practical. At the same time her son, Frank, who had recently been baptised also sought membership and visitors were appointed. Frank subsequently emigrated to Australia where he trained for the Baptist ministry and became pioneering pastor of the church at Cohuna followed by a second pastorate at Stawell. Subsequently he served as an active layman whilst his expertise in psychology took him into government service.

However, the second column on the tribute board in the vestibule, remains starkly empty, with the latest date of overseas service being 1955, but as chapter 16 will demonstrate that is not the end of the story, for mission is not now to be seen narrowly in terms of a simple act of "sending" and "receiving", but of creative relationships with vigorous indigenous churches, all working together for the coming of God's kingdom, in a search for justice, peace and respect for the whole created order. The Baptist Missionary Society now works in many more countries than formerly but even that does not describe accurately the range of Tyndale's engagement with Christian communities across the world which now becomes a task where the search leads out into an ever-changing context.

Chapter 11.

W. E. Whilding and Reconstruction

David Bell

> From your warm-hearted letters we believe that you have a deep
> sense of guidance in this event; while we are sure that the Divine
> Hand has been directing us toward you.

So wrote the Revd William (Bill) Evan Whilding to the church at Tyndale in
the magazine of January 1951. It goes on to announce that "he will begin his
ministry on Sunday 4th March". At the Deacons' Meeting in May of the
previous year, there was an indication that an invitation had been made to
Whilding who was enjoying a markedly successful twelve-year ministry at
West Bridgford, Nottingham, during which he had both secured a BSc
degree in economics and served for a time on the Urban District Council.
Initially Whilding replied to the deacons' invitation to preach at Tyndale,
saying he feared that he was not free to visit Bristol that autumn. The
Secretary replied, hoping Whilding would be able to come in the New Year.
Names of a possible to successor to F. C. Bryan had been requested from
the members, and as late as August 1950, H. L. Taylor suggested the name
of Dr Leonard Champion of Rugby to the deacons, who decided to ask him
for a Sunday in January. However, by then things were settled between the
church and Bill Whilding, for he preached at Tyndale on October 22nd and
made a deep impression.

Harry L. Taylor, elected by the church as Chairman and Moderator for the
interregnum, urged the deacons to "take some action as quickly as
possible". They were unanimous that Whilding was "a man of great
spiritual gifts". Several mentioned his sincerity and spirituality clearly
apparent in his beautiful reading of the Scriptures, his prayers, his whole
conduct of the services, his outstanding preaching. A large number of the
congregation had expressed their great appreciation of Whilding – "not one

The Revd Bill Whilding

adverse criticism had been heard". Already it seemed that Tyndale had found a worthy successor to Bryan, whose "seventeen years of great ministry", said Taylor were "of such a high spiritual level". Following the vote to invite Whilding, a message from Bryan was read, saying "in what affection and esteem he held Mr Whilding and how happy he would be to see him at Tyndale". This may explain why the settlement process was so short: just over six months compared to the interregnum of almost two years between G. W. Harte and F. C. Bryan. A manse was purchased at 10 Cavendish Road, Henleaze for the new minister, his wife, Joyce, and their children, Rosemary and Roger, and his salary set at £600 p.a. with an additional £50 as a car allowance, a sign of changing times.

Bill Whilding began his ministry on Sunday 4th March 1951, preaching in the morning on John 3 v 16 – "the Gospel the Church must proclaim". His evening text was "Lord, teach us to pray". The welcome tea at Redland Park, and the induction service followed on Tuesday. Next day, the front page headline in the *Western Daily Press* read, "Tyndale can show Bristol", referring to remarks at the induction by Prof. L. H. Marshall, Principal of Rawdon College, that there were "so many different social classes represented in Tyndale that the Church could show how these should be welded into a real fellowship and be an example to the city". Whilding commented later, "Our opinion is that this has already largely been done. The warmth of our welcome from all directions indicates a united spirit of friendship". In three days, Bill Whilding's own stated principles of ministry and church life had each been introduced – he wrote, "three things will bring God's blessing on our church: the faithful preaching of the Gospel; the relationships between us; and remembering one another in our prayers."

Tuesday 13th March saw church and congregation welcoming the Whildings. Donald Yeo, soon to be church secretary writes,

> We have taken them, not only right into the family circle of the Church, but to our hearts. The gladness and warmth of our welcome were happily voiced by every organisation of the Church, led by Peter Bradford for Children's Church and Ruth Bodey for the Youth Fellowship – and how delightfully they did it – while the choir gave their welcome in song. We could never repay the debt of gratitude we owe to Harry Taylor as moderator.

Three others in particular were thanked for their part in the interregnum: the Revd H. W. Burdett as ministerial visitor, the Revd J. I. Carlyle Litt of Westbury, who led the Tuesday prayer meetings, and Dr Arthur Dakin of the Baptist College who led worship on the first Sunday of every month and presided at communion. "We were glad to hear from Mrs Whilding and her words make us feel that she brings us much good". Whilding spoke of "the Tyndale tradition and of its continuing, though possibly in a different form".

Off the mark quickly

The "different form" began to appear immediately at his first Deacons' Meeting, where he suggested having "slow soft music played while the bread and the wine were distributed at Communion... a long discussion followed... to some this was a distraction, while to others a very definite help, much appreciated... Perhaps it would help if the bread and wine were taken together... music might be played during the distribution, and then complete silence for prayer". Further discussion was postponed to the next meeting. Bill Whilding also suggested that the church magazine, known to everyone as "the leaflet", be larger so as to include news and activities at Tyndale, information on the World Church and an article by the minister. It was decided to experiment with this. At the same meeting, Braille hymn books were ordered, paid for partly by money already collected by the choir. At the same time the name of the bank account was to be changed from Tyndale Chapel to Tyndale Baptist Church. At the April church meeting – the annual meeting – the Finance Report for 1950 showed a balance of only £6, and the Secretary's report a membership of 250, a net loss of 14.

Returning to the matter of communion, the deacons, and later the Church Meeting, "unanimously agreed that after the bread had been distributed all should partake together, the same order being observed for the wine". The music question was left in abeyance "because opinion was divided, and no vote was taken". Change, but not at the price of unity! At the May Church Meeting he asked for support for the choir; announced the start of an Enquirers' Class; and asked that "we should join more heartily in the 'Amens' at the end of the prayers. He himself found this helpful". (A year later a sung "Amen" was introduced at the end of hymns, the "Amen" at the close of the Benediction remaining said.) He agreed to a request for discussion after the Bible Study on Tuesday evenings, and at his suggestion, a time of hymn singing after the evening service on the last Sunday of the month began in September. This was "appreciated and helpful". Bill conducted this himself in order to improve the congregational singing; his daughter, Rosemary Cooper, recalls that during worship, if her father thought the congregation could do better, he would call a halt to the singing of the hymn, and a fresh start was made! In October an annual service to

Tyndale lecture hall used for services after the bombing of the sanctuary in 1940

commemorate William Tyndale was instigated, and an experiment for the organist to play "very softly while the offertory prayer was offered" began.

From the induction through to the end of the year, the minister's letter in the church magazine centred largely on the three themes of proclamation, personal relationships and prayer, always emphasising togetherness with God and togetherness with each other. In August 1951, Bill and Joyce Whilding issued an invitation to church and congregation to visit them in their home to get better acquainted.

> But we also want the people of Tyndale to know one another. There is, of course, a limit to intimate friendships, but we ought to be aware of each other's existence, and concerned about each other's welfare. A true church is a fellowship... there is ample evidence of this spirit at Tyndale, and we want to encourage it.

There would be a series of eight "At Homes", grouping people alphabetically, from September through to March.

Whilding proposed to welcome new deacons at the December communion service, when "all Deacons should sit at the Communion Table". This would have been a formidable array, but yet another way to foster togetherness and team spirit. Sadly, Harry Taylor would be missing, having died the previous month. The church had lost its Life Deacon, but recognised immediately that

> there are two members who have been in membership since 1886 whom we should delight to honour by offering them to become life deacons – Miss C. A. Culross and Miss D. F. Glover. The proposition was carried by long and loud acclamation.

The new year, 1952, began with the minister suggesting a special Deacons' Meeting to consider the spiritual life of the church. In September 1952, 39 people from Tyndale travelled to Bill Whilding's home church at Fownhope, Hereford, where he had served as lay pastor for five years before going to college, for a thanksgiving service for "a liberally redecorated Chapel and Manse". He recalled the start of his ministry at the age of eighteen when he voluntarily took a service for an absent preacher; also "the faithful few who had the courage to make it possible for him to go on to Rawdon College, and so set him on his way".

Towards rebuilding

The national go-ahead for re-building blitzed churches had been announced in November 1949, and Tyndale had immediately appointed Eustace Button as architect. In March 1951, the church also decided that any stained-glass windows in the re-built church were to be by Arnold Robinson whose work had been destroyed in the bombing. By February of 1952, all church building had slowed down, so that "now that there was no chance of rebuilding the new church at present"; nevertheless the architect deemed repairs to the church tower, saved in the blitz, should go ahead. These were claimed as war damage. It was about this time that baptismal services in the ruins ceased because of fears regarding the safety of the old church walls. In

April 1952, the first meeting of the Building Sub-Committee reported that Button was making good progress with the plans. However, Harry Taylor "gave a word of warning that we must not be overconfident that a [building] licence would be granted, but that we must be ready", and repeated references by Whilding in the magazine expressed his and the church's frustration.

After six months of uncertainty, in August the Licences to Build Committee confirmed Tyndale's priority on the list of Free Churches to be rebuilt, Redland Park now being second. Tyndale's costings to the Ministry of Works amounted to £33,500. Relief came with the letter from Button dated 18th November 1952 stating "that on that day he had received a building licence in the sum of £36,850 for the rebuilding of Tyndale Baptist Church". The money from the War Damage Commission would prove to constitute 83% of the rebuilding costs, the church finding the rest.

At the November church meeting, Bill Whilding put forward four principles he thought should now be followed: "to build a spiritual church was of far greater importance than to erect a building; that we should build a worthy church; that there should be bold giving; and that we should go forward in faith". He concluded the meeting by reading Malachi 3 v 10, "Bring the full tithes into the storehouse, that there may be food in my house; and thereby put me to the test, says the Lord of hosts, if I will not open the windows of heaven for you and pour down for you an overflowing blessing". Sub-committees set up included Building, Heating, Windows, Chairs & All Woodwork, Furnishing, Housekeeping, Garden, Outside the Church, Opening of the Church, and Book of Remembrance.

The contract for the new church was awarded to Messrs Stone & Co Ltd. Originally, a large vestry and new Children's Church were planned, but the War Damage Commission determined the new church had to be on the old foundations, using as much of the old structure as possible. This meant that more space would have to be given over to seating than first thought, for Tyndale's congregation had been steadily growing since Whilding's arrival. By May 1953, this growth in numbers produced a seating problem in the lecture hall, and the deacons urged that something be done immediately to relieve congestion, especially on Sunday mornings. To make space, the platform was replaced by a smaller, lower rostrum for the communion table, the pulpit moved to the side, and a sectional platform made for use when necessary. The communion table was new, partly paid for by the War Damage Commission, the rest from an anonymous donor. It was dedicated in memory of Mr and Mrs Edward Sargent as was the former table lost by enemy action. The alterations to the lecture hall cost three times the original estimate, and were an unpleasant reminder of rapidly rising prices in post-war Britain.

The treasurer reported that general giving had not risen in proportion to the increased congregation. Among the deacons, some thought the debt on the manse should be cleared before going forward, or should the two funds be merged? The Finance Committee was charged with making further recommendations. In the meantime it was decided to place an immediate order for an organ from Rushworth and Dreaper, who said a year before that they would need three years to build it. However, now the order could be met in 18 months. The kind and price of organ would be decided later. (Eventually it was decided it would be an "extension" organ, one that could be added to subsequently if desired.) Notice was also received from the Town Clerk that he had agreed to the removal of the static water tank in the ruins of the old church. This had been installed after the bombing to help with local fire-fighting. What could be more appropriate than a Baptist church housing such a huge amount of water!

Beyond Tyndale

In all these domestic church arrangements, Tyndale, as usual, did not forget wider concerns. Those new to Tyndale were afforded a special welcome by two appointed deacons on Sunday mornings, in addition to the stewards on duty. Cards were made available for visitors to record their names and addresses. For imparting news locally, new notice boards were erected on the corner of Whiteladies Road and Imperial Road. The front wall was lowered, a corner pillar removed, and a tree cut back to ensure visibility. This was, of course, dealt with by a sub-committee! Tyndale's morning service of Sunday 11th May 1952 was broadcast by the BBC. Tyndale was entitled to six representatives on the Folk House Council. At the end of

1951, the Folk House was "as flourishing as ever, with over 800 members attending classes". Tyndale supported the appointment of a full-time secretary for the Bristol & District Baptist Churches Association which of course had further financial implications. Bill Whilding's obituary records his popularity with other members of the local Ministers' Fraternal and the support he gave to fellow ministers.

Thinking still of the "bigger picture", Whilding urged the church not to let the rebuilding "affect in any way our obligation to the church overseas". Missionaries abroad were, of course, not forgotten – the annual Everybody's Effort in November 1952 was divided, as usual, with two-thirds going to the BMS, and one-third to the Manse and Maintenance Fund. A service to remember Tyndale's friends overseas was arranged for the evening communion in December. On Christmas Day, at a united service with Redland Park at Trinity, a little known and very appropriate carol with the refrain "happy day" was sung by Whilding. In January 1953, Whilding reported on a Bristol Council of Christian Churches' retreat which had considered "equipping Christians to answer the challenge of the World". As a result two classes to consider such matters began at Tyndale. The Annual Church Party in January was "one of the most successful Tyndale has ever had".

New year, new realities

In January 1953, the Finance Committee outlined methods of fund-raising for the new church building. There was also an outstanding debt on the manse of £1,500. Letters were to be sent to all members of the church and congregation, all friends of Tyndale at home and abroad. One of the first donations to the Building Fund was £1, which came with best wishes and greetings from Herr Falkenhauer, pastor of the Lutheran church in Hanover. Through a Bristol Council of Churches link, he had visited Tyndale the week before, speaking at the evening service and Tuesday prayer meeting "with power and sincerity, his presence much appreciated and his fellowship valued". In April, a Gift Day at the manse raised £676 for the Manse Fund Appeal, leaving £620 outstanding. Copies of the church accounts were printed for church members' understanding. In May, the

City Engineer approved the rebuilding plans, "subject to Tyndale agreeing to the widening of Whiteladies Road at some future date", which would mean the pavement coming up to the front porch. Fortunately that proviso has never been invoked! The Finance Committee further recommended that in September – the anniversary of the first Sunday services in 1868 – a service of prayer and praise be held in the ruins or the garden, followed by a meeting to inform the church of the exact amount required for reconstruction.

National reconstruction: the "New Elizabethan Age", children, young people and men

The Festival of Britain in 1951 pointed people's thinking very much toward the future. The accession of the young Queen Elizabeth II in 1952 reinforced this forward-thinking mentality. On the Sunday following the death of King George VI, Whilding

> most helpfully led the congregation in conspicuously able fashion, and at an early point in the morning service included the children. In the evening, speaking more of the new reign opening up under Queen Elizabeth, he urged the young people to support her and the nation in loving God and serving their fellows.

Now Coronation fever swept the land, although overshadowed for Tyndale by the death of Miss Culross. "The flagstaff on the tower was in place, and the Union Flag was ready. Dr Dakin was ready to lead a service of prayer on the eve of the Coronation, assisted by some of the young people." On the Friday before the Coronation, Tyndale hosted a tea for the mothers of the neighbourhood and their children, and on the Sunday before, the Sunday School staged a Coronation Pageant. This was arranged to help the children understand the spiritual significance of the great day, and the meaning of the symbols used in the ceremony, replicas of which had been made by members of the church. For the great day itself, 2nd June 1953, 50 ticket-holders gathered in the church parlour to watch events on a television lent by Harold Hockey.

However, in June Sunday School superintendent F. W. Matthews made

> a somewhat sombre statement to the church meeting. Referring to
> the great social changes that had come over the life of the district
> served by the church he told of the efforts made by the staff of the
> Sunday School to meet them. We heard of great difficulty securing
> teachers: fourteen persons had been invited to become teachers
> all of whom for one reason or another had refused.

In March 1952, eighteen young people from Tyndale gathered for a day
conference where Bill Whilding addressed them on the life of the church
and the part they could play in it. Young people's leaders Rowland Brake
and Geoffrey Fisher declared the meeting "most encouraging". Only a few
years before, Tyndale Youth Fellowship was struggling with only seven or
eight young people, but by the autumn of 1952 "our young people have been
greatly encouraged by many new members and inspired by Mr Whilding's
regular meeting with them week by week". Maybe this was something to do
with table tennis! In March, young people from St John's, Redland Park,
Trinity and Tyndale took part in the annual competition for the Whiteladies
Road Churches Cup. The "Tyffers" team, the holders, played Trinity
Methodist in the final, the deciding match being between Revd F. Hickling
and Bill Whilding. "A great shout went up as Mr Whilding won by two
games to love". Difficulty in dealing with a very wide age-range in youth
work, led to a decision that those aged from 14 to 20 would continue as
TYF, under the leadership of John Bodey, assisted by Ruth Bodey; those 21
and over would form the William Tyndale Society, to be led by Rowland
Brake. The purpose of the new Society was "study, fellowship and service".
Each would have its own programme, but would be under one committee.

At the start of 1953 it was decided that the children too young for Children's
Church would be looked after in the Ladies Vestry, which was decorated by
the Tyndale Youth Fellowship. "Kindergarten Church" opened on Sunday
19th April 1953, allowing the mothers to remain in the morning service. To
help in the work with students, lists were drawn up, easier for the Edward
Terrill Society and University, but more difficult for Redland Teachers'
Training College with which links were not so close. Bill Whilding was
himself involved as the Free Church Chaplain to the University of Bristol.

A new member, Tom Dunning, took over as Sunday School Superintendent on the resignation of Matthews in September 1953. In July 1954 general appreciation was expressed of the evening service for the Sunday School Anniversary. Whilding had planned it as "a little less formal than normal". He wondered if this kind of pattern could be employed more often. In September 1954, 15 boys from a Muller home in Westbury Park began to attend the Sunday School, and later another 15 from a Muller home in Hampton Park also came, two men from Tyndale offering themselves as additional teachers. In December 1955, Tom Dunning moved away from Bristol, and for a short time Leslie Tweeney was Superintendent. Concern for work among boys had been expressed in the autumn of 1953. Work among girls had always been easier and more successful. Discussion centred on whether this should be uniformed, or more of a boys' club. Eventually a boys' club was started under the leadership of Tom Dunning.

With regard to men's work, Whilding recognised that

> the next few years will make big demands upon our financial, physical and spiritual resources, and I particularly wish to meet with the men of our Church to help them towards a growing confidence in God's resources.

A conference held in October 1953 at the Methodist Guest House in Weston-super-Mare, "away from business and mundane affairs", proved an enriching experience with "inspiring leadership" from Bill Whilding. Recommendations were made: that it be made easier to approach the minister about spiritual concerns after a service; useful books be available to lend at the minister's discretion; training be given whereby all members should feel themselves to be ministers; and each magazine should contain, as well as the minister's letter, a short article on a basic Christian truth. Another conference was held the following year, with the theme "A New Church: what is required of me?"

"Reconstruction" of the music at Tyndale

In the same month that Bill Whilding had been inducted, Walter Maker's successor as organist was appointed. Whilding was quick to meet with

View through the trusses of the new roof during the rebuilding

Reginald Flew, a deacon of Buckingham Baptist Church, who was appointed Tyndale's organist in March 1954. At the same time Miss Balmond, well-known singing teacher, offered to build a new choir. Both these appointments led to long and happy associations with Tyndale, and a dependable quality of music at the heart of the church's life and worship. Also, by September 1954, the price of a new organ had risen considerably owing to an increase in wages at Rushworth & Dreaper.

The rebuilding work begins

Rebuilding began on 15th September 1953, five months later than first planned. On September 29th (the day before the anniversary of the opening of the church in 1868)

> A large company met in front of the Church to give praise to God...
> and pray for His guidance in all we should attempt. Mr Whilding
> led us in prayer, read verses from Haggai chapter 2, where the

> prophet asks "Who of you is left who saw this house in its former glory? But now be strong for my spirit has not left you, so I will fill this house with glory, and the splendour of this latter house will be greater than the glory of the former house and I will make this a place of peace" and as his voice rang out above the noise of the traffic we were confident all would be able to hear in the new building! ... we closed by singing "In heavenly abiding" and re-dedicated ourselves to follow "wherever He shall guide us".

At the meeting that followed in the lecture hall, each person received a copy of the Tyndale Report laying out the church finances. Harold Bodey, as chairman of the finance committee, outlined the plan to raise the £5,000 needed. Dr Dakin then spoke of the importance of the site of the church as a strategic spot for attracting folk in all walks of life. Letters and promise forms had gone out to friends of Tyndale, near and far. Whilding announced that December 1st (the day before the anniversary of the bombing in 1940) was fixed for receipt of donations towards the target of £5,000. At 8 p.m. on that day, a large gathering heard Whilding announce that gifts and promises received that day amounted to £7,765.

> In stunned silence Mr Whilding reminded us the church was free from financial anxiety... to help others at home and abroad. After the singing of a hymn Mr Whilding closed this wonderful occasion in a beautiful prayer of thanksgiving and rededication. Thus closed one of the most thrilling days in the life of the Church.

At this time Whilding began a time for silent prayer on Monday mornings from 7.45 – 8.30 a.m. "to pray for the men working on the building of the new Church and for the church which is to be". He hoped that members and others would stop for a while on the way to work. This proved, he said, to be "a real experience of worship" and despite its time, continued to within two months of the opening.

Making everything ready

As 1955 began, and Tyndale's building was nearly complete, Redland Park were planning to lay their foundation stone. It was testament to the long and close association of the two churches that Bill Whilding was invited to offer the dedication prayer at the stone-laying on Easter Sunday.

Dorothy Porteous caught the mood of the lead-up to the awaited day anticipated for fifteen long years:

> Demolition began and no beauty remained – nothing but dust and rubble and it seemed impossible that we should ever see a new church arise. Did you see the stone masons picking over the old stones, discarding some, and finding others they could use again? Did you see the man putting the mosaic into the baptistry piece by piece? Did you see the men laying the floor, on their hands and knees, fitting one block into another, rather like children playing with bricks? Did you see the golden pipes of the organ arrive? Did you know that Mr Woods, Bristol representative of Rushworth and Dreaper's, our organ builders, spent two nights alone in Tyndale before the opening, so that in the silence he could get the organ tuned exactly to the right pitch? What a day when the stained-glass windows arrived and we saw the sun shining through the beautiful colours. What a hive of industry it was, the last week! who polished the floor? – ask the minister and deacons; who dusted the furniture? – ask the ladies; who laid the gravel on the paths? – ask members of William Tyndale Society and again the deacons. And all the time our good caretakers, Mr and Mrs Bracey, went quietly on with their tasks with the utmost courtesy. And we were ready for March 5th.

The new interior

The planning authorities had determined the outside of the new church would resemble the old, blending in with the tower, which survived the Blitz. The greatest difference now outside was the floodlighting, the estimate for which greatly exceeded expectations, so Miss Katherine Robinson made a gift of it to the Church, bringing "great joy to us all". The building was to be lit up only on Saturday and Sunday evenings, but later that year this was also done for all public meetings. On entering the vestibule, the new tablet in memory of Dr Richard Glover was to be in the

The sanctuary of the rebuilt church

middle of the wall facing the entrance doors. The list of ministers was on a side wall in the vestibule. The new room above the entrance porch was to be named after Harold Bodey who had died at the end of 1954.

On entering the sanctuary, the new interior looked quite different from the old. Gone was the heavy-look of the stonework, the new arches having clean lines with no decoration. Gone was the stone pulpit, replaced by one of wood. The greatest change was the replacement of the brooding mock-Gothic hammer-beam roof of dark wood by a simple, modern lower ceiling. Access to the space above the false ceiling was via the spiral staircase in the tower, to the clock room on the second floor which houses the clock mechanism itself. Instead of proceeding upward to the bell chamber, a small wooden door leads across the roof to another door, giving access to the space above the false ceiling. This is a sight few people, even from Tyndale, have ever seen. The space is immense, and from the doorway a metal walkway stretches to left and right, turning to run the length of the church immediately above the sanctuary's ceiling lights. It is from here that the bulbs are changed.

In the sanctuary below, the cross on the rear wall was in gilt, the same colour as the organ pipes, and was an anonymous gift. It was thought a risk worth taking to paint the walls "so they would look so much more beautiful for the opening". Colour came mainly from the stained-glass windows, and the deep blue curtains around the bottom of the apse behind the baptistry, with a cross in the centre. The new organ was installed in the north transept, with the south transept given over to much-needed seating. A great deal of discussion had taken place whether there should be pews, as before, or chairs. There was a post-war shortage of suitable timber for pews, but the extra cost of £2,000 made the decision in favour of chairs an easy one. 500 chairs were ordered "for the present" but at some later date the desirability of replacing these by pews should be considered. Also, twelve hearing aids stations were installed at various points in the sanctuary.

The communion table stood in the apse, where the floor level was higher than that of the sanctuary, accessed by wooden steps. The pulpit Bible was donated by a Mr Glassco of Montreal, Canada, in memory of his wife, Gladys (née Hoffman) who had attended Tyndale as a girl. The lectern Bible was a gift from Tyndale's daughter church at Westbury On Trym. The mosaic in the new baptistry was a memorial to Mrs Bryan, and the hymn-board was given by the builders, Messrs Stone & Co. A decision had been made that no memorial plaques were to placed on any of the furniture in the new church.

The Re-opening

The minister and deacons issued the following statement:

> We, the Minister and Deacons, wish to place on record our unbounded gratitude to Almighty God, who has inspired and led us in the rebuilding of our Church and its opening on March 5th 1955. Throughout all our planning and its fulfilment we have been deeply conscious of Divine Guidance. The enterprise has called for human thought and energy, but through the Holy Spirit, God has

given a oneness of mind and motive; difficulties have been
wonderfully overcome; and throughout the Re-Opening Services
we were aware of a Presence which hallowed all that was said and
done to the smallest details. The experience was commented on by
many. We, therefore, look to the future with confidence, believing
that if we seek only to be the instruments of God's purposes, we
shall see many more signs of His glory among us.

497 ticket-holders attended the opening service on the afternoon of
Saturday 5th March 1955. 409 attended the tea which followed in the Drill
Hall, opposite the BBC, the only near-by hall big enough, and 395 were
present at the evening celebration at Tyndale. 100 chairs were hired from
the Folk House. The Press were notified that "there could be no posing for
photographs either before or after the Opening ceremony" and the AA and
RAC were asked to deal with cars!

*Bill Whilding, Dorothy Glover and Robert Glover (son of T.
R. Glover) at the re-opening [Bristol Evening Post]*

Katherine Robinson's offer for someone to take a film outside the church at the opening was gratefully accepted. The opening service was relayed to the lecture hall by Cranbrook Radio Ltd. The Revd Basil Sims of Redland Park lent his "recording machine" and Tom Dunning found a friend who could operate it. No collections made on Saturday, and at the Sunday services the offerings were for Bristol's Baptist Extension Fund. The Secretary was charged with the responsibility of ensuring there were sufficient communion glasses. Large numbers in the new church raised the question of whether fire extinguishers were necessary, the decision being left to the church officers. 1,500 good-quality brochures provided those attending with details of the weekend's events, with a separate leaflet for the Children's Service on Sunday afternoon.

Dorothy Porteous describes the two days of celebrations, beginning on the Saturday outside the front of the Church:

> There was a great company, but no confusion, for every detail had been considered and our stewards were magnificent. Not everybody could see the doors opened nor hear Miss Glover's speech which ended with the words, "May God, the God and Father of our Lord Jesus Christ, meet every soul that enters these doors. Thanks be to God." But everybody could hear and will not forget the thrill of Mr Whilding's voice as he announced from the back of the Church, "Praise, my soul, the King of Heaven" – the procession started up the aisle. I wanted it to go on and on. How the soprano voices went soaring up and up, and what good bass the men gave us. It was moving to hear Mr Bryan's dear familiar voice as he dedicated this new church to God, and what a challenge Dr Dakin gave us, and how gracious and kindly and inspiring were the words of Bishop Cockin. We had a great family tea-party, didn't we? And all sorts of complimentary things were said. It was noticeable how each one who had had the responsibility passed on the honour to the next. We congratulated our architect and the builders. The day was, as we had hoped, a demonstration of our unity in Christ.

On Sunday I went into the church quite early, when it was empty and quiet. The echoes of the opening day were in every part. Did I say empty? God was there before any of us, waiting for His people to come again to worship. And a great day we had. I heard more than one say, "Mr Whilding was at the top of his form". He was indeed inspired. How many of you saw the boys and girls lined up in Chertsey Road on Sunday afternoon, and heard the band of the Sea Cadets? It was a grand sight and an unforgettable experience. The boys' eyes fairly danced with glee, and their legs kept in time with the drums as they marched behind this splendid band, and the girls were no less thrilled. We marched all around to Whiteladies Road and the police held up the traffic and the band played us into the Church. Then there was a hush. The atmosphere caught the children at once. Do you realise some of them had never worshipped in a real church before? It was a receptive congregation for Mr Litt and he was more than equal to it.

As the day drew to a close, and as the candidates came forward for baptism, gradually the church building seemed to fade from my mind. We were a great company standing on holy ground as Mr Whilding had reminded us in the morning, and we were encompassed by a great cloud of witnesses, as he had told us in his evening sermon. Those who had gone before, those of today standing before the baptistry, and all of us witnessing their confession of faith, were joined together with those who follow after.

The March church meeting heard that "many expressions of appreciation regarding our opening ceremonies had been received", including about Reginald Flew's fine playing of the organ, and Brian Kemp's splendid work as Chief Steward. Starting two weeks later, the Church was open during the day for the many people who wished to see it.

What next?

"Now that all the activity preceding the re-opening was over, what next?" This was the question Bill Whilding asked in the church magazine:

> We have not arrived at an end, but at a new beginning. When a goal is material it is not difficult to define, as for example the building of our Church. When the aim is not material it is harder to put into words. Shall we set out to increase our membership or fill our Church? I hope we shall do both, but there is something much more fundamental for each of us to do. Well expressed by Saint Paul in Galatians 1:15, 16 – God "called me by His grace to reveal His Son in me"... Could there be a higher or worthier objective? – that when people have anything to do with us they find Christ, that when people come into the life of our Church they know they are in touch with Him. What a remarkable idea – Christ incarnate in us!

A week after the opening, 13th March, saw the dedication of the Harold Bodey Room, with the Bodey family, the deacons and a number of young people present. Bill Whilding moved the Tuesday evening meeting to the Harold Bodey Room, "a much better setting than the church". Later in the year he was anxious to make this meeting "more alive and vital" to the life of the church, with a shorter address, and the four Tuesdays of the month centring on Tyndale's work at home, overseas, then world events, and the fourth, the church meeting. He appealed for more deacons to be present, which received a sympathetic response. A year later the Tuesday meetings were being held in the south transept. There was a great deal of thought and discussion among the deacons about the character of Tuesday evenings. Should it be a midweek service rather than "free prayer", which was deemed by some "difficult" at such a meeting.

In April, Whilding read the deacons an article by F. C. Bryan about the church service and the communion being considered as one. The complete break before the communion, allowing non-members to leave would be replaced by a slight pause, with the deacons taking their places at the table during the last hymn. This was introduced on Sunday 5th June 1955. The bread and wine were still to be taken when received.

Following the Church Meeting in May, the members adjourned to the lecture hall to see the film of the Opening Service which had been gifted to the church by Katherine Robinson. She also arranged for photographs to be taken of the inside of the church. These furnished a request from the Baptist Union for photographs of the church for a Baptist World Alliance Exhibition.

As well as the spiritual life of the church, there were the hard financial facts to be considered. A year before the Opening, the treasurer, Ronald Cooke, had been able to say in his annual statement "what a pleasure it was to present such a satisfactory report". But what would be cost of having larger premises again? Would a full-time caretaker be needed? Just before the Opening, the estimated expenditure for 1955 was compared to the previous four years. There was a need for increased giving. The envelope system was under-used, and only a few subscriptions were covenanted. Expenses for running the church would be £8 per week more than the previous year. Fees to visiting preachers were reduced. However, over-subscription to the Building Fund allowed the remaining debt on the manse of £700 to be cleared.

After the Opening, Bill Whilding and the deacons outlined a scheme to further improve the lecture hall. Much time and effort, mainly by Ron Cooper, aided by the Fuel Committee was spent researching what would be the most cost-effective method of a new heating system. The organ in the hall had been a gift from Harry L. Taylor in memory of his first wife, and his family were happy for it to be given to Counterslip Baptist for their church hall. The missionary board was moved from the lecture hall to the church vestibule, where the board recording past ministers had also been placed. The Book of Remembrance, bound by the Oxford University Press, was a gift from the minister and the deacons, and would record past Tyndaleans if their family wished. It began with a record of the beginnings of the church, the writing paid for by Dorothy Glover. A small oak table to take the Book of Remembrance and the Offertory was given in memory of former minister, G. W. Harte by Mrs Harte and her daughter Ruth. This was made to match the Communion Table. A Book of Record for dedications, baptisms and marriages was the gift of H. G. Taylor and his daughters in memory of his wife. There was "a desire on the part of many" for prayer stools or mats, but lack of space made their use impracticable. In June 1955, the plaque gifted by Westbury was placed on the north side wall of the new porch. It had been generally felt that "there should be some wording on a stone to mark the fact that two churches had arisen from the ashes of the old". Westbury's original wording had been revised slightly at Tyndale's request "as we did not want the words 'generosity of Tyndale' to appear".

In November 1955, the church welcomed Michael Dennison from the Baptist College as student minister, settling the following summer to the pastorate of Victoria Park in south Bristol. Also in November 1955,

> thanks to the William Tyndale Society, we had a very special evening of Music in the Church which included three scenes from Mendelssohn's Elijah sung by Mr Whilding. How well interpreted they were and how they stirred one, with all the richness of art and true emotion. A final thrill was to have Roger Whilding beside his father singing the part of the servant.

For some time work had been proceeding on the garden, and now "owing to the generosity of some friends" the whole scheme was able to be put into operation. Two garden seats in memory of Spencer Murch, former church secretary, were the gift of Mrs Murch and her daughter.

In the new year of 1956 the deacons discussed the spiritual side of the church's work, "wonderfully led by Mr Whilding". Bill Whilding let it be known that he would welcome a small group to meet with him each week to think over the subject of the sermon for the following Sunday. To make new worshippers feel welcome, it was suggested that a social hour be held once a month after the evening service.

The Finance Report for the previous year showed an adverse balance. However, there was a good number of members, and covenants and envelopes were not being used to full effect. Ronald Cooke had been treasurer eight years and would serve another ten. The auditors passed these comments: "the accounts were so clear and Mr Cooke's explanations so adequate, there were few questions". They expressed their "unbounded admiration for his complete accuracy, good writing and clear figures, and the masterly way the various accounts had been kept throughout the year, so that the auditing of them was a pleasure". The amount received from War Damage and covenanted gifts, if all were realised, would give a balance in hand of £700. The fact that an extension organ had been installed meant that extra stops could now be fitted that made soft playing possible during prayer, one of the things that Whilding looked for to enhance worship when he first arrived.

In October 1956, Leslie Tweeney was unable to continue as Sunday School Superintendent. The teachers expressed their wish that Michael Smith be invited to lead them. He had arrived at Tyndale a year before, as Tom Dunning was leaving, having come from university to teach at Henbury School. Whilding was "impressed by Mr Smith's whole-hearted desire to give himself to the work, and the plans he had for the School. How fortunate we were because Mr Smith had the right training and possessed the right spirit". Michael Smith was granted permission for the School to meet in the Church itself first on Sundays at 3 p.m. and then move to classes in the lecture hall.

Tyndale's influence far and wide: broadcast services

Being ideally placed near the BBC, several services had already been broadcast from Tyndale in the post-war years. A member of Tyndale acted as liaison officer with BBC as the church's feedback on religious broadcasting. The morning service of the 11th May 1952 was broadcast – "the service was part of our Tyndale Missionary Sunday and a cogent forceful missionary sermon was preached by our minster on 'Be ye reconciled to God'". A service was broadcast to the South Atlantic area on 6th December 1953, and later to North America. The service was heard by friends of Tyndale in Brazil, the Congo and Northern Rhodesia. In February 1955 Bill Whilding took Children's Hour Prayers on the four Wednesdays in February. The morning service of Sunday 2nd October was also broadcast.

The arrival of television brought a new dimension, with the morning service on Sunday 18th March 1956 broadcast live on BBC television. Whilding reflected on the experience:

> There may have been some who wondered whether it was fitting to televise a service at all, whether it could be a real act of worship or only a performance, as the rehearsal seemed mechanical. But on Sunday morning... [our] efforts and gifts were taken hold of by the Holy Spirit, and fashioned into a demonstration of spiritual power. I have received by letter and telephone many appreciations; people felt they were actually with us at worship. We have seen what this wonderful medium, television, can do – an experience we shall never forget.

The evening service of Sunday 9th December was broadcast overseas, led by Dr Champion.

A Good Samaritan Ministry

In October 1951 the Lord Mayor asked for support for a house the city had purchased – Tudor Lodge in Ashley Down Road – for eleven Displaced Persons, the legacy of the 1939–45 War. "The letter was received most sympathetically, and Mr and Mrs Stride were asked to interest themselves in this work". Arthur Stride subsequently became treasurer to the organising committee, and Tyndale committed itself to sponsor one refugee for seven years at an annual cost of £120. In a month £75 was raised and furniture and bedding donated. Such was Tyndale's response that by January 1952 one of the large rooms in the house was named the Tyndale Room, then with two female occupants, one a Latvian and the other a Hungarian, with a third expected. Five refugees recently arrived from the continent were among those invited to a united Christmas party by the Women's Fellowship and the Wives' Comradeship. Entertainment included a "solo beautifully rendered by Mr Whilding". A year later, recent arrivals brought the number to eight. One male refugee had found work, and his daughter was being educated at Badminton School free of charge. Tyndale's support for Tudor Lodge brings to mind the church's running of the "Belgian House" during the First World War, and the sponsorship of several "Tyndale beds" in a mission hospital in India. In January 1954 there were still 8 million Second World War displaced persons living in camps across Europe. In the autumn of 1956, Tyndale supported a national campaign to raise hundreds of thousands of pounds to help such refugees.

The January 1954 issue of the BMS newsletter in India contained an article headed "Everybody's Effort with acknowledgement to Tyndale Baptist Church, Bristol" which tells of a united money-raising effort by all the Baptist churches in Delhi. This resulted in a gratifying financial result, but also enjoyed was "a heightened sense of fellowship which brought joy and happiness to every church in the city".

March 1955 saw a tribute paid to a "20-year-old kindness" at Hawthorn Baptist Church, Pontypridd by the Revd Richard Jones, present at Tyndale's re-opening a week before. He said that "in the days of unemployment this church had taken a deep interest in Pontypridd, particularly Hawthorn. They stretched out a helping hand to us in our time of need". As a symbol of "the tie that binds", the Hawthorn congregation sang the hymns sung in Tyndale at the re-opening service. Jones concluded,

> as I came out of the church that afternoon into the wan March sunlight I looked up at the building – at the clock in the tower which never stopped through all the blitz – and I felt a great thankfulness that this church of the Good Samaritan, itself once wounded, was now whole again.

Church Relations

Tyndale had long associations with Redland Park Congregational and Trinity Methodist churches further up Whiteladies Road. The three Sunday Schools shared important occasions.

In June 1955 the ecumenical grouping of churches brought this "Whiteladies Road Group" to an end. Redland Park, Trinity Methodist, Downs Congregational and Tyndale now joined Christ Church, St Paul's, Victoria Methodist and Buckingham Baptist churches in an expanded Clifton Group. Each church in turn would host a quarterly united worship service on the evening of its ordinary week-night service. The first of these at Tyndale came in December 1955 with

> Congregationalists, Methodists, members of the Church of England and Baptists worshipping together, with real fellowship at the social half-hour after the service. This surely is the way Church union will grow.

For some years, at the request of the Baptist Itinerant Society, Tyndale had a special partnership with the church at Woollard in the Chew Valley, seven miles from Bristol. Tyndale provided a preacher one Sunday a month, but as the congregation had reduced to only two the partnership came to an end at the beginning of 1956.

Cotham Grove Baptists opened their rebuilt church on Saturday 5th May 1956. In a short speech Katherine Gotch Robinson said:

> I have heard about Cotham Grove since I was a little girl. My Robinson grandfather, Elisha, had laid the foundation stone. My grandfather, Dr Gotch, used to come here. My mother and father were married here; and one of my aunts, Mrs Dickie, taught in the Sunday School for many years.

However the rebuilt church closed in the mid 1960s, its congregation joining with the Methodist and Congregationalists to form Christ Church, Cotham, which itself sadly closed in 1989, the Baptist remnant of the congregation joining Tyndale, a possibility first mooted in 1935.

In July 1956, Bill Whilding sailed on the Queen Mary to the United States of America for a seven-week tour of churches of various denominations in a number of states. This was by invitation of the Baptist Union, under the auspices of the British Council of Churches. It was during this visit that he suffered a bad fall which left him in considerable pain, the cause of his going into hospital on his return to England. On his "Welcome Home" gathering on 11th September he gave an account of his travels, including references to the divisions in American society. A specially-written welcome song was sung by a special choir.

"Everybody's Effort" in November 1956 raised £630 (two-thirds to BMS). J. W. Brighton, standing in for the minister who was indisposed, named two people in particular for their work: Joyce Whilding, whom he called "our assistant minister", and Mrs Cooke "our secretary, whose efficiency and care, attention to detail and unrelaxing effort were in admiration of us all".

Tyndale week by week

The weekly pattern of church activities that all the above fitted round during Bill Whilding's pastorate was:

Sunday	Worship at 11 a.m. and 6.30 p.m.; communion on 1st Sunday morning and 3rd Sunday evening; Children's Church in the morning and Sunday School in the afternoon; the Club (founded originally for women in domestic service) for tea before the evening service; Young People's Fellowship (14–21 years) after the evening service
Monday	Monthly Women's Fellowship in the afternoon; Young People's Fellowship in the evening (from September 1955)
Tuesday	Evening Prayer and Bible Study, giving way to Church Meeting once a month
Wednesday	Brownies; Boys' Club; William Tyndale Society (over 21s), with the first Wednesday being Whilding's "Padre's Night"
Thursday	Wives Comradeship (for young wives and mothers) in the afternoon (fortnightly); The Club in the evening; Choir Practice
Friday	Guides; Men's Contact Club (Whiteladies Road churches), fortnightly at Redland Park; monthly Deacons' Meeting
Saturday	Prayer Meeting (from September 1954, at first led by Burdett)

In the spring of 1957 the Women's Fellowship and the Wives Comradeship amalgamated. They had for years held various joint meetings, one being the Christmas Party to which the Folk House and Tudor Lodge were regularly invited. Regular annual events included a Church Party in January; the

Church AGM in March (reporting for the previous calendar year); BU Home Work Sunday; BMS deputation and Missionary Supper in May; Sunday School Anniversary in July; Church and Congregation Social in September (to begin the church's year of activities); and Everybody's Effort in November (two-thirds of the proceeds going to the BMS, one third to church fabric). There were annual services for the Edward Terrill Society, the Bristol Guild of the Handicapped, and the Collegiate School.

Lawrence Weston Baptist Church

Two or three months after Tyndale's re-opening, the Bristol Association was considering selling land it had purchased from the city council to build a church in Lawrence Weston, where a very large council estate was under construction, because of the difficulty of raising funds. Tyndale expressed their concern, and authorised Bill Whilding to ask the appropriate committee "to take no step toward selling the land which had been allotted for building at Lawrence Weston until we at Tyndale had had a chance to see if we could pledge adequate support". Having launched its daughter church at Westbury on its way, seen through its own rebuilding and facing greatly increased costs, it was natural to think Tyndale might now, for a while at least, concentrate on its own affairs.

However, when the Association invited Tyndale "to explore the possibilities at Lawrence Weston", Bill Whilding said how keenly he felt "this work to be a call to us at Tyndale". Dr Champion, who had succeeded Dr Dakin at the Baptist College in October 1953, expressed his willingness to co-operate in the work if undertaken and that the Baptist College students also would help in visiting and taking services. "It was obvious that the whole mind of the meeting was in tune with the idea of this adventure" and a unanimous decision was taken "to explore the position with a view to accepting responsibility for the work".

The Lawrence Weston Committee, appointed by the deacons, first met on 24th October 1955 at the home of Mr and Mrs Nicholson. Mr Hares was elected secretary, and in his report to the Church Meeting, said how sure and right it seemed to go ahead and establish a church at Lawrence Weston. The Sunday School of 180–200 pupils had been going for 6 years, but it was not certain it could go on meeting at Kings Weston House.

Tyndale's Ron Cooper had started to draw up plans, and had explained them to the committee. At the November Church Meeting in 1955, Tyndale unanimously resolved that "we pledge ourselves to assume the responsibility of the work at Lawrence Weston and the founding of a church there on the site already available". Application was made to the Baptist Union to be put on the list for financial assistance as an initial pastorate. The Lawrence Weston estate numbered 2,000 homes, with another 1,000 planned. By the following May, however, Sunday School numbers were falling because it was meeting a long way from the estate.

Serious fears about the suitability of the site for building were overcome, Ron Cooper drew up plans for a church building, two small halls, with offices and other rooms. Including furniture, heating and lighting, this was costed at £17,500. £1,000 had already been covenanted and appeals were planned. Space for a manse was set aside, should it be needed later. Because of the urgent need for housing the Sunday School, the building needed to prioritise that function. At the same time it was crucial that no heavy debt be incurred. However, Lawrence Weston was in a queue for help from the Baptist Union Home Work Fund for an Initial Pastorate Grant, and even then such special help would only be for three years. Dr Champion would arrange a team of students to assist. A Lawrence Weston Finance Committee was set up, and appeals made to all connected and interested at

Lawrence Weston Baptist Church

Tyndale and Lawrence Weston, and to all 6,000 members of Baptist churches in Bristol, and businesses in Lawrence Weston and Avonmouth. By October, total costs had risen to a staggering £25,000. As visitors from Tyndale reported "how impressed and delighted" they were with all they found at the Sunday School, it was agreed to go ahead with the school room at a cost of £13,000, leaving the building of a church proper to a later date, and plans for the building of the Sunday School were passed by Christmas of 1956.

Tragedy hits church and family

Bill Whilding was absent from the October Deacons' Meeting, "still out of action and having such a bad time" due to a slipped disc. He returned to chair the Deacons' Meeting in December. But that would be his last, for tragically Bill Whilding died during a routine operation on 28th December 1956, aged only 44 years. Dorothy Porteous wrote

> January 2nd was a sad grey day, and yet just at the end of the service, the sun came shining through the south [Tyndale] window, lighting up the great bank of flowers, especially the golden cross of flowers, and it spoke to us of hope... and we knew even in our sadness that all was well.
>
> May he not have spoken to us in vain – may God be glorified through us.

The W. E. Whilding Memorial Fund was set up to honour his commitment to found a church at Lawrence Weston. The Gift Day on 3rd May 1957 brought the total to date to £4,793, enabling building to begin immediately.

Let two people speak who knew Bill Whilding well – firstly, Dr Arthur Dakin from his funeral address:

> He was essentially a GOOD man. People soon got to know him; to know him was to like him; and to know him well was to love him. There was nothing intricate, complicated or abstruse about him. His was a plain, open nature that the common man could understand. He had room in his heart for all sorts of folk; he could

be at home with all sorts of folks. He had gifts – he could preach and pray and sing. But his gifts didn't separate him from his fellows; rather they the more endeared him to them. I have no hesitation in saying that the secret of his success – and his life was a success – was a very real and devoted attachment to Jesus Christ. It was a pleasure to talk with him about the Lord Jesus... and there again was the simplicity – a simple faith, not sentimentalism; a strong love based on conviction and insight.

Mr Whilding always preached as he believed, that the Gospel was for everyone, that everyone needed the Gospel. He believed in... and valued the visible church, the church on earth – in THIS church. He believed in the after life... of eternal splendour, and because he believed that, he could minister to us at the deepest levels of our personality. On Sunday morning when I met her before the service, Dorothy Glover – shrewd as ever – said to me, "He ministered to me", and she put an emphasis on the word "ministered" which conveyed her meaning. He ministered in the things of Christianity. He could be sociable, jovial and happy-go-lucky, crack a joke, but that doesn't make a minister. But he was a minister and he could speak to our state – he could lift us to the presence of the Great Physician that we might me healed. He had no ambition but that. He sought no honours for himself, but always for Christ. His call to Tyndale raised him in our denomination above his fellow ministers, but he never had the slightest consciousness of that. One little intimacy I would like to reveal. When he sat in his plaster jacket he said to one of his visitors that one of the blessings of the illness was that it was allowing him to enjoy his own family. An interesting side-light on a minister's life.

Bill Whilding saw Tyndale through a time of physical reconstruction, spiritual renewal, and continual readjustment to a rapidly changing world. On his own admission, the reconstruction of the people of Tyndale was far more important than the building that housed them. He had said that numbers alone will not make a church, yet the figures speak for themselves – three months before Bill Whilding arrived, Tyndale's membership was

250; this had risen to 280 by the end of 1953; and a year before his death stood at 326. Always looking to the spiritual, with a vision which looked beyond buildings and meetings to the people whose lives could be empowered by God, and who could in turn transform the lives of their fellow men and women, F. C. Bryan had spoken of the times as the "Era of the Common Man", whilst his successor spoke of the need for everyday saints even more than great leaders, himself having "the common touch" in relating well to people and inspiring them.

Dorothy Porteous shares her memories:

> The first time Mr Whilding preached for us in the Lecture Hall before he was our minister, I remember looking up in the middle of a hymn, hearing the new, rich baritone voice, and finding him completely absorbed. He was singing and praying every word. His eyes never left the book. This was a real and vital part of the worship he was leading. I knew in that moment this man was a gift of God to us.

All agreed that in proclamation he was a powerful preacher, much praised. In prayer he was sincere and inspirational. In personal relationships, warm and friendly. Dorothy Porteous further writes:

> The last words our minister wrote to us as a Church were these: "A happy New Year. May God be glorified through you"... he could not have been more inspired, or written anything more stirring and challenging for us. He wanted joy and happiness for us, he believed in it, he was so full of joy himself. He wanted even more that God should be glorified through us. And, as always, he practised what he preached, in this case unconsciously. Mr Whilding has gone in and out among us for five-and-a-half years, and even in his serious moments we have known that he had an inward and abiding joy; and we have seen in a remarkable way God being glorified in him. Has anyone caught him in an off moment, on a bad day? Whenever we met him, whenever we heard him speak, whether from pulpit, platform or in private conversation, the radiance of his personality shone through his words, glorifying God.

At the Welcome Tea in March 1951, Bill Whilding had said he had no fears for the future, quoting God's assurance to Moses, "Certainly I will be with thee". If by "thee" he was thinking of himself, then God certainly was with him. But if by "thee" he was thinking of the church – of Tyndale in its ongoing work – then this was also certainly true, but all the more so because of his own spirituality, leadership, example and personality. At the beginning of his ministry he had "made it clear that Christ calls us to no easy task and that hard demands will be made upon us by the gospel he will preach and our own deeper fellowship with Christ". The hymn "Christ of the upward way" was sung at his induction, and the line "Like one who would not bring less than his best" seems entirely appropriate to sum up Bill Whilding, the man and the minister. His was a short ministry but one with a long-lasting impact.

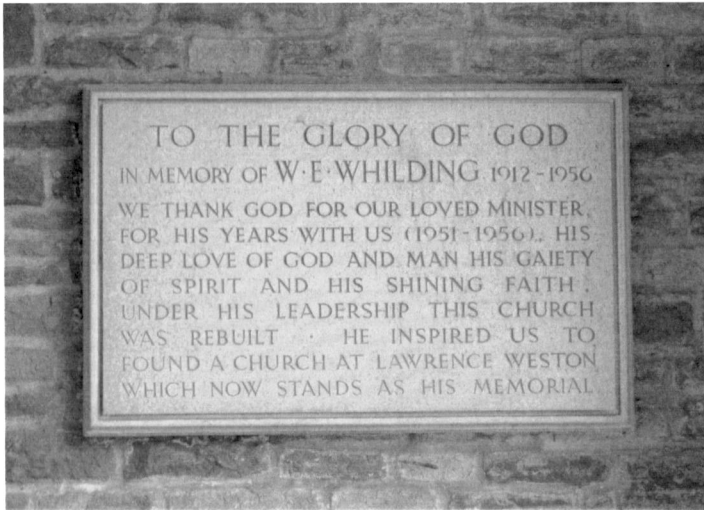

Memorial tablet to Bill Whilding in the Tyndale porch

Chapter 12.

History in Stained Glass

John Briggs

Nobody entering Tyndale can ignore its splendid array of stained glass, all associated in one way or another with the craftsmanship of the Robinson family. Arnold Wathen Robinson (1888–1955), son of Mr and Mrs Kossuth Robinson, was educated at Clifton College and the Royal West of England Academy, and afterwards served an apprenticeship with the distinguished Roman Catholic artist, Christopher Whall. Back in Bristol he worked for the well-established stained-glass manufacturers, Joseph Bell and Son, becoming first a director of the company and then, from 1923, its owner. As part owner from 1918 he also brought new life to the rather flagging Bristol Guild of Applied Art (The Guild), originally founded to implement William Morris' Arts and Crafts idea in Bristol. Arnold Robinson's work in a very graphic way enables a large number of west-country churches to tell the gospel story, and nowhere is this more clearly seen than in Tyndale. Tellingly in his obituary for Robinson, who served for many years as a deacon of Tyndale, F. C. Bryan writes of the great themes depicted in his art highlighting the theme of the Redemption of Man represented in the windows in the apse:

> The preacher from the pulpit cannot see it, but may he never forget it. In Adam and Eve we see ourselves, with Moses we are thankful for the law, yet owning that we cannot keep it; in the Incarnation we rejoice, for God has come down to us sinful men; in the cross we know our sins atoned for and forgiven, in the Resurrection we are made "more than conquerors through him who loved us".

There are basically three sets of windows in the church – those in the apse illustrating what biblical scholars call "Heilsgeschichte", a German term for "salvation history". Here the Bible story is seen as describing God's redemptive work in the Biblical record with its focus on the life, death and resurrection of Jesus Christ. The first double window depicts the act of creation and then the giving of the Law. On the extreme left in the creation window there are found Adam and Eve with Cain and Abel in front of a tree in whose branches there is a coiled snake. Adam is busy digging and Eve holds in her hands what appears to be some sort of utensil. Plants grow at their feet but already a good creation has been spoilt and humankind is struggling with a sin-infected universe. Paired with this window is that which demonstrates the gift of the Law given through Moses. Here the law-giver with a halo around his head emitting rays of light stands on a rocky path which leads above the clouds to Mount Sinai, boldly displaying the God-given scroll containing rules as to how humankind should conduct itself. Significantly, broken tablets lie at Moses' feet on account of the Israelites' sin in worshipping the golden calf (Exodus 32–34). Biblical scholars are anxious to stress that the law does not stand alone but rather is part of God's covenant with his people: "I will be your God and you shall be my people". In the giving of the law there is as much grace as demand and that is why this is the second scene depicted in the apse.

In the middle window are depicted the incarnation and ministry of Jesus. Mary is seen here kneeling before the Christ child who is lying in a crib at the very bottom of the window – so low had he come to be with his people. In the middle ground stands Joseph holding a lantern; to the side is seen the head of a cow. Above them is an angel holding a cross-shaped scroll on which is inscribed the word "Emmanuel", interpreting the birth of Jesus as "God with us", but already the potential cost of that process is shown with a suggestion of a cross. The other half of this window depicts Jesus teaching from a boat with hand uplifted in blessing. Two disciples are attentive, one standing and one kneeling, but a third man appears to be running away, indicating differing responses to Jesus even during his lifetime.

The third pair of windows focus on the crucifixion and resurrection. Crucifixes are rarely found in Baptist churches, given the argument that Christ is risen, the representation is normally of an empty cross but here the representation of what happened at Calvary is central to the story being told. A nail-pierced Christ, scantily clad is shown pinned to a cross which is

Apse windows

depicted with some continuity with the tree that appears in the creation window, and which bears the inscription "INRI", the common abbreviation for "Iesus Nazarenus, Rex Iudaeorum" or "Jesus of Nazareth, King of the Jews". In the rear middle ground is depicted the city of Jerusalem and at the foot of the window there are three soldiers playing dice, who provide continuity with the final window which depicts the Risen Christ which again has three Roman soldiers in the foreground, this time asleep. Dominating the window is a large figure of Christ, dressed in a white robe with a golden outer garment but still showing his wounded hands and feet. He dwarfs the empty tomb which He has left behind and beside Him we see a young tree starting to grow. The salvation story is complete – a broken world is giving way to the fruits of a new creation.

Whilst these windows were designed by Arnold Robinson they were not executed by him but, because of his age, by artists at the North Dean Studio near High Wycombe where his son, Geoffrey Robinson, also a stained glass window artist, was working. For example, Geoffrey himself cut the glass for Adam and Eve and for Christ preaching from the boat, but the execution of the whole sequence was under the direction of Patrick Reyntiens, who collaborated with John Piper in producing the great baptismal window in Coventry Cathedral.

If the windows in the apse are concerned with the message of the Bible, those in the transepts reflect Christian history, focusing first on the life of locally-born (near Wotton under Edge in South Gloucestershire) William Tyndale (c. 1494–1536), which is of particular importance since it is after him that this church is named. Tyndale's fame is well established as one of the earliest translators of the Bible into English, but that achievement, as well as his suspected association with continental reformers, made him the object of hostility from the leaders of the English church, who did all they could to prevent the spread of his translation, buying up copies of his New Testament only to have them burnt. No less a person than Sir Thomas More denounced Tyndale's scriptures as heresy, and Tyndale himself as "worse than Luther", "a hell-hound in the kennel of the devil".

Tyndale's years of relatively safe and peaceful study in Antwerp, working on further translations, came to an end in May 1535 when a debauched young Englishman named Henry Phillips, anxious for cash, betrayed Tyndale to the imperial authorities, who imprisoned him in Vilvorde Castle on the outskirts of Brussels, where he was to remain incarcerated for the next sixteen months. During this time he was tried by the Inquisition and condemned as a heretic in August 1536. In October he was brought out to an open space outside the castle where a stake surrounded by brushwood had been prepared. Tyndale was not burnt alive, as, out of respect for his work as a scholar, he was strangled first before his body was burnt. Foxe records that his last words were "Lord, open the King of England's eyes". And indeed Tyndale's martyrdom was not in vain, for John Rogers, chaplain to the English merchants in Antwerp, assembled an English text of the Bible using Tyndale's translation wherever that was available and Coverdale's where it was not, and this, printed in Antwerp, appeared in England, with the inscription "Set forth with the King's most gracious license" at the foot of the title page. However as the name of a convicted heretic Tyndale's could not appear in the title, so the Matthew's Bible was launched in 1537, named after two of Tyndale's disciples, one named Thomas, and the other, Matthew. The 1,500 copies imported into England were swiftly sold, leading to the preparation of the Great Bible of 1539, a copy of which was required by law to be placed in every parish church in England. In such a way Tyndale's prayer at the beginning of his translation work almost came true: "If God spare my life, ere many years I will cause a boy that drives the plough to know more of the Scripture, than the pope does". The Bible was indeed made available to plough-boys but at the cost of Tyndale's life.

In the south transept is a later version of a window Arnold Robinson had undertaken at the end of the First World War for the old Baptist College in Woodland Road, donated by his aunt, Katherine Robinson, in memory of her father, Dr F. W. Gotch, one-time president of the College, in part to celebrate his contribution to the Revised Version of the English Bible published in 1885. In the church's window (see the frontispiece, page 2) a figure of Tyndale holding a Bible takes centre place surrounded by eight subsidiary images illustrating Tyndale's life and mission. At the top left is reference to his life in Little Sodbury. Following his graduating BA from Magdalen Hall, Oxford in 1512 and being ordained priest in London in April 1515, he returned to Gloucestershire to become tutor to the children of Sir John Walsh. It is suggested that left him the time and facilities to embark on the preparation of an English translation of the New Testament, so beginning to implement his conviction that he had a vocation to make the New Testament widely available to Englishmen using the new technology of printing. Surmounting the scene is a depiction of a town or castle conspicuously set high up on a hill for all to see, and beneath this is written out the plough-boy text. Below this, Tyndale is seen in conversation with a priest with Little Sodbury manor in the background. The next panel to the right shows Tyndale exercising a wider ministry preaching on College Green in Bristol with the tower of the cathedral appearing in the background. A mixed crowd listen to what Tyndale has to say including a shepherd with his crook and children seated on the grass. The third scene on the top row is set beneath the symbol of an open book – the scriptures readily available for all to consult. Below, a printer is at work with a ready supply of paper on the table being watched by Tyndale with a completed testament in his hands. Incorporated in the picture is the name of Peter Quentel who was Tyndale's printer in Cologne where Tyndale had taken refuge because of threatened persecution in England; the whole scene is labelled "Printing the New Testament".

On the left in the second row, Tyndale is depicted about to board a ship carrying precious sheets of paper. A sailor is in process of adjusting the rigging, clearly underlining the importance of cross-channel trading in the supply of the scriptures to English readers. The title is "Saving Half-printed Sheets". By contrast the scene on the right hand side is of Bishop Cuthbert Tunstall, the Bishop of London, preaching at St Paul's. Below him on the ground, a pile of New Testaments are in process of being burnt with a naked flame rising to the skies – what are the congregation to make of the contrast between sermon and action? The divergence between left and right at this level, between creating and protecting and destruction, is clear to see.

The three scenes across the bottom spell out the cost to Tyndale of his pioneering work: betrayal, imprisonment and the stake. Thus at the bottom left we have the wretched Henry Phillips betraying the peaceable Tyndale to the imperial police armed with a variety of weapons. The middle scene is of Tyndale's castle prison with the night sky visible through the barred window, showing Tyndale sitting at a table with a book propped up in front of him transcribing text into another book. "Tyndale works in Prison" is the description, though historians are not sure that this happened because of the close scrutiny that the forces of the inquisition exercised over him, and the lack of any evidence that his request for a lamp was ever granted, though John Foxe says he converted "his keeper, the keeper's daughter and others in the household". The final scene depicts the burning of Tyndale's body, the fire well-stoked with one flame ascending heavenwards, with the accurate description "Tyndale's body is burned". Across the bottom of the window is written "As a city set on a hill cannot be hid even so the light of Christ's gospel may not be hid as though it pertained to some holy persons only" which now explains why the little cartouche of the city on a hill appears in the top left hand corner.

The window in the north transept features John Bunyan's *Pilgrim's Progress*. Accordingly what is depicted here is the Christian journey, as Bunyan saw it, though like Tyndale, for conscience sake, he suffered from imprisonment for 16 years in Bedford gaol. As with Tyndale a Bunyan window is particularly appropriate for this church whilst Bunyan believed in believers' baptism, he also wrote in one of his books,

John Bunyan, north transept

"Differences in Judgment About Water Baptism [should be] No Bar to Communion", and this is the churchmanship of Tyndale, namely that whilst it practises believers' baptism, membership is open to all who acknowledge Jesus Christ as their Lord and Saviour. In the centre of this window Bunyan stands carrying a copy of the *Pilgrim's Progress* and what appears to be a hammer which may refer to his background as a tinker or tinsmith. The legend below simply reads, "JOHN BUNYAN, 1628–88". Not surprisingly this window should be read from the bottom upwards tracing Christian's travel from the terrors of the City of Destruction to join angels in the joys of the Celestial City, and this is explained by the words across the bottom: "As I slept I dreamed a dream". The story starts with Christian, whose former name was Grace-less, engrossed in reading a book which is clearly the Bible, leaving the City of Destruction under a banner posing the question "What must I do to be saved?" which contrasts with the message below, "Graceless leaves the City of Destruction", and in the background there is the city with the word "Destruction" on one of the buildings though this is partially hidden. In the next scene Christian is rescued from the dangers of the quagmire which has engulfed him up to his thighs by a handsome youth, called "Help" in Bunyan's allegory, with the slogan written out: "The Name of the Slough was Despond". The dangers of the journey are not over for in the background it is seen that Christian's path leads on to a formidable wall with firmly closed gates. The next scene is ambiguously entitled "He comes to a place somewhat ascending" but it clearly witnesses a change of fortune as Christian falls upon his knees before the cross, and as he does so the straps of the burden on his back snap apart and the burden rolls away, and there is no ambiguity about the banner overhead "He hath given me life by His Death".

Notwithstanding this new life that Christian has received, the two middle panels emphasis the ongoing dangers of the journey. On the left Christian, with sword raised, encounters the fearful green monster, Appolyon, who appears in Revelation chapter 9 as an angelic Destroyer, which is how he is depicted by Bunyan in this window. Whilst Appolyon throws an arrow, Christian deploys his sword firmly stabbing the wild beast; above is the motto, "Appolyon straddled the Whole Way", in other words there was no avoiding him and Christian did well to stand his ground until the wounded fiend flew away. In the panel on the opposite side Christian encounters two hungry lions on either side of his path, under the crisp pronouncement: "Difficulty is Behind; Fear is Before". Their appearance is threatening enough to have caused some travellers to turn back on their journey. What is not, quite properly, shown in the window, for Christian did not see this, is that the lions are in fact chained and are therefore only an apparent threat and not a real one.

The final three images are interlinked and appear above the text: "Blessed are they that do his commandments that they may enter in through the gates of the city". On the left are angelic figures with trumpets matched by similar figures on the right hand side together bearing the message: "Holy, Holy, Holy is the Lord". This is the end of Christian's journey with "trumpets sounding for him on the other side". In the centre panel two more fully defined angelic figures help pilgrims, each bearing their scroll of assurance, out of a river setting them on a path clearly lit with a great beam of light which leads them up to the gates of the city, through orchards of fruit, to the celestial city beyond. In this way both transept figures are united by the prospect of arriving at the heavenly city.

The third set of windows link the Biblical scene to the world of the rebuilt Tyndale, a world only slowly recovering from the worst that human conflict had inflicted on humankind. On the south wall of the nave are two memorial windows – the first is a replacement for the war memorial window in the old church and features St John the Divine and David. It is very personal in that Arnold Robinson is here commemorating the loss of his three brothers and three other church members: only members of the church are commemorated in this window, several more who were associated with the church, the Mission or the Sunday School or were not members at the time of their death, are not commemorated. In the book of Revelation John writes a lot about spiritual warfare and the end of all conflicts, whilst David is the country lad who overcomes the forces threatening the life of the people of Israel. St John is seen looking to the right with pen in hand as if checking names on a scroll, whilst above him in a separate cartouche is the dove of peace, beneath which is inscribed the text from Revelation 21 v 4 that spells out the end of all wars: "And there shall be no more death", but beneath John's feet another small roundel

War memorial, south wall of the nave

depicts St Michael slaying the dragon reflecting the story recorded in Revelation 12. In the second window the dove of peace is paralleled by a very small representation of Noah's ark, presumably symbolising the salvation secured for Noah and his family. David is a ruddy lad still holding his sling and the pouch in which the stones from the brook were carried. At his feet is the large head of a fallen Goliath, and above is the text from Psalm 37 v 15 "Their sword shall enter their own heart". A small circular window at the bottom shows David slaying a lion. Although this was executed in 1955 it confines its concern to the 1914–18 war, listing three of Kossuth Robinson's sons: Second Lieutenant Edward Colston Robinson, Lance Corporal Clifford Kossuth Robinson and Lieutenant Geoffrey Wathen Robinson, together with Arnold St John Leger Kerry, Cyril Prewett and Alfred Rutherford Whitewright. Geoffrey Robinson writes that his father's intention in executing this window was to illustrate the principle of "Triumph through Adversity".

Adjacent to the War Memorial window is a further window executed in 1960 by Geoffrey and Daphne Robinson as a tribute to their father's work, given to the church by Arnold Robinson's widow, Constance, and her children, Geoffrey and Daphne. This window features John the Baptist as the last of the prophets and Stephen as the first martyr of the Christian church. A bearded John the Baptist, belted and clad in camel's hair, holds his left arm and hand out in blessing, a gesture emphasised by being repeated in a lozenge above, whilst his left hand holds a staff which carries a banner inscribed, "Ecce, agnus dei", which is visually suggested by a lamb gently standing at John's feet, all reminding the viewer of how John first greeted Jesus, "Behold, the Lamb of God". Over the whole display is written the text, "He shall baptize you with the Holy Ghost", and at the bottom in a separate lozenge John is shown baptising Jesus, and below that there is a plain inscription reading "Arnold Wathen Robinson, Master Glass Painter, 1888–1955", although it has been argued that the real tribute to Arnold Robinson's work is to be found in his windows themselves, including those in Tyndale and those to be found in the nave of Bristol Cathedral.

The second frame shows a youthful or angelic Stephen wearing cream, green and blue drapes, holding a palm (the symbol of martyrdom) in his right hand and a Bible in his left. Reflecting Acts chapter 7, he is said to be

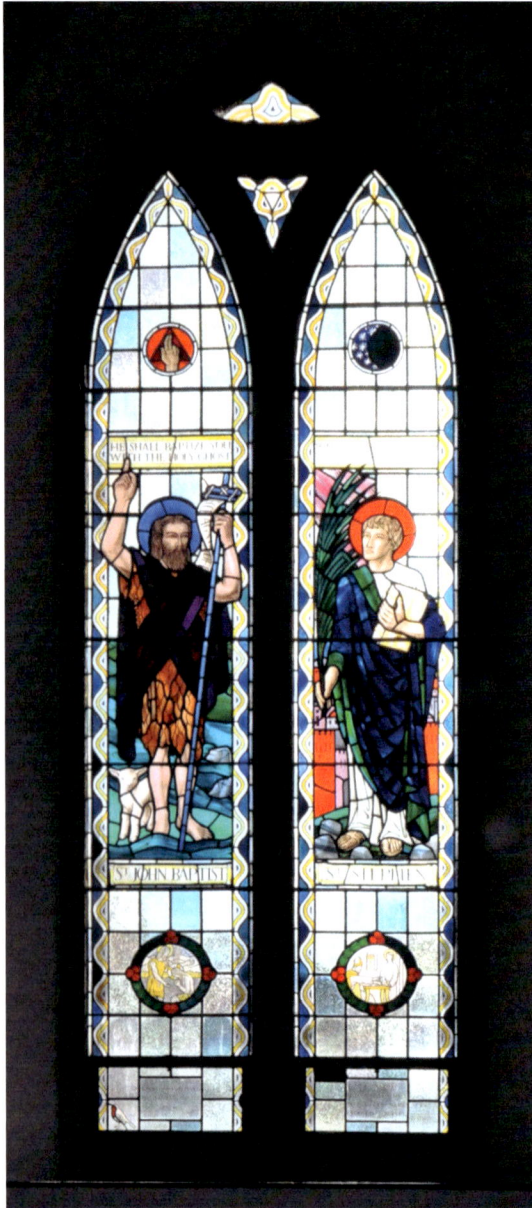

John the Baptist and Stephen, south wall of the nave

preaching a sermon tracing the faithfulness of God in contrast to the continued disobedience and infidelity of the Jewish people – "a stiff-necked people with uncircumcised hearts and ears". Such preaching caused the rabble to take up stones with which they pilloried the fearless Stephen to death, and such stones can be seen at Stephen's feet whilst in the background is Jerusalem, its towers and walls red with anger, underlining its bloody crime against an innocent saint of God. In the roundel at the bottom Stephen is shown appearing before the Sanhedrin and below words from Ecclesiasticus 41 v 13, "A good life hath a few days but a good name endureth for ever". Above Stephen are Luke's words describing Stephen's vision of heaven, "Behold I see the heavens opened, and the Son of Man standing at the right hand of God", which is also said to be represented in the apex of the window where the separation of light and darkness is symbolized.

A second window by Geoffrey Robinson executed in 1970 is situated on the opposite wall. Whilst the donor remains anonymous, the artist entitles the composition, "Sickness and Suffering", which from the Old Testament is seen in the life of Job, and from the Gospels in the woman suffering from an incurable haemorrhage. Both subjects are set under a depiction of symbols of healing, a mortar and pestle in one, and in the other the ancient symbol called a caduceus, consisting of a staff entwined by two snakes over which are set a pair of wings, which is often used as a symbol of healthcare organizations and medical practice. The left-hand panel depicts "My servant Job", set under the text, "Blessed be the name of the Lord", underlining Job's patience and faith, for whatever disaster became him he was still able to praise God. In the window he is depicted as a sick man with shaved head and skin disfigured by boils, surrounded by his three false friends but his face is surrounded by a dramatic shaft of comforting light emanating from the hand of God signifying the Almighty's ongoing care of Job even though his body is assaulted.

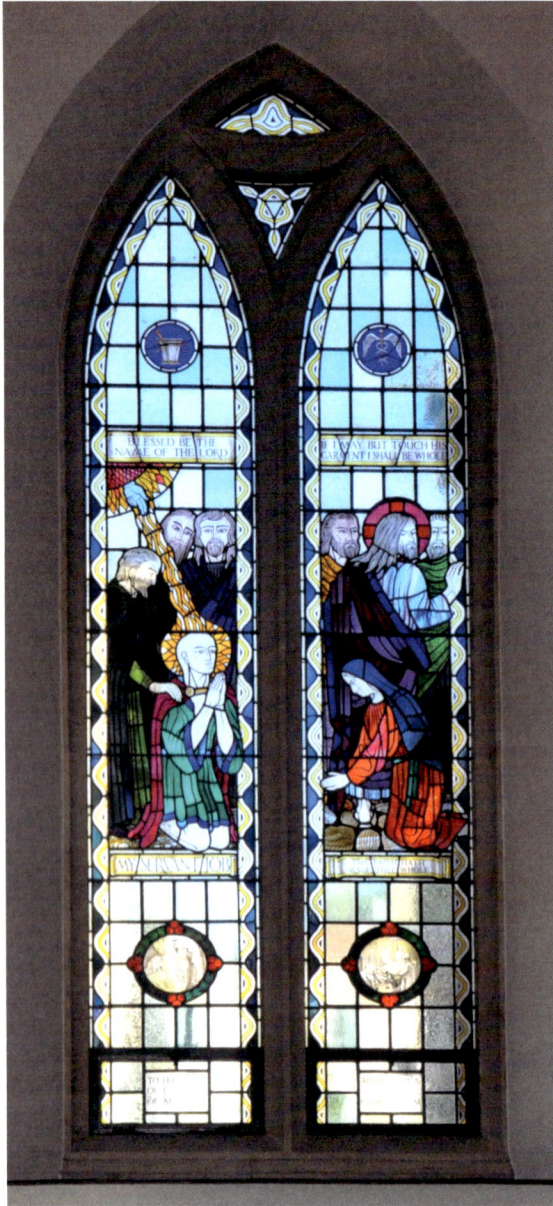

*Job and the woman healed through touching Jesus'
garment, north wall of the nave*

Paralleling Job is the woman who could find no cure for her haemorrhages, who like Job had such great faith that she believed if only she could touch the hem of Jesus' garments she would be healed, so the commanding text, "If I may but touch his garment I shall be made whole". The woman is accordingly shown kneeling doing just that. Jesus is accompanied by two stern-looking disciples who argue that Jesus' question, "Who touched me?" is unreasonable given the crush of the crowd, but Jesus knowing that this was a special contact, says to the woman the words written beneath the image, "Thy faith hath made thee whole". Below the main portraits are two small images reflecting the modern-day medical profession at work, although they are now almost half a century old. On the left nurses attend to a patient receiving a blood transfusion, while the picture on the right is of an operating theatre with an operation in process. At the foot of the window are inscribed the words, "TO THE GLORY OF GOD AND TO ALL WHO THROUGH PAIN AND SUFFERING GIVE GLORY TO HIM". In such a way the faith of God's people from ancient times to the present day, notwithstanding adverse circumstances, is portrayed.

Finally, two much smaller exercises in stained glass are to be found in the vestibule, each dedicated to a Miss Porteous. Coming into the church from the forecourt on the right is to be found a representation of Jesus at his carpenter's bench with saw and timber in his hands demonstrating his youthful skills, a goodly supply of wood shavings on the ground. As Jesus took pains to do his everyday work well, so members of the church are called upon to be workmen never ashamed of the quality of the work they undertake. The motto at the bottom says, "To the glory of God and in loving memory of ELLA MARY PORTEOUS, 1954". Ella Porteous was a devoted member of Tyndale, "dependable as a rock". Of her F. C. Bryan wrote: "The light that was in her illuminated dark places for many a troubled spirit". A unique combination of Martha and Mary, she combined spiritual insight with a readiness to undertake both menial and leadership roles in nearly every aspect of

Ella Porteous, vestibule

church life: the choir, the sewing group, arranging flowers in the sanctuary and then after Sunday services taking them to the sick and those who were confined to their homes with a cheerful greeting reminding them they were not forgotten by their fellow church members. But her special concern was for work with children and young people. Donated by a Mr and Mrs Sandys of Lincolnshire the window was executed by Arnold Robinson and originally graced the walls of the Children's Church where it was unveiled in November 1954.

Dorothy Porteous, vestibule

The theme illustrated in its pair is the children of the world: it shows a group of three children, one white with fair hair, and behind him an African or Caribbean child in a white robe, both of them looking down on a younger bare-chested Asian boy with the inscription "To the Glory of God and in memory of DOROTHY A PORTEOUS". Given her concern for work with children and the worldwide mission of the BMS which she supported so energetically it eloquently illustrates the good relations naturally existing between children of all colours and races, all of whom have a right to receive, whatever circumstances they find themselves in, equal and proper respect from adults. The window was dedicated in early 1981 in honour of one who tirelessly gave her time and energies and substance for the good of Tyndale.

Chapter 13.

Ron Cowley: Continuing Ministry in a Questioning Age

Keith Clements

"You've never had it so good" was the slogan with which Harold Macmillan won the general election in 1959. In purely material terms it could hardly be denied by people of any political persuasion, and the words chimed in well with the national mood of the time. The welfare state was in full swing, post-war austerity was being left behind, living standards were rising, the consumer society was blossoming. Whatever anxieties loomed over the world at large, symbolised by the image of the nuclear mushroom-cloud, at home there was optimism in the air. That was true, for the most part, in the churches too. At any rate there was a measure of confidence which today we may look back upon with some envy. It was not just that church attendance was still relatively high – the steady if slow decline that had begun before the First World War was in fact continuing – so much as the way in which the churches felt they had an accepted and respected place in society, a society which by common consent was founded on Christian values. That consensus was in part a legacy of the Second World War and the widespread belief, even among many who would not call themselves "churchgoers", that the war had been fought and won at great cost for those values, and that Christianity therefore had a right and duty to teach, witness and embody them for the common good. In 1954 Dr Billy Graham led the first of his British evangelistic crusades, three months long, in London amid huge publicity (the final overflow rally at Wembley Stadium was broadcast live on radio and attended by both the Archbishop of Canterbury and the Lord Mayor of London). The broad consensus on religion was codified in the provision of the 1944 Butler Education Act for both religious education and a daily act of Christian worship in schools.

Likewise religion had an assured place in the media, and the voice of Christian conviction was welcome even in secular discussion: the Abbot of Downside and the Methodist Donald Soper, for example, were regular panellists on the BBC's *Any Questions*, while few writers and speakers of any persuasion enjoyed more widespread attention than C. S. Lewis. Christianity was itself enjoying a kind of mini-boom in the never-had-it-so-good society.

Tyndale moving forward – to what?

Tyndale's own rightful share in this mood was of course expressed in the beautiful restoration and rededication of its building in 1955, together with its role in founding the churches at Westbury On Trym and Lawrence Weston. But few at Tyndale or anywhere else could have discerned that this decade was seeing the high summer of Christianity's post-war come-back rather than its springtime. By the mid-1970s English society, Bristol as a city, its churches and among them Tyndale, would all present a rather different picture. Indeed, already in the mid-1950s tremors were being felt from several directions, foreshadowing uncomfortable changes ahead that would end the easy consensus both in the churches and the wider world. In 1956 the "angry young man" walked on stage in John Osborne's play *Look Back in Anger*. Protest was on the way to becoming the style of a new generation. The advancing spread of the media, television especially, into daily life was enormously significant. It was not just that television provided an entertaining alternative to Sunday worship (though of course it did, a familiar complaint in the churches), but more than any other medium it brought, every day of the week, a different world right into people's homes, a world of new imaginings, of challenging views and debate, very different from the orderly ethos of conventional church life where people mostly sat and listened deferentially. "The mid-1950s", argues Adrian Hastings, "can be dated pretty precisely as the end of the age of preaching: people suddenly ceased to think it worthwhile listening to a special preacher". Not of course that preaching as such was finished but, in an age when people were being encouraged to think more for themselves and explore the questions they themselves wished to ask, its place in worship and the expectations that people had of it were changing. A vital factor in all

Tyndale in the 1960s

this was the huge expansion in secondary and higher education. The 1944 Butler Education Act had indeed sought to safeguard the religious element in education, but in promoting the sciences and humanities education overall was not operating on religious presuppositions. It was a religiously neutral if not humanistic affair. Just how far society was moving towards a new kind of consensus on values was signalled in 1960 by the obscenity trial which removed the ban on D. H. Lawrence's novel *Lady Chatterley's Lover*. Freedom of thought, not deference to traditional authority, was becoming the order of the day.

Then came the new wave of satire, and the 1960s youth culture energised especially by pop music, which expressed what young people were wanting for themselves instead of what their elders and betters thought would be good for them. Nor could the churches be insulated from the enquiring mood. In the early 1960s the tide of radical theology and debate swept in, opening up even the most basic questions like the meaning of "God", most famously seen in Bishop John Robinson's *Honest to God* (1963).

The scenery on the wider stage was shifting too. The Suez Crisis of 1956 shocked many people into realizing that, however strong politically and militarily Britannia might still appear to be, she could no longer rule the waves as of old. Former colonies and territories were in any case gaining their independence. "Empire" was becoming "Commonwealth". This called for a re-thinking by the churches, too, of what the missionary enterprise, which had a long and at times questionable relation to western imperialism, now meant in the contemporary world where "new" nations and "younger" churches were calling for equality with those in the West. Moreover that wider world was no longer simply "over there". Immigration, at first especially from the Caribbean, was bringing new ethnic communities into British cities, including Bristol. In 1958 the race riots in Notting Hill, London, showed how Britain was not as tolerant as it often liked to think, and that issues of racial justice had to be faced at home as well as in the Deep South of the USA or in South Africa; and racial issues would be highlighted in Bristol itself during the Bus Boycott of 1963.

In all denominations there were some prophetic minds and voices calling for the churches to face the new challenges. That meant disturbing any complacency, any assumption that the status quo was adequate. New experiments in worship and in ways of relating to daily life and problems in the cities, were under way mainly in the Church of England, but also in some Free Church circles. The ecumenical movement was growing in importance, and a wholly unexpected new vista in inter-church relations opened up when the Second Vatican Council, convened by Pope John XXIII, opened in Rome in late 1962. For their part the Free Churches might still feel reasonably buoyant at the start of the 1960s but, again, among the younger generation were those critically impatient with what they saw as a dangerous complacency overtaking what was still called "Non-conformity" but was now itself far too conformist in its attitudes. Christopher Driver, a young Congregationalist journalist, wrote a book with the disturbing title *A Future for the Free Churches?* published in 1962. Highly critical of what he saw as the prevailing ethos of Free Church individualist piety and preaching, which bore little relation to the needs of people's lives in society, and a too complacent attitude to the need for Christian unity, he particularly highlighted the way in which the pulpit now had to address a far more educated congregation than ever before. The products of Butler 1944 would be wanting far more than pietistic pleasantries and moralising. He concluded:

> If the rising generation in the Free Churches begins to feel that no significant change can be expected in its lifetime, we expose

ourselves to a new stampede out of the chapels, no less injurious
than the one that has already occurred.

A church in the mid-1950s and a minister beginning a pastoral charge at
that time were therefore, perhaps more than they realized, about to step
into a markedly uncertain and challenging phase of their pilgrimage. Some
familiar landmarks were about to fade or disappear, new routes would have
to be assessed and tried. Some problems continued as before. Tyndale's
membership in 1956 stood at 318, by 1976 it would be 220: overall a decline
of about 100 in the course of 20 years. In one sense that tells us very little
except that it was of the same order as that for Baptists as a whole in
England during that time. More important and interesting is the question
of how, regardless of numerical size, a church relates to the issues that bear
upon it from its setting, locally, nationally and internationally. Does it try to
ignore or deny these, retreating into a world of its own? Does it achieve
apparent success by creating a new kind of culture of its own, very
attractive and supportive for those who belong to it but essentially existing
alongside the world without seeking to engage with it and transform it? Or
rather, does it keep its eyes, ears, doors and heart open to that world,
engaging with it in the love of Christ, with all the cost and risk which this
entails?

It is with this perspective that we shall survey some aspects of the life of
Tyndale, for the twenty-year period roughly corresponding to the arrival of
Ronald Cowley as minister in 1958 up to the arrival of Peter Webb in 1975.

Ronald Cowley

Ronald (Ron) Austin Cowley accepted the call to the Tyndale pastorate in
1958. Following the sudden and devastating loss of Bill Whilding, any new
pastor would have been acutely aware of what he would have to bring in
ministering to what was truly, little more than a year after that tragedy, a
whole bereaved community. Ron Cowley not only had the pastoral
sensitivity to match that situation but proved that he had the gifts of mind
and heart to lead the church in facing the new context of uncertainty and
change which, as just described, marked the late 1950s onwards. He came
with fourteen years of ministerial experience behind him in the London

The Revd Ron Cowley

pastorates of Norbury and Bromley; and before that, during the war years, ministerial training at Manchester Baptist College where he had been one of the youngest students on record. Ron Cowley always wore an air of calm, easy affability and thoughtfulness. That gentle demeanour however was attached to a notably athletic frame. In his native Buckinghamshire he had made his name as a soccer player, and during his London years he captained the leading amateur side, Dulwich Hamlet. In fact he was a natural at almost any ball-sport and although by the time he came to Bristol it was the golf-course rather than the rigours of the football pitch that exercised him, any younger minister who rashly invited him for a game of squash was apt quickly to end up exhausted and reeling in amazement as well as defeat. With his sporting instincts, his gift with words and his conversational style he would have made an excellent football commentator, and indeed there were rumours that the BBC were for a time interested in him with just that in mind.

He did not come alone but with his wife, Maureen, and their two sons, Howard and Peter. Maureen, stylish and energetic, was a teacher of drama and dance. During the war she had worked in the highly secret but now famous de-coding operation at Bletchley Park. Between them the Cowleys brought a shared appreciation of how, in church as in any sphere of life, creative leadership involves listening, careful observation, imagination, and encouraging people to discover and use their talents: above all an openness to the wider world, and fostering relationships with others by word and example. What we see in Ron Cowley's sixteen years at Tyndale is a remarkable combination of diligent, close attention to pastoring this local congregation week by week, with a breadth of vision that embraced other churches in the immediate locality of Tyndale and in Bristol as a whole, both Baptists and others, together with the wider Baptist and ecumenical worlds. Equally, we see a fellowship of people with diverse gifts, ready to explore new paths in worship and service. Together, pastor and people continued and enhanced still further the Tyndale tradition.

Ron Cowley confessed that it was with some diffidence that he had first considered the call to Tyndale. One can imagine that a "university church", that is, a church with the university on its doorstep and a number of teaching academics in membership, not to mention critically-minded students in the term-time congregation, would be a quite new experience for him especially as he would be expected to be the Baptist chaplain in the university. If so, it was a feature which was to draw out much of the best he had to offer.

While he had a London BD to his name he would never have described himself as a scholar; but he valued scholarship highly and continued to read widely, keeping abreast with whatever output he thought relevant in theology, studies in pastoralia, mission and ecumenism; and often commending in the monthly magazine what he had found valuable. Not only so, but on occasion he asked readers of the magazine for their suggestions on what he should be reading. The minister, in other words, was still a student himself and no doubt this added to his appeal in the student constituency. It also greatly affected both his pulpit style and indeed his sermon preparation too. Roger Newman, assistant minister during 1964–68, says:

> It's interesting that I can't remember a single sermon by Ron –
> perhaps that's how it is for all of us. I do however remember the
> process of producing our sermons, since we had regular periods of
> collaboration when Ron, myself and Philip Lucas, from Lawrence
> Weston, met and hammered out series of sermons on a given
> theme. This must have been quite innovative for its time.

There was indeed here a creative response to the changing expectations of
preaching from the mid-1950s onwards. Ron Cowley was essentially a
pastor, even in the pulpit, and pastoral theology remained his chief
academic interest. In 1973 he was awarded the Bristol MA for his
dissertation "The Concept of Guilt in the writings of St Paul, in the light of
some contemporary psychotherapists". It was the fruit of some ten years'
thinking and study. As he told the Tyndale congregation:

> For most of my ministry I have been interested in the relation of
> theology to psychology which I have felt to be important not only
> as an academic exercise but in the realm of pastoral ministry. It is
> increasingly necessary to relate the Christian Gospel to
> contemporary thought.

Tyndale and Bristol Baptist College

One of the factors making for continuity in Tyndale's life during these years
was its relationship with Bristol Baptist College. From 1916 the college was
Tyndale's nearest Baptist neighbour, having that year relocated from Stokes
Croft to Woodland Road, a few minutes' walk away from the church. In fact,
as has been seen, right from its founding Tyndale had been closely
connected with the College. Richard Glover's service as the College
secretary from 1871 until – long into his retirement – 1919 was but the start
of a long and mutually rewarding relationship. Throughout the course of 76
years (1924–2000) there was at any one time at least one College Principal
(in post or retired) in membership: Arthur Dakin (Principal 1924–53),
Leonard Champion (Principal 1953–72), Morris West (Principal 1972–87),
John Morgan-Wynne (Principal 1987–1994) and Brian Haymes (1994–
2000). As well as being involved – sometimes intensely – in the life of the
church it is notable that three of them played roles at particularly

significant points when the church was in need of counsel and guidance. Arthur Dakin preached the sermon at the tragically poignant memorial service for Bill Whilding; Leonard Champion served as moderator in the ensuing interregnum which led to the call of Ronald Cowley; Morris West served likewise after the departure of Ronald Cowley (1974); and the 2001–2002 interregnum between the ministries of Robert Ellis and Michael Docker was moderated by Ernest Lucas, Vice-Principal of the College. Harry Mowvley became a member at Tyndale on the closure of the church in Cotham Grove and Keith Clements on his appointment as a College tutor in 1977.

A steady stream of students of the college worshipped at Tyndale, perhaps from a variety of motives. According to Roger Newman, in the 1960s the old joke was still standing: "If you're cold on a Sunday evening, go along to Tyndale and sit between two fur coats". But the appeal was not wholly due to proximity and a (physically) warm welcome. Peter West who entered the college in 1965 speaks well for those who wanted both thoughtful preaching and dignity in worship:

> Tyndale satisfied, at least for the time being, two "itches" I then had in my mind:
>
> First was the quest for some good open-minded theology. I had been raised in a Bedfordshire village chapel belonging to the Wesleyan Reform Union (an off-shoot of the Wesleyans that had never found its way back into Methodist Union). That had offered me what I would now call a rather disorganised evangelicalism, with enough loose ends to provide plenty of room for me to think for myself... So, feeling a call to ministry, it appeared that I would be more at home with the Baptists. I had also been reading John Robinson's *Honest to God*, which introduced me to Bonhoeffer, Bultmann and Tillich. When I was interviewed by the Northants Association ministry committee I was foolish enough to mention this. One older ministerial member of the committee apparently said that I clearly had not understood what I was reading. He was probably right. So Tyndale, with Ron Cowley's creative thinking

and preaching, was a good place, along with the College, to discover more.

The second "itch" was that I had begun to appreciate some aspects of Anglo-Catholic worship which I had discovered in a few Parish Churches near to my home village. While Tyndale could in no way be described as "Anglo-Catholic", its sense of worship, with a structure and drama of its own, answered to that need in me very well.

There was one further "itch" that Tyndale, however, could not satisfy. My own experience in the village had shown me that by the 1960s churches were having great difficulty in connecting well with working-class people in modern industrial society. Reading Ted Wickham's *Church and People in an Industrial City* about Sheffield showed me that this was no new problem. That was a question which would have to wait until later.

But I value very much the four years I spent at the College and in contact with Tyndale. It was there, also, that I met Mary Pettis, a student at Redland Teacher Training College. Ron Cowley married us at the end of her course (though only half-way through mine). Now, fifty years later, with four children and nine grand-children, it's clear how good those years at Tyndale were.

The proximity of the college was certainly a benefit to Tyndale. During the 1960s occasional evening lectures by Leonard Champion and tutors Norman Moon and Harry Mowvley were open to all, and from 1972 the college's Lay Training Programme provided regular weekday evening lectures and study groups, and Saturday seminars, on a wide variety of subjects including biblical studies, lay leadership, ethics, broadcasting, and Christian responsibility in industry and ecumenism. In May 1973 Tyndale closed its normal midweek Bible study meetings so that people could attend the college course on "Worship Today".

In turn, during these years Tyndale through its members made a major contribution to the life and work of the college at every level. In the lay training programme, Ron Cowley led a Saturday seminar for deacons, and in 1974 he with Dr John Roberts led a weeknight course on "The Church as a Healing Community". In the teaching of college students, from 1982 Tyndale member Amanda Bratt, a classics graduate, taught in a cheerful and humane way that dread subject in many a new student's life, New Testament Greek. Robert Ellis taught philosophy of religion after Keith Clements left the college staff in 1990, and he served as a College tutor 1995–2001. In the 1980s, pastoral theology classes drew on the medical expertise of Michael Whitfield, and on David Roberts for his experience of parental bereavement. Classes on worship brought in Eric Sharpe, for his knowledge of hymnody, and Pam Fisher from the Tyndale Dance Group. Michael Garnier found himself in an ethics class making the case for Christian pacifism.

Moreover, Tyndale members continued to be involved in the executive and governance sides of the college, in the tradition of Richard Glover as secretary and of Edward Robinson, H. L. Taylor, and Harold Bodey as treasurers: the Revd George Byrt, in his retirement a member of Tyndale from 1965, was college secretary from 1965 to 1975. Ministers of Tyndale almost as a matter of course served on the college committee, as did Derek Parsons, who was a member of the candidates' committee and much involved in personal interviews with prospective students. Michael Docker became chairman of the newly structured Council of Trustees from 1998. During his retirement Geoffrey Fisher gave voluntary assistance in the library, as later did Pauline Roberts and Derek Parsons, whose wife Miriam helped Freda West in the domestic work of the college for several years. Like other churches Tyndale took its turn at hosting the college meetings at the start of the college year, and for many years from the early 1970s each June the church was the regular venue for the students' valedictory service. The Tyndale–College relationship was certainly to the benefit of both.

Students: the Edward Terrill Society and beyond

When F. C. Bryan became minister of Tyndale in 1933 one of his first initiatives, in co-operation with some university students attending Tyndale, had been to found a society for Baptist students. Such societies already in existence at other universities were customarily named after a

Edward Terrill Society, 1952, on the way to Oxford for a meeting of BSF societies

historically eminent Baptist figure, preferably associated with the city or university in question. The Bristol society took the name of Edward Terrill, the Baptist layman of the 17th century whose deed of gift of 1679 made possible the founding of what would become Bristol Baptist College, the oldest Baptist theological college in the world. Twenty-five years later at the start of Ronald Cowley's ministry the society was still flourishing, with a membership of some 40 students, mainly from the university but also including some from Redland Park Teacher Training College, as well as nurses in training. The vast post-war expansion of higher education was presenting university-related churches with new opportunities and challenges for pastoral care, evangelism and Christian nurture, and the student Christian societies whether denominational, inter-denominational, or non-denominational were key to what could be accomplished. The Baptist Union had recognised this as early as 1947 when the Baptist Student Federation (BSF) was formed with the assistance of the Young People's Departments of the BU and the BMS. In BSF the various societies were fully autonomous but linked for purposes of fellowship and mutual support, and joint enterprises such as missions with local churches during the Easter or summer vacation. The annual BSF conference at High Leigh, Hoddesdon, just before Easter became a regular and popular feature.

From the late 1950s through to the 1980s Tyndale continued to take seriously its relations with students. Student matters feature regularly not only in the monthly magazine of the time but in the Deacons' and Church Meeting minutes. The Baptist Union ran a scheme whereby shortly before the start of each new academic year a list of the Baptist societies with contact details of their secretaries or chaplains was published in the *Baptist Times*, so that local churches or their ministers could commend any new students from their fellowship for a welcome on arrival. Without fail, not only did Tyndale and the Edward Terrill Society (ETS) hold a welcome tea meeting for "freshers" each October, but the church meeting was reminded well in advance, as early as June or July each year, what the church's responsibility was towards the new intake (as well of course as the already existing members of the society). Ron Cowley was the recognised Baptist chaplain to the university, and to the ETS in particular.

The ETS had already proved its worth to students coming up to Bristol – and its value as an investment for the Baptist future including Tyndale in particular. Its president in 1951–52 was Michael Smith, and its secretary in 1953–54 was David Roberts, both of them later to become familiar and important figures in Tyndale. The ethos of the ETS a little later, in 1959, is well conveyed by the then secretary, Alison Soddy:

> The Society exists to provide Christian fellowship among students in Bristol. It purposes to provide a background for people to think out the implications of their Faith, and, linked with this, to provide an atmosphere in which people may develop spiritually. We feel, however, that members of the Society should also be aware of the need for taking part in the life of the Church.
>
> The programme of activities is planned with these things in view, and probably the most important items are the Sunday meetings. In the afternoon we have a discussion group in which a variety of topics are discussed informally. This is followed by the evening service when the whole Society normally worships in Tyndale. Our Sunday evening meetings after the service would not be possible

except for the generosity of Tyndale's members, for we have been meeting in members' homes. Here we have discussed Society matters or had talks on various subjects...

Other Society activities include preaching engagements; open meetings, to which we try to invite other students; and a weekly Prayer Meeting. Social activities include some rambles and theatre parties, and visits to Baptist groups in other Universities.

In all these ways we aim to promote a deeper knowledge and following of Jesus Christ.

May I add how indebted we are to you in Tyndale for your welcome and continual interest in us. It is wonderful for us to be able to feel so "At Home" with you, and we are indeed grateful. We also rejoice that Mr Cowley has accepted the post of Chaplain to ETS, and we hope that this will enable us to feel even more at one with you during our stay at the University.

While some changes took place in the weekly programme, this picture of life in ETS remained remarkably consistent over the next twenty years. For many years the "preaching engagements" referred to included, once a year, a Sunday evening service at Tyndale conducted by the ETS. It was however a matter for repeated discussion in Tyndale as to just how closely involved the students should be expected to be in the life of the church itself beyond attending Sunday worship. Tyndale's main role was clearly to provide a welcoming space and an appropriate measure of pastoral care. But just what should that that "welcome" entail? Again and again, we read of requests in the Church Meeting that members volunteer to open their homes to students and it is evident that some members did, and that some students greatly appreciated this. Ron Cowley, however, interestingly remarked at the start of the new academic year in October 1969:

Sometimes [church] members have commented to me that students do not really "get in" to the life of the church here. They come to services, but have their own meetings and we don't really get to know them. No doubt we ought to get to know them better. And yet they belong to an academic community in which they

> study and live and, if they apply themselves, will find opportunity for Christian witness and service. I believe it would be wrong to draw them away from this opportunity.

Ron Cowley clearly gave great care and attention to his pastoral role among the students. This was quickly appreciated at Baptist Union level too. In 1960 he was invited to represent Baptist chaplains in the UK at the third International Conference for Pastors to Students, arranged by the World Student Christian Federation at the Ecumenical Institute at Bossey, Switzerland. Meanwhile ETS itself gave its members an enriching and educative experience at many levels. In addition to its regular weekly programme there were retreats at Weston-super-Mare and student missions to Cowley, Oxford (1965) and Doncaster (1967). ETS continued to be a good training ground for future responsibilities. Two presidents of ETS in the 1960s, Michael Wotton (1960) and John Clark (1964), following study at the Baptist College would go on to give notable service with the BMS in Brazil. Special occasions included ETS hosting a conference in October 1964 with Albert van den Heuvel, youth secretary of the World Council of Churches, who preached at the service in Tyndale on 4th October. In March 1969 permission was requested from the deacons for Tyndale to be one of the Bristol church venues for a 48-hour student sit-in and fast, in protest against world poverty. Permission was granted "so long as proper supervision and control were exercised".

New ministries for a new student world

There were indeed continuities in ETS but the early 1960s also saw significant changes on the pastoral side. Chief among these was the appointment of assistant ministers at Tyndale who were given major student chaplaincy roles both to ETS and the university student community as such. Roger Newman was the first (1964–68), followed by Keith Lamdin (1969–73), Barry Vendy (1974–76), and Ian Millgate (1977–80). Roger Newman's residency – followed by the others – in the university student hall of residence Badock Hall, signified the start of a greater identification with the university student community, not just with Tyndale and those who were members of ETS. This was not a diminution of the significance of

Tyndale but rather an extension of Tyndale's ministry into the secular university constituency. It was also in 1964 that the ETS renamed itself the "Baptist Students' Society" (BapSoc): not a trivial change if the aim was to communicate an identity in a context where names of denominational saints of old counted for little if anything at all.

The year 1968 marked the start of the wave of student protest in Britain as elsewhere. Not all students of course took part in demonstrations against the Vietnam War or in sit-ins against the university authorities, but nevertheless overall a significant change in student attitudes and culture was under way. The age of deference and assumed compliance was over, and any form of ministry to that constituency would have to engage with it on its own terms, not on assumptions brought from outside. Tyndale's new ventures in student chaplaincy were therefore a creative response seeking to understand and identify with the new generation from the inside. Ron Cowley agreed with Keith Lamdin, whose work was supported by a three-year grant from the Baptist Union (BU), that his ministry was primarily to the university, with Tyndale as an adjunct. In due course questions on the continuing financial support of such a ministry began to loom. Could the BU be convinced? Would it answer the scepticism of those Baptist circles which demanded to see signs of successful "evangelistic outreach"? As the last year of Keith Lamdin's ministry approached, a searching discussion about the future of the student chaplaincy took place in the Tyndale Deacons' Meeting in June 1972. The minutes demonstrate just how fully the church was taking on board the newer concept of such a ministry as being a matter of service to the world, not primarily the church seeking to build itself up. Keith Lamdin gave the deacons a full report on what his work involved, and the range of pastoral, counselling and advisory roles he undertook both to individuals (staff as well as students) and to the corporate life of the university: "It could be said that he had a church of some 150 people with whom he is in close contact and a parish of 400". In the discussion a series of deacons spoke about how vital this work was for the future of both society and the church, and how damaging it would be if Tyndale withdrew from it. A question was raised about evangelistic outreach.

> Mr Lamdin said it was a problem to decide if you spent your time with those who were committed or were not. Students these days do not like to commit themselves to anything.

But he stressed the importance of continuity in the work for two or more years at a time. Finally:

> Mr Gareth Jones moved that we open negotiations with the Baptist Union for a grant for continuing with this work and we must look for ways to carry on. We should tell the Baptist Union and local Association and area superintendent that we wish this Christian service to continue and that the essence of Mr Lamdin's report be conveyed to them.

It was carried. That can be noted as a defining moment when Tyndale underlined its commitment to ministry in the world as it is now, not as it was, or was imagined to have been.

A thing of the past?

By this time also there were ecumenical developments in student work. The denominational societies in Bristol formed an Association of Christian Societies (ACS). This was more than just a loose federation on paper. An ACS retreat at Lee Abbey in March 1972 drew 80 students. A number of joint activities appeared in the programmes of the societies and BapSoc was fully involved in these. In 1972 Tyndale had been running with BapSoc a series of small "house groups", and now these were being opened to all ACS members. "The groups have special topics, such as producing some programmes for Radio Bristol, Bible study, worship, and various others". There was also a new magazine produced by some Christians in the University, SPOKE. Within a few years, BapSoc itself disappeared as a name, succeeded by the ugly-sounding but affectionately regarded BURCSOC, the Baptist and United Reformed Church Society, formed out of BapSoc and its student neighbours just up the road at Redland Park. Numbers might diminish but the former ethos was maintained. A highlight of each autumn was the weekend spent at Boxenwood cottage in the Quantocks. Conditions there were somewhat Spartan but for their

Baptist and United Reformed Church Society

combination of fresh country air, times of serious reflection and debate, and riotous fun, those weekends will long be recalled with affection by those who participated.

The kind of student Christian activity represented by ETS, BapSoc and BURCSOC might now be a thing of the past, but former members remain adamant about the value of that experience. It provided a network of friendships which could be both supportive and challenging in the strange new environment of university. It led to a wider appreciation of the varieties of Christian outlook and belief. Those who attended Tyndale (or Redland Park, or both) were privileged to hear preaching of a kind not always enjoyed elsewhere, and to share in worship which uplifted because it also stretched the mind. It encouraged members to discover and develop their own gifts whether in leadership, organisation or lay-preaching. It enabled people to mature in understanding of themselves as they encountered others. It was a most vital part of Tyndale's service over the years. And of course student chaplaincy still continues, on an ecumenical basis – and with Tyndale's strong support.

Chapter 14.

Wider Relationships: Baptist and Ecumenical

Keith Clements

On 25th June 1957 the Tyndale Church Meeting was told that the Baptist church at Downend, on the northern edge of Bristol, had just suffered the destruction of their newly built hall by fire. The meeting immediately resolved to send a letter of sympathy and a cheque for ten guineas (equivalent to about £240 today). Some members asked that more be done, with a collection on the following Sunday. There was evidently at Tyndale an instinctive sense of concern for other Baptist churches, which has to be set against the image which others might have had of it had as an affluent and comfortable church, spared the problems of council estates or isolated villages. Certainly Tyndale wore an affluent image. Recalling his surprise at the start of his time as assistant minister in 1963, Roger Newman says: "I had never been to a Baptist church where a Rolls Royce and a Bentley were a run of the mill experience". Yet what is very apparent during the period 1957–1975 is how actively Tyndale engaged with the whole Baptist scene in Bristol, taking into account also that the Westbury On Trym church had been parented by Tyndale, and the Lawrence Weston cause likewise was taken under Tyndale's wing from 1956 onwards (and the Lawrence Weston pastor was for a number of years counted as an assistant minister at Tyndale).

The benefits of fellowship

Two factors helped to counter any tendencies towards condescending benevolence. For one thing, Tyndale as a church was never quite as financially fortuned as might be imagined from the odd Rolls Royce turning up on Sunday morning. More important, many Tyndale people and its ministers saw that fellowship with others brought real benefits to the church as well as wider opportunities for service. This was seen at several levels. For example the annual Bristol Baptist Eisteddfod, a competitive festival of arts and crafts and music, regularly drew Tyndale entrants and continued until the 1970s. There were regular joint youth events including weekend camps and gatherings, sometimes under the auspices of the Bristol Baptist Association; at other times, it seems, organised more spontaneously by two or more churches with their ministers taking the lead. Peter Hofman has happy memories from the later 1950s of such get-togethers between the youth of Tyndale and the Horfield and Downend churches, and the happy cooperation between Ron Cowley and the ministers of these other two churches, Arthur Liston and Bill Dixon respectively. But underlying it all was a definite understanding that to be the church meant being in solidarity with other churches. In March 1959, in the context of the annual appeal for the Home Work Fund (HWF) – today's Home Mission Fund (HMF) – Ron Cowley highlighted the urgent need for support for ministers on low stipends, and for initial pastorates: "This represents, I am sure, the growing realisation that as Churches we are members one of another." A year later, having pointed to the significance of "mergers" and "strength in unity" in the world of business, he continued:

> Baptists have always tended to stress the independence of the local Church... But sometimes independence has been interpreted as exaggerated individualism, as isolationism, as self-interest which turns a blind eye to the needs of others. Now, I think, it would be accepted by almost all our Churches that a failure to seek fellowship with other Churches would be a serious failure in churchmanship and a disobedience to Him who is the Head of the Church.
>
> It might be preferable to use, not the illustration of mergers but the Biblical principle of the strong helping the weak. Fellowship with other Churches implies the carrying of burdens which others are too weak to shoulder. This we at Tyndale must continue to do. Do you realise that there are over 400 churches which could not afford ministerial oversight without the help of others?

Tyndale gave regular and consistent support to the HWF, observing the annual HWF Sunday, though during this period the annual giving was greatly outmatched by support for the Baptist Missionary Society (BMS). In addition, no doubt, the support given to Lawrence Weston Church was justly counted as giving to "home work" in principle.

The Bristol Baptist Association

The Bristol and District Association of Baptist Churches (to give it its full and proper title) at this time comprised over 70 churches, remarkable in the variety of their membership, size and social setting, covering not only the city of Bristol and its suburbs, together with the city of Bath and the seaside towns of Clevedon, Burnham and Weston-super-Mare, but also the outlying villages of the southern part of Gloucestershire and the northern part of Somerset. The Association existed to promote fellowship and cooperation among Baptists, organising support for the Home Work Fund, overseeing the use of that fund among its churches, and organising joint activities wherever appropriate, not least for young people. The secretary from 1940 was Revd Ernest Durant, succeeded in 1971 by Revd Fred Bacon. Tyndale had a long tradition of participating fully in Association life. As has been seen, it supported well the annual giving to the Home Work Fund. Many members attended the annual spring meetings of the Association, Tyndale taking its regular turn at hosting these two- or three-day events (as in 1958 for instance) while the autumn rally, usually held at the Broadmead Church, was a regular and popular feature in the Tyndale calendar.

The Revd Dr Leonard Champion [Bristol Baptist College]

Leonard Champion was elected President of the Association for 1962–

63. The next Tyndale holder of the office was Ron Cowley (1966–67). It was at this time that some significant changes in the governance of the Association were carried through – very much with Ron Cowley's support and very likely at least partly his initiative. The Association Council would comprise representatives of all member churches. The Council would then elect its committees and sub-committees. Ron Cowley saw this as more than administrative tidying-up. He wanted the Council to be both more representative of all the churches yet at the same time taking on responsibility for the actual decision-making, which hitherto had been left in rather cumbersome fashion to the whole of the annual Assembly. The Association would then be better enabled to fulfil its cooperative aim. Ron Cowley posed the question, why have an Assembly at all? In June 1966, he answered:

> Not, I think, merely to preserve an ancient institution, nor for the sake of fellowship alone, that is, if by fellowship we mean the cheerful, hearty greetings we receive from fellow Baptists. All who have attended previous Assemblies have appreciated this element and long may it continue. But true fellowship is a sharing in Christ in His ministry to the world, and I believe that we shall come closer to one another as we pursue more diligently together the common task of witness and service in His Name.

Urgent common tasks, he said, required the Assembly's attention, and the sharing of insights and encouragement.

> This year we take a tentative and small step in this direction. I would have liked to have gone further, and I think we need to go further, but I recognise that we need to feel our way and progress slowly.

He chose as the Assembly theme "The Congregation in Mission", which reflected the current ecumenical programme "The Missionary Structure of the Congregation" and its study material emanating from the World Council of Churches. An Association President, however, was President for a whole year and not just an assembly, and as such was expected to chair meetings of the Council and its big autumn rally, attend as necessary its various committees, and represent the Association at important events like the induction services of incoming ministers. Ron Cowley did all this yet much more. He gave notice of his intention to visit personally as many of the churches as possible and this he did throughout his twelve months in office, reporting in the Tyndale magazine on what he was finding. It was a pastoral interpretation of his role and an expression of his firm belief, as seen earlier, that belonging to an Association meant being members one of another in Christ.

In succeeding years Tyndale provided the Association with five more Presidents: Morris West (1977–78), Peter Webb (1984–85), Keith Clements (1989–90), David Roberts (1997–98), and Robert Ellis (2001–2). Moreover, David Roberts was Association Secretary 1984–1992.

Tyndale and the Baptist Union

Tyndale and the Baptist Union of Great Britain ("and Ireland" as it was until 1988) were no strangers to each other. By the time of the Second World War two BU Presidents had been supplied direct from Tyndale: Richard Glover (1884) and H. L. Taylor (1937), together with that son of Tyndale, T. R. Glover, who by the time of his election (1923) was a Cambridge don. F. C. Bryan, minister of Tyndale 1933–1950, was in his retirement elected BU President in 1960. As late as the 1960s, to be President of such a body, was to occupy a high-profile position not only within the denomination but among the churches generally and indeed, on occasion, in national life too. Along with the General Secretary (from 1951 to 1967, Dr Ernest A. Payne), the President might well be expected to attend state occasions, or might even hope for lunch at Buckingham Palace. But beyond the formalities of presidencies, Tyndale ministers and laypeople throughout this period made very significant contributions to the work of the BU, and in turn the church as a whole was always being encouraged to take a well-informed interest in what the Union stood for and offered to the denomination. Tyndale habitually sent two delegates to the Annual Assembly in addition to the minister. The Home Work Fund, as we have already seen, was for Tyndale a major nexus in this two-way relationship between Union and local congregations.

Baptist Union Council meeting at Tyndale in 1991

Ron Cowley was a member of the BU Council from the early 1960s and was a member of the Youth Department Committee. Quite apart from his direct involvement in BU affairs, he took it upon himself to keep Tyndale up to date on BU matters especially as they pertained to the life and mission of local congregations. Indeed one could almost compose an outline history of the Union over the 1960s and 1970s from his brief reports in the monthly Tyndale magazine. The years 1959–62 saw a concerted movement by the BU to consolidate and renew the life, mission and worship of Baptist churches, in a programme centred on the 150th anniversary of the founding of the Union in 1812: the "Ter-Jubilee Celebrations". In June 1959 Ron Cowley reported on the launch of the three-year programme at the Baptist Assembly in London the previous month, stressing the importance of the three-fold thrust of the programme: evangelism, education and the creation of the Ter-Jubilee Fund to fuel the next phase of cooperative Baptist witness. Large-scale meetings were held in every area of the country to raise awareness and stimulate giving, and the Bristol meeting was hosted by Tyndale in July 1960.

Ron Cowley however was not the only Tyndale member on the BU Council. By virtue of his office as Principal of the Bristol College Leonard Champion was also a Council member, and was widely respected in the denomination not only as a scholar and a mentor of those training for the ministry, but as one who in his quiet and dignified way took a deep interest in every aspect of Baptist life and work, and especially saw the seriousness of the challenge of communicating the gospel in the contemporary world. In 1963 appeared his book, *Baptists and Unity*, and the same year he was elected Vice-President of the BU. He was welcomed as President at the Assembly the following year, and gave his presidential address "The Resurrection of Christ". Tyndale unsurprisingly led the congratulations, subjecting him to a "This Is Your Life" evening of celebration the week before the Assembly. Mrs Marjorie Champion, too, took office as President of the Baptist Ministers' Wives' Fellowship.

Tyndale continued to be kept informed and challenged at its Church Meetings and in its monthly magazine by information and appeals (including financial ones) from Baptist Church House and these were taken seriously. At New Year 1966 the BU issued a "Call to Prayer and Mission", which Ron Cowley interpreted as a call to repentance on the part of the churches. As we shall see later in this chapter it was at precisely this time that Tyndale was being led by its minister to a radical rethinking of what "mission" meant for a local congregation in its contemporary social setting. Further change at the BU itself was under way. Dr Payne retired from the general secretaryship in 1967 and was succeeded by Dr David Russell. In 1968 Tyndale celebrated its 100th anniversary and the BU President for that year, Dr George Beasley-Murray, Principal of Spurgeon's College, preached at the actual anniversary service. The church took on board for discussion the BU report *Baptists and Unity* (1967), and the somewhat controversial strategy paper, *Ministry Tomorrow* (1968), which Ron Cowley believed merited serious attention – even by the deacons! Interestingly, there is no record of reactions, if any, to the controversy following the address given at the 1971 Assembly by Principal Michael Taylor on "How Much of a Man was Jesus Christ?" In March 1974 Ron Cowley devoted the whole of his pastoral letter in the church magazine to the recent BU report, *Working Together*, which called for urgent thinking on strategy, in the emerging scenario where matching demand and supply for full-time ministers was becoming more difficult, and the costs of new buildings and of maintaining existing ones were escalating. The proposals in *Ministry Tomorrow*, dismissed by many at the time, for full-time and "supplementary" ministers were now surfacing again. The only way forward, was that of working more effectively together as Baptist churches, and with those of other denominations. "The matter is urgent and there are no easy answers. But try we must", argued Cowley in 1974.

This was to be Ron Cowley's almost last word to Tyndale, as later that year he took up his appointment as Superintendent for the Western Area of the Baptist Union. During his sixteen years as pastor Tyndale had contributed much to the Union, and equally had been a receptive ear and mind for it at local level. Meanwhile, in 1971 Tyndale acquired a new member who provided perhaps the most active link that the church ever had with the Union and its inner workings: Dr W. M. S. (Morris) West was appointed Principal of the Bristol College in succession to Leonard Champion on his retirement, and was formally inducted to the post in October 1972. He and his wife, Freda,

The Revd Dr Maurice West [Julian West]

became members at Tyndale. His close involvement with the Union had begun while he was tutor at Regent's Park College, Oxford – he was co-opted onto the BU Council in 1958 – and his contribution to Union work deepened during his pastorate at Dagnall Street, St Albans, 1959–71. Indeed he was to serve a total of 42 uninterrupted years on the Council till the year of his death in 1999. By the time he came to Bristol he had chaired the Commission on the Associations and the Young People's Department and had served on the General Purposes Committee, and the group which produced *Ministry Tomorrow*, chairing also the Structure Group which after David Russell's appointment made proposals for a new, tripartite organisation of the Union's work into sections dealing with Mission,

Ministry and Administration. After his arrival in Bristol West's BU workload if anything increased, including the handling of the Baptist responses to the "Ten Propositions" unity proposals, and chairing the search committee to find a successor to David Russell. He was, in the apt title of an essay by Neville Clark in the volume presented to him on his retirement in 1987, best described as "Servant of the Union". But in retirement he seemed to become even busier on behalf of the BU: chairman of Council; chairman of the Superintendents' Board; member of the Pensions Committee; and involvement in the proposals to move Baptist headquarters from London to Didcot. Well might he say towards the end of his life:

> I realise that I have spent many hours, if not the equivalent of days in serving the Union. In fact I once began to work it out and I reckon, counting a working day as eight hours, I must have given two years of my life to the Baptist Union on various committees and that, I think, is a low estimate.

It might be thought misleading to list Morris West as a contribution of Tyndale to the Union, since he would undoubtedly have made his kind of contribution wherever his home base happened to be. But being a member of Tyndale was not incidental to him. He enjoyed and took his membership responsibilities seriously, a regular worshipper whenever possible, not to mention attending all kinds of functions whether BMS and Home Mission suppers, or socials and a home group and of course the Church Meeting where he was a diplomatic but alert poser of pertinent questions. As has been noted, he gave wise counsel as moderator in the interregnum following Ron Cowley's departure, and his last ever sermon was preached at Tyndale just a few months before his death in 1999. If Tyndale cannot fully claim him as one of their contributions to the Baptist Union, it nevertheless might well be said that he was a great gift of the Union to Tyndale.

Tyndale's involvement with the Union through it members continued. From 1984 Keith Clements was secretary of the committee which produced the hymn book *Baptist Praise and Worship* (1991) and was a member of the BU Council from 1987 to 1991. David Roberts served on the Council from 1985 to 2010 and throughout this period was heavily involved in much of the Union's committee work: General Purposes and Finance Executive (Moderator 1994–97); BU Corporation and Legal Committee (Moderator 1998–2004), Finance Advisory Committee, Education Committee, Doctrine and Worship Committee… and more. In 2004 Tyndale acquired into membership yet another principal of the College, Brian Haymes, who both as an ex-President of the Union (1993–94) and as a college principal was a member of the Council. Robert Ellis also served on the Council during his later years at Tyndale.

Tyndale and ecumenical neighbours

A photograph taken at the dedication of Tyndale's restored building in 1955 shows the Bishop of Bristol, Frederick ("George") Cockin, standing among the dignitaries about to enter the church. At that time some would have been surprised at the sight of an Anglican bishop at such a ceremony in a Baptist church. But this was in Bristol, already with a reputation as one of the most ecumenically progressive cities in the land, and Bishop Cockin even before he came to Bristol in 1946 had a notable record in the cause of Christian unity; and this was Tyndale, a church which, while firm in its Baptist and Free Church commitment, had over many years in its ministers and many of its laypeople manifested an openness to the kingdom of God wherever it was to be found, however far beyond its own Baptist doors. Bishop Cockin was to retire in 1958, succeeded by perhaps the most ecumenically eminent Anglican of his generation, Oliver Tomkins, who from 1945 was closely associated with the emerging World Council of Churches (founded in 1948) in Geneva where he became secretary of the Faith and Order Commission. "Bishop Oliver", as he became known to Bristol, continued his involvement with the ecumenical movement at international level but was equally concerned with grass-roots ecumenism in his own diocese, particularly with the establishment of "Areas of Ecumenical Experiment", later called Local Ecumenical Partnerships (LEPs). By the 1970s it was reckoned that there were more such projects in the Bristol area than any other part of the country, and this owed much to his influence and leadership. It is a sign of Tyndale's openness to the wider church that in September 1958 a letter of appreciation was sent to Frederick

Cockin on his retirement, and one of welcome to Oliver Tomkins soon after his arrival. The latter responded:

> I have certainly made a very happy start with the ready friendship that is being held out to me, and look forward to seeing something of the members of your Church as time goes on. How lucky I know myself to be in following Bishop Cockin.

At Ron Cowley's induction – which coincided almost exactly with Oliver Tomkins' arrival – among those who brought welcoming greetings was the Revd P. G. Reddich, archdeacon of Bristol and chairman of the Bristol Council of Christian Churches. Talking of "friendship" was not trivial, for one of the factors in generating active ecumenism in Bristol was the quality of personal friendships that grew among the leading clergy at this time. It has been said, with some reason, that this grew on the golf course as much as in church meeting rooms – certainly Ron Cowley affirmed this.

The Bristol Council of Christian Churches was in fact one of the earliest of such British bodies to have been founded, in 1924. Ron Cowley soon found himself actively involved, joining the executive committee in 1960, and for a time serving as honorary secretary. Tyndale gave strong support to the council's work, notably the collections for Inter-Church Aid (later renamed Christian Aid); appeals for refugees; day conferences on Christian unity, care of the elderly; lectures on nuclear warfare... and much else. There is, however, no trace of any response in Tyndale to the Bristol Bus Boycott of 1963 which was one of the landmark events in race relations in Britain, and on which the Council of Churches at one point drew controversy by its comments. Tyndale took its relationships to the council seriously enough to consider its work at Deacons' and Church Meetings, for example in May 1962 when the council undertook some changes to its governance to enable more adequate representation from participating churches, and set up a financial base to secure a part-time secretariat.

Also in the field was the Free Church Federal Council. In the late 1950s at both national and local level it still played an important role for Baptist, Congregational, Methodist and Presbyterian churches but its profile slowly diminished in face of the wider ecumenism that was gaining ground in the 1960s and 1970s. Its specific significance now lay mainly in the provision of chaplaincies, attention to educational issues and, at local level, homes for the elderly. In 1970 the National Congress was held in Bristol at Horfield Baptist Church. The following year Ron Cowley was elected president of the Bristol Council, and Leonard Champion became moderator of the National Council, taking as the theme of his moderator's address, "Freedom and Responsibility". Meanwhile an important contribution to the National Council's work was that of Michael Smith who served on the Council. Tyndale's last conspicuous link with the National Council came with Morris West's moderatorship in 1982.

Neighbourhood ecumenism

In Bristol itself, however, and not forgetting its participation in such councils, Tyndale's most concerted ecumenical endeavours during these years focused on relationships with the churches in its immediate neighbourhood. On Whiteladies Road four Free Churches – Victoria Methodist, Tyndale, Trinity Methodist and Redland Park Congregational (later United Reformed) stood at short walking-distance intervals from each other, with a Quaker Meeting also at the northern end of the road. St John's Anglican was situated almost opposite the Redland Park Church, St Mary's Anglican was a few minutes' walk from Tyndale on Woodland Road, with St Saviour's on Chandos Road, Redland. In the Clifton area west of Whiteladies Road there was St Paul's which also served as the Anglican university chaplaincy church, All Saints' Church on Pembroke Road, and the Roman Catholic Pro-Cathedral which in 1973 was replaced by the new Clifton Cathedral, also on Pembroke Road. Four of the churches – Tyndale, Trinity Methodist, Redland Park and All Saints – shared a common history of having all been destroyed during the Bristol Blitz of 1940. Of all these churches it was with Redland Park and its minister Cyril Grant that Tyndale enjoyed the closest and longest-standing of relationships. (At the induction of Peter Webb in 1975 Cyril Grant wryly commented that he hoped the arrival of this new minister would prompt some people, among the students especially, to make up their minds one way or another which church they wished to belong to). The story of the efforts to relate the Clifton and Redland churches as a whole more closely together makes an intriguing chapter in local ecumenism, combining vision, frustration and disappointment – yet also wisdom and at times even gracious humour on the part of Tyndale.

In the January 1963 Tyndale magazine Ron Cowley wrote:

> Unity is difficult to define. It does not mean one denomination swallowing up all the others, but for all Christians a listening to the Spirit of God and a moving forward into a deeper fellowship with Christ and with fellow Christians. This is what we pray for.

He was speaking about the forthcoming Week of Prayer for Christian Unity, during which there would be a special service at Tyndale conducted by himself with Archdeacon Reddich as guest preacher. There would also be a united prayer service at Redland Park. Such observances of the Week of Prayer were by now regular features of the Clifton and Redland local churches' calendar, as also for example was the Women's World Day of Prayer at the beginning of March, but thanks to developments on the wider scene the years 1962–64 saw heightened expectations in the quest for Christian unity. In 1962 the Second Vatican Council convened by Pope John XXIII opened in Rome. It was clear from the start that this would open up a whole new era in inter-church relations, as the Holy Father called for the Roman Catholic Church to enter a dialogue with other Christians, "our separated brethren", and a new dialogue with the world. This would greatly transform ecumenical relations at every level, right down to the local. Then in the summer of 1964 there took place in Nottingham the British Faith and Order Conference under the theme "One Church Renewed for Mission". It was attended by 500 delegates from all the main British churches, together with Roman Catholic observers; and among the Baptist delegates was Ronald Cowley. Most notably, if controversially, it resolved that the churches should "covenant together for the inauguration of union" by an agreed date, under obedience to God, and suggested that this date be Easter 1984. Whatever Ron Cowley's own impressions and thoughts about the conference, and this particular resolution, there is no mistaking his continuing commitment to pursuing closer unity among Tyndale and its neighbours.

The "Clifton Group" of churches not only held united services during the Week of Prayer for Unity but arranged quarterly prayer services hosted by each church in turn. Free Church united services on Good Friday were also a regular feature. In 1964 there started to appear the Bristol churches' monthly newspaper *Contact* which included an insert for a particular area of the city. Redland Park were enthusiastic for the project and Cyril Grant came to talk to the Tyndale deacons about it, but Tyndale was wary about taking on a share of the production costs and responsibility for distribution.

Then in 1964 a development took place which promised to open up new possibilities of closer cooperation within the Clifton Group but was to turn into a rather tangled and frustrating tale over the next ten years. Discussions took place on forming a new South Clifton Group comprising the Friends Meeting House, the Roman Catholic Pro Cathedral, St Paul's, Tyndale, and Victoria Methodist. The proposals were finalised at a meeting at Victoria Methodist on 30th October. Each congregation would appoint three representatives to the committee, and an organizer for Christian Aid would be appointed. Two aspects of the membership list were significant. First, it marked the advent of the Roman Catholic Church fully into local ecumenical life (it did not even wait for the Second Vatican Council's epoch-making Decree on Ecumenism but preceded it by three weeks!) and the Roman Catholics were asked if they could arrange a prayer service in the Pro-Cathedral during the forthcoming Week of Prayer in January 1965. Second, Redland Park with which Tyndale had greatest affinity was not part of the grouping and remained in the "Redland Group".

There followed an undoubted new lease of ecumenical life, especially in the new relationships with the Roman Catholics. The Tyndale magazine reported on the Week of Prayer Service on 21st January 1965:

> It was indeed a deeply moving religious experience to find oneself worshipping in the Pro-Cathedral with our Roman Catholic friends. We are grateful to them for the opportunity to join with them during the week of prayer for Christian Unity, grateful, too, for the simple yet beautiful order of service which they had arranged. It made it easy for us to feel at one with them and to worship together.
>
> We sang hymns that were in their hymn book and ours, and we knew that they were THEIR hymns long before they were ours.

> During this time of worship Church Unity seemed a much nearer possibility than we sometimes think.

Not quite everyone approved. The Tyndale deacons received a letter from one church member objecting to Tyndale people attending worship in a Catholic church. No action was taken. Tyndale as a whole was very positive towards the South Clifton Group. Excellent reports were received at the Church Meeting of the Lenten Bible study meetings. So it continued for the next three years. In early 1967, however, a set-back occurred. The British Council of Churches had launched a nationwide programme, *The People Next Door*, involving Lenten study groups and suggestions for encouraging churches to look outwards to one another and to those around them in society. It was being widely taken up, aided by press, radio and television. In January 1967 Ron Cowley wrote enthusiastically about the prospects it offered for "a rich experience of spiritual renewal" for those who would share in it. "The idea is that it should be approached on an inter-church basis, and our South Clifton Group has planned the course which will take place in the seven weeks before Easter." But soon after writing this he was clearly dismayed to discover that nothing had in fact been arranged by the South Clifton Group, so Tyndale would have to carry out its Lenten studies on its own.

It would be wrong to suggest that this disappointment by itself led to a disillusionment with the South Clifton Group. But the Redland Group of Churches was on Tyndale's doorstep in the other direction, and with Redland Park Church in particular Tyndale was in constant and friendly contact. It was therefore a genuine question, to which geographical area Tyndale most appropriately belonged. In fact overtures from the Redland Group were now coming to Tyndale; for example in April 1966 the Group had asked for volunteers from Tyndale to help in a visitation programme in the area. Ron Cowley and Cyril Grant were evidently having informal conversations about cooperation between their churches. In March 1969 Ron Cowley presented to the Tyndale deacons a memorandum drawn up by himself and Cyril Grant on the possibility of Tyndale and Redland Park planning together their respective building projects. The Tyndale deacons warmly and unanimously approved the idea and appointed three of their number to serve on a joint committee of the two churches. The joint meetings took place, and included discussions on whether cooperation might centre on a joint use of the Trinity Methodist site if and when that church closed. This was thought in the end to be unrealistic. But the exchanges with Redland Park widened into whether Tyndale should in fact transfer from the South Clifton to the Redland Group. This Tyndale decided to do in October 1969. The earlier hesitations notwithstanding, it was even decided to take up the Redland edition of *Contact*.

If it was now clearer to which local ecumenical grouping Tyndale most usefully belonged, the form of that grouping was within eighteen months thrown into question thanks to an intervention by Bishop Oliver Tomkins. Consistent with his ecumenical convictions, he was disconcerted by the church scene in the Clifton and Redland areas: a seeming plethora of churches – of all denominations – and their buildings, each pursuing its own way. Were they all necessary? Should there not at least be greater coordination in their use? In 1971 therefore he proposed a commission to assess the situation, and

Bishop Oliver Tomkins

called a round table conference of all the churches in the Clifton–Redland area, "to consider the use of the ecclesiastical buildings in the Clifton/Redland area in the light of the Ecumenical Movement, and in particular the possibilities implicit in the Sharing of Church Buildings Act 1970". The Tyndale deacons and Church Meeting received the bishop's letter with great interest, and in fact it resonated in timely fashion with Tyndale's own embryonic building plans and the conversations with Redland Park – and indeed with a discussion in the Redland Group as a whole about a possible housing project. But of course some of the implications could be threatening if any existing places of worship were being called into question.

It was agreed that Ron Cowley and Derek Parsons should represent Tyndale at the initial discussions. Tyndale dutifully filled in the questionnaire sent out for the collation of facts about the buildings, membership and activities of each church. The report of the commission came out in the summer of 1972. At Tyndale it was discussed fully at both Deacons' and Church Meetings in September. In general terms, both meetings agreed to take the issue of buildings seriously. The minute continues more specifically:

> Considering our Redland area the suggestion is that the following look at this together:– St Johns, St Saviours, Redland Park, Trinity and Tyndale with The Society of Friends and the Lutherans continuing on their own...

> The Report suggests that Redland Park and Tyndale, with the most suitable premises, might become the two buildings on which all the work in our area might be based and this would include the holding of services of different traditions. There is no suggestion that the services would in any way merge or change. Each present denomination would maintain its own identity and traditions.

It was agreed that "Mr Cowley and Messrs, Bass, Brown and Bodey" should represent the church at future discussions of the commission.

This was a radical, even dramatic, proposal: that two of the present Free Churches on Whiteladies Road, Tyndale and Redland Park, should provide the main base for all future church activity, including worship, in the area. Tyndale and Redland Park were "safe" in these proposals but the implications were nevertheless huge. How would those churches whose separate physical existence was being queried react? This particularly concerned the three Anglican parish churches (the viability of Trinity Methodist was already doubtful according to the Methodists themselves). The strong implication was that at least one of the Anglican churches should close. Further, whatever was being said about each denomination keeping its tradition and identity, occupying the same house was bound to have effects (welcome or otherwise) on each congregation in the shared space. First reactions in the Tyndale church meeting varied:

> Mr F. thought that we should consider building up our own Church rather than taking on those whose church was running down. He thought there was a danger of the various beliefs and traditions being watered down if the various churches started to merge their services. You may then finish up with no one really believing in anything... Mr C. felt that this reluctance to unite was the greatest blot on Christendom and unless such a joining together had a group ministry arrangement then sectionalism would continue and no real progress [be] made.

But more important, Tyndale actually resolved firmly to continue the explorations with the other churches cited.

These discussions did indeed begin – and continued tortuously for nearly two years. As had been half-expected Trinity Methodist closed anyway, which removed one piece from the puzzle. The real sticking point proved to be the reluctance or inability of the three Anglican churches to come to any conclusion among themselves on their future, whether to close or unite with each other (let alone come closer to the Free Churches). A proposal for a new parish to be created utilising the disused Highbury Chapel was debated for some time. In such an uncertain atmosphere much of the work of the Redland Group as a whole was stymied, beyond holding united services as before (and even then there was in the Tyndale Church Meeting in November 1973 a long discussion on the purpose and effectiveness of such services). Time and again Ron Cowley confessed his frustration to the Tyndale deacons. Each of the Anglican churches was sticking out for its own continued existence. St John's, for instance, maintained that it was essential for a distinctly Anglican church to be present on Whiteladies Road, and St Saviour's likewise argued its case for Chandos Road. It was being suggested that St Johns and St Saviours buildings be demolished and a new purpose-built church placed on the St Saviour's site. St Mary's might go to Highbury and become a new parish church. At the Tyndale Deacons' Meeting in June 1973 it was reported that the situation was getting even more confused among the Anglicans. The use of Highbury Chapel was now in question. There was irony in the fact that it was the Anglican bishop who had called for a rationalisation, and it was members of his own flock who were now resisting the calls for closer cooperation. Such wilful "congregational" independence, Baptists were used to being told, was their own besetting weakness, whereas the Anglicans now "appear to be exerting their independence against the general wishes and plans of the bishop". One Tyndale deacon remarked, "The Anglicans are more like us than we are!" It should be noted that at the same time as these discussions were taking place, serious thought was being given to the possibility of the Lawrence Weston Church forming an Area of Ecumenical Experiment with the local Methodists and (for a short time) the Anglicans.

The Redland Group was proving ineffective at moving the situation forward. There was even talk early in 1974 of re-linking the Group with South Clifton. Some further Redland Group discussions took place during 1974–75 on possible joint projects (help for the elderly, Sunday luncheon club, etc). After one such Redland Group conference in October 1975, Derek Parsons told his fellow deacons that he felt that only two churches, Tyndale and Redland Park, had come prepared for it, and that only these two churches "would initiate any new schemes and get them working". It was a disappointing end to the high hopes and imagination engendered by Oliver Tomkins' commission in 1974, and equally it is intriguing to picture what might have resulted if all the Redland churches, especially the Anglicans, had grasped the opportunity (and taken the risks) that had been created. But Tyndale, with Redland Park, had at least kept the ecumenical standard flying high throughout. In February 1975, assistant minster Barry Vendy, musing that the local ecumenical movement seemed to have reached a "plateau", commented:

> The potential is still there – but the dangers of impatience, frustration and cynicism grow. Whenever I walk to Tyndale on a Sunday morning, past the Mount of Olives, St John's, and especially Redland Park, and see my fellow-Christians heading in the opposite direction for worship, I cannot help wondering, is this wise stewardship of the resources God has given us?

It is important to note that for Tyndale the presupposition of all local moves towards unity was, to use the title of the 1964 Nottingham Conference, "one church renewed for mission". Hence the parallel discussions with Redland Park and other churches about joint action in the community. In fact as early as November 1959 Ron Cowley announced a conference for Tyndale members to consider the church's work in its neighbourhood. This was based on a new and deeper concept of mission. Inspired by the Baptist minister, Lewis Misselbrook, and the veteran Dutch missionary and ecumenist, Hendrik Kraemer, he asked for a move away from mission purely in terms of evangelistic "campaigns", towards a real meeting with real people in their needs after the manner of Jesus Christ who became completely involved in the lives of others, bearing their needs and sufferings: "In short, we are going to try to care for people and this means being totally involved. We are going to love them and, as Mr Misselbrook says, we may find ourselves painfully out of practice".

The wider ecumenism

Tyndale could never be left in any doubt that its local ecumenism was a strand in the great web of manifesting the oneness of the body of Christ in all the world. Ron Cowley in 1965 participated in a team visit of clergy to the USA arranged by the British Council of Churches, and in 1968 was invited to take part in an ecumenical visit of Bristol church leaders to the Holy Land. In November 1966 the founder and leader of the Iona Community, Dr George Macleod, was invited to preach at Tyndale and doubtless made his listeners, and the pulpit too, quake in face of his prophetic delivery on justice and peace. But furthermore, continuously from the mid-1950s onwards until 2006, at any one time at least one member of Tyndale was directly involved in the ecumenical movement at international level. Leonard Champion was a member of the World Council of Churches Faith and Order Commission from 1958 to 1972, and in addition to meetings of the Commission attended the WCC Assemblies at Evanston (1954), New Delhi (1961), and Uppsala (1968). Back home in Bristol from these meetings and events he made every effort to share his experiences and comment on their significance. After New Delhi for instance he shared with Oliver Tomkins and Ann Coe, an Anglican youth delegate from Bristol, in a youth conference at Penscot on "New Delhi – Over to You!". In August 1967 the Faith and Order Commission met in Bristol and Leonard Champion had the pleasure of introducing some of its members to morning worship at Tyndale on 6th August when Dr Emlyn

Thomas, a member of the Commission and minister of Yorkminster Park Baptist Church, Toronto, Canada, preached.

When Morris West arrived in Bristol in 1971 he had already served seven years on Faith and Order, and continued to do so until 1983. He attended the Fifth WCC Assembly at Nairobi (1975), and among the Faith and Order Commission meetings in which he participated none was more significant than that at Lima, Peru, in 1982, which finalised the text of the paper *Baptism, Eucharist and Ministry*, reckoned by many the most important ecumenical text of the latter twentieth century. Keith Clements followed him into Faith and Order, among other meetings attending the Fifth World Conference on Faith and Order at Santiago Compostela, Spain, in 1993. By then he was working as secretary for international affairs in the Council of Churches for Britain and Ireland (CCBI), and in 1997 moved to Geneva where he was general secretary of the Conference of European Churches until 2005. He attended the WCC Assemblies in Harare, Zimbabwe (1998) and Porto Alegre, Brazil (2006). Another significant Tyndale contribution to the wider ecumenism was that of Dr John Roberts who with his wife joined Tyndale in 1964 when he became lecturer in psychiatry at the university. He worked for a time in Geneva on the WCC's *Humanum* programme. This, following the 1968 Uppsala Assembly, was a major study led by David Jenkins (later bishop of Durham) on the need for a new Christian understanding of human nature as it faced the threats and opportunities posed by rapid social change and burgeoning new sources of conflict in a world struggling for justice.

In the spring of 1973 much of the atmosphere of the wider ecumenical movement was brought to Bristol in the South-West Ecumenical Congress (SWEC) which saw nearly 2000 participants from all over the West Country and from further afield gather for a weekend of worship, celebration and group study, plus plenary meetings in the Colston Hall. Archbishop Michael Ramsey, Cardinal Suenens of Belgium, and former secretary of the WCC Wim Visser 't Hooft were star attractions. Tyndale folk helped to provide hospitality for the guests, as they did again for the next SWEC in 1976 at which Phillip Potter, "new" general secretary of the WCC, was the literally towering presence.

Chapter 15.

Tyndale and the World

Keith Clements

Tyndale from the mid-1950s onwards continued to combine a commitment to local mission with a worldwide outlook, a feature of the church from its beginning. This chapter relates how this global consciousness and activity was expressed in three ways: through support for the Baptist Missionary Society; in contacts with Tyndale-related people working overseas while also receiving people from overseas into the life of Tyndale; and in active engagement with issues of international justice, peace and humanitarian aid.

Tyndale and the Baptist Missionary Society (BMS)

"What will the next fifty years bring? How will the continuing story unfold? What names will be added to the list?" So Leonard Champion concluded his section "Tyndale and the Baptist Missionary Society" in his 1968 centenary booklet. Tyndale does indeed have a long and inspiring record of members who have served overseas with the BMS, as the list of no fewer than 29 names on the "Missionary Roll of Honour" in the church vestibule testifies (see Chapter 10). Yet no name has been added to that list since that of Miss Barbara Gadd who served in Ceylon (now Sri Lanka) 1944–1954. In that sense the story might be thought to have folded up, rather than unfolded further. But while Tyndale since the mid-1950s may not itself have sent members to the "mission field" the story of the church's strong support for the BMS certainly continued, together with a variety of involvements in many overseas situations.

Indeed, throughout the 1960s and 1970s, as regards all outside organisations, Baptist or otherwise, Tyndale gave more financial support, time and effort to the BMS than to any other body or cause. The church budget for 1964 is instructive:

		£
General Expenses (maintenance of ministry, heating, lighting, cleaning, etc		3,372
Fabric expenses of church and halls		940
Baptist Missionary Society		**1,800**
Home Work Fund		425
Christian Societies (Bible Society, Baptist Colleges, etc)		180
Contingencies		200
		£6,917

As well as an allocation from church finances in general the fund-raising for the BMS took several forms. Everybody's Effort, the annual pre-Christmas fair, was one major source. Another was the annual "missionary supper" combined with a gift day. F. C. Bryan had started a tradition of holding this on or near the minister's birthday, and Ronald Cowley enthusiastically continued the practice in February each year, until about 1972. Often a well-known BMS missionary or officer of the BMS would speak at the supper (for example David Grenfell in 1957, Dr Stanley Thomas, 1959, Clifford Parsons, 1960). In 1962 Leonard Champion spoke of his impressions of India gained during his attendance at the World Council of Churches Assembly in New Delhi the previous year, and of the BMS work he had been able to see at first hand there. As was the practice in many Baptist churches of the time, the first communion offering each year was devoted to the support of the widows and orphans of Baptist missionaries, and retired missionaries. This was discontinued in 1964 when it was decided that a specific sum should be placed within the overall amount budgeted for the BMS. Sometimes special events were held for particular causes: for example in 1959 a garden party for work in Angola. From 1969 onwards, a portion of the harvest thanksgiving offering, as well as going to Christian Aid, was devoted to Operation Agri, the BMS agricultural programme. A close eye was kept on reports from the BMS about the

World Council of Churches, New Delhi, India, 1961 [WCC archives]

changing financial situation, such as the difficulties caused to the Society in 1968 by the fall in the pound. Tyndale's giving was responsible and informed.

In fact a huge amount of information on the BMS and the contexts in which it was working was constantly made available to church members. The BMS Bristol Auxiliary was active and supported by Tyndale (interestingly in 1964 its annual meeting was even held in the Colston Hall). Many read the BMS monthly *Missionary Herald* but there was also much in each month's Tyndale magazine, often highlighted in Ron Cowley's pastoral letter. Ron and Maureen Cowley also showed their devotion to the cause by leading at least one (Bexhill, 1960) of the ever-popular BMS summer schools for young people. Up-to-date detailed information was provided on the crisis in Congo which followed the country's independence from Belgium in 1960, and particularly on the resulting needs of refugees identified by the United Nations, the International Missionary Council and the World Council of Churches – the overall international effort within which the BMS was working. Likewise with the Angolan crisis in 1961, following the revelations – thanks largely to some BMS missionaries and a group of concerned younger ministers at home – of atrocities being committed by the Portuguese military. "The last chapter of [Angola's] story has been written in blood and tears", wrote Ron Cowley. Again there was a huge refugee crisis, with 125,000 crossing over into Congo. Inter-Church Aid was asked to take responsibility for 25,000 of the refugees. Tyndale responded very quickly with gifts of clothes and individual donations which were channelled through Inter-Church Aid.

Congolese refugees [WCC archives]

Tyndale's contribution to the governance of the BMS was renewed in 1976 when Elizabeth Webb began her long-standing service on the General Committee, and she also became chair of the Bristol BMS Auxiliary. Furthermore, over the years Tyndale continued to enjoy a number of live links with missionaries, if not always from its own membership or indeed BMS ones. Michael Wotton was a Bristol University student who, having recently recovered from polio which left him significantly disabled, was baptized by Ron Cowley at Tyndale, following which he trained for the ministry at the Baptist College, and became President of the Edward Terrill Society. After pastorates at Chichester and Bournemouth, in 1970 he and his wife Jill went as BMS missionaries to Brazil where they served for fourteen years. They kept in touch with a number of Tyndale members and reports from them appeared in the magazine. Another President of the Edward Terrill Society, John Clark (1964), also worked in Brazil with the BMS for more than twenty years. In 1973 Tyndale welcomed into membership Daisy Fowles, sister of Tyndale member, Mrs Vera Hofman, on her retirement from 42 years' service with the BMS in Kalompong, North India. Then there was Christopher Lamb, whose family was Anglican but who often worshipped at Tyndale during the time he was a pupil at Clifton College in the 1950s. He was much impressed by the preaching of Bill Whilding, and long afterwards recalled a sermon he heard on Christian attitudes to Muslims. Christopher in due course entered the Anglican ministry, and in 1969 went to serve for six years with the Church Missionary Society in Lahore, Pakistan, from where reports of his work in that challenging context for the Christian church frequently found their way to Tyndale. On his return to England he became a leading Anglican and ecumenical thinker on Christian–Muslim relations. Nor are personal links with the missionary story only a thing of the past. In 2018 Lesley Fuller, who from 1958 served for twenty years with the BMS in the Congo, came into membership at Tyndale.

People going overseas

Though not technically as missionaries, a number of people associated with Tyndale from the 1950s through to the 1980s went to work overseas for longer or shorter periods. They sought to use their knowledge and experience, imbued with Christian faith, in the service of the communities in which they went to live. Moreover they kept in touch with Tyndale, and although not given to parading their work whether in teaching, business or medicine they certainly kept Tyndale in mind of the international scene, especially in what was becoming known as the "Third World". Among these were David and Pauline Roberts who had attended Tyndale while students at the university. In 1958 they went to Sierra Leone for two years where David was History Tutor at Union College (a teacher-training college) in Bunumbu, and Pauline taught science part-time. Frank Matthews, brother of Vera Hofman, with his wife, Winifred, after a spell with the International Labour Office in Geneva travelled to a number of developing countries as a consultant to governments on the establishment of national insurance schemes: Nigeria, Tanzania, Cyprus, Singapore (where he came to know Prime Minister Lee Kuan Yew very well), Guyana and the Bahamas. His nephew, Robert Hofman, spent a year (1965–66) in Kenya on Voluntary Service Overseas (VSO). John and Chris Hayter went to work in Malawi. "We came because perhaps we felt we wanted to give something. We know that we have received far more than we have given", they wrote to Tyndale in 1969. In the early 1970s Ian and Alison Love were in Zambia. Eric Stride, a member of the Tyndale Young People's Fellowship who went into banking, worked in Ghana. In 1980 Derek Parsons spent several months in Nigeria under the auspices of the British Council, to teach at the University of Ife in Ibadan and to share current ideas in academic physics teaching with physicists in Nigerian universities. That same year Juliet Campling, a

World Council of Churches, Harare, Zimbabwe, 1998 [WCC archives]

fifth-year medical student who had come into membership with both Tyndale and BURCSOC went to the BMS hospital at Berhampur, Orissa, India, for a ten-week elective term in her clinical training. As recipient of a grant towards her travel costs she was the first person to be financially supported by the Dorothy Porteous Trust, the fund created by Tyndale in memory of the church's former secretary to assist younger people in widening their experience and furthering their education for Christian service.

People coming from overseas

The traffic was not all one-way, not least because Bristol was an important university city with an international reputation. In the autumn of 1961 two educationists from Ceylon (Sri Lanka today), Mrs Indanie Premawardhana and Mrs Leili Karunaratne, were welcomed to Tyndale whilst spending a year in the university's Department of Education studying teacher-training. At around this time the Adegbite family from Nigeria made itself at home in Tyndale. Dr Adegbite was a minister also studying in the university who on the occasion he preached at Sunday morning service startled the congregation by his vigorous style of delivery. In 1962 Ken Manley arrived from Australia to study at the Baptist College for two years, with his wife

Margaret; they became close friends with a number of Tyndale folk. Ken later became Principal of Whitley College, Melbourne and a Vice President of the Baptist World Alliance. The Revd Daniel Mompoko of Ntondo, Congo, came to Bristol in 1964 under the auspices of the BMS to spend four months at the Baptist College, and was welcomed to Tyndale. He also spent time at Lawrence Weston with its minister, Philip Lucas. Today he is remembered in the Congo as a wise pastor with a gift of leadership from his student days, becoming regional secretary first in the Middle River and then at Kinshasa. In 1972 Jamaican minister and chaplain to students, Revd Ambrose Findlay, came to study at Bristol University and was welcomed to the pulpit.

No less welcome were those on shorter or passing visits from overseas. In July 1964 a team of American preachers was touring Great Britain and spent a weekend in Bristol. Revd K. Shelford, executive secretary of the North Carolina Council of Churches, preached at Tyndale. In October 1974 three Ugandan Christians (two of them bishops) came to Bristol to speak at Broadmead Church and in the Colston Hall. Although as far as is known they did not actually visit Tyndale Barry Vendy wrote in anticipation:

> What I hope is that we shall be on the receiving end of something unfamiliar and unexpected and refreshing, new insights from a different culture, faith in a different guise. This is an example of a reversal of the old-style missionary trend. Instead of taking our message to them, we become the recipients of the message. This reversal has been on the way.

There was good reason to remember their visit when, less than two years later, Archbishop Janani Luwum was done to death by forces of President Idi Amin, and another name was added to Uganda's already long list of Christian martyrs.

International issues: the UN, refugees, hunger, justice, peace and development

Following its commitment to the League of Nations between the wars, in May 1963 Tyndale became a corporate member of the United Nations

Association (UNA), affiliating to the Bristol West branch following the approval of the deacons and the church meeting. Tyndale's support continued into the 1970s, with full publicity being given to branch meetings, films, visiting speakers etc. A regular feature was the annual garden party which in 1971 was given special importance by the presence of Lord Caradon, former UK permanent representative to the UN. Brian Sears, Tyndale's representative on the Bristol West Branch, organised Tyndale's stall on the occasion and appealed for gifts in kind or cash. H. K. Compton, also active for UNA in Tyndale, stressed its importance:

> The UNITED NATIONS need informed world public opinion and support. The UNITED NATIONS ASSOCIATION is the official body to provide this and it in turn needs your support and money.

Tyndale's membership of the UNA went hand in hand with the intense interest shown by many in the church over a wide range of international issues and crises, in addition to those directly involving the BMS. Christian Aid appeals and the annual Christian Aid Week collections drew consistent support from Tyndale, and in addition the Harvest Thanksgiving collections were regularly denoted to Christian Aid, as also to the BMS Operation Agri work. But from 1959 to 1973 no issue was more highlighted at Tyndale than the successive refugee crises. 1959–60 was designated as "Refugee Year" by the UN. Fifteen years after the end of World War II survivors of concentration camps were still living in the famous refugee camp at Linz, Austria. A member of the Westbury On Trym Baptist Church, Joy Elworthy, worked there for several months and not only shared her experiences with Tyndale but put the church in touch with the relief supervisor, Bob Cambridge.

> Both Joy and Bob Cambridge emphasize the heartening effect on old and young of even a postcard received by the refugees in Camp. Is it too much to ask that members of our Fellowship at Tyndale will reach out to these people, and extend to them a little of that fellowship we all enjoy? We commend these people to your prayers. Perhaps in the moments of solitary prayer the call will come; to some for money, to others for the "adoption" of a refugee

> family by correspondence, and possibly some young vigorous
> heart may be called to volunteer for relief service in the Camps.

The famous refugee village of Rennies Mill, Hong Kong, was still crowded with those who had fled communist China. Then came the succession of refugee crises in Africa: Congo (1960); Angola (1961 and after); Congo again in 1963; and Biafra from 1967. Collections for Christian Aid, garden parties, concerts, all played their part both in information-sharing and fund-raising. The Middle East, South Africa and India (BMS work in Orissa for example) were among situations highlighted particularly at meetings of the William Tyndale Society (see chapter 11) which was evidently a valuable forum for both educating members and stirring up concern in the wider world. For example in October 1970:

> The first meeting of "Christian Concern" – the monthly series –
> considered the problem of the Middle East. An additional interest
> was the presence of two visitors from Baghdad, who were able to
> give some local views on the situation. After Mr Cowley had given
> a very fair exposition of the problem – with roots going back to
> Old Testament times – the main concern focused on the hopeless
> plight of the refugees, war victims whom no one seems to want. It
> was suggested that a resolution should be sent to the various
> Governments and organisations involved, stating our Christian
> Concern for these unfortunate people.

Britain and Europe, relations with Islam (including a discussion with Muslim guests), and the work of Amnesty International also featured in the Society's programmes during the 1970s.

Through two of its members, in the 1980s Tyndale was brought into relationship with two of the most fraught scenes on the international stage. In September 1985 Keith Clements was a member of the British Churches' Delegation to South Africa at a most critical phase in the struggle against apartheid. On his return he co-founded the group Baptist Concern for Southern Africa which among other projects sought financial and moral support for the Baptist anti-apartheid body in South Africa, the Fellowship of Concerned Baptists. John Daries, a leader of that group in Cape Town, came and spoke about the situation at Tyndale and in other churches in the

UK. Generous support came from Tyndale members. In 1989 David Roberts was on a similar delegation of the British Council of Churches to the growingly violent scene of Israel and the West Bank. In the 1990s the wider ecumenical concern for the whole world and all life upon it found expression in the "Justice, Peace and Integrity of Creation" project launched by the World Council of Churches, and Tyndale set up its own JPIC group to monitor and bring before the church these wider issues. Gordon Luton was a key player in founding and leading the group.

From 1983 until 2009 a major means of Tyndale's contribution to overseas aid were the Thursday "Drop-In Lunches". These were three-course meals (not "hunger lunches"), open to all, the proceeds from which enabled donations totalling around £5,000 each year to be given to overseas development, medical and educational work. The causes supported included Baptist World Aid, Feed the Minds, Christian Aid, Water Aid, UNICEF, the Leprosy Mission, the Bible Lands Society, Baptist Concern for Southern Africa, and many, many others. The background to such an effort was the deep and long-standing concern that Tyndale had with world hunger expressed through support for the BMS and also for Christian Aid, use of its educational materials, and study groups focusing on the causes of world poverty and the challenge presented to responsible lifestyles.

But among the causes funded from the Drop-In Lunches was one with which Tyndale had an especially close link: the Whiteladies Health-Share Project (WHSP) and its support for basic healthcare for the people of Pachod, Maharashtra State, India. The WHSP was conceived as a way of enabling both staff and patients at the Whiteladies Health Centre to becoming involved in the needs of others in a very different context – for the good of all concerned at both ends of the project. The priority was not just a matter of providing the hospital with the latest equipment (though much essential equipment was indeed provided) but of providing access to basic health care and teaching preventive medicine in the surrounding rural area. Much of the work at the Institute of Health Management at Pachod (IHMP) was initially funded by Oxfam but of course funding was needed to cover the costs of many aspects of the work both in Bristol and in Pachod itself. Fairs and garden parties were organised. In October 1985 the autumn fair was held at Tyndale and over £700 was raised.

Tyndale members visiting Pachod; IHMP director Dr Ashok Dyalchand stands at the right

Dr Michael Whitfield, who was in general practice at the Centre, and his wife, Mavis, were instrumental in enthusing Tyndale people with interest in Pachod and enlisting support and were able themselves to visit the project a number of times. The written history of WHSP makes reference to support in Bristol:

> Many people and organisations donated small and large sums to the charity over the years, some on a regular basis. One that merits special mention were the hundreds of pounds raised by the weekly lunches at Tyndale Baptist Church that continued from the start of the project until 2009.

During four of those years alone a total of £2,000 was donated from the lunches to the WHSP. In 2005 Tyndale made a different, but very significant, kind of gift: a group of thirteen people from Tyndale were able to visit Pachod and see the work at first hand.

Institute of Health Management, Pachod

Chapter 16.
Tyndale Servants in the Wider Community

Keith Clements

One of the books which excited Ron Cowley, to the point of strongly commending it in the Tyndale Magazine of April 1965, was *God's Frozen People* by Mark Gibbs and Ralph Morton. It was a powerful and provocative call to recognize that the church comprises the whole people of God, not just the clergy, and that laypeople have a vital role not only in the internal life of the congregation but, even more, in mission through fulfilling their "secular" vocations in the world of work and the community. The whole duty of the Church is to offer worship to God:

> This is true, if we remember that this worship is expressed in all we do and not only in our special acts of worship. For the church is not the only place [people] can worship God. They can worship him in the work of their hands, in their solitary prayers and in their corporate activities.
>
> And the place of worship is not the place of witness or of work. It is not the primary place for the preaching of the Gospel or for the healing of the sick. Paul knew that the place for the preaching of the Gospel was the market place and even the prison. The work of preaching and of healing had to go on outside, wherever [people] were.

Accordingly, as with any local church, the life and witness of Tyndale comprised not just what took place in Sunday worship, and in weekday gatherings, at a certain spot on Whiteladies Road, but the activities of its members dispersed throughout the week in their homes, at work, at leisure, and wherever and however they mingled with their neighbours. As was seen in earlier chapters, from its founding days Tyndale had among its members people who played a very prominent role in civic affairs and in the commercial life of Bristol. In more recent times such public eminences may have been fewer but the involvement of members in vital areas of society – especially education, business, and healthcare – has remained strong. It is appropriate therefore to mention some representative figures who not only earned great respect in their secular engagements but saw these as channels of expressing in action their Christian commitment in the world. Firmly rooted in Tyndale as the gathered church, they also represented Tyndale the servant church dispersed to be the salt of the earth.

The University – Derek Parsons

Not surprisingly, as well as with the student chaplaincies and Christian societies, Tyndale's close relationship with the University of Bristol has been seen in a succession of lecturers in its various departments. On present reckoning the longest such engagement was that of Dr Derek Parsons (1933–2013) in the Physics Department from 1961 till his retirement in 1998. Derek and his wife, Miriam, joined Tyndale in 1961, having moved from Sheffield where Derek had gained a first-class degree in physics, followed by his

Dr Derek Parsons

PhD and four years as assistant lecturer. As lecturer in Bristol, he continued his research speciality in the low temperature physics of metals and electronic structure. In collaboration with colleagues he made ground-breaking advances in studies on metal surfaces and indium alloys, supervising eight PhD students in that field, as well as undertaking all the normal round of undergraduate teaching. He was not, however, just a brilliant researcher and outstanding popular teacher, not to mention an able administrator. His senior colleague Professor Robert Evans wrote of him in the *Bristol University News* (9th September 2013):

> In his early days at Bristol it was clear that Derek had exceptional personal qualities. A former Head of Department writes: "Derek's wise and temperate advice was constantly sought by staff and students alike". This statement understates the quality of Derek's contributions. Undergraduates, postgraduates, technical, secretarial and academic staff benefited enormously from their interactions with Dr Parsons. Derek served with distinction for many years on Science Faculty Progress, Undergraduate Studies and Technical Staff Committees, and on Senate.
>
> In 1982 Derek was promoted to Departmental Administrator in Physics. The title is misleading. Whilst Derek did have an administrative role in supporting Heads of Department on matters related to arranging teaching duties and oversaw secretarial support to research groups... he also acted as Senior Tutor in Physics. As such he had overall responsibility for pastoral care. Many generations of students appreciated enormously Derek's generous support. Guidance was given patiently but firmly. Wise and kind are adjectives that students and colleagues used in describing Derek. Just before he retired Derek served (1995–96) as Dean of Graduate Studies in the Faculty of Science. I was Director of the Physics Graduate School at the time and I recall the skill with which Derek handled problems. He cared about each individual; he would make efforts to get to know the particular student, the supervisor and the detailed circumstances. Moreover, his unfailing good humour and his font of anecdotes ensured many committee meetings and interviews were not as dull as they might have been? Old fashioned virtues? Yes, indeed.

Many Tyndale people will recognize this picture of Derek Parsons as the same person who manifested exactly the same qualities as church member, deacon, Church Secretary (1973–77), Junior Church teacher, friend of young people, choir member... and much else. It is impressive how in the secular world of the university his colleagues appreciated and respected him for the way he lived out the worship he shared in at Tyndale, to the great benefit of the university.

Since the 1960s from time to time others from Tyndale have been glad to follow in a similar path in the university: Dr Adrian Beaumont (Music); Dr John Roberts (Psychiatry); Dr Ian Holyer (Computer Science); Dr Judy Holyer (Mathematics); Dr Michael Whitfield (General Practice, Social Medicine); Dr Debbie Pinfold (German). In addition, during their time as staff at the Baptist College the Revd Dr Leonard Champion, the Revd Dr Harry Mowvley, the Revd Dr Morris West and the Revd Dr Keith Clements lectured in the Department of Theology and Religious Studies.

Since the 1970s however the higher academic scene in Bristol has developed and changed enormously. Bristol Polytechnic was constituted in 1970, and in 1992 was granted university status as the University of the West of England (UWE). By 2015 UWE's total enrolments (30,000) outnumbered Bristol University's (23,000). Margaret Clements (Mathematics, Statistics and Computing) and Michael Garnier (Modern Languages) taught at UWE since its Polytechnic days. Also on the scene over the same period has been the Open University (OU) which was granted its charter in 1969, making higher education accessible, through distance learning and local tutorials, to many people unable to benefit from the conventional universities. Tyndale people made significant contributions to the OU. For fifteen years from 1970 David Roberts was Deputy Regional Director in Bristol, his responsibilities including coordinating the team of academics and organising the annual summer school in Bath, while Margaret Clements and Dr Sarah Dodds taught as tutors. In addition, a number of Bristol OU students became familiar with the interior of Tyndale when it was used as a venue for examinations!

Education for life and work – Michael Smith

Tyndale members over the years have indeed given much to the educational scene, not just at university level but as primary and secondary school teachers as well. The huge expansion of education after the Second World

Michael Smith

War required teachers of great ability and commitment, and for many Christians this provided their natural avenue of service to society (it also provided their churches with additional expertise in children's and young people's work). It would be a fascinating if impossible exercise, to estimate just how many classrooms in Bristol over the past 70 years have had a Tyndale teacher in them at one time or another. But if education had to be expanded, it also had to be asked what education was for in the modern world, and how that purpose could best be served. What was it actually preparing children and young people to face when they left school?

That is a challenging and often controversial issue. One person who was not afraid to ask it, and who took the lead in looking for creative answers, was Michael Smith (1931–2002), secondary school head teacher, member of Tyndale for 44 years, a deacon, and leader of its Junior Church during the 1960s.

Michael (Mike) Smith first came to Bristol in the 1950s as a university student and graduated in history. As noted in chapter 13 he took a leading part in the Edward Terrill Society. It was during his short service commission in the RAF's educational branch – which he followed up (again at Bristol) with a postgraduate certificate in education with distinction – that he became deeply interested in education itself. He was to remain based in Bristol for the rest of his life. His first post was in the history department at Henbury School, a pioneering comprehensive, followed by six years as deputy head at Hartcliffe School on the large new council estate of that name. While he was at Hartcliffe, Tyndale people were among the first to become aware of how his educational vision was taking shape, how it arose out of his Christian convictions and how it was being noticed in the wider world. In 1964 he wrote an article "Education and National Life" for *Focus*, the journal of the Bristol Social and Industrial Mission:

> In the schools, a quiet but significant revolution has been going on... Experiments are being tried to make the world of work relevant to the society of the future... Much more thinking has been going on as to the purpose of our education.

The article was also taken up and published by the journal *World Christian Digest*, and the significance of this was highlighted by Ron Cowley in the Tyndale magazine. It was in collaboration with Canon J. B. Chuter, the Social and Industrial Advisor to the Bishop of Bristol, that Michael was at this time closely involved in the "Learning to Earning" scheme which arranged day conferences for those soon to be leaving school for the world of work. Michael spoke about the scheme at both Church and Deacons' Meetings during 1964–65, and one conference took place at Tyndale in April 1965. He was already becoming known as an able writer, and he was to produce a whole series of books for the Careers Advisory Centre.

In 1968 Michael was appointed head of Filton High School, a grammar school in process of becoming a comprehensive. Here he remained until he retired in 1993. He was much more than just an able head. He pioneered careers guidance courses (hitherto the Cinderella of many schools curricula) and course choice methods. He developed Certificate of Secondary Education (CSE) courses, and for one of these drew on his own main academic interest, history through architecture. He established team management as a model for researchers, colleagues and countless visitors, and pioneered the development of vocational courses for students over sixteen years of age. With the early 1970s came also local government reorganisation with major consequences for education. Michael wrote the *Towards Avon* report that summarised good educational practice from the four constituent local authorities. In 1976, during her silver jubilee year, the Queen visited the school. Michael not only took this occasion in his stride but invited Sir Keith Joseph, secretary of state for education in the Conservative administration, to present their academic awards to the Filton students. "The fact that he persuaded Joseph to extol the virtues of a comprehensive school was a tribute to Smith's powers" wrote the author of the very informative obituary that appeared in the *Guardian* on 19th September 2002.

Mike Smith became a leading figure in the Secondary Heads Association (SHA), for which he wrote or edited many publications on school leadership, and he was personally sought by many school heads for advice. "His contribution to the development of school leadership was an inspiration to many and, like all great educators, his commitment to his pupils was total". The year following his retirement he was awarded the OBE. He continued in active concern on educational matters, especially on behalf of the Secondary Heads Association (SHA):

> Since retiring from headship in 1993, Michael Smith guided school governing bodies in many maintained and independent schools through the difficult process of appointing headteachers. As leader of the headship appointment service of SHA, he developed an analytical process of selection, in marked contrast to the lack of rigour with which most of nation's headteachers had previously been appointed. He persuaded governing bodies to think more clearly about what they required in a headteacher and, using well-researched methods of need and skills analysis, he advised them on which candidates fitted their description and which did not. His calm but authoritative manner produced sincere expressions of gratitude from many governing bodies in England and Wales.

That "calm but authoritative manner" was well seen at moments of decision-making in Tyndale too; as when for example he and another church member reported to the Church Meeting on their interview with an applicant for church membership, a case which presented some very difficult issues of both propriety and pastoral sensitivity. That he was able to carry that same spirit and wisdom into the increasingly pressured and often combative milieu of education is a prime example of how Christian integrity and consistency can be put into serving the world well beyond the church door. Michael Smith had many other interests as well. He was, as noted earlier, on the National Free Church Council, where educational matters were always matters of concern. His wife Ruth, whom he met while they were students in Bristol, was a dermatologist and also a pioneer in family planning, helping to set up the Bristol Brook Advisory Centre in 1968. Michael took a strong and supportive interest in her work with Brook and as a trustee was a leading member of its executive committee.

Business – the Cooper family

While the production of our daily bread, our basic foodstuffs, comes from agriculture as it has done for many centuries, in the modern world agriculture has come to rely heavily on industry, and particularly engineering, for supplying the tools and machinery that are now employed on the farm. One Tyndale family has been at the centre of this crucial development for the life and well-being of everyone today, not just in this country but in many places overseas including the developing world.

From just after the end of the Second World War, when he transferred his membership from East Street Baptist Church in Bedminster, till his death in 1990 Ronald (Ron) Cooper was a central figure in Tyndale. He was both a deeply committed and loyal church member and, thanks to his business and financial skills (he was treasurer for many years and was made a Life Deacon) and practical wisdom, was hugely important in the care and renewal of the fabric and in ventures such as the founding of the Baptist church at Lawrence Weston and the Tyndale Housing Association. But what was notable about his concern and work in and for the church – his professional diligence combined with a vision for the future – was equally true in the place where he spent most of his time and energy on weekdays: the work-a-day world of manufacturing business, and in his desire also

Ron Cooper

to put his expertise into the service of the wider community, especially in the care of the elderly.

The firm of H. Cooper and Sons (Bristol) Ltd traced its origins to 1889, when a young man, Harry Cooper, after being apprenticed to a tinplate worker, began his own business making a range of dairy utensils – milking pails, milk buckets, churns, cheese moulds and vats. After the First World War larger premises were acquired on Redcliffe Hill in the centre of old Bristol, and Harry took into partnership his sons Henry Ernest (father of Ronald) and Horace Norman. Ronald was apprenticed to his father in 1927 and in 1936 joined him as a partner in the business. During the Second World War the business was directed into munitions work. With the end of the war came a return to supplying the needs of dairy farming – but in a rapidly changing scene as new processes were coming into operation. Milk heat treatment, pasteurization, farm and dairy equipment sterilization became a growth industry. H. Cooper and Sons were soon at the forefront of supplying the new technology required. In particular, a new stainless steel holding type Pasteurization Vat proved a great success, and the company extended its work into the design of complete dairy installations. By 1949 the demand for these was so great that a new and larger site proved necessary, and the firm moved out of Redcliffe to a new factory, in St Philips – designed by Ronald. Henry Cooper died in 1951, at which point the firm became a Limited Company with Ronald appointed as Managing Director.

Colin Cooper

The range of products widened still further in 1953, when the firm was approached by the patentee of grain- and grass-drying machines. Before long, drying machines of all types and sizes were being dispatched word-wide: Western Europe,

Africa, Australia and even communist Eastern Europe. This expansion necessitated yet another move of the factory, to Yate, just north of Bristol, the new premises being designed, again, by Ronald. Further diversification took place during 1969–70 with the manufacture of grain storage and handling, in association with Brice Baker and Co. Ltd.

Ronald Cooper retired as chairman and managing director in 1978, his son Colin taking over these roles and so the long family tradition continued. So too did the ventures into new products. As the journal *Farm Buildings Digest* described it:

> By this time the grain silo manufacturing business had developed into a sophisticated market, comprising round storage bins, maxibins and industrial installation up to 54 feet diameter, fabricated catwalks, square bins, Econostores, hopper bottom silos, main air ducts, laterals and drying systems and various methods of grain handling. The products also led to some business in the field of water conservation and fish farming enterprises.

All this of course was not technology for its own sake: it was aimed at developing better methods of feeding an ever hungrier world and therefore carried a great responsibility for the wider community. As was said in 1981:

> Mr Colin Cooper feels that the company has come a long way since that day in 1887 when his great grandfather, having only finished his apprenticeship 10 years before, began his path to achievement, but in doing so the firm has not lost its individuality and philosophy of personal service which made Coopers a household word in engineering and farming circles throughout the West.

Sometime in the 1950s another member of Tyndale, a young engineer by the name of Brian Pratt, who had worked for a time on machinery for the aircraft industry, was looking for work which would not take him away so often from home and family on trips to Munich. He was introduced to Ron and Colin and was to work for the firm – as well as devotedly serving as deacon and in other various capacities in Tyndale – for over 40 years. One of his main responsibilities was in developing standards of construction for the ever-increasing size of storage silos, which came to be implemented throughout the industry.

Ron's retirement from leadership of the firm in 1978, far from being a journey into inactivity, released him for still closer involvement in the Tyndale Baptist Church Housing Association (TBCHA). Not only did this initiate the Tyndale Court project, but it was under Ronald's vision and expertise that the Avonlea home for the elderly at Yate was established as a TBCHA project (see chapter 19). This was on land close to the Cooper factory, made available and sold to the TBCHA by the Cooper family trust. This along with other projects set up by TBCHA was run by Ron until the association was handed to the Bristol Churches Housing Association. Others at Tyndale, as well as Colin, became involved in the company. As well as Colin's wife Rosemary (daughter of Bill Whilding), in 1994 Colin's daughter Alison and her husband Bruce Lloyd joined the board of the company, and Bruce in turn became Managing Director, whilst also serving as Church Secretary from 2006. The company was sold in 2008.

Healthcare – Janet Gerrish

One of the windows on the north side of Tyndale's interior depicts the suffering figure of Job, and the woman who came to Jesus for healing and touched his cloak. As well as the inscription "To the Glory of God and of all who through pain and suffering give glory to him", the window in two small panes depicts a patient receiving treatment in a hospital bed, and an operating theatre at work (see chapter 12). That is a reminder that healing and relief of suffering, regardless of social status, nationality, race or

Janet Gerrish MBE

creed has been central to Christian mission since the time of Jesus himself. It is also an appropriate sign of appreciation for the many Tyndale people who throughout the church's story have served in healthcare in Bristol and beyond, and in some cases overseas. Right down to the present, nursing, general medical practice, psychiatry, physiotherapy, ancillary hospital services (such as education for hospitalised children), and health service management and administration, have all drawn upon the gifts and character of Tyndale people for whom a commitment to wholeness of life is rooted in their faith in Christ the healer and servant of all. Such commitment is never to be romanticised. In a scene where healthcare at every level is beset by increasing pressures on staff and resources, and often fierce debate about priorities and values in healthcare, it is especially challenging for people who believe that "people matter" above all, and that every person is entitled to the humanly most caring as well as professionally most skilled attention possible.

One Tyndale person who embodied this commitment in the National Health Service and as a result was highly respected at every level on the hospital scene, was Janet Gerrish (1936–2015). A lifelong Baptist born and brought up in South Wales, she came into membership at Tyndale in 1983. Her devotion, sharp mind and practical gifts quickly became evident in the life of the church, and she served as Church Secretary from 1994 to 2005. But these features had long been put to use and developed in an already outstanding career. On leaving school she had trained as a nurse in London and undertook midwifery training in Southampton. Returning to London and the Middlesex Hospital, within a few years she was appointed a ward sister at the Middlesex, and managed nursing in a variety of capacities before moving to Bristol in 1975. Here she moved progressively into the very highest levels. She was matron of the Bristol Royal Infirmary (BRI) during the time that the Radiotherapy and Oncology centre was being re-organised. Much else in the NHS was about to undergo change and restructuring, including its funding and management. It was a testimony to the respect in which she was held that she became Director of Nursing for the Bristol and Weston Regional Health Authority, General Manager of the BRI, and in due course supervising nursing for the planning department of the Bristol and Weston Authority. When she retired in 1992 she was awarded the MBE for her services to nursing. That was not however an excuse for doing nothing more, as she continued to serve on and chair Community Health Councils until they were abolished in yet another round of restructuring in 2003.

Tyndale member Rachel Molyneux worked as a nurse and then ward sister at the BRI. Her first sight of Janet, very brief and formal, was when this new matron was taken on a first round of introductions in her new domain. Rachel was not aware that she had any church connection and so was surprised to meet her again the next Sunday evening at Tyndale. Not expecting to be recognised or remembered at all, Rachel was somewhat taken aback when told, "Yes, I know who you are – Sister Ward 22!" Michael Docker in his tribute at Janet's funeral made clear that she could certainly fit the image of the "formidable" matron, yet a deeply caring one:

> And all this through the years of change, ferment, growth and challenge in the NHS. Janet, an "old-style" matron – fiercely efficient, in control of everything, ruling their territory with that winning combination of carrot and stick, loved, feared and respected.

Yet essentially she was a very gentle, unassuming person, never speaking for speaking's sake but only saying enough for what was needed to prompt action or elicit an answer. Michael Docker also recounts how after working at the highest levels of management, even in retirement she never lost her sense for detail and the way things needed to be done at the immediate and personal level:

> Part of my work is regularly to visit places such as the BRI. I'd sometimes mention which ward I'd been on to Janet – she knew it of course. I reckon she knew just about every nook and cranny in the place. I'd occasionally mention something I'd come across on a ward and she'd roll her eyes, just a small amount – and not say anything, but you could be fairly sure she'd formed an opinion about what was going on in the place that she'd influenced so greatly.

She was known not for wanting to make an impression, but for wanting to make a practical difference to how people were treated: true servant-hood in the world.

One life, five careers – Gordon Luton

The people we have highlighted in this chapter were typically those who pursued a continuous professional career within an established institution or business. Not everyone, however, has had either the opportunity (or wish) for such a single, clearly marked path within which to live out their Christian life. Nevertheless there are those who have felt God's leading at the very different turns their life has taken, and have found a variety of ways of expressing their faith whether in the community of the church or out in the world, and whether in paid or in voluntary work.

The Revd Gordon Luton

Gordon Luton, who became a member of Tyndale in 1981 and served as Church Secretary from 1984 to 1994, was a notable example. In fact it was said of him at his funeral that he had had five careers. Two years before his death in 2016, and prompted by a remark that being a single person he must have had "a very lonely life", in order to rebut such an idea he wrote a brief autobiography for the Tyndale magazine. In his own words:

> There is a general idea around that a man who remains single all his life is "not normal", but that is not the way I see it, nor how I evaluate my own life.
>
> I have the same kind of feelings, instincts, hopes and fears as other men, and I have had a varied, interesting and fulfilling life. I am not "gay", nor have I ever chosen not to marry. I had a number

of girlfriends earlier in my life, but, for various reasons, none of these attachments ended in marriage. Now in my old age, I regret that I have no family to leave behind.

After I left school, I was called up for National Service in the Army, after which I joined the family bakery business, which my grandfather founded in 1893.

I worked in this for ten years, by which time, I had come to feel a sense of calling into the Christian ministry. I spent four years [1958–62] as a student at Bristol Baptist College and the university, before my ordination. Then [1962] I was introduced to the pastorate of Stocking Farm Free Church, Leicester, a relatively new church, serving three estates in the city. Seeking a change of pastorate after five years there, I discovered that most Baptist churches at that time preferred a married man as their minister, and this left me with a very restricted choice for my second pastorate.

I decided to break into school teaching, and after a year at a college in Birmingham, was appointed [1967] Head of Religious Education at a large comprehensive school in that city, with some 1,750 pupils. I moved into a flat in Sutton Coldfield, and transferred my membership to the Baptist Church there.

Some twenty-five percent of our pupils came from immigrant families, and this was the time when multi-faith RE was increasingly being turned to. It seemed to me to have much to commend it in the circumstances. But I had not been trained with this in mind, so had to avail myself of various in-service courses on the subject. I have never regretted having done so. Children from Muslim families were generally much more literate about their faith than those from local families. Prior to this I was frequently asked, "Sir, why do I have to do RE? I don't go to church. I don't believe in God!" The same pupils were later asking, "Sir. When are we going to do our religion?"

Some years later, the minister of Sutton Coldfield Baptist Church received an appeal for help from the Baptist church in Four Oaks, a suburb in the north of the town whose members were no longer able to support a minister of their own. He asked me if I would lead a pastorate team of four men from his congregation, to provide a ministry there, each preaching one Sunday in four, and taking a quarter of the congregation for pastoral visitation. So I found myself back in the ministry while still a serving school teacher.

In 1980 I was looking to move to another school but was finding it difficult to get an appointment. Meanwhile, back in Bristol my father had died, and the man who had assumed control of the bakery business was due to retire three years later. There was no one to replace him, and I found myself facing the most difficult decision of my life. Should I solve my dilemma by leaving the teaching profession, returning to Bristol and, of all things, rejoining the bakery business? It took me six months and much hesitation, before I finally decided that I should do so.

The consequences were not what I had anticipated. After two years recession struck the country. Now private bakery businesses had to contend with supermarkets equipped with in-store bakeries, selling fresh bread made on their premises. Our shops faced fierce competition which we could not counter. Providentially, I was approached by a baker whom I had met in trade circles, looking to expand into Bristol. He knew of Lutons (his father had met mine years before) and I was able to negotiate the sale of the business to him.

This left me looking for employment. It came when I heard that the Bristol branch of the Royal Commonwealth Society was looking for an administrator and was given an introduction to their chairman. I served in this capacity for nearly ten years, after which, on my retirement, I was made a life member of the Society.

A lonely life? Not at all.

The Royal Commonwealth Society exists to promote through education and discussion the values of the British Commonwealth, especially human rights, democracy and peaceful conflict resolution among the member countries and in the world at large. Gordon's appointment was not just an opportune lifeline of employment (its home in Bristol is on Whiteladies Road). It made a piece with his long-standing internationalist interests and sympathies, as seen in his teaching in multi-faith Birmingham, his love of travel to distant and exotic places overseas and, in Tyndale, his leadership of the Justice, Peace and Integrity of Creation group. The fact that at on his retirement he was also invited actually to become the Society's chairman testifies to how he had gained the respect and affection of its non-church and varied constituency, who appreciated his quiet, gentle and sincere humanity.

Chapter 17.

Towards the Millennium

David Roberts & Michael Whitfield

For the last quarter of the twentieth century Tyndale was served by two ministers with similar backgrounds. Both Peter Webb and Robert Ellis had been members at Llanishen Baptist Church in Cardiff and both were trained at Regent's Park College, Oxford.

In June 1974 the Revd Ron Cowley left Tyndale to take up his duties as Superintendent of the Western Area of the Baptist Union. Ten months later, on 9th April 1975, the Revd Peter Webb was inducted as Tyndale's new minister, having moved into the Manse with his wife, Elizabeth, and children Stephen, Jeremy and Kate. Before going to Oxford he had first studied at Cardiff University. In 1964 he married Elizabeth Robertson. Before coming to Tyndale Webb had already served in two pastorates – at Biggin Hill in Kent for three years from 1965 and then in Edinburgh at Morningside for seven years. In Tyndale he later recalled that he found "a strong church with a lively congregation". Writing in *The Link* magazine soon after his arrival he said: "My task is not to be some kind of clerical 'head cook and bottle washer', but to share in the work as part of a team, and co-ordinate people's gifts for the building up of the body of Christ."

Already in that team was the Revd Barry Vendy, who had been at Tyndale since September 1973. His principal ministry was to the university students. When the time came for his departure, in the summer of 1976, the church had to consider very carefully, not only who would replace him, but also what type of ministry had priority. At the same time Ray Smith, a ministerial student, who had been there for a couple of years, left Lawrence Weston. Tyndale had for many years supported both the work among students and also the ministry at Lawrence Weston. A succession of ministerial students served Lawrence Weston for the next few years. In

Barry Vendy's place Alison Overton (née Logan) came to Tyndale with a special interest in students. She had recently completed her studies at the Baptist College and had married Grenville Overton. He would not be seeking a pastorate for another year, so her appointment to Tyndale was only for that one year. Because of this the ministerial rules would not permit her to be ordained as she would only be at Tyndale for one year and would have to await ordination until she settled for a longer period (in the event the Overtons were called to a joint pastorate the following year and both were then ordained). In the circumstances she was called "Minister's Assistant", although for all practical purposes she was an assistant minister! It was also seen as desirable for Lawrence Weston to have the benefit of a more permanent ministry than could be provided by a succession of students. It was beginning to become clear that very soon there would probably not be the resources to support both the ministry to university students and also Lawrence Weston with full-time ministry.

Over the next few years the church tried to balance these priorities. When Alison Overton left, the church thought long and hard about whether another minister should be called to work with the students. In the event the decision was positive and the Revd Ian Millgate, who had just completed his training at Spurgeon's College, accepted a call to be the Associate Minister and Student Chaplain. Like his predecessor, he was provided with accommodation in a university hall of residence, Badock Hall. However, after two years he married Jill Prime, a Tyndale member, and moved out of halls. Although it was considered desirable for the "University Chaplain" to live in one of the halls, it had already been agreed that this was not essential should he or she be married. Millgate served Tyndale for three years before moving to a pastorate in Birmingham. On his departure the whole issue of the ministry to students was again under consideration. While acknowledging the good work that Millgate and his predecessors had done, Peter Webb was of the opinion that ideally such a ministry could best be fulfilled by a minister with some pastoral experience. One suggestion was for a joint appointment with Redland Park URC, which also exercised a ministry to students. Since 1964 the Baptist student society had dropped the name "Edward Terrill Society" in favour of the more prosaic "BapSoc" and it then merged with the URC student society into

The Revd Peter Webb

what was popularly known as "BURCSOC". This was part of a national trend. Denominational societies were going out of fashion among students in the 1970s – the Baptist Student Federation, which was the core of the network of Baptist student societies, was wound up in 1977. When Robert Ellis arrived at Tyndale in 1987 there was still a lively BURCSOC, attended by twenty or so young people with some links to Baptist or URC churches. A number of the Baptist students worshipped at Tyndale on Sundays, while URC students often went to Redland Park. BURCSOC continued apparently thriving, with a number of able and committed student leaders. Then suddenly, as if realizing belatedly that denominations were passé for their generation, the society went from thriving to nothing within a couple of years in the mid 1990s.

Some reservations about the idea of a joint chaplaincy were expressed in the Church Meeting and there was a hope that the Association might become involved. In the event, not least for financial reasons both within Tyndale and the wider denomination, the eventual outcome was to create a Free Church Chaplaincy, towards which both the Association and the Baptist Union Home Mission Fund would contribute. After complicated negotiations with the URC and Methodists at national as well as local level, a scheme was agreed and the Revd John Fail was appointed in March 1983. He was a Methodist who had been an army chaplain, so came with relevant experience of ministering to young people. Sadly his ministry was cut short after little more than a year by his sudden death. Unfortunately the financial arrangements between the denominations then had to be renegotiated before a new appointment

The Revd Tim Pittock

could be made, but eventually the Revd David Pittock (who later adopted the name "Tim"), another Methodist minister, was appointed. Tim worshipped at Tyndale and was elected to the diaconate. Following his resignation as chaplain, he served as a member of the counselling team in the University.

Lawrence Weston had a much smaller membership than Tyndale and from time to time had difficulty in finding people who were willing to take leadership roles. Therefore it was essential that some form of pastoral oversight was provided. In 1976 it was hoped that Tyndale's other "daughter" church, Westbury On Trym, might help, but this did not materialise. In 1979 the student pastor, Bruce Morgan, was invited to remain at Lawrence Weston as its minister after he completed his studies at the College. However he declined and was called to his first pastorate in Coventry.

Then in 1980 the Revd Jacqueline Triggs accepted the pastorate on completion of her college course. There was some concern at the prospect of a single woman living alone in the Lawrence Weston manse, but she did have another woman companion to live with her for much of her time there. The following year the relationship between Tyndale and Lawrence Weston was reviewed by the Tyndale deacons, since it was far from clear. The outcome was a Memorandum which acknowledged that Lawrence Weston looked to Tyndale for support, that the Tyndale minister might attend

Lawrence Weston Church Meetings and that membership decisions should be reported to the Tyndale deacons. At the same time Tyndale appointed two of its members to serve on the Lawrence Weston diaconate. Crucially it was Tyndale that would issue any call to the pastorate and the Lawrence Weston minister would be designated an Associate Minister of Tyndale. In fact Triggs frequently attended Tyndale Deacons' Meetings. To underline Tyndale's commitment to Lawrence Weston, in 1983 it was made clear that financial support for it took priority over university chaplaincy and the strong links between the two churches were confirmed. Her years at Lawrence Weston were not easy for Jacqueline Triggs. Increasingly she had to deal with community problems and there were few in the membership who could offer her support in pastoral work, while at the same time some of the older members were beginning to drop out of active involvement and also finding it more difficult to give financial support. Added to that, she found little support from other churches on the estate as ecumenical relationships were weak. Perhaps it is not surprising that in the spring of 1984 Triggs felt it was time to move on and she accepted a call to be Associate Minister at Stony Stratford.

In 1979 the Revd Stuart Fuller came to Bristol (where he had been a student at the College in the 1950s) to take care of family business interests in Bristol, and became a member of Tyndale. On Triggs' departure he accepted a call to be part-time minister at Lawrence Weston. As he had his own house, the manse was made available for a student of the College, and Michael Stanbridge lived there until 1987. Fuller fulfilled this role for the next nine years, joined in 1986 for three years by Mrs Pat Battarbee, a Tyndale member who was studying at the College to be a Supplementary Minister and who went on to be part-time Assistant Minister at Westbury On Trym.

Tyndale's concern for young people was by no means restricted to students. Throughout the years of Peter Webb's ministry there were a substantial number of teenagers, mostly, but not all, the children of church members. At the beginning of Webb's ministry there were two youth groups which were designed to cater for the older children from church families. There were also a number of younger children who were in the crèche or Junior Church – a number which grew from about 30 in 1973 to 50 in 1977, and which remained fairly stable throughout the following ten years. A member of the Junior Church in the late 1970s recalled:

> Each class catered for a different age group which included Phyllis Payne who for many years, a Tyndale institution, led the youngest group. During my time in Junior Church I attended classes led by Brian Pratt, Derek Parsons and Geoff Molyneux. All classes reflected their particular personalities: Brian using popular culture to reflect on a Christian theme, Derek often drawing on his love of literature and Geoff using drawing and creative arts. Geoff's classes were particularly memorable because of his encouragement of us to express ourselves creatively. Whilst he would give a critique of our work and advice, he was unfailingly positive and encouraging unless we misbehaved when you were quickly reminded that he was a school teacher!

Many of these children moved into the youth groups as the years passed. A popular activity for the young people was the occasional residential weekend at Boxenwood, a cottage in the Quantocks frequently made available by Canon (later Bishop) Peter and Donata Coleman (there were also occasional weekends there for students as well). One who went there a number of times recalled:

> The cottage was basic and included a barn which we used as a dormitory and for entertainment. The setting and surroundings of Boxenwood are glorious and as ever with childhood memories I remember endless picnics, barbecues and French cricket or rounders in the sunshine. As we got older we began to use Boxenwood for youth club weekends and for more independent trips, for instance Martin Jones, Chris West and a few others went one weekend for one of a number of attempts to form a band taking drums, guitars and a synthesiser. We demonstrated enthusiastically that everyone has not actually got talent but luckily Boxenwood has no close neighbours!

It was during this period that the first of a series of pantomimes was performed, some of the later ones involving older people. Elizabeth Webb, quite early in her time at Tyndale, established the "Tyndale Dancers" for the

Humpty Dumpty pantomime in 1983

older girls, and in later years a number of older people (of both sexes) became involved (see chapter 18). However, as is so often the case in so many churches, there was frequently a problem of finding sufficient leaders. Over these years a number of very dedicated and talented people were involved in youth work. The organisation of the youth work also changed from time to time; as the young people grew older so it became necessary to split them into different groups and there were several re-organisations of the structures. Many of these young people were baptised and became church members, although frequently they were lost to the church as they left home, often for university, and settled elsewhere. Others remained and in time came to fulfil leadership roles in the church.

Most of the baptisms were of younger people, but there were also a number of more mature people. As well as infant dedications, baptisms were always incorporated into the Sunday morning service, or occasionally the evening service (a contrast with Richard Glover's years, when they were always on a Wednesday evening). Between 1973 and 1987 there were about 60 baptisms in all. In addition there were people who came into membership on confession of faith or by transfer from other churches. Yet the number of members remained fairly constant throughout at around 240. Partly this was, as in most churches, because of members moving away and transferring their membership to other churches, or, sadly, allowing their membership to lapse. However there also appears to have been rather a large number of deaths, some 75 during those same years – the minutes of most Deacons' Meetings and monthly editions of *The Link* report one or more deaths. Several of these were of people who had played a significant role in the life of the church including Dorothy Porteous, Harold Hockey, Milford Kemp, Rex Hopes, Joyce Whilding and Katherine Gotch Robinson. The death of Katherine Robinson in 1985 marked the end of an era for the church – for the first time in the church's 116 year history there were no members of the Robinson family in membership.

In 1979 the whole church was shocked by two sudden and untimely deaths. In July, Judith Roberts (daughter of the Church Secretary) died suddenly of a brain haemorrhage at the age of only 15, and in November Gareth Jones (son-in-law of the late Harold Bodey), aged 54, fell to his death in the Avon Gorge. The two tragedies were linked in that Jones' children were close friends of Judith and her brothers. Reflecting on both these tragedies, one of Judith's brothers later wrote: "Tyndale friends were there to provide a level of love and support usually not found in other walks of life".

Tyndale had always been closely involved with the life of the Bristol Association. This continued during these years, not only hosting the Annual Assembly. In 1977 the Revd Dr Morris West and 1984 Peter Webb served as Association President, as did Robert Ellis in his final year at Tyndale. Then in 1985 David Roberts resigned as Church Secretary on being appointed as Association Secretary, an office he held for the next seven years.

The Revd Dr Robert Ellis [Regent's Park College]

As seen in earlier chapters, Tyndale has been associated with Bristol Baptist College for most of the church's existence. But Robert Ellis' ministry at Tyndale was the first in which Tyndale's minister has held a formal teaching position at the College – serving as part-time tutor at for the last six years of his ministry at Tyndale (1995–2001). This is, perhaps natural in view of his impressive academic qualifications, for he studied theology at Regent's Park College, Oxford and Colgate-Rochester Divinity School, New York, before ordination in 1981. His doctoral work was concerned with modern "Process Theology". Ellis started teaching at the College in the autumn of 1990 when John Morgan-Wynne invited him to teach Philosophy of Religion and Christian Doctrine following Keith Clements' departure. Following Brian Haymes' appointment as Principal in 1994, this teaching was put on a more formal basis when Ellis was appointed Tutor in Christian Doctrine and the "salary" for this helped Tyndale afford other ministry costs.

There were various attempts to reach out to the local community. In 1976 there was talk of a local mission jointly with other churches, but this eventually came to nothing. The buildings which had been created by the Centenary Project provided a large area in the basements beneath the rear halls and Tyndale Court. This opened up a number of opportunities and in 1976 a scheme was agreed to provide a supervised workshop for the benefit of elderly people who might not have facilities at home for their hobbies. This was named "The Richard Glover Centre". Another project was to open the church on weekdays for any who might wish to use it for quiet meditation. However, this did not last very long as it proved to be very little used and was discontinued after about 18 months. More positively, after much careful thought, in 1983 it was agreed to make the Harold Bodey Room available for meetings of the local Alcoholics Anonymous group, a facility which was later extended to other "Anonymous" groups.

Another very successful venture around this time was what were first called "Ecumenical Lunches" (because other local churches, notably Redland Park URC, provided some of the voluntary helpers) but soon became known as the "Drop-In Lunches". These proved very popular for many years. As well as being appreciated by many in the local community, the funds they raised went to support overseas development, medical and educational work. Large sums were raised to support developing-world charitable causes, particularly the Whiteladies Health-Share Project supporting the work of a clinic in India, with which the church had close associations (see chapter 15). Initially meals were cooked at home and brought in to church by volunteer cooks, but changes in legislation meant that this no longer conformed to food hygiene requirements. The kitchen had already had a major makeover, with stainless steel fittings making it a much more professional and appropriate space. But now a deal was done with health service providers to buy-in cook-chill meals, and so new regeneration ovens were required to make it possible to re-heat these for serving in church. Drop-In Lunches provided a valuable place for shoppers, locals, and some who craved a bit of company, with a valuable service.

Tyndale's support for Billy Graham's "Mission England" in May 1984 was less than whole-hearted and Peter Webb expressed some reservations about this approach to mission. Nevertheless a coach was hired to take people from Tyndale to the Ashton Gate football stadium where the rallies were held and there were a few referrals of possible converts, at least one of whom was baptised.

In 1986 a project was launched under the title "Tyndale Tomorrow". Various meetings of small and larger groups led to the formulation of priorities for the church in the future. Education, pastoral care and social action were high among these and there were a number of suggestions for children's work. To launch some of these ideas a programme, "Tyndale Together", was launched at a "Church Day" in September that year, with classes in Christian Basics and Bible Study. To strengthen the prayer life of the church "Eighth Day Prayers" had also been launched whereby groups of people undertook to follow a suggested pattern of prayer every eighth day, thereby avoiding this simply becoming a routine attached to a certain day of the week.

It was in 1919 that the first women deacons had been elected, but it took another 57 years before, in 1976, they were invited to serve at communion, and even then one of the women deacons declined to serve. At the same time a number of women were added to the stewards' rota for the first time. In leading worship it was Webb's practice to wear a clerical collar, cassock, tabs and academic hood. The form of Sunday morning services remained largely unchanged throughout this period, including the chanting of a Psalm and the singing of an anthem by the choir (contributions to worship which were later dropped – but some of the 21st century congregation still miss them). The new *Praise For Today* hymn book was introduced and the evening services followed a more varied pattern. To the long-established choir, which now came under the leadership of Mrs Gwen Sharpe, was added a small music group. Despite wearing a "dog collar" in a 1989 photograph of the minister and deacons, it was rarely apparent during Robert Ellis' ministry. Sunday worship slowly became less formal, not only in the dress of the minister, but in the music that was used and the structure of the services. Modern songs started replacing the chants and some of the hymns and he would sometimes accompany these on his trumpet.

The diaconate in 1988. Front: Christine Bodey, John Elliott, Robert Ellis, Gordon Luton, Ron Cooper; middle: David Roberts, Suzanne Elliott, Pam Fisher, Elizabeth Benson, Janet Gerrish, Mary Baseley, Freda West, Michael Whitfield; back: Dave Morris, Bob Jones, Miriam Parsons, Brian Pratt, Michael Smith, Eric Sharpe, Geoffrey Fisher.

Gwen Sharpe and her husband, the Revd Eric Sharpe, came as wardens of Tyndale Court. Both played a very active role in the church for many years and Eric Sharpe served as a deacon. Over much of its history Tyndale has numbered Baptist ministers among its membership – some retired, others in non-pastoral roles – and at this time they included the Revd Dr Morris West (the Baptist College Principal) and the Revd Dr Keith Clements (College tutor), as well as the Revds Albert Oakeley (with his wife, wardens of Tyndale Court before the Sharpes), Harold Roberts, Walter Bottoms, Michael Pitts and Gordon Luton.

One of the interests of Eric Sharpe was "Stewardship" in which he had been involved at national level. So he was able to give the minister a good deal of support when a Stewardship programme was launched at Tyndale in 1978. It was made clear from the start that this was not simply about finance and a wide spectrum of the church's activities was looked at in various ways. However the church's financial arrangements were seen as needing to be brought up-to-date. Thus a number of changes were made, during the course of which Reg Stephens retired as treasurer and his place was taken by John Elliott. With the active support of Webb it was decided to bring decisions about the minister's remuneration to the Church Meeting, whereas this had largely been in the hands of the Finance Committee with some involvement of the deacons. Around the same time, in 1978–9 there were two other changes – an "all in" budget, eliminating virtually all special appeals, and moving the financial year from the calendar year to April– March. Over these years there were no financial crises, although both income and expenditure went up and down – mostly up! There was generally a good response to requests for increased giving and there were a few legacies, including one of over £26,000. This was of significant help in meeting the costs of a number of fabric problems which needed attention.

There were a number of "one-off" special events – the Christmas Day service was broadcast on Radio Bristol in 1978, an Association Assembly met at Tyndale in 1983, Civic Services were hosted in 1986 and 2000 and a televised morning service in 1986. There were also two final events. The Bristol Guild of the Handicapped (a charity begun in 1896 as "The Guild of the Brave Poor Things") joined the Tyndale evening service once a year for many years. By the 1980s most of its beneficiaries were very elderly and, although Tyndale members organised their cars to bring them to the service, its last service at Tyndale was in May 1986 and the Guild itself closed in 1987. There was also an end to another long-running traditional service. For many years the Collegiate School had joined morning worship on the occasion of its former pupils' reunion. However the Old Girls' Society disbanded, these reunions came to an end in 1986 and so ended the visits of the school to Tyndale.

In July 1987 Peter Webb announced that he had accepted a call to be minister of College Road Baptist Church, Harrow. He subsequently moved to South Street Exeter in 1995, until he retired in 2005. Peter and Elizabeth Webb remained in Exeter for several years before returning to the Bristol area in 2014 and renewing their membership of Tyndale.

At Peter Webb's final service at Tyndale he was able to announce the name of his successor! This was unusual, but the "search process" had started as soon as he had announced his call to Harrow and had proceeded very smoothly. So it was only four months after Peter Webb's departure that the Revd Dr Robert Ellis was inducted on 21st November 1987. He was married to Sue, a primary school teacher, and they had three children: Gareth (6) Timothy (4) and Ceridwen (2). They moved into the manse in Upper Cranbook Road. Ellis had held his first pastorate at Spurgeon's Baptist Church, Bletchley, Milton Keynes.

The Revd Alan Smith

The Revd Alan Smith was called to minister at Tyndale in 1992, following his retirement from New Road, Oxford. Smith was employed half time with little responsibility for Sunday worship and no general pastoral care involvement and was termed "Associate Minister" as a replacement for the Assistant Ministers associated with student care. His proved to be an inspired appointment, investigating local needs as he spoke with local social workers, schools, health professionals, and others. Soon a distinct need came into focus and the Tyndale Circle took shape. This day centre for dementia sufferers was a bold venture and became possible because Smith did excellent preparation and got people on board – it would have been impossible without the enthusiastic commitment of volunteers from Tyndale (and from other local churches) and without credibility in the eyes of professionals serving in the area. It opened on 3rd November 1995 to provide care on Thursdays in the basement, with professional leaders and lunch provided from the kitchen above.

Tyndale Coffee Shop began on Tuesday mornings during Alan Smith's ministry as another way of connecting with the local community. It attracted "passing trade" and quickly developed a regular clientele. Miriam Parsons was the moving force in this, but again a pool of volunteers gathered to make it viable. The area at the entrance of the church was used for this work, with tables set out on the church forecourt during better weather. This modest venture was, and continues to be, a clear success, showing how pastoral work and outreach go closely together.

Other initiatives during this time were partaking in National RE (Religious Education) week, led by Michael Smith, where classes from local schools visited the church and were challenged to look around the sanctuary and answer questions about what they saw. David and Pauline Roberts were largely responsible for the Open University using the church as an examination centre from 1996 to 2002, where some 2,000 people visited the church over a two week period. It was not easy as Tyndale's catering volunteers nobly set up shop at the kitchen hatches providing hot drinks from 9.00 a.m. for the students gathering in the church. They would be there again for an hour before the afternoon exam. This was much appreciated, as many candidates had had long and difficult journeys to reach the exam centre. At the weekends volunteers would stack the exam furniture and reinstate the church chairs. After the Sunday evening service more volunteers would restore the exam layout once again.

Other community outreach initiatives that lasted into the new millennium included the start of the Saturday Soup Run (providing food and drink to homeless people in central Bristol) organised by the Clifton group of churches, where Tyndale took responsibility for the month of September each year. The house-to-house delivery of *Tyndale Tymes* to houses in the immediate neighbourhood, a leaflet detailing work in the church and inviting householders to visit, was another.

When Alan Smith retired in 1998 and with the Tyndale Circle still going strong, the church decided that the next associate minister should have a slightly more general remit. The Revd Jane Kingsnorth was appointed with more Sunday responsibility and more pastoral care work than Alan Smith had, and she worked on making closer links with people coming in and out of the building. She continued in post when Robert Ellis left, and helped smooth the transition during the pastoral vacancy, aided by Janet Gerrish as secretary, Edward Duffield, as treasurer and Julian West as administrator.

With a young family, it is not surprising that work with young people was important for Robert Ellis. In the early years of his ministry the church considered professional help in this area by funding a youth worker, but this never proved possible. The difficulty of a widely dispersed congregation showed itself in young people's work, where few of the young people attended the same school so had little contact between Sundays. Despite much commitment from those involved in leading it, with teenagers especially there were real difficulties. Junior Church continued on Sunday mornings and there were three main initiatives away from Sundays. "MOB" – a name chosen by the teenagers involved – was led by Dave and Cilla Morris, and then by Richard and Ruth Ward, and also Julian West. They met with the young people on Sunday evenings in their homes, and also took them off once a year or so for a weekend away. One of the purposes of youth work is making healthy relationships, and it appears that on this count MOB worked well. "TYC" (Tyndale Youth Club) was aimed at the pre-teens, and met each week on Friday evenings. Games figured prominently, and much energy was expended. Most successful, perhaps, in terms of helping the young people feel a sense of belonging was the church's decision to allow all children and young people to attend the annual Church Weekend free of charge – so enabling families to come with less concern about costs, and giving prolonged time together for the youngsters. Ellis reflected that young people's work always felt a bit precarious and this state of affairs, unfortunately, continues.

The Church Weekends from 1989, initially at Malvern, then at Swanage and more recently at Brunel Manor, Torquay, were important for young people, but also for the whole communal life of the congregation. A mixture of working together on a given theme, allied with games and entertainment, free time to enjoy the area or just one another's company, and very experimental worship together on Sundays, proved an excellent vehicle for building and deepening relationships in the church.

One of the more successful one-off projects during Ellis' ministry was Tyndale Arts 2000. It lasted two months and began with a drama workshop by the travelling theatre company Riding Lights Roughshod and included a performance of their new play "The Story of God's Mutineer" and "Mary Magdalene" performed on Sunday evenings by members of local churches. The festival included art exhibitions, dance, drama, film, music, and more. Schools and community groups were involved, some working with disadvantaged groups, as well as the Bach Choir and a professional singer – Martyn Joseph. It took huge effort, but was generally thought a success. It enabled the church to establish itself as a partner in promoting the arts with groups from around the city. In total the audience was over 2,000 and they were able to donate just under £5,000 to local arts groups. Robert Ellis described the festival's vision:

> God gave human beings a share of his own creativity, and the arts are one form in which we humans express, enjoy and explore what it is to be human. In becoming, albeit briefly, a centre for arts we become a centre for expression, enjoyment and exploration of a precious divine gift. And through it all, this creativity honours the Creator himself. Every contributor to this festival will be praising God, knowingly or otherwise, through his or her artistic endeavour and expression.

The ecumenical cooperation along Whiteladies Road was considerable though always limited. Victoria Methodist, Redland Park URC, and Tyndale were a natural geographical and theological triumvirate – but nobody really asked the daring question about the future, and whether the area would be able to continue to support three churches whose traditions might be different but whose ethos was so similar. Levels of cooperation waxed and waned a little according to who was in post in each church, but relationships were always good with occasional minor turbulence. With Colin Baxter (URC), Ellis developed a peculiar relationship where each would goad one another into eye-catching Christmas morning services. Because of the Chaplaincy connection, which also brought these churches' ministers together, the relationships between these ministers was continually nourished. St Paul's Church of England, just off the bottom of Whiteladies Road, became a fourth member of the local group – with Woodlands Christian Fellowship, an evangelical student-oriented church, occasionally pitching in. Cotham Parish Church would also prove good ecumenical neighbours, especially in Neville Boundy's time.

In 2000 Robert Ellis was encouraged to apply for the job of Principal at Bristol Baptist College. He was not appointed but his elder brother, the Revd Dr Chris Ellis, was. Inevitably this was not easy to manage and in exploring his options he felt that he and Tyndale needed a change. In March 2001 he accepted the position of Tutor in Pastoral Theology at Regent's Park College, Oxford, succeeding to the Principalship in 2007, where he has deployed his rich gifts in preaching and pastoral care in the formation of a new generation of Baptist ministers. Before he left Tyndale Ellis suggested to his eldest son, Gareth, that he set up Tyndale's website which was the start of something really new – an appropriate innovation in a new millennium!

Appendix 2: Traffic at Tyndale – The Ministry of Space

Edward Duffield

Location, location, location – Tyndale's halls have always been attractive to outside users and, of course, their location makes it no surprise. With five bus routes, a train station and in the middle of a popular residential and shopping area it might indicate that something was wrong if there was not a constant interest in hiring the halls. Since there are a surprising number of sets of rooms to hire in the area, it is a competitive market place. Typical amongst those looking for a regular venue are clubs and societies and small-scale entrepreneurs trying to get their business off the ground. Rather limited cash is a common factor for them all, so it has created quite high price sensitivity in letting charges. If not managed carefully this can become a most unwelcome problem. In the early 1990s the treasurer, after sending many unhappy letters demanding payment for a year's unpaid rent from one organisation, was knocking on the door of the last known address of the organisation's proprietor. It was an unproductive attempt, other than to establish that Tyndale was not the only agency left without payment!

What picture then emerges over the years of who, apart from church-connected activity, actually uses Tyndale's halls and does a change of usage reflect anything about the shifting scene and changing life in this part of Bristol?

The starting point must be with the Classical Dance Studios whose principal, Deborah Sims, opened ballet school classes at Tyndale in 1981. Her classes on four days a week have continued without a break to the present time. Many of her students progress to achieve very high standards and some have gone on to join the Royal Ballet. Other major customers going back twenty to thirty years have been the Bristol & District Flower Arrangement Group, the Townswomen's Guild, the Open University, the University of the 3rd Age, the National Youth Orchestra audition centre, the Red Cross and Bristol Intermediate Technology. On an occasional-booking basis the Labour Party, Bristol European Movement and MPs' surgeries can be added, but apart from the Ballet School none of them continue to meet at Tyndale now.

Throughout this period the Harold Bodey Room on the first floor at the front of the church has been used by various "Anonymous" or "Anon" support groups. With its own front door and access to toilets and a kitchenette, it is a perfect venue for groups wishing to be self-contained and is hugely appreciated by them. In the 1990s there were four groups, today there are fifteen. There are meetings every day of the week, most lunch-times and at least one every evening. About 220 people per week attend these meetings which speaks volumes about the need and the remarkable support being provided through this one part of Tyndale's premises so that this part of the story is not just a commercial transaction but a compassionate ministry in its own right.

The completion of the basement refurbishment in the mid-1990s enabled a substantial area with five separate rooms to be brought into use. One by-product of this was the research by the Revd Alan Smith into the needs of the community which might be served by the basement accommodation. It was from this that the Tyndale Circle Day Centre was founded as a joint venture with the four Whiteladies Road churches in 1995. The Day Centre continues to use the whole of the basement every Thursday, serving the special needs of up to 12 people with dementia who are still being cared for at home. It is a double win, providing the carer with a day's respite and the patient with a stimulating, fun day in safe and supportive care. But there was disappointment too! It had been expected that demand for rented space would apply to this area in just the same way as for the ground floor. There were a number of short term lettings but none survived as viable projects until 2011 when the Bristol Language School was established. From very small beginnings at Tyndale it has steadily grown and now runs classes in many European and Oriental languages on four evenings per week plus Tuesday mornings. In 2017 there were 3,816 student attendances. That's a lot of learning!

Another major change for the halls happened in 2000 when we were approached by the Bristol Chinese Christian Church. After a short experimental period, Tyndale became their home for Sunday services in three languages. They very quickly grew and occupy every inch of space on Sunday afternoons until early evening.

What else then is different today? The biggest change is reflected in the weekly use of the sanctuary. From rarely being used during the week it is now used for two Bristol choirs on Mondays and Thursdays, by Slimming World on Tuesdays and our own time@tyndale mid-week meeting on Wednesdays. Saturdays are regularly booked for choirs, musical theatre rehearsals, Come & Sing events and concerts. Our halls are booked on a weekly basis by Music With Mummy on Wednesdays and Thursdays, Les Petits Zouzous on Thursdays as well as the Tyndale Babies and Toddlers Group on Mondays. The Ladies Painting Group meet on Friday mornings and piano lessons take up the afternoon. The Coffee Shop on Tuesday mornings in the sanctuary has expanded to three days a week and makes a special connection with children and parents attending other groups on Wednesdays and Thursdays. Even the vestibule sees considerable traffic in the run-up to Christmas as those selling charity Christmas cards set up their wares there.

Today's usage has quite a different flavour from that of yesterday with a noticeable emphasis on children and music coupled with service to needs in the community. In 2004 Tyndale's Halls Steward, Charity Hamilton, concluded her annual report with:

> I know it's only a building, but it is a building, which is a tool of ministry, it is a space which has had the presence of God in it for many years and which is effective in engaging with others. Not only does it enable groups of people to practise community, support and engagement with one another, the buildings also offer opportunities for us to engage with Christ in the form of the stranger. The offering of this space not only benefits Tyndale's worshipping community but also benefits the hundreds of people that pass through every week, it is possible they catch a glimpse of God as we do when we meet them. It is an outreach ministry which I am privileged to be part of.

She called it the "Ministry of Space" and as those before have exercised this ministry the present generation seeks to continue in that spirit.

Chapter 18.

Music, Dance, Drama and the Arts at Tyndale

Michael Whitfield

Tyndale's organist in 2018, Dr Sarah Dodds, provides a useful introduction to what she calls a "Theology of Music", when she identifies two biblical texts as justification for the place of music in Christian worship:

> It is good to praise the Lord, to sing psalms in your honour, Most High, to tell out your devotion in the morning, your faithfulness each night, accompanied by a ten-stringed lute and the playing of a harp. (Psalm 92 vv 1–3)

> Praise him with trumpet sound; praise him with lute and harp! Praise him with tambourine and dance; praise him with strings and pipe! Praise him with clanging cymbals; praise him with loud crashing cymbals! (Psalm 150 vv 3–6)

Fortified by such Biblical authority she underlines the fact that:

> A significant portion of our worship consists of music. Many Christian traditions have quite explicit teaching about the role of music in worship and what expectations people should have of it. Anglicans have a strong sense that music is an offering they bring to God in worship, whereas Methodists have a rich heritage of hymn singing. Martin Luther gave more thought than any other theologian to the role of music in worship, and his ideas inspired the richest musical traditions the Church has ever known, culminating in the work of J. S. Bach who has become known as "the fifth evangelist".

Whilst acknowledging that it is not possible to please all the people in a church all the time, accepting that the church has a role to play in music education has challenged Tyndale to question its own beliefs about the role of music in church. There is no doubt that music has played an important part in the life of the church and that Tyndale has experienced crashing cymbals and all sorts of percussion instruments at various times! But there has been so much more.

When the church was opened in 1868, the choir was seated at the back of the chancel, their seats forming three sides of a square, with an open front. It would appear that initially an organ was hired for £10 a year. What kind of organ it was is not recorded, but it was at least superior to a harmonium, since a succession of organ blowers were employed (at 1/3d a Sunday). However, in 1877 it was decided to have a two-manual organ built at a cost of £400 plus £120 for the case. The design by W. G. Vowles was accepted with "front pipes of spotted metal" but "omitting the figures of angels". The organ, which stood behind the pulpit was "opened" in October 1877 with a recital by the Cathedral organist (who had advised on the specification) and a performance of Mendelsohn's *Hymn of Praise* by an augmented choir.

The first organist was J. B. Miles, appointed in time for the opening of the church at an annual salary of £30. He had been organist at Arley Chapel (Congregationalist) and served Tyndale for 10 years. His service might have ended sooner, as in January 1877 he was given notice by the deacons. However, this was withdrawn when he agreed to be "responsible for the conduct of psalmody at Tuesday evening services". As there was no Baptist hymn book 100 years ago, the church first used *Bible Tunes and Chants* and frequently discussed the introduction of new tune books. *The Bristol Tune Book* was used as was the *Congregational Hymnal* before the first *Baptist Church Hymnal* became available in 1900.

Before the first organ was installed in 1868, at the first bazaar in aid of Tyndale, the band of Messrs Derham Brothers played throughout the evening and "enlivened the proceedings" and the next year there was a soiree in the Victoria Rooms celebrating the settlement of Richard Glover at Tyndale. In the gallery there was a select choir conducted by Miles that "sang at intervals with great taste and ability". Over the years, music formed a crucial part of money-raising, for instance in aid of the "lecture hall building fund" in 1882 there was a soiree as part of the programme of the Tyndale Literary Society where piano recitals and numerous songs were given by members. On another occasion R. J. Vosper and his band of 30 performers with a choir of 100 voices, gave a sacred concert of Farmer's oratorio *Christ and His Soldiers* and Mendlessohn's *Lauda Sion*. The choir comprised the members of the Tyndale Chapel choir assisted by the choirs of all the neighbouring chapels. Next year there was a Male Voice Glee concert given by a specially selected choir in aid of the building fund.

The newly formed Bristol Choirs Association met at Tyndale in 1883 for their spring festival, when the anthem *Raising the daughter of Jairus* by Stainer was sung. In 1885 there was a concert in aid of the city's Penny Dinner Fund, which included singing and violin solos. There was also a choir of 30 voices. The Bristol Choirs Association met again in January 1886 for a talk by the Revd John Curwen, a Congregational minister from the Tonic Solfa Association on the subject of "Church Psalmody" in the Tyndale Hall. After the talk there were various solos and choral works performed. To help fund the mission school being built in Deanery Road in 1888, there was a concert in the Church Hall. Both professional and amateur musicians gave their services freely and performed a cello solo (Bocherini's *4th Sonata*), a couple of harp solos and an "exquisite performance of Beethoven's *Moonlight Sonata*". Various songs were sung, and two songs from Gilbert and Sullivan operas proved very popular.

Miles was succeeded as organist by A. Bruton in 1878, but he resigned in 1882, and Henry Warner was appointed organist and choir master in the autumn of that year. By 1892 Tyndale's choir had 27 members, fourteen single ladies, two married and eleven men. There was a congregational practice of psalmody on Wednesday evening after the service (7.30 p.m.) and a choir practice on Friday evening at 8 o'clock. Warner's appointment lasted until 1893 when he was succeeded by D. W. Rootham until September 1900. On 15th October 1900 Rootham was presented with a silver salver and his wife with a silver tea service after their faithful and valiant service to the church over the previous eight years.

Of the 22 applicants for the post of organist in 1900, the organist at the David Thomas Memorial (Congregationalist) church in Bishopston was eventually selected and so Walter F. C. Maker, FRCO, began his fifty years of service. He was the son of the organist at Redland Park, F. C. Maker, who composed many hymn tunes, seven of which were in the *Baptist Hymn Book*. Walter Maker became a church member in 1902 and was recorded as the Sunday School Superintendent of the Tyndale Mission in 1913. He died shortly before his planned retirement in 1950 and was followed for two years by Anthony Gibbon, ARCM, ARCO.

Various concerts were given, one of which in aid of the Bristol City Mission, was held in the church hall in June 1915. The musical portion of the evening was undertaken by choirs from the several Mission stations under the leadership of the Senior Missionary. After World War I, a Service of Praise was held on Friday 4th April 1919 with Phyllis Lett, Madame Katharine Gerrish and Seymour Dossor as vocalists, the violinist, Maurice Alexander and cellist, Lt Leonard Dennis. The choir was conducted by Henry Dennis and Bartlett Hunt was at the organ. The programme included the *Hallelujah Chorus*, *The Easter Hymn* and *Parry's Jerusalem* and donations were given for the Jubilee Fund. During Christmas 1922, after the evening service, an augmented choir sang carols on the steps of the church's portico and a collection was made for the Lord Mayor's Fund. The church Jubilee scheme which was implemented in 1935 involved moving the organ to the north transept and creating the open baptistry in the centre of the church. The choir sang from the balcony at the rear of the church. At the evening service on the 14th October, Maker gave an organ recital on the renovated organ. During 1937 an advertised Sunday service included the name of the minister and also the soloist (Elsie Balmond).

In December 1940 the church was gutted and that organ destroyed. The loss of the church during World War II meant that worship had to take place in the church hall. The Church Secretary wrote in 1947 that for seven years,

> our good little piano has striven valiantly to fill the gap... We are now being presented with a pipe organ by some friends. It is a dear little organ, good looking, possessing two manuals, a pedal

> board and a good and varied range of stops. It was formerly in the
> hall of the Bush family home in Stoke Bishop and should be just
> about the right size for our hall.

In spite of being restricted to the church hall, Tyndale was invited to be one of a series of churches who had their evening service broadcast on the radio in March 1947. The other places of worship included St Mary Redcliffe and Gloucester and Salisbury cathedrals! The choir did well at both morning and evening services and an anthem was sung during the evening service. There was another broadcast service the next year, this time in the morning, and the congregation was instructed to be at church at 9.20 a.m. with the service starting at 9.30. Walter Maker played the organ and Elsie Balmond and her friends helped with the singing. On Christmas Sunday afternoon, in the church hall, a warm welcome was given to Elsie Balmond and her talented St George's Institute Choir on the occasion of Tyndale's Carol service. It was reported that "Their visit is developing into a popular annual event and their kindness in coming so regularly is much appreciated". Balmond was eventually appointed choir mistress and clearly had many talents as exemplified by a report of the annual church party:

> After an early tea, the "musicians group" won a series of
> competitions and Mr Motson sang to us and then the
> entertainment was taken over by Miss Elsie Balmond and Mr Rex
> Hopes who gave duets in a style brilliantly parodying a Victorian
> musical evening. Those who heard them will smile reminiscently
> at the laughter they provoked, especially during the flying visit of
> the Spanish girl, who was naughty, but very nice!

The period after World War II was not so good for the quality of music at Tyndale and some negative comments appeared about the willingness of choir members to turn up for practice and of the poor congregational singing. The rebuilding of the church, the new organist and "choir-master" certainly effected a change. After Tyndale was rebuilt, the present organ was built by Rushworth and Dreaper. It has two manuals and a pedal board with 656 pipes in all. Reg Flew was appointed on 20th February 1954, having been "on trial" (his own phrase) from 17th January. Elsie Balmond was appointed choir-mistress until 1962 when Gareth Jones took over, until he became treasurer in 1966. After that, Reg Flew ran the choir. Flew's annual salary was £75 a year and he was contracted to play for two services and the choir practice each week; Balmond received £52 a year.

There was a broadcast service from Tyndale in 1959 and another in 1961 when the Palm Sunday morning service was transmitted. The order of service was as follows:

Conducted by the Minister, The Revd. Ronald Cowley

Preacher, The Revd. Dr. Donald Hudson

Sentences and Invocation

All glory, laud, and honour (B.C.H. 107)

Prayer of Confession

First Lesson: 1 Corinthians 2, vv. 1-9

Te Deum

Second Lesson: St. Matthew 27, vv. 33-51, 54

Children's address

There is a green hill (B.C.H. 752)

Prayers of Thanksgiving and Intercession

The Lord's Prayer

Thou art the everlasting Word (B.C.H. 77)

Sermon

Presentation of Offerings

In the cross of Christ I glory (B.C.H. 118)

Blessing

Choirmistress, Elsie Balmond

Organist, Reginald Flew

Reg Flew

Evening concerts continued in the 1960s and in April 1961 there was an evening of music in church arranged by Irene Burrow, one of the church members, and her family, with programmes costing two shillings, proceeds given in aid of refugees.

April 1962 saw the arrival of the new hymn book, the *Baptist Hymn Book*, and this was followed by singing practice in the church, especially concentrating on singing chants – a chant and an anthem were usually sung each Sunday morning. The Hymn Society of Great Britain held its annual conference in Bristol and the annual Hymn Festival was held in Tyndale on 18th September. The hymns were led by a united choir from Anglican and Free Church choirs in Bristol. The annual Christmas service of carols and readings was replaced that year by the *Christmas Cantata* by Julius Harrison. In 1965 Adrian and Janet Beaumont gave a musical evening for the William Tyndale Society. Adrian was on the staff of the Music Department of the University, Janet (née Price) was an opera singer and these two church members made an impact on music at Tyndale; having Janet singing a hymn behind one at a morning service, was a real joy! The inaugural concert of the Bristol Bach Choir took place in Tyndale church on Saturday 1st July 1967. The music was by Bach and Britten, Adrian Beaumont was the conductor and the Telemann Ensemble provided the music. The ensemble consisted of Klemi Hambourg (violin), Daphne Webb (cello), Adrian Beaumont (oboe) and Alan Farnill (continuo). *Rejoice in the Lamb* by Britten was the final piece and the programme cost 3/6d.

For Tyndale's centenary celebration the next year (1968), the Bach Choir under Adrian Beaumont performed the appropriately named lyric drama *Tyndale* by Francis Jackson, with John Stuart Anderson speaking his original text as narrator and Brian Runnett doing wonders with what was described as "the limited tonal range of the organ". The reviewer in *The Musical Times* added that

> Tyndale Baptist Church, has acted as host to the Bach Choir since
> its foundation, and the building's clean lines and clear acoustics
> proved helpful in a work that does not always cope successfully
> with the problems of a sung and spoken text.

The Bach choir continued to use Tyndale for its concerts until June 1973 when they moved to the larger Clifton Cathedral.

Music at Tyndale was not only a vital element in weekly worship, with the people of God offering of their best to him in a sacrifice of praise but, alongside art, as part of God's good creation, it was a natural element for the people's enjoyment and recreation. Because God has given his people ears, eyes, lungs and mouths, Tyndale has over the years provided opportunity for members of the church and congregation, young and old, to enjoy excellence in both these areas both as participants and well-rewarded audiences and spectators. In the early 1970s the young people of the church performed *The Mikado* one year, and *Cinderella* the next, in the newly built hall under the direction of Geoff Molyneux. There was also a concert to raise funds for the new manse in 1975. Not only were funds raised but a sense of community and common task was strengthened, another dimension of Everybody's Effort.

The Revd Eric Sharpe and his wife, Gwen, moved to Bristol in 1977, Gwen having been appointed warden of Tyndale Court, and a new phase in Tyndale's music history started in collaboration with Elizabeth Webb. Eric Sharpe had been

Eric and Gwen Sharpe

chairman of the music advisory committee as well as serving on the main committee of the *Baptist Hymn Book* that was published in 1962. In like fashion F. C. Bryan had served on both the main and music committees of the *Baptist Church Hymnal (Revised)* in the 1930s. Elizabeth Webb had been involved in the ministry of Dance in Worship at their previous church in Edinburgh and, in addition to other church activities, decided to start a similar group in Tyndale. Gwen Sharpe wrote in the church magazine after an early dance:

> How fortunate we are in Tyndale to have a group who can portray the Christian faith in such a modern way as the Tyndale dancers, with their presentation of John Bunyan's "Pilgrim's Progress" on a recent Sunday evening.

Some of the congregation may have viewed it a little apprehensively beforehand, expecting a performance or a production, and wondering how it would fit into a service of worship. Instead they found themselves sharing in an inspiring interpretation of John Bunyan's message. The congregation was challenged by the fact that the problems and difficulties which Christians had to face then are the same as those which face Christians today, when they, too, can find themselves in the Slough of Despond, or diverted from the straight and narrow of the King's Highway by Mr and Mrs Worldly Wiseman. However, at the end all were assured that with faith and hope and the power of the Holy Spirit they can tackle the Dangerous Journey with confidence and reach the Celestial City. It was a very moving sermon, which made a deep impression, and, of course, the story is already clearly depicted in the church's Bunyan window by Arnold Robinson (chapter 12).

The church started using *Praise for Today*, the new supplement to the *Baptist Hymn Book* published in 1974, in the mid 1970s. Eric Sharpe wrote:

> Regrettably there are some folk (even in a Christian Church) who have a built-in resistance to anything that is new or modern. But most who see their hymn book, not as a historical record of eighteenth-century or even Victorian piety, but as an expression of today's faith, will find that these hymns speak directly to the present age in a fresh and stimulating way.

He introduced many of the new hymns to the congregation. Gwen Sharpe was appointed choir-mistress in 1980 and in April 1982 the choir achieved Membership of the Royal School of Church Music. Not only was music in worship being led by an invigorated choir, in 1978 a junior orchestra had been started by Tina Parsons, with annual concerts for a few years, and the first pantomime *Snow White and the Seven Dwarfs* had been produced from 15th to 20th May, with proceeds for the BMS hospital at Chandraghona in Bangladesh. Pantomimes then became almost an annual event with performances of *Cinderella, Aladdin, Humpty Dumpty, Jack and the Beanstalk* (directed by Chris West and Paul Roberts), *The Ousting of the Ogre Bogle*, and *Tom and The Crooked Sixpence* (directed by Cilla Morris and Jill Prime with Tina Parsons as musical director).

A week of events titled "Through the church's year in Flower and Song" took place from 31st May to 8th June 1980. A Flower Festival was held on the Saturday, Sunday and Monday, with the main floral arrangements depicting hymns for the various seasons of the Church year from Advent onwards. A selection of the hymns was sung at the Songs of Praise on the Sunday evening when a united service of the Redland Group of churches occurred with a full church and a choir of about fifty voices.

The next year, twenty members of the congregation joined the choir to sing Stainer's *Crucifixion* on Palm Sunday evening which was the fourth occasion in the year when the choir had been augmented for special services. The regular church choir continued and an anthem was sung at most services as well as providing strong leadership in the singing of hymns and psalms. Choir practice took place on Thursdays from 7.00 to 8.45 p.m. In 1982 the short cantata *The Last Supper* by Eric Thiman for solo soprano and baritone soloists, chorus and organ was sung at the evening service on Passion Sunday, 28th March. In October 1982 the Tyndale Festival of Arts and Crafts took place and it included the dance, *Captain Noah and his Floating Zoo* as well as drama from visiting groups. On Passion Sunday, 5th April 1987 parts 2 and 3 of Handel's *Messiah* were sung at the evening service, following a 3.00 p.m. rehearsal, conducted by Adrian Beaumont with Janet Price as the soprano soloist.

The Tyndale Dancers, April 1978 [Bristol Evening Post]

Meanwhile, the Tyndale Dancers became recognised nationally and as their repertoire grew they found themselves being invited to contribute to worship in other churches and also Cathedrals, at conferences, and at various celebrations including weddings! Through movement they brought the gospel stories to life, such as the Sower, the Good Samaritan, and the story of Ruth. They performed dances of praise – lively and joyful – but also quieter dances of prayer using gestures of offering, praying and interceding. Other dances expressed concern for particular issues: *Forgotten People* dealt with the subject of those taken against their will and tortured, while another dance focussed on the atomic bomb. Other dances looked at the theme of Christian unity, while others had a more theological subject such as *Yours is the Kingdom* prepared for the Baptist Assembly in 1983. The

Tyndale Dancers performed twice at the Edinburgh Festival Fringe, whilst two other occasions remain as high points in their history. These were both performances at The Royal Albert Hall for the Women's World Day of Prayer: the first was to celebrate its Golden Jubilee in 1982, and the second was five years later at its World Centenary. Elizabeth and Peter Webb left the church in 1987, so Pam Fisher became the Tyndale Dancers' leader for the next period. When she retired, the group of dancers largely led by Gillian Collins, Cilla Morris and Ali Lloyd carried on working along the same lines as before with the other members of the group having input. The 32nd birthday of the Tyndale Dancers was reached in 2007 and the small group who were still involved in it decided that it was time to hang up their leotards and go out with a bang! So a celebration service was planned with dance and Holy Communion. Many who had taken part over the years attended for this reunion.

Robert Ellis' induction service on 21st November 1987 had included an item by the dancers and Ellis' ability with the trumpet added to the Tyndale musical scene. He also played a key role in the performance of a musical *Pilgrim's Progress* entitled *Let's Go,* written by Peter English, in October 1989. This was a magnificent production with tiered seating and excellent staging. The full houses and excellence of the performance somewhat overshadowed the exhibition mounted by national and local organisations, such as Relate, The Samaritans, Amnesty International, and Shelter.

The Tyndale Festival in May 1989 included a concert on the evening of Friday 19th given by children, soloists and the choir concluding with a Musical, *The Maker of Things* by Edmund Banyard and Graham Bishop. The children took part in singing and mime and the guest soloist was Janet Price accompanied by Adrian Beaumont and the choir concluded with the triumphant piece *The Heavens are Telling* from Haydn's *Creation*. Two months later, Eric and Gwen Sharpe with an ecumenical choir and orchestra led a Bristol Festival of Hymns at St Mary Redcliffe, as part of the annual Redcliffe Festival of Music – with every hymn and or tune being the work of a writer who has lived and worked in Bristol. In September that year Reg Flew retired as organist ending a magnificent period of service and, as finding a replacement was difficult, it was decided to employ an organ scholar, recruited from the University of Bristol's music department

Bristol Bach Choir with Adrian Beaumont conducting

– these included Ian Abbott, Richard Vandy and Matthew Redman. The popular radio programme of hymn singing, BBC Sunday Half Hour, was broadcast from Tyndale on Sunday 17th December 1989. A united choir of over 100 voices conducted by John Bishop took part. Pantomimes continued at the end of the 1980s: *Robin Hood and the Royal Seal*, *Lucy Loose in Pantoland* in December 1990 and *Aladdin* in the early 1990s.

In 1991 the Psalms and Hymns Trust produced *Baptist Praise and Worship*, which was to prove to be the last in a long line of denominational hymn books stretching back over more than 200 years. Keith Clements served on the Editorial Committee and Alan Smith on the Worship Advisory Committee. Their task was to produce a hymn book for a new generation in which "the ecumenical and charismatic movements had challenged many of the more rigid traditions of worship" whilst the proliferation of modern translations of the Bible called for modernization of language, with "Thee-s and Thou-s" no longer corresponding to modern usage whilst the dominance of masculine forms were less than helpful. At the same time the hymn book sought to make available the liturgical riches of the church throughout the ages and from all around the world. Within the collection, Keith Clements' *Father of glory whose heavenly plan* provides an excellent example of a hymn expressing a Christian response to issues of race and colour within the context of a wide embracing creation theology.

Gwen Sharpe retired in 2000, having completed 20 years as choir director. It was said that during her time, music enhanced the worship – choir practice was never dull and invariably spiced with laughter, triggered by some witty comment, intentional or otherwise. There was a range of musical activity from Sunday worship, through special services, to RSCM workshops and Hymn Festivals. Change brought a new hymn book (with no chants) and choir numbers decreased. Although relationships between organist, choir-mistress and minister were generally good, Robert Ellis wrote:

> As in many churches then and now, worship became something of a power struggle at times. The choir sang twice each week, the only accompanist was on the organ, and the choir mistress' insistence on having musical choices in hand by Thursday evening's practice effectively allowed her to subvert my intentions by changing musical arrangements and sometimes even items on occasion. I do not think that this was done deliberately – there was simply an inability to comprehend why the existing tradition of church music might need to be changed or enlarged. In time I began to introduce a music group led by a pianist. It helped that she and her husband were choir members too. Matters came to a head with a BBC Radio 4 live broadcast on Easter Day in 1989, when I insisted on a range of music, some of which was new to the church. It was high risk, but our musicians, including eventually, a cooperative choir, pulled it off. Previously, I got the impression that *Praise for Today* was considered a little avant garde so some of my choices must have seemed strange at first to some. The music group grew in importance and settled into part of the church's life, even as the choir began to wane – first dropping Sunday evening singing, and then making other changes. Chanted psalms were one of the first casualties – though I kept selecting them for a while, if not every week. Many in the choir clearly

enjoyed them – and sung well they were beautiful. However, most members of the congregation, even those who had been singing them for years, were baffled by them – and they were not at all "welcoming" for most newcomers. I had chosen a modern psalm setting (the Dam Busters, no less) for my "preach with a view", so the demise of the chant after a few years cannot have been a huge surprise. The "freeing-up" of music in worship was a significant step, and allowed the expression of a wider range of gifts and the participation of a wider range of people, as well as giving the church's musical tradition a more contemporary feel. Ministries are often marked by strong personalities and Gwen Sharpe was certainly one of the strongest. Despite my battles with her, her support and insistence of high standards were enormously helpful.

Tyndale members were involved in three musical productions at Broadmead Baptist Church, including taking lead roles and directing. First *Terrill*, about the life of Edward Terrill, played by Geoff Molyneux. Second, *Kyrios*, which told the Easter story and was directed by Maureen Cowley with Geoff Molyneux playing Jesus. These were followed by *Knibb*, the story of William Knibb. This production in 1992 marked the bi-centenary of the BMS and was directed by Maureen Cowley and Pam Fisher, with Robert Ellis playing the title role and many other Tyndale members taking other parts. There were also productions of several of Roger Jones' musicals: *Greater than Gold* (about Mary Jones and her bible), *Away in a Manger* and *Mary Magdalene*. Drama was also used in worship from time to time; for example, a dramatic portrayal of William Tyndale's story *Open the King of England's Eyes* by John Coutts formed an evening service in October 1994 and was repeated as a dramatic reading in a service in 2011 to mark the 475th anniversary of Tyndale's death, and again the drama put into action the story already enshrined in Arnold Robinson's transept window.

The 2000 Arts Festival was broadened to include art as well as music with the participants exploring what it was to be human, with every contributor praising God through his or her artistic endeavour. About this time Tyndale hosted a visit from Tblisi dancers as part of a civic visit and another dance evening with Sarah Dodds and a group of Flamenco dancers. In about 2010

Tyndale choir after their final performance in 2006

Tyndale hosted an "Artist in residence" for a year, when Mark Hughes, who worshipped at Tyndale throughout his degree course, took on this task during his Masters course at Bower Ashton.

In September 2016 Bruce Lloyd and his team transformed the sanctuary into a beautiful art gallery to mark ten years since Geoff Molyneux's death and the reopening of the sanctuary after its refurbishment, with which Molyneux was very much involved (Molyneux and Rex Hopes were members of a group of artists called the Bristol Savages).

The music group was formed in 1989 during Robert Ellis' ministry, to lead worship hymns and songs which are not well-suited to organ accompaniment, and has been playing in the morning service since then. It is led by Rachel Molyneux (pianist), with many other musicians playing an array of different instruments, including Alison Lloyd (clarinet), Michael Docker (guitar), David Bell (percussion) and Russell Corfe (trumpet and organ). Dr Sarah Dodds was appointed organist in 2000 and she also plays

376

the violin in the music group. Roger Kirby has been the assistant organist since 1987.

In 2006 the Tyndale choir came to a natural end by mutual agreement and since then a singing group, organised by Rachel Molyneux, often leads the singing of new or less well known songs on Sundays as required. The singing group also learn particular pieces which are sung for occasions such as Christmas and Easter. Tyndale is well blessed with talented singers, several of whom are willing to sing solo alongside the musicians. The church also boasts two hymn writers within the congregation, the most prolific is Michael Docker, but Keith Clements also contributes. But with the ability to project suitably illustrated words onto the church's twin screens, the congregation is no longer limited to hymn books. In addition to the rich heritage of Christian hymnody bearing witness to the witness of the church across the ages which is to be found in *Baptist Praise and Worship,* hymns and songs are sourced from the best of modern evangelical songwriters such as Graham Kendrick and Stuart Townend with their joyful affirmation of the fundamentals of the faith together with that which enables the congregation to offer heart-felt praise to Almighty God. Material from the Iona community brings into theological focus many of the challenges of discipleship in the modern world. Michael Docker follows in the tradition of early non-conformist hymn writers by composing hymns arising out of the day's Scripture readings and sermon theme.

For many years there has been a nativity play performed on the Sunday morning service before Christmas. These have been mostly led by Junior Church leaders, but have included some adults. Many musical versions of the nativity story have been performed by the Junior Church accompanied by the Music Group, such as *Hosanna Rock*. December 2008 saw a production of Keith Clements' nativity play *Time to Sing* with music written by his son Peter Clements. More recently, nativity plays have taken different forms and been largely performed by adults.

"time@tyndale" began on Wednesday evenings in September 2009 as Sunday evening services ceased. Its programme throughout the years since then has regularly included music, poetry and prose evenings, and many concerts, especially in recent years by students from the Bristol University

Music Department and the Royal Court Players. Many of these have raised significant sums for various charities. Concerts and pantomimes continued being produced, although the latter were more difficult to find cast for, with fewer young people attending worship. Nevertheless there were excellent performances of *Snow White and the Seven Dwarfs* (2003), *Aladdin* (2005) and *Godspell* in 2008 during which Michael Docker, as John the Baptist, walked through the audience and up onto the stage singing *Prepare Ye the way of the Lord*. In 2010 Bruce Lloyd directed the incredibly successful *Joseph and the Amazing Technicolour Dreamcoat* with members of both Tyndale and Horfield Baptist churches. Concerts have included a further performance of *Come and Sing Messiah* in 2003 at Tyndale with Adrian Beaumont as conductor and George Lang leading the orchestra, in aid of the Whiteladies Health Share Project, and in 2017 *Swingtime into Springtime* when three of the church family and two visitors enthralled a full church in aid of the Tyndale Circle and the community ministry. Sarah Dodds' Baroque ensemble *No Shrinking Violets* have had two excellent concerts in 2014 and 2018.

Chapter 19.

Mission and Ministry to Senior Citizens

Michael Whitfield

The population around Tyndale in the latter part of the twentieth century contained two peaks in age range; the first being young adults of 20–40 years and the other being the elderly – those over 60 years of age. Tyndale members had been supporting work with the elderly for many years, such as in the residential home, Terrill House, in Apsley Road, that was an initiative of the Bristol Free Church Council. This warden-supported home for 28 people existed from 1964 until the end of the century and housed many Tyndale members including the Revd H. W. Burdett towards the end of his life. Tyndale supported various other initiatives such as the fortnightly Sunday lunches that were run at Redland Park United Reformed Church during the 1970s and 1980s as part of the Redland Group of Churches' initiative, as was the short Elderly People's Service that took place monthly on Thursday mornings at Tyndale for those who could not sit through a normal Sunday service.

The centenary of the church in 1967 was an opportunity to review Tyndale's future direction. After the church had been rebuilt following the war, Ronald Cowley encouraged the members to look at the rear premises that had largely escaped war damage. Were the premises adequate for purpose? They had been constructed about twenty years after the original church and had many deficiencies, for example they had overhead gas heating and were not easy to maintain. They were cold and damp. They were useful for Everybody's Effort and for hosting missionary suppers and for young peoples' meetings including badminton on one evening a week run by Rowland Brake, one of the deacons. The high pitched wooden ceiling made some shots easy, but sometimes the metal heaters interrupted the flight of the shuttlecocks! Was their condition and usage the best use of the land in the church's ownership?

Tyndale Court

The church was aware of many elderly people in the area who needed special care. There was sheltered accommodation in Clifton but all homes had long waiting lists. Ron Cowley wrote recalling the fact that

> Tyndale has always been engaged in caring ministries to those in special need, such as the Tyndale Mission, the Belgian House and the "Maids Club" for women in domestic service from the "big" houses in Clifton. Caring was at the heart of the Church's ministry and providing housing for the needy was in keeping with that tradition.

The idea was that flats for the elderly would be built around new church premises and the creation of a Housing Association would enable government funding for the flats to help defray some of the cost. Walter Millard and his wife had moved to Bristol after his retirement, and Walter became a deacon in 1967 just as the church began their deliberations about changes to these rear premises. In January 1968 Millard applied for the church to become registered with the National Federation of Housing Societies. Tyndale Baptist Church (Bristol) Housing Association Limited was registered as a charity in order to:

> provide housing and any associated amenities for persons in necessitous circumstances upon terms appropriate to their needs and

> provide for aged persons in need, housing and associated amenities specially designed or adapted to meet the disabilities and requirements of such persons.

The centenary celebrations of 1968 were completed by October but the plans for the building project were running into problems. The plans had been drawn up by the architect, Antoni Poremba, who was married to one of the church members and worked for Sir Percy Thomas and Partners, but the Planning Department rejected the first set of plans. Plans were re-submitted and rejected again. The church was advised to appeal to the Ministry of Town and Country Planning and the Inspector also rejected the scheme. However, the Minister of Housing and Local Government

Demolition of the old lecture hall (left) and the new Tyndale Court that replaced it (right)

intervened and gave permission to proceed, describing the project as "meritorious".

The cost to the church would be about £40,000 and the cost of Tyndale Court would be £115,000. The Housing Association would pay an annual rent to Tyndale of about £700 which was the rental agreed by the District Valuer for the portion of the site occupied by the housing project. The Church Meeting in December 1970 agreed unanimously to proceed and gifts and loans were sought to finance the project. A significant loan was provided by the Bridgewater Society arranged with the help of the manager, who was a Baptist. Tyndale Court would have thirteen bed-sits, four flats and a warden's quarters, a guest room and a communal room. Many people paid £1 for a share in the Tyndale Housing Association but two members, in particular, brought wisdom and technical skills to the project with Cowley: Ron Cooper, the chairman of the Planning Committee, and Walter Millard. By December 1971 the residents were selected, including some who came from the Bristol Corporation Housing List, and the selection of a suitable warden was a crucial decision, with Elsie Chapman being chosen. The official opening took place on 20th May 1972 by the Lord Mayor of Bristol, Alderman Edwin Roberts. The architects were Sir Percy Thomas and Partners and the builder was Henry Willcock and Co. Ltd. One of the interesting features of this development was the roof garden that is tended by some of the residents, situated on the top of the church hall. This is overlooked by many of the flats. In 2005, after the housing scheme had been taken over by the national organisation, Places for People, all the bed-sits were converted to one and two bedroomed flats.

Further developments: Richard Glover Centre

A proposal was made to adapt the basement area of Tyndale Court for work among the elderly, specifically to set up an elderly persons' activity centre and the Richard Glover Centre opened on 22nd March 1977. Funding had been obtained from various charities and the leader was Alan Sadler. Helpers were recruited to help instruct various crafts. Walter Millard said that this would be part of the outreach of the church and would start in the mornings – as "this encouraged the elderly to get up from bed"! Unfortunately, in the middle of 1977 it was reported that the Richard Glover Centre was not getting much support, especially from women, but business picked up a little and later that year ten people attended on average and soft toys, wooden waste paper containers and wooden trains were being constructed. By 1992 the management committee of the Richard Glover Centre reported that as no-one was now using the workshop and fewer ladies were meeting for knitting and a chat, a decision was made to close the centre.

Avonlea and Porteous House

In 1977 Walter Millard told the church that the Housing Association had got permission from the Department of the Environment for the "Avonlea" development to go ahead. This was an exciting project, with the Yate shopping complex only ¼ mile away. The site was part of land owned by H. Cooper and Sons that included the factory and a large lake.

Avonlea

One hundred trees had been previously planted on the site by Ron Cooper, the grandson of the founder of the firm. A sum of £485,000 had been applied for – nearly twice as large a sum as was required for Tyndale Court. The funds would come from Government sources and 80% was loaned by a Housing Association grant. Only 20% had to be raised by mortgage. Chipping Sodbury Baptist Church took a great interest in the project and it was managed by a local committee involving that church. By October 1980 several of the bungalows were occupied and three residents had taken residence in Oak Lodge.

Porteous House

Dorothy Porteous left her house in Chertsey Road to the Housing Association and this was converted in 1979 into seven flats with those at the top being suitable for single young people.

Administrative Change

In 1985 it was reported that there would be a merger of the Housing Association with the Bristol Churches Housing Association. Millard reported that the management of 78 flats in Tyndale Court, Avonlea and Porteous House and the 113 people housed within them had become increasingly onerous since the 1980 Housing Act, and Ron Cooper was now spending about four days a week on this. Slowly, Tyndale's involvement with Tyndale Court and Porteous House became more distant, although the Court still houses some who worship at Tyndale. Although present-day costs and administrative demands have made a purely Tyndale charity no longer possible, it remains that it was the energies, vision and sacrificial giving of the church community that initiated this important provision for a needy group of people, providing a comfortable, secure and economical space they could call home.

Drop-In Lunches

Mavis Whitfield had visited a church in Cheltenham that had been providing simple food for passers-by, in support of Oxfam and reported this to Peter Webb. He suggested that Tyndale should do something similar so "Drop-In Lunches" started on Thursdays in 1983 to provide contact with people living and working locally. About 90% of customers were senior citizens. The lunches were staffed by volunteers from local churches and local people and provided hot meals for many years. Proceeds from these were donated to many different development projects throughout the world. Gwen Sharpe, who had been a warden of Tyndale Court and was choir-mistress at Tyndale, was heavily involved in the Drop-In Lunches and was known to encourage passers-by in Whiteladies Road to come in to sample them! The lunches started in a simple way with bread and soup but quickly became known for superb cooking and very tasty meals. A typical menu included: steak and kidney pie, meat cannelloni with cheese sauce, mushroom and pepper flan, apple and mincemeat pie, and fruit flan. One year they catered for 150 people for a Christmas lunch, including 20 from the Tyndale Circle. In 2000 it was decided to change the name to "Thursday Lunches" and to lose the term "Drop-In".

Thursday Lunches closed at the end of December 2009 after running for 27 years, as it was becoming increasingly difficult to recruit helpers. The total amount raised over these years for overseas aid was just over £127,000. The range of charities supported was considerable and large sums were paid to Christian Aid and other work associated with various church members such as the Whiteladies Health Share Project based at the health centre in Whatley Road, that supported the Institute of Health Management at Pachod in India and Dr Graham's Homes in Kalimpong, India.

The Tyndale Circle

The Tyndale Circle

In 1994 the Revd Alan Smith was appointed as the half-time associate minister of Tyndale and set about helping the church to determine the future direction of outreach. Following several lunchtime meetings involving local professionals and church members, it became clear that there was a need for helping those supporting relatives with memory loss. On 2nd November 1995 the Tyndale Circle opened in the basement premises on Thursdays from 9.30 a.m. to 3.30 p.m. Pamela Wall was appointed as a professional organiser and a grant was obtained from the Local Authority to help pay her. An average of ten clients a week attended and about 22 voluntary helpers from Tyndale and the other local churches looked after the clients. Lunches were bought from the Drop-In Lunches which were taking place in the hall above, with continued provision of lunches for the Tyndale Circle after the Drop-In Lunches had come to an end. The twentieth anniversary celebrations of the Tyndale Circle in 2015 were an opportunity to celebrate the on-going work of this inspiring initiative.

Coffee Mornings

Tuesday coffee mornings started in the church in June 1993 from 10.00 a.m. to 12.00 noon and provide a regular time for church members and visitors to meet. These coffee mornings met also on Saturday mornings for a time and now in 2018 also take place on Wednesdays and Thursdays. Tables and chairs are provided in the sanctuary, and outside in good weather, and many enjoy the opportunity of sharing in conversation, listening to music and even knitting.

Chapter 20.

Today and Tomorrow

Michael Docker & Rachel Haig

The Revd Michael Docker, Minister (2002–), writes:

Being asked to take up the ministry of Tyndale Baptist Church in 2002 presented me with an enormous privilege and challenge. I had, for the previous ten years, been the minister of Stoneygate Baptist Church, Leicester – a church similar in outlook and style to Tyndale. Prior to that a much shorter period (just three years) at Swaythling, Southampton, had given me the opportunity to "cut my teeth" in ministry and had introduced me to a number of "circles" of involvement that would become firmly a part of my approach and that would come to play an important part in Bristol. Before Southampton I had been a student at Bristol Baptist College and spent the last of four years there, as a College-based student, on placement at Tyndale. The church had termed this placement a "student-in-ministry" and, under Rob Ellis, I had learned much and been given the opportunity to practise various aspects of ministry – preaching, leading worship, pastoral visiting, being part of the life of a church as a minister – in ways that, I now realise, were to become central to my own ministry and that would, in large measure, come to a full and fresh expression when I became Rob's successor in 2002.

In Swaythling I became involved in the life of the Free Church Chaplaincy at Southampton University, serving on its committee and writing a report for an ecumenical review, which led to a decision by the Baptist Union, the Methodist Church and the United Reformed Church, to continue funding a Free Church Chaplain post. As a probationer I was not allowed to function as a chaplain, but I was appointed the Baptist Chaplain to Leicester University and, later, the Baptist Chaplain to the University of Bristol.

Again, from shortly after leaving the College in 1989 I had become involved in its committee life, first as a member of the then Publicity Committee, later as a member of the General Committee. During my time in Leicester, Roger Hayden approached me about becoming the Chairman of the General Committee; I eventually did so in the late nineties, continuing in that role after moving back to Bristol and remaining active as the Chairman of the College Council (the body that succeeded the General Committee after a re-drawing of the Constitution) until 2018, proving some continuity in the relationship between the College and Tyndale.

Worship

Rob Ellis had enthusiastically imparted to me a liking for a liturgical approach to worship; this had not really suited the worship style of Swaythling Baptist Church but found some expression at Stoneygate and was something that I relished exploring and developing at Tyndale. Discussions with the Tyndale diaconate ahead of my appointment had emphasised the church's "change with continuity" approach, and this accorded with my own. The worship style of Tyndale Baptist Church, which had been heavily influenced by the Liturgical Renewal movement of the 1960s, continues to the present to maintain a clear structure, with the reading of Scripture, preaching and intercessory prayer as major elements. The monthly morning communion service, in which bread and wine are "offered" (along with the financial offering), the

The Revd Michael Docker

Peace shared and the "elements" distributed by the deacons, stays, I think, close to the style that the church has practised for decades. An innovation I have introduced has been the inclusion of "bidding and responses" before the bread is broken.

There have been changes – there has been a steady increase in the number of contemporary songs sung (though a strong commitment to organ-led hymn singing remains). The formal choir, that for many years provided anthems, hymnic accompaniments and occasional sung pieces, was closed down in the summer of 2006, but a much less formal singing group regularly participates in current services, along with a music group (consisting of piano, drums, clarinet, violin and guitar – and occasionally flute and trumpet). All pertinent material for each service – hymn and song words, responses, video clips and pictures – is projected. All this, together with the careful way in which services are constructed and led, ensures that the heart and "engine" of the church's life continues to provide what it has always provided and the changes are, I believe, true to the church's history.

Congregation

Over the last decade, there have been marked changes in the make-up of the congregation of people who gather for worship at Tyndale Sunday by Sunday. Ageing is, of course, a factor but on its own is far too crude a way of describing what is going on. Of more significance, perhaps, is the relationship between the "indigenous" congregation (historically those in membership of the church) and the present congregation of people, somewhat in flux, who feel a deep attachment to Tyndale, but who are not, formally, in membership of the church. Yes, the historic membership is depleted in number, though still made up of many active, energetic and "engaged" individuals. Yes, too, the present congregation comprises many individuals who contribute considerably to the life of the church, though in informal ways – attending events, helping to make those events happen and so on. The challenge arises in creating and deepening the sense of belonging and "ownership" of the church from both sides – members whose considerable efforts in the past (and still) have made the Tyndale church what it is – financially well-set, physically well provided for, spiritually generous and theologically "open" – but who are less involved in other-than-Sunday activities as they have moved to live at some distance from the church; and "non-members" who, for all their considerable loyalty to and involvement with the other-than-Sunday life of the church, do not play an active part in the decision-making "Church Meeting culture" of Tyndale. But it is in Church Meeting that the church as a fellowship of the children of God in covenant relationship with one another becomes visible in the pastoral reports which are on the agenda of every meeting and the quite natural way in which they lead into intercessory prayer. There has been some success in holding "open meetings" where both members and non-members can share news and express views and preferences, but as yet there is no clear trajectory along which the church might proceed towards an integrated modus operandi.

A Baptist church is not a club, of course, nevertheless its congregational and independent character requires that a membership exists to conduct essential business, hold officials accountable and effect the life of the church. Increasingly Charity Commission requirements bear down on churches, widening the scope of decision-making, policy setting (everything from Safeguarding to Data Protection, and various other aspects of governance) for which charity trustees are responsible – in the case of a Baptist church, those trustees are the church's deacons; they are elected; elections require meetings, and membership.

Demographic changes in the area

During the last decade and a half there have been noticeable changes in the commercial and residential environment around the church. Of course, the Whiteladies Road of the 1900s is hardly recognisable today (though many fine buildings remain and the basic layout, leading up Blackboy Hill to the Downs has changed little). The mix of retail outlets along the Whiteladies Road is in constant flux; traditional butcher-baker-grocery-type shops have given way to specialist retailers, customer-facing insurance and banking outlets and an increasing number of furniture and interior design outlets and food-related businesses, restaurants and, in line with a national trend, coffee shops – of which there are upwards of ten within a few hundred metres of Tyndale. The "strip" to the south of the church had developed, by the early 2000s, into a major part of the Bristol nightclub scene. Nowadays it is less focussed on nightclubs *per se* though restaurants, pubs and bars abound.

Residential housing in the immediate area around the church, which began and continued through the first half of the twentieth century as an area of large, semi-detached and terraced family properties, is now "bed-sit land" of a particular type. A number of the frankly enormous homes, many of them with three stories and a basement, have been divided up into flats. Most of these are rented, to young professional people, a small number of which are being purchased. There has been an explosion of student accommodation across the

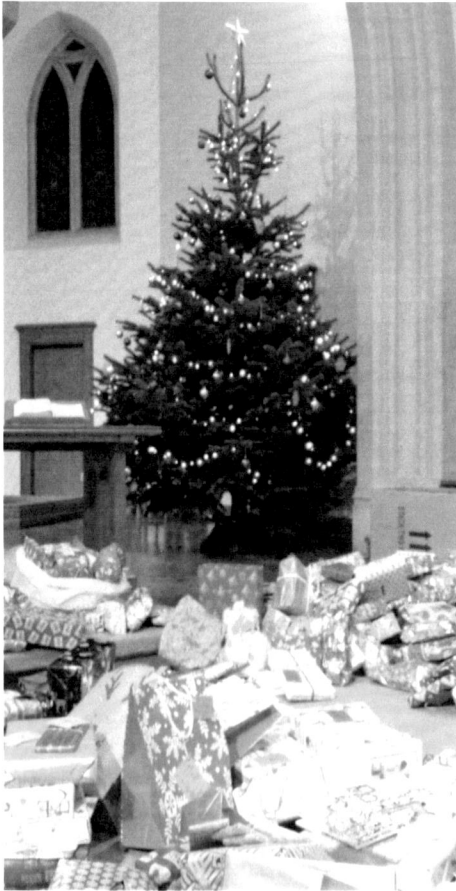

The Christmas Giving Tree service, organised by the Whiteladies' Road churches and Tyndale's David Bell, collects Christmas presents for local charities

north and centre of the city, much of it purpose-built. Whiteladies Road is the major route for students living in the University of Bristol's main student halls, by which they make their way to the university precinct. There have been proposed developments of some of the nearby properties for student accommodation, though as yet none have come to fruition. A smaller number of large, private residential homes remain in the vicinity.

All of this means that the Tyndale "catchment area" has changed hugely over the course of its history, from the days when it was at the centre of a growing, prospering suburb – and attracted a congregation of prosperous people – to today when it is at the centre of a lively "street scene", with a large number of people passing by the church daily, though it now has less of a profile amongst the residents of the area. To be sure, numbers of those residents find their way into the church, either to avail themselves of the church's facilities and activities, or as adherents of local "special interest" groups, that occasionally or regularly use the premises. But increasingly the challenge to the church is to relate to, and engage with, the variety of people whose daily lives are conducted in close proximity to the church. These include homeless people who sleep rough on or near the church premises; shoppers and visitors to the area; local residents (some of whom visit the church as members of various user groups); local business people; others.

That last category raises an issue that is becoming increasingly pertinent. Clifton and Redland, part of the wealthiest area of the city, have, besides the resident population of well-off families and single people, a "hidden" population of people who are far from well-off. Some are elderly, isolated, "asset rich, cash poor" who find themselves widowed, perhaps, with family members living elsewhere in the country. Charities working in this sector are beginning to identify the need and allocate resources accordingly. Some have learning difficulties and are housed in the several hostels not far from the church. Some live a little further away but come into the area to attend, maybe, one of the many "Anonymous" groups (several of which hold meetings on the Tyndale premises), find friendship locally, and stay around during the day.

The challenge is being responded to by the church's current expression of associate ministry, the Community Ministry, which has, under the ministry of the Revd Rachel Haig, been playing an increasingly significant role in the life of the church and the lives of many individuals over the last five years.

Youth Work

Traditional forms of church-based youth work — youth clubs, young people's fellowships, "junior church" — had long been a part of the Tyndale scene, but in recent years, these have not much featured in the church's life. The last rising generation of church family young people moved through from crèche to YPF and on to career and university in the first decade of the 21st century, and has been followed by no more than one or two individual children and young people at any one time. In any case, given the demographic situation described above, there is not a local population of young people looking for "something to do" — which in so many places has been the source of youth-club-type activities. The last functioning club of this kind reached a natural point of closure, again in the first decade of the century.

Historically, the Tyndale Baptist Church minister has served as the Baptist Chaplain to the University of Bristol. For a long time this was in recognition of the fact that the church acted as home to numbers of students from Baptist churches who came to Bristol to study. A denominational (joint with the URC — BURCSOC) student society existed until the 1990s. Many of those students belonged. Now, as denominational loyalties have changed and with them expectations amongst students of what constitutes a "good" church (a term used by the Evangelical Christian Union to describe the churches it commends to students — a combination, one understands, of a certain kind of theological outlook, style of worship and various student-orientated activities) few students make their way to Tyndale. In many ways, though, this has opened up and challenged the understanding of what a chaplain actually is. Both Tyndale's current ministers share in the work of the University's multi-faith chaplaincy team, which is offered as a gift to the University and gratefully received, acknowledged and indeed integrated.

Renewed Fabric

Whilst in common perception, a church is a building, for Baptists the church is a body of people, who may or may not meet in a particular building, but that building as such is without theological significance. Yet, in practical terms, most Baptist churches are closely identified with the building in which they worship. What is generally true is particularly true in Tyndale's case — the traumatic event described elsewhere in this book, the bombing of the building in the Second World War, illustrates this full well. The subsequent rebuilding, the care and maintenance thereof and various developments since, all reinforce the depth and closeness of the identification. It is difficult to imagine Tyndale Baptist Church — the people — existing at all without the building that bears its name.

Such a close identification gives rise to feelings of affection, even love, which helps to shape and form the worship and service that the church offers. The building also gives shape and form to the theology of the church and to the story it tells itself — see, for instance, the story of the Tyndale stained glass windows in chapter 12. All of this came into play when, in the first decade of this century, discussions began about refurbishing Tyndale's interior. The need was clear: paintwork was looking tired; the ranks of heavy, old-fashioned chairs were in need of replacement; temporary staging that had been built for a pantomime production years before and left in place was creaking. Beyond this was the desire to make the space more welcoming and "user-friendly" and to provide facilities for socialising and for projection.

The church, through discussions, came up with a new scheme but it is fair to say that none of this would have been possible without Geoff Molyneux. As an artist he had a vision for an integrated colour scheme and layout that only someone of his extraordinary skill and insight could have imagined. As a thinking Christian he presented this scheme to the church with a full theological rationale, and as an intensely practical and collaborative leader, he involved several students in the making of a model to display his ideas. Geoff was also very persuasive, but in reality such was the level of trust in his abilities that the church took little persuading to accept, without any dissent, his scheme. It is doubtful if the bold use of colour would have been accepted had it not been presented so effectively and creatively by someone so trusted and highly thought of as Geoff. The centre piece of the scheme – rather the focus – was a mural, to be secured to the wall, linking the open baptistery to the stained glass window above. This mural, at the centre of which is a white cross surrounded by shades of blue, ensures that in this Baptist church an understanding of baptism as both a "dying and rising with Christ" is depicted. As the central focus, some twelve years later it still catches the eye. Geoff's vision was to see this all of a piece with a central blue band leading from a new dais to the baptistery, so linking Word and worship, with communion and baptism. The dais, also covered in the same blue colour, stands under the very cruciform centre of the building so that a theological sense of completeness pertains – the Word received from God leads to the communion table, to water, to death and resurrection.

Michael Long painting the mural in the sanctuary, to a design by Geoff Molyneux

The mural was painted by Geoff's friend Michael Long, with Geoff involved closely in the production. The communion table was altered so that the eye is drawn through it to the baptistery and mural. New lecterns were purchased to provide both symmetry and a suitably elegant finish to the worship-leading area (the pulpit remains in place but is no longer in use). New chairs were purchased to provide flexibility; they also complement the terracotta colour of the ceiling panels. A new lighting and sound system was installed at the same time, as well as high-mounted twin projectors to facilitate the projection of song words, pictures and video clips onto the front wall either side of the central arch (since upgraded with new screens fitted).

The other major aspect of the refurbishment is the provision of a galley kitchen in the main worship space (a storage area on the opposite side of the building mirrors its design). This has proved its worth in making it easy to provide refreshments after services on Sunday and at regular mid-week daytime and evening events, which is proving a particularly useful development for, by way of example, funeral and thanksgiving services. Extensive internal scaffolding was required to allow for the painting and alteration, and for the period of work the church met for worship in the Hall. A "grace-filled tragedy" accompanied this challenging project. Geoff Molyneux saw the project through to completion, seeing the finished project shortly before his sudden death, adjacent to the re-opening of the building, in September 2006. We worked very hard to ensure that the refurbished building would be well-used from that time forward and so it does not so much stand, but sighs and sings in Geoff's joyful memory.

Associate Ministries

Tyndale enjoyed a hugely influential Associate Ministry — that of the Revd Alan Smith — in the nineties. He retired from New Road Church, Oxford, and brought his considerable gifts and insights into the life of Tyndale. He developed, amongst other things, the Tyndale Circle day centre for people with memory loss, that still provides a high quality, widely recognised facility that is greatly appreciated by clients and their carers. When Alan retired from this post, the church decided to appoint an Assistant Minister. The Revd Jane Kingsnorth was called to take it up as she finished her preparation at Bristol Baptist College. She carried out her role in the areas of pastoral work and in leading worship and made a significant contribution in relation to Junior Church issues during her time at Tyndale, 1998–2002.

Students in ministry

In the 2000s the church was approached by Bristol Baptist College, which was keen to develop its congregational placement scheme for college-based students. A succession of students-in-ministry (a designation Tyndale had long used for such people) spent periods of their time at the College on placement at Tyndale, taking part in pastoral work, leading worship and preaching and undertaking various forms of outreach. Successive students including Andy Scott, Caroline Brown and Eleanor Kelsey and two students from overseas, Christine Ritter from Germany and Maki Mico from Albania, have all enriched the life of the church, helping it in its mission to being open to the local community. Each in their own way have helped Tyndale to outwardly express the life of the Christian gospel.

Towards the next 150 years

How, then, does Tyndale Baptist Church appear as it celebrates its 150th anniversary? In many ways it is in good heart. A lively and varied congregation of people gather week by week for worship and some of them meet during the week for the varied programme put on by "time@tyndale". Some of them provide staffing for the church's regular mid-week coffee shops and occasional activities of outreach. They also support the variety of things that are emerging through the Community Ministry. The building is very well kept and maintained, and used extensively by local groups. Outreach brings the church fellowship into contact with an increasing number of individuals – who receive extensive pastoral support and who, from time to time, discuss and express interest in different aspects of Christian faith. As the motto "Open to God, Open for All", which is today incorporated in the church's logo, comes to shape and express many aspects of the church's life, theological issues are much to the fore, as well as matters of social concern. As described above, the Community Ministry has initiated many activities that bear directly on some of the social problems of the day, such as homelessness and alcoholism. Alongside this we as a church are engaging in debates such as those that emerge from the changing and challenging scene of human sexuality – and taking those debates outside our own circle, to, for instance, the West of England Baptist Association. At the same time we are seeking to remain informed about things that are emerging on the wider scene nationally, such as the "Safe Passage" campaign, which highlights the plight of unaccompanied refugee children.

The church's worship life continues to keep abreast of contemporary trends in the use of music and song and multi-media, whilst at the same time keeping alive the tradition of hymn singing. Preaching remains central, and seeks always to engage with the Christian scriptures and the modern world and to inspire a wide range of people (of many Christian backgrounds and none) to live by faith. Carefully structured and sensitively led, such worship, we believe, expresses the church's values of openness and welcome and provides an effective "engine" driving our commitment to Christian service.

There are, of course, challenges. Denominational loyalties have changed substantially in recent years, so that being Baptist *per se* is no longer a sufficient reason either for attending a Baptist church or else for serving through one. Many new non-denominational churches have grown up, some of them within a short distance of Tyndale. Since they belong to the now well-established Evangelical culture in this country, they provide a natural home for many especially young people (not least students) who, in previous generations, might have found their way to a church such as Tyndale. The church was, in the 1960s and 1970s much more in the centre of Christian and Baptist denominational life than today; its commitment to ecumenism, and to an attempt to make the historic faith relevant to an emerging generation of socially and politically-engaged people, ensured that it was lively and well attended.

The story of the church told in this book is a story of a church that, throughout its history, has always sought to be open to the commercial, social and political world around it and to express, shape and inculcate Christian values in that world. For most of that time the surrounding area was populated with people who related to churches such as Tyndale, not only for their own and their family's sake, but because those churches were part of the value system and indeed the culture to which they belonged. In today's more secularised and, one might say, multifarious world this is no longer the case. Yet Tyndale has not been affected to the same extent as some other similar churches by some of the physical changes that also belong to that world. It has not become marooned on one side of a major arterial road. It has not become an isolated – attractive yet underused – city centre building, surrounded by commercial outlets, with difficult or expensive access. It has not found itself trying to keep up a Christian presence in a multi-cultural or other-than-Christian faith community. Tyndale Baptist Church (like any church firmly identified with its building – the "Holy and Beautiful House" of which its erstwhile minister, F. C. Bryan, spoke) occupies what has been described as a "strategic location". It is certainly a landmark, and with its policy of being physically open as much as possible, one that is increasingly well-known and used by passers-by and local residents alike. The excellent condition of the buildings, their user-friendliness and good management, ensure that a large number of local groups use the premises for regular and occasional meetings.

A question was asked some years ago, as to whether anyone would build a church such as Tyndale where it is today. It is, perhaps, a question that cannot be answered straightforwardly, but Tyndale's presence on the Whiteladies Road gives contemporary expression to a challenge for all Christian churches. It is a challenge that emerges from the writing of Dietrich Bonhoeffer: "the church is only the church when it exists for others". That challenge is particularly acute for Baptist Christians who have always sought to distance their life of discipleship from any particular building or location. Still, in today's world, where a congregation worships and how it serves there shapes, as much as it is shaped by, its location and its building. Tyndale Baptist Church – its building and its people – is located in the very centre of a busy, various, lively human community. Businesses trade close by, well-heeled folk live within easy reach, homeless people shelter in its grounds and people with various addictions, learning difficulties and social interests come in and out of its doors. They bring all manner of human life with them and, hopefully, intentionally, they encounter the welcome, comfort and challenge of the Christ-shaped God through its ministries, its mission, and its life of worship.

Such things have always been part of its history. May they always be so in its future.

The Revd Rachel Haig, Community Minister (2013–) writes:

After 16 years at Horfield Baptist Church, situated on the Gloucester Road about as far out from the city centre as Tyndale, the call to be Community Minister at Tyndale came as an opportunity to use the experience gained in traditional ministry to be purposefully missional and less institutionally focussed. Whilst I am not sure that many at Tyndale understood what they were inviting someone to do, one of the initial tasks was to work out who and what Tyndale was, and what was Community Ministry supposed to be. To be a minister without the usual tasks of preaching each week and a pastoral care list to attend to, meetings to arrange agendas for, suddenly clears the diary but what would be the new agenda? To fill the diary with outreach programmes or to fill it with people? What were people going to be invited to be part of? What were the best ways of enabling people to find a greater engagement with the life of Tyndale? But more than that, how to help them understand God in their midst?

The Human Face of Ministry

At the point where Community Ministry began it was apparent that there were many people of different ages and stages using the buildings during the week and a lot of good will towards Edward Duffield, as the Halls Manager. As the face of Tyndale for outside groups, Edward presented Tyndale as welcoming and caring, which was vocalised by group leaders. However, the majority of the time the buildings were empty. Tuesday Coffee shop, Wednesday time@tyndale, and Sunday morning were the opportunities when the Church met. There was no one to answer the telephone or the door. So the starting place for Community Ministry was about being present. Being present around the buildings and visible to meet people and give some life to the buildings

The Revd Rachel Haig

during the day. This was a simple place to begin with a focus on establishing relationships; being present to begin conversations, to offer encouragement, to answer the phone, offer a smile, or respond when someone was in need. If you like, Tyndale began to have a face.

It was just after the Community Ministry began that people arrived one day to find a large Gromit had been placed right in front of the doors of Tyndale. So over the course of the summer the footfall outside Tyndale vastly increased. Thousands of photos of Tyndale's front doors were taken and people were happy to stop and chat. The natural thing to do was to join in, and so Tyndale held its first bring your dog to church Sunday and had a handful of faithful friends who shared in Sunday worship. One of the members afterwards said to me, "when it was suggested, I had no idea how you could do something meaningful with this dog service, but I was wrong". We explored the idea of faithfulness, devotion and that very doggy trust that they will receive the love, as well as food and shelter that they need if they wait. Gromit came and went but our Dog Services translated into other opportunities with links to the doggy day care shop around the corner from the church on Cotham Hill that had just opened. Two further doggy nativities took place subsequently. In a way the dogs tested out the willingness to think outside the box and to respond to those around us, as did the introduction of sofas and a play area into the sanctuary. This gave the coffee shops more relaxed informal space. It also was a strategic way of saying that children are welcome to be in the space and part of it, even whilst there were no other children present.

Open to God, Open for All

The development of a new logo and vision of "Open to God, Open for All" tried to capture all the conversations and discussions about how we presented ourselves to others with the invitation to join us. It was a chance to stand back and look again with fresh eyes at what people encountered both inside and outside the buildings. It was also a time to try to encapsulate the ethos of Tyndale in today's world and answer the question, "what at this time in Tyndale's story are we trying to express about God and ourselves?" A more overt invitation to join Sunday worship led to some new faces appearing and it was not long before the need for opportunities to explore ideas about God and faith and church became a regular monthly daytime Faith Exploration group. The mix of understandings about God, religion, the Bible and spirituality made for rich and deep conversations.

Being open is not just a physical thing. It is also a willingness to think about how others can access the ideas and perspectives on life that faith offers. With new faces on a Sunday, and aware of the missing element of children and young people, Tyndale adopted a new way of working through the Bible story using Godly Play. This is a way of nurturing spirituality that empowers individuals to own their faith journey and encourages people to place themselves into the Bible story and see how it all fits together. Appropriately, the space under the Tyndale window was cleared of chairs and developed into storytelling and prayer space. Over the weeks and months it filled up with stories of Advent and Easter, Creation to the Prophets, and the Parables of Jesus to the Life of Paul. This significant development was an attempt to introduce something a little less formal to the morning service, as well as making the Bible more accessible for all, and for the service to seem a little more child friendly at the point where Tyndale began to have children in its midst again. It means that whenever Tyndale worships, the Bible is present in a tangible form, ready for connections to be made. There is so much more that can be developed from this space for both children, families and older adults.

Tuesday Coffee shop was well established. Being present in the week to greet people and enable them to feel at home. There are always new faces appearing. It was one of these new faces, a small woman who turned out to be Hindu, who came into Tyndale to pray one day and I stopped to chat to her. She asked if we knew of a knitting club anywhere near Tyndale. So Knit Club was born and soon had a large group of people sitting, chatting, knitting, teaching new tricks, inviting others to join in. It contributed blankets to Age UK and Aid Box. Similarly Tyndale began to have a number of quite musical people ask if they could sit and play the piano. They stayed and most weeks now Coffee Shops have someone or other serenading people while they consume their drinks and chat together.

Clearly being open was the simplest of ways to meet new people and build relationships, and so the Wednesday Coffee Shop opened in early 2014 and was intended to be very child friendly and become a place

Jonah and the Whale, with Circo Rum Ba Ba

where the successful "Singing with Mummy" groups could meet up and chat with safe play space for the children. Very quickly it was heavily used by the groups who welcomed the space and made themselves at home. Again, one of the outcomes was the way that being at home in the sanctuary bridges the gap between church and ordinary life with families feeling at home and enjoying being in a sanctuary, opportunities to celebrate new births, birthdays, as well as the offering of support to struggling mums, and getting alongside the toddlers with drawing and stories.

Subsequently Tyndale had a couple of successful "Messy Church" experiences and, more recently, Christingle services on Christmas Eve to which to invite parents. Other family and child friendly events were done jointly with the other Whiteladies Road Churches. These included "The Whale Project" where a giant whale was placed in the playground at St John's Primary School and arts and crafts themes around Bible stories, together with dramatic presentations of these stories, attracted around 70 kids from the school and their families, all working together having fun with the Bible stories. Tyndale's contribution was a giant Goliath made from scrap which the kids were encouraged to knock down at the end of the day by way of defeating the giants of which they are afraid.

"Get in the Picture" was another Christmas initiative. We set up a stable in the market place on Whiteladies Road and encouraged passers-by to dress up as nativity figures and get their photo taken. They could then download the photo and get a little potted message about Christmas and an invitation to the churches. More recently "Christmas Through the Keyhole" has sought to engage families by enabling them to explore the homes of Mary, the Shepherds, the Kings and finally meeting the characters from the story in the Stable. Giant gazebos filled Tyndale, as well as a replica of Christmas Present complete with fireplace, Christmas tree and stockings, as the starting place for the trail. Year 3 and 4 classes from St John's, the Cub Scouts from Redland Park all visited, as well as holding open days on the Saturdays that again encouraged some of the families from Coffee Shop to come and join in. The donkey outside on the forecourt was eye-catching, and along with the burger stand, helped to capture attention of people going by. Further opportunities to engage with children on behalf of Tyndale have been off-site with the invitation to take Key Stage 2 Assemblies at Elmlea Junior School around five times a year.

If Community Ministry is to engage with Clifton, Redland and Cotham then the University of Bristol is one of the key constituents for Tyndale to continue to engage with. So it was natural to join the Multi-faith Chaplaincy team and find appropriate ways to get involved with University life, both formally with Graduation Services and the Annual Service of Thanksgiving for bodies donated for medical research and the

University Christmas Carol Service, as well as being available to get alongside students during the week when they drop into the chaplaincy centre to study, to ask for help, or more recently where I have helped with the Monday Soup Lunch. Being present, one day, as I was heading out for a walk around the area near Tyndale I noticed a young man peering in through the front window of the tower room and stopped to see if I could help. The young man was part of Bristol University Music Society, or BUMS for short. He was looking for venues where students could perform in order to gain experience. This chance meeting led to a series of lunchtime and Wednesday evening concerts, again, with a view to opening Tyndale up to the community. Similarly it was during the Welcome Week BBQ in 2017 that Mike Wilshaw stopped for a burger and during the course of the conversation came into Tyndale. By the end of the conversation we had begun to talk about how the Royal Court Players could perform at Tyndale. So music concerts have become a regular part of the Community Ministry story of Tyndale.

The needy on Our Doorstep

Tyndale's porch area often has a body or two sleeping in it overnight. When the church gathers, the openness to all meant offering cups of coffee or soup to those who we walked past to enter through the front doors. "Sock it to 'em" was started in 2015 so we had some useful items like fresh socks, gloves, hats and scarves that could easily be given away when needed. We welcomed many of the homeless into services and coffee shops and tried to build relationships and offer help to those whose lives seemed to have reached such a low place. Alongside Tyndale's long participation in the Churches Together Soup and Sandwich run, the opportunity arose in September 2016 to offer a night a week to be part of a new Churches' Winter Night Shelter. Here was an opportunity to do something more practical to help people off the streets, alongside

The soup run [Roger Hockey]

other Christians in Bristol. Tyndale responded wholeheartedly and in January 2017 we opened our doors for four Tuesday nights for the pilot scheme with beds for up to 15 people referred by St Mungo's Charity. We provided a two-course evening meal, space to relax and play games, a bed for the night and breakfast in the morning alongside six other church venues around the city. Tyndale hosted the media evening and a good number of the church volunteered to help on one of the shifts alongside others from other churches to make up the team each night. It was a great experience for everyone involved and led to the Nightshelter being extended to 12 weeks in 2018 with more churches coming on board as venues. Tyndale did six weeks this time starting from the second week of January, offering a warm welcome and safe space. It ran like clockwork and was another example of Tyndale's working alongside others in the city to show God's love to those in need. So the decision to make community ministry its outward face has drawn Tyndale into greater engagement with city life and as it has done so life continues to flood in to Tyndale itself.

In 2017 Fareshare came into Tyndale's life, linking Tyndale to Waitrose and Tesco in Clifton. This scheme is trying to address both food poverty and food waste. It began with two days each week receiving texts on my phone to say that there are crates available for collection of bakery, fruit or vegetables. We pick them up and distribute the food rather than let it be wasted. The act of giving things away for free seems to express something of God's love that is given so freely for us. A new Soup Lunch began out of Fareshare on the first Tuesday of the month. Tyndale does a free lunch and it is open to anybody who wants it.

In the prevailing difficult economic climate of welfare upheaval and austerity Tyndale's ongoing relationship with a variety of Anonymous groups, meeting in the Harold Bodey Room, deepened as individuals came through the doors and the Community Minister was able to work alongside them to help particularly challenging people around Tyndale's porch. In fact, it was particularly encouraging that the first baptism to take place for a while in December 2016 was a member of one of the AA groups who had originally made her way into Tyndale in Holy Week 2014 when the doors had been opened up for prayer and reflection during the mornings.

Community Ministry has meant looking for ways to do as much stuff outside the doors as inside, so the task is to go out to where people are with the intention of being welcoming and friendly and giving things away. For example, Holy Week 2017 we went outside and put up a gazebo each morning and invited passers-by to write prayers on leaves. On Maundy Thursday and Good Friday we used the leaves, the prayers of our community, in our joint services with the other Whiteladies Road churches. Being outside means being willing to open to the unexpected. Similarly in 2018, we created an Easter garden over the course of Holy Week, inviting passers-by to stop and make a flower to add to the garden. On Easter Sunday morning we filled the sanctuary with the flowers and again held the community around us close in our worship.

This constant movement of going out and holding close seems to mirror an understanding of an incarnational God who is always calling his creation forwards towards new life. Sometimes the simplest things say the most. However, the story would not be complete without counting the cost of this kind of openness. Success is not a word that sits easily with gospel values. How is

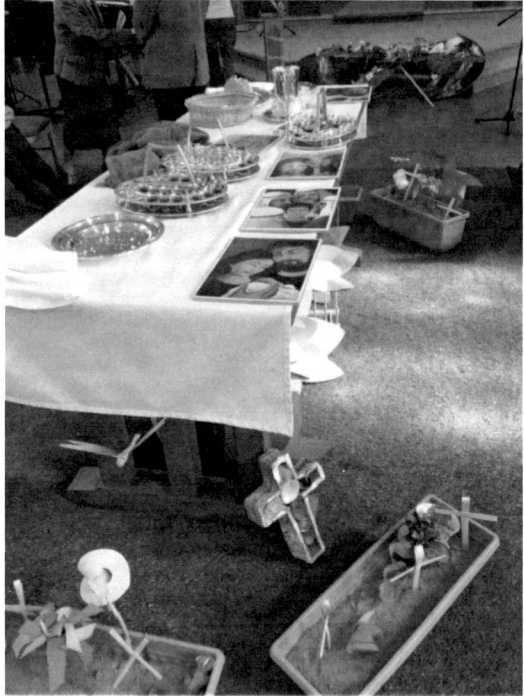

Easter garden communion service

it measured? Quite early on I was assured that it was not about "bums of seats" on a Sunday morning. Yet, ultimately we desire that people would want to become part of God's family and find shelter, strength and love through an increasing sense of being part of Tyndale which might include worshipping the living God together.

The Hopes and Heartbreaks of Community Ministry

Thus for every face that we have welcomed on a Sunday morning or through the doors of coffee shop or into a music concert is the possibility of building relationship. Some of those relationships bring chaos and turmoil. Some of the lives we engage with bring heartaches and a little anger at the way life is so very challenging and difficult for some. Community Ministry has raised all kinds of questions about faith and about how God chooses to work in a broken world. Can God help people overcome their addiction to alcohol or drugs and what does it mean to overcome addiction? Can God make it go away completely?

Here my thoughts go to a man who had been addicted to alcohol and drugs since he was a teenager. He told me he took his first drink at 6 years old. He carried with him a deep sense of rejection and in many ways he remained a child who was hurting and felt unloved. He found his way into Tyndale via chatting outside waiting for a group, and then through coffee shop. On and off, he shared some of his triumphs and joined the Faith Exploration Group. He joined in with our first "Christmas Through the Keyhole", agreeing to be Joseph. He helped with the new Thursday Coffee Shop when it opened. He started to come on Sundays and even came on the Church Weekend away where he was delighted to read the part of the Prodigal Son on the first evening. But he was always fragile, experienced great highs and lows. He had been clean for seven months, and had asked for baptism. In the last conversation I had with him, he talked about discovering how God loved him and how much he wanted to learn more about the life of Jesus while he stood and looked at Pilgrim's burden rolling away at the foot of the cross in the John Bunyan window in the sanctuary. Then he failed to appear for Thursday Coffee Shop when he said he would. Messages were not answered, and on the following Tuesday, just a week after his baptismal classes began, one of the other coffee shop guys came into Tyndale to say he had been found dead in his flat after taking some drugs. Why? What happened? No one knows. Did God love him? Yes, I know he did and the addicted man knew it. Just at the point where life seemed happy, it ended.

Community Ministry is being there to pick up the pieces and offer comfort whilst struggling with a sense of Good Friday. Community Ministry is hugging the people who found his body, out at the café over the road as they stare in shock at each other and wonder about the fragility of their own recovery. Community Ministry is receiving the call from the police in Gloucester on the same morning about concerns over a suicide message left for me by someone who was baptised two years before and responding to it, while toddlers want you to continue the game of musical statues in the sanctuary. Community Ministry is constantly wiping the spit or the thrown-up soup off the doors of the church and still welcoming the same face who has lived on the streets for 30 years and prays for us all too, over and over again, with the possibility that it will happen again tomorrow or next week. Community Ministry is waiting for the police and ambulance to arrive to take away the drunk who is peeing over the church steps and himself in full view of passers-by and then refusing to move. It is pouring away the alcohol stashed in the bushes and even sometimes picking up human faeces from where the mothers and toddlers walk to enter the church buildings. It is also sitting with the same person whilst they weep and apologise and ask what life is about and ask you to pray for them.

Community Ministry is having to board up the front porch in order to move on people who have begun to use it as their home and be abusive of church members when they go in and out of the buildings for meetings. Community Ministry is herding out the woman with deep mental health issues who is shouting about being abused because you won't let her steal the food bank food in the sanctuary. Community Ministry is arriving back from a break to find that someone has left you a divining stick as a gift, or being patient when someone thinks it is a great idea for the church to buy a laptop for an alcoholic to encourage them to get into their music. Community Ministry is trying to bring the conversation back to the Bible and your planned discussion on the cross after someone has led it onto the idea of reincarnation. Community Ministry is listening attentively when complete strangers tell you about their sexual habits and desires, or when a Hindu asks you to teach her to pray.

Servants of a Generous God

As I write, Tyndale has just finished a pilot for a holiday club for adults, with a special concern for isolated senior citizens, something like a holiday at home. Two weeks of activities, three days each week with trips out to Berkeley Castle and the Bishops Palace and Gardens in Wells, bread-making, wood sculpture, a music workshop, a tour of Royal West of England Academy, not forgetting canoeing and rowing on the harbour side with a tour of the MShed. It epitomises the way ahead for Tyndale: a great way to build new relationships with lonely people beyond the borders of the church, and working alongside the Whiteladies Road churches.

Tyndale has also gone outside and given away cakes to passers-by as part of the Good Neighbours Weekend that arose out the murder of MP, Jo Cox. Trying to convince people that free means free, no expectations, just to make them smile was an interesting experience. How then do we convince them that God's love is also free and all they need to do is accept it? Is it without conditions? I am reminded of an old book by W. H. Vanstone, *Love's Endeavour, Love's Expense* that I read in college days. God can never make anyone respond to love without ceasing to be loving. There is the cost of Community Ministry. For all of it there are no guarantees of "bums on seats". But then Tyndale's story demonstrated this time and time again.

It seems to me that Community Ministry is anything that enables a connection to be made with people's lives beyond the walls of the church's buildings. It is looking for ways purposefully to engage with the creativity, social consciousness, spiritual awareness and the need for meaningful relationships of anyone we come into contact with, whatever age, stage, background, status, ethnicity, sexuality, religion, and to do so in the name of the God made known to us in Jesus Christ. This is deliberately broad because once the doors are open there is no telling who will walk through, and the cost of an open door is most likely closer to the experience of Good Friday than Easter Sunday. Yet, we must have a message of hope. There must be the hope of resurrection however long a journey that is.

Church weekend away at Brunel Manor, Torquay, 2016

Appendix 3. Ministers and Office Bearers

Ministers	
Richard Glover	1869–1912
Herbert Morgan	1912–1920
George Harte	1921–1931
Frank Bryan	1933–1950
Bill Whilding	1951–1956
Ron Cowley	1958–1974
Peter Webb	1975–1987
Robert Ellis	1987–2001
Michael Docker	2002–
Rachel Haig (Community Minister)	2013–

Assistant and Associate Ministers	
Herbert Burdett	1908–1912
Ian Thompson	1962–1963
Roger Newman	1964–1968
Keith Lamdin	1969–1973
Barry Vendy	1973–1976
Alison Overton (Minister's Assistant)	1976–1977
Ian Millgate	1977–1980
Alan Smith (part-time)	1992–1998
Jane Kingsnorth	1998–2002

Assistant and Associate Ministers (Lawrence Weston)

Philip Lucas	1963–1969
Morgan Williams	1969–1973
Ray Smith	1974–1976
Jacqueline Triggs	1980–1984
Stuart Fuller	1984–1993

Secretaries

E. G. Clarke	1869–1871
C. Townsend	1871–1892
J. Davis	1892–1900
F. A. Jenkins	1900–1919
D. F. Jenkins	1919–1924
S. H. J. Murch	1924–1947
A. J. Finch	1947–1949
Miss D. Porteous & R. P. Motson	1949–1951
Miss D. Porteous & D. Yeo	1951–1964
Miss D. Porteous & G. Fisher	1964–1970
D. Bodey	1970–1973
D. Parsons	1973–1977
D. T. Roberts	1977–1984
G. Luton	1984–1995
Miss J. Gerrish	1995–2005
J. West	2005–2006
B. Lloyd	2006–2018
B. Lloyd & Mrs D. Lewis	2018–

Treasurers

J. Eyre & W. Polglase	1869–1880
J. Eyre & W. Sherring	1880–1882
J. Eyre & E. Robinson	1882–1890
E. Robinson	1890–1935
E. Davies	1935–1941
C. R. Dickens	1941–1946
W. H. Parsons	1946–1949
R. M. Cooke	1949–1966
J. G. Jones	1966–1972
R. Stephens	1972–1983
J. Elliott	1983–1993
E. Duffield	1993–2006
J. West	2006–

Life Deacons

J. Davis	1903–1907
C. Townsend	1903–1908
R. Padfield	1929–1950
E. G. Sargent	1929–1934
H. L. Taylor	1946–1951
Miss C. Culross	1951–1953
Miss D. F. Glover	1951–1961
S. Murch	1954–1955
J. W. Brighton	1958–1967
R. M. Cooke	1970–1975
Miss D. Porteous	1970–1977
Miss K. G. Robinson	1970–1985
Mrs C. Bodey	1977–1992
R. Brake	1979–1981
R. Cooper	1983–1990

Appendix 4. Membership

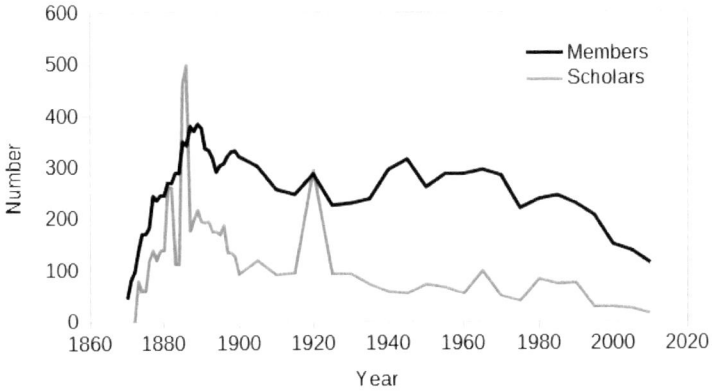

Tyndale Baptist Church members and scholars from 1868 until 2010

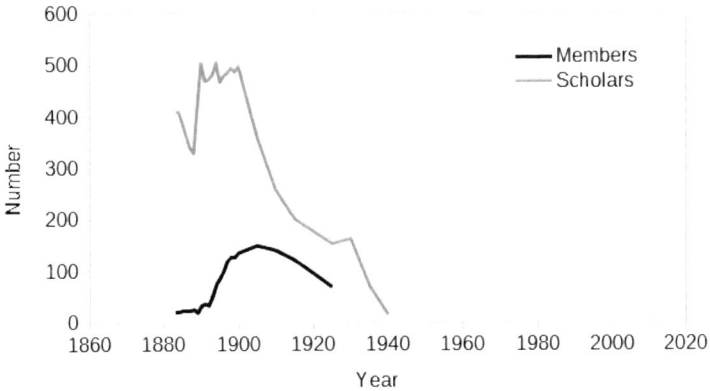

Members and scholars at the Tyndale Mission from its commencement in 1880 until it separated from the church in the 1930s

Index of People